Financing
Income-Producing
Real Estate

Financing Income-Producing Real Estate

Second Edition

Eric Stevenson Editor in Chief

Senior Staff Vice President
Mortgage Bankers Association of America
Washington, D.C.

Edited by Wallace B. Katz

Sponsored by Mortgage Bankers Association of America

McGraw-Hill Book Company

New York St. Louis San Francisco Auckland
Bogotá Hamburg London Madrid Mexico
Milan Montreal New Delhi Panama
Paris São Paulo Singapore
Sydney Tokyo Toronto

Library of Congress Cataloging-in-Publication Data

Financing income-producing real estate/Eric Stevenson (Mortgage
  Bankers Association of America), editor. — 2nd ed.
        p. cm.
    Includes index.
    ISBN 0-07-061311-7
      1. Mortgage loans—United States.   2. Real estate development—
    United States—Finance.   I. Stevenson, Eric.   II. Mortgage Bankers
    Association of America.
    HG2040.5.U5F49 1988   87-32043
    332.1'753—dc19   CIP

1234567890   DOC/DOC   893210987

ISBN 0-07-061311-7

*The editors for this book were Martha Jewett and Barbara B. Toniolo, the
designer was Naomi Auerbach, and the production supervisor was Richard
Ausburn. The book was set in Baskerville. It was composed by the McGraw-
Hill Book Company Professional and Reference Division Composition Unit.*

Printed and bound by R. R. Donnelley and Sons Company.

Contents

Preface

Financing Income-Producing Real Estate is designed primarily for those who are new employees of mortgage banking firms or lending institutions and who are interested in financing commercial, industrial, and multifamily housing real estate as a profession. Unlike a college text in mortgage finance, this book is filled with useful and practical suggestions about how business is conducted from authors with considerable working experience in the topics they describe.

The use of different authors for each chapter results in different styles of writing and some limited duplication of subject matter. Some reiteration of essential points should be helpful, because it is unlikely that any reader will sit down and read the text from beginning to end. The book's chapters, however, are arranged in a useful sequence.

Part 1 describes the steps taken by a developer, a mortgage banker, and a financial institution to finance income-producing real estate, also known as income property. The last chapter in Part 1 briefly describes the process of property analysis.

Part 2 covers what information has to be obtained before the property can be financed. The decision on the form of ownership for the real estate is a legal issue, discussed in Chapter 5. Chapter 6's analysis of the owner's credit is conducted by both the mortgage banker and the lending institution and covers not only the owner's net worth, but also the owner's experience and skills in developing real estate. The market feasibility study and the appraisal, discussed in Chapters 7 and 8, help determine the viability of the project. Because any income-producing property

is subject to leases, Chapter 9 covers the essentials of a lease transaction.

Part 3's topic, "Analyzing Income and Expenses," gives many beginning professionals great difficulty. Nevertheless, determining the net
operating income from property, described in Chapter 10, is the key to
knowing how much debt financing may be obtained. Chapter 11 describes a few important mathematical ratios, and Chapter 12 covers the
techniques used to put a value on the investment—not just when it is
built, but over a period of years. The final chapter on federal taxation
is a brief introduction to the topic and must be prefaced with the warning
that tax laws are always subject to change.

Part 4, "Underwriting Properties," covers the particular characteristics
of the different types of property that a mortgage banker or lender will
be asked to finance. Multifamily housing, also known as apartments,
deserved a somewhat longer discussion, in two chapters, because of the
federal housing programs and the secondary market for multifamily
housing mortgages.

Part 5, "Structuring the Loan," outlines the various types of mortgages
in use during the mid-1980s. The types of lenders making the various
types of mortgages will likely change over the years, but the basic forms
of mortgage lending will probably remain because they permit infinite
variations.

Part 6 begins with what information a mortgage banker should include
when submitting a loan to a lender and then turns, in Chapter 25, to a
detailed description of how the mortgage loan should be closed. Chapters
26 and 27 apply once the loan has been made. One covers how the
lender administers the construction loan, and the other describes the
basic principles involved when a mortgage banker services a loan for a
lender. Sometimes the loan is not as successful as the parties hoped:
Chapter 28 discusses how to prevent and cure problem loans.

Increasingly, lenders seek to sell a mortgage loan or loans in their
portfolios, and other institutions choose to buy existing loans from others. Chapter 29 describes that market, including how mortgages can
occasionally be transformed into securities sold to a wider group of
investors.

The final chapter is a thoughtful look at the trends and changes in
income property financing. The author, Ronald F. Poe, CMB, was president of the Mortgage Bankers Association of America during 1986, the
year that this book was started.

The Appendix is a glossary of terms used in income property finance.

The use of particular interest rates in any examples does not imply
the status of current market conditions. In addition, the authors have

no intention whatsoever of offering any legal advice, even though some of the chapters touch on legal issues. The authors' opinions are their own.

Enough of caveats. The Mortgage Bankers Association of America hopes that this book will be useful to its readers.

ERIC STEVENSON
Senior Staff Vice President
Mortgage Bankers Association of America

Acknowledgments

In 1977, McGraw-Hill published *Financing Income-Producing Real Estate*, edited by James A. Britton and Lewis O. Kerwood; the book consisted of 30 essays and 11 case studies by professionals in real estate financing. The Mortgage Bankers Association of America (MBA), the book's sponsor, used the book for nine years for correspondence courses, and the book was sold widely by McGraw-Hill.

This, the second edition, is entirely new, although several authors who contributed to the 1977 book also authored chapters in this book: Daniel S. Berman, Esq.; Angelo L. Dentamaro, CMB, MAI; Jess S. Lawhorn, CMB; J. Thomas Montgomery, CRE, MAI; Robert F. Plymate, CMB; Ronald F. Poe, CMB; and David C. Tolzmann, CRE.

This book follows an outline developed by Eric Stevenson and Wallace B. Katz with help from three of the authors, Henry S. Kesler, CMB, MAI; Donald H. Schefmeyer, CMB, SRPA; and Thomas Z. Minehart, III, CMB. Wallace Katz edited the book; John B. Nicholson, Eric Stevenson, and Lynn M. Harvey were responsible for the final manuscript. The manuscript was read by a review committee headed by Donald H. Schefmeyer, CMB, SRPA, president of the Action Mortgage Corporation in South Bend, Indiana; the committee included William F. Cozzens, CMB, senior vice president of Covenant Mortgage Corporation in Brentwood, Tennessee; Angelo L. Dentamaro, CMB, MAI, executive vice president of Margaretten & Company, Inc. in Perth Amboy, New Jersey; D. R. Schwartz, CMB, vice president of Pacific Southwest Mortgage Company in San Diego, California; and Howard M. Stearns, CMB, president of Institutional Investors of America, Inc. in Paramus, New Jersey.

The initials *CMB*, which appear after many of the authors' names, stand for "Certified Mortgage Banker," a designation awarded by the MBA to those who meet certain professional requirements over a period of years and pass the necessary examination. *MAI* and *SRPA* or *SREA* refer to professional appraisal designations awarded by the American Institute of Real Estate Appraisers and the Society of Real Estate Appraisers. Those who have any of these appraisal designations have passed the necessary tests as appraisers of income-producing property. *CRE* is a designation for "Counselor of Real Estate," awarded by the American Society of Real Estate Counselors.

John Libby, Larry Team, Mildred Brooks, William DeCarlo, and Ricardo Blanco prepared the manuscript for the publishers.

The Mortgage Bankers Association of America is fortunate to have members who contribute their time and skills so generously for the education of real estate financing professionals. It is particularly grateful to those who wrote the chapters of this book.

PART 1

Parties to the Transaction and the Property

1

Parties to the Transaction: The Developer

David C. Tolzmann, CRE

President, Hayden, Tolzmann & Associates, Inc.
Bloomfield, Connecticut

The business of the developer can be expressed very simply: *the creation of value*. Unless a completed development, in which the developer has invested knowledge and years of effort, is worth substantially more than the total of cash, kind, and time contributions to it, the developer has failed. Chapter 1 discusses what the developer does to create that value.

Planning and Design

The first phase of the development process involves planning and design. The process begins with the developer's concept of a specific project located on a specific site, whether it be relatively simply garden apartments, a single office or industrial building, or a complex mixed-use project including, for example, offices, retail, hotel, residential, and parking components.

As developers refine the concept, they must get the site for the proposed project under control, ideally expending as little up-front money as possible. The most frequently used option is to purchase the property for a specific price to be paid at some point in the future. Such an option, usually requiring payment of some relatively small portion of the agreed-upon purchase price, should allow the developer sufficient time to do all of the necessary studies to determine whether the project is feasible before the purchase of the site must be completed.

During the planning and design phase, the developer must also select an architect to begin to translate the development concept into preliminary plans for the specific project. These preliminary plans are essential, since they will begin to firm up the actual square footage of the project, both for economic modeling purposes and for use in the approval process, which will take place later.

Concurrently with the development of the concept and the preliminary plans for the project, the developer must qualify the market into which the project is to be placed, and thus must make a detailed market analysis. This analysis, whether done by developers and their staffs or by outside experts, will carefully study that component or components of the market with which their projects will compete, including analysis of historical supply-and-demand trends for the past several years. Beyond that, future rental and market absorption rates must be projected, and potentially competing projects must be studied to determine if the proposed project has a reasonable chance of being financially successful. Pro forma economic models of expected operating results must be developed and analyzed against anticipated development costs before the decision is made to proceed with the project.

Some key questions the developer must consider at this point are:

- If the project is constructed within a market with certain supply and demand considerations, can a profit be expected?
- Does the project have a reasonable return on its projected cost?

The second phase of the development process involves necessary regulatory approvals. Depending on the project's jurisdiction and complexity, obtaining the necessary approvals by the regulatory bodies can range from a relatively simple process accomplished in a matter of weeks to an extremely long and complicated process involving literally dozens of regulatory agencies and years of time. (In one particular case, the approval process on a multiuse project to be developed on the banks of a navigable river involved approvals by 38 local, state, and federal bodies, including the Army Corps of Engineers, and took over four years before construction commenced.)

During the approval process, the developer's architect must proceed from preliminary architectural drawings to much more detailed plans for use in work with the various regulatory bodies. Also at this point the developer will need additional consultants, including traffic engineers, specialists who will prepare the required environmental impact statements, and soils engineers to report on potential hazardous wastes in the soils. Of prime importance at this juncture is expert legal counsel skilled in the specialized section of the law dealing with zoning.

Financing Alternatives

When the necessary approvals are in place, the next phase of the development process—the arranging of financing, which includes not only permanent mortgage financing but also construction financing and the raising of the required equity capital over and above mortgage financing to complete the project—must be accomplished. Some financing alternatives the developer may explore are the following:

- Develop the project for its own account, supplying any equity dollars required over and above debt financing secured
- Develop the project and retain an interest as general partner, bring in equity investors as limited partners, and obtain third-party debt financing
- Develop the project as a joint venture with an institutional financial partner providing all dollars required
- Develop and sell—obtain a preconstruction commitment to purchase the project when completed

When the financing arrangements are in place, the next phase of development can begin—that of constructing and leasing of the project.

Construction and Leasing

As the project moves into the construction phase, the developer must decide whether the development firm will also serve as general contractor or will select a general contractor or construction manager to build the project.

The developer who serves as general contractor must take these steps:

- Select and award contracts to the 20 or more subcontractors who will perform the various components of the construction process
- Set up the timetable for construction and closely monitor progress and coordination among the subcontractors
- Initiate and participate personally in periodic reviews and updating of

significant project elements, such as development schedules, market forecasts, financial modeling, and marketing strategy

If the developer's firm elects to engage an independent general contractor or construction manager to build the project, the developer's firm must still monitor and coordinate controls as if it were the general contractor and must also set up periodic reviews of all elements of the process.

Meanwhile, the marketing of the project and the actual leasing of space must be accomplished. Some large developers have their own leasing staffs, but the majority of developers engage an outside firm specializing in leasing. Whether leasing is done in house or by an outside firm, an overall marketing strategy must be developed and implemented by the developer and staff. Although the developer can and must delegate tasks to its own staff and to outside contractors, the overall responsibility for coordination and oversight cannot be delegated. There is no substitute for an experienced, knowledgeable, highly involved and motivated developer.

Management

Once construction of the project has been completed and the building is leased and occupied, the project moves into the operational phase. Again, the developer must choose whether to serve as the operational manager of the project or to hire an outside management firm.

Whichever choice the developer makes, there are certain functions which must be performed by the developer's firm that cannot be delegated. It must be responsible for overall planning, annual budget preparation, monitoring of actual performance versus budget, approval of all leases and their terms, capital improvements, and a host of other items. Whether, at this point, the sole owner, the general partner of the owning entity, or a joint venture participant, the developer is responsible for the operations of the property.

To summarize, the role of the developer includes conceiving the project, acquiring the site, obtaining regulatory approvals, arranging financing, constructing and leasing the facility, and operating it. For the typical income-producing project, the developer must put in and pay for anywhere from two to five years of work from the usually small but highly skilled staff who makes all this happen.

Clearly, the developer's role requires an individual possessed of very broad competencies and unusual interests and motivations. Although the overriding interest is, most assuredly, that of substantial personal financial gain, it seems certain that a person possessing such wide-ranging skills, experience, and motivation could do just as well financially in less complex and safer forms of endeavor.

The developer's job, simply stated, is to ensure that the proposed development is completed both on time and on budget and that it meets the three tests imposed by the Roman architect Vitruvius over 2000 years ago—commodity, firmness, and delight. What did Vitruvius mean? *Commodity,* to my way of thinking, means that the product will suit both the purses and the purposes of those who own and those who occupy it. *Firmness* means that the project stands up in fire, flood, and earthquake—and keeps out the rain. *Delight* means that it pleases the eye of the beholder, the owner, and, again, those who live or work in it.

2

Parties to the Transaction: The Mortgage Banker

Angelo L. Dentamaro, CMB

Executive Vice President
Margaretten & Company, Inc.
Perth Amboy, New Jersey

The mortgage banker serves as the intermediary between borrower and lender. Acting for the borrower, the mortgage banker negotiates and places financing with a lender on the borrower's real estate. For the lender, the mortgage banker serves as a source of income-producing loans. Certain lenders service their own loans, but many other lenders have correspondent relationships with mortgage bankers under which the mortgage banker services the loan. Servicing means that, for a servicing fee, the mortgage banker collects and remits to the lender the mortgage payments, inspects the property, and advises the lender both on the continued ability of the borrower to make the payments and on the changing value of the property. If the borrower fails or is likely to fail to make the mortgage payments on time, the mortgage banker represents the lender in the effort to bring the payments up to date or to negotiate another solution to the problem.

The spectrum of activity in income property finance for the mortgage banker begins with the solicitation-origination process and proceeds to the taking of an application, after which a loan submission or offering is developed and is usually delivered to a lender with whom the mortgage banker has a correspondent relationship.

The lender, in turn, analyzes, underwrites, and reviews the loan offering and issues a commitment which the mortgage banker must then deliver to the borrower. Once the commitment is unconditionally accepted by the borrower, the mortgage banker then coordinates and assists in closing the loan. After the loan is closed, the mortgage banker is responsible for servicing and administering the loan until it is paid off.

In this process, a multitude of talents and abilities are focused on the task of satisfying both the borrower and the lender to deliver quality service to all parties.

Solicitation-Origination

In the solicitation or origination process, the mortgage banker must seek out borrowers and convince them that the services being offered are worthy of consideration. These services include knowledge of the market area, of costs of land and buildings, of interest rates and financial trends, and—above all—an intimate knowledge of the desires, needs, and pricing requirements of lenders.

The mortgage banker's function is to develop a steady stream of quality business, and to do that the primary contact should be directly with the borrower and not through other parties who are on the fringes of the ultimate transaction. Too often valuable time is wasted by the novice mortgage banker who gets side-tracked into contacting architects, civic officials, planning and zoning board officials, lawyers, insurance agents, and accountants. Occasionally, product (meaning loan applications on real estate) is developed from these secondary and tertiary sources, but, in the final analysis, nearly all the product will be developed with the actual borrower and not through some other intermediary.

As mortgage bankers gain experience and develop skills, they will find it less difficult to go directly to the borrower to explain the services the firm has to render. In this face-to-face confrontation, the mortgage banker must convince the borrower that a significant service is available, and that working together the two parties will obtain the financing needed to develop the project.

One key to being a successful mortgage banker is the ability to ferret out the objectives of the borrower and determine and prioritize those objectives. For example, a borrower may need maximum dollars and not be concerned, unduly, about rate. Another borrower may have the capacity to infuse equity and is very rate-conscious. Another borrower may be concerned more with timing and will accept a higher interest rate provided that the timing needs are met.

Having discovered the needs of the borrower, the mortgage banker must discuss alternatives and offer suggestions for the type and structure of financing that best suits the borrower's needs.

I would caution the novices that many developers will pick their brains about lenders and mortgage rates but will be unwilling to sign a loan application. Mortgage bankers must keep clearly in mind that they must obtain an application or authorization from the borrower to arrange financing. All the talk, discussion, and demonstration of knowledge and ability is for naught if the mortgage banker cannot get the borrower to sign on the dotted line.

The form of application or authorization has been a topic of discussion for as long as there has been mortgage banking. Some firms prefer a long detailed application which covers interest rate, term, amount, amortization, prepayment, insurance, escrow and reserves, guarantees, assumption and alienation provisions, fees to all parties, and whatever else might come to mind. Others prefer a shortened form giving the mortgage banker authority to arrange financing in a certain amount, at a certain rate, with the borrower agreeing to pay all the costs of closing, appraisal, and surveys for a specified fee. In this shortened version, interest rates and lender charges are spelled out, together with the amount of financing desired, the term, and the amortization.

Some mortgage bankers believe a too-detailed application may well scare off a potential client. Others, having had problems collecting fees and perfecting their application, go to great lengths to "legalize" this first step. The novice should not be surprised to discover that some borrowers, particularly those who develop the larger properties, may deal directly with lenders rather than have a mortgage banker or broker arrange the financing. Although the solicitation-origination process is the most difficult part of the entire function performed by the mortgage banker, there is little excuse for a transaction not to come to fruition if the mortgage banker is capable of finding a knowledgeable, sophisticated borrower with a project to be developed in a quality location with physical real estate that meets the tests of architectural appeal, functional utility, and excellent construction.

Preparing the Loan Submission

Once the authorization-loan application has been finalized, the mortgage banker must proceed immediately and dutifully to prepare a complete and quality loan offering for the lender. This package must contain as complete information as is necessary, tempered by the size of the transaction, the knowledge the lender may have of the area, and the confidence the lender has in the particular mortgage banker.

The package, without exception, must contain area, neighborhood, and site information, including trends, strength of the market, rentals, construction activity, services available in the area, transportation, police, fire, zoning, and any other matters that may be important to understanding, analyzing, and underwriting the transactions. (For more detail, see Chapter 23.)

Financial information and background information on borrowers, including their capacity as builder, lessor, manager, and owner, should be fully explored. The lender must come to know the borrower thoroughly from the information presented in the loan offering. (See Chapter 6.)

Every offering includes a valuation. It is here the mortgage banker, either directly or through a separate appraisal, develops the three approaches to value and a final estimate of value. Even in those cases where the lender may require an independent fee appraisal, the mortgage banker develops a physical indication of value, a market indication of value, and an economic indication of value, and expresses a final value estimate. (See Chapter 8.)

It behooves those new to mortgage banking to develop those appraisal skills needed to understand these three approaches to value and to express the facts uncovered in the marketplace clearly and definitively. Value, like beauty, may be in the eye of the beholder, but some solid factual basis must exist for the mortgage banker's final value estimate.

Underlying the valuation process is always the question of demand. This demand for the product that the lender may finance must be demonstrated clearly and accurately. This demonstration may require independent feasibility studies, market studies, and absorption studies. Again, depending on the size and sophistication of the transaction, the detail and scope of these studies is the responsibility of the mortgage banker working with the borrower to satisfy the needs of the lender and convince the lender that "demand" does, in fact, exist for this product at the time and place in question. A feasibility study is outlined in Chapter 7.

The loan offering should contain sufficient maps, photographs, demographics, land comparables, rental comparables, and sales comparables to satisfy the lender and present the product in its best light. The mortgage banker should be sure that all inconsistencies are eliminated or explained in order not to confuse the lender.

Always remember that the loan offering is one basis upon which the mortgage banker's honesty, integrity, judgment, and abilities will be viewed. The assessment of the lender viewing the loan offering will ultimately determine the degree of success the mortgage banker will have in placing loans with the lender.

The process of structuring the loan actually began with the very first meeting with the borrower. It becomes perfected through the process of preparing the loan offering.

Many times, mortgage bankers—after completing their market study, area analysis, and review of the financial statements of the borrowers—come to realize that what was originally believed attainable is no longer valid. Thus an increased loan amount and/or a lower interest rate or a decreased loan amount and/or a higher interest rate may be mandated by the facts developed in preparing the loan offering. At this point, the mortgage banker may have to return to the borrower and have the original authorization or application altered.

Included in the loan submission should be copies of actual leases, if any exist, and/or copies of the standard form of lease the owners intend to utilize for their project. The mortgage banker must review these leases and spell out, in detail, who is responsible for each and every expense and what the base rent will be. Any average rents, increases in rent, renewal options, and any other details such as common area contributions must be fully explained. Many mortgage bankers develop a "brief" of lease form and fill out this form for each and every actual lease. Incidentally, many lenders require such a form. (See Chapter 9 on leasing.)

The mortgage banker should also explain accurately and in detail how the rentable area was calculated. In various parts of the country, different techniques are used, and various jargon and terminology are used. (See Chapter 10 on income and expenses.) For the mortgage banker submitting a loan to a distant lender, it is imperative that the lender understand completely the methodology used by the borrower and portrayed in the loan offering. There is no shortcut to lease analysis and, certainly, no shortcut to accurate rentable area calculations.

In many firms, the chief executive officer or the officer responsible for production will sign off on every loan offering which leaves that firm, regardless of the experience of the loan officer who developed the loan offering. Some firms require the originating loan officer to find the deal, prepare the loan offering, and sell the deal to the lender. Other firms may partition out these various functions.

An integral part of the loan offering is the underwriting function. Most mortgage bankers develop the criteria for loan-to-value ratios, debt service coverage, methodology of developing capitalization rates, acceptable loans per square foot for various types of property, net worth requirements for the borrower, preleasing, and other risk analysis factors, hand in hand with the lenders. (See Chapters 11 and 12.) Consequently, mortgage bankers must be constantly aware of their lenders' needs, attitudes, desires, and requirements—and the underwriting process.

It may be wise from time to time to discuss with lenders, frankly and openly, their thoughts concerning the mortgage banking firm's loan offering package. There may be ways in which to improve upon the loan offering package in order to facilitate a lender's needs. Many times, unknowingly, mortgage bankers decrease their odds of receiving a favorable reply by not doing, or caring about, those small details which may be critical for loan approval.

As transactions become more complex, the mortgage banker in the underwriting process may have to use computer programs for lease analysis, cash flow analysis, and developing internal rates of return. These should be considered tools for better understanding of the transaction rather than ends in themselves.

When using feasibility studies and other sophisticated analytical tools, remember that the underlying assumptions must be clearly explained and all work must be detailed in the loan offering.

Completing the Transaction

Initial contact has usually been with the lender to determine the lender's interest in a loan before the completion of the loan package. Once the loan offering has been completed, it must be delivered to the lender as quickly as possible. Many mortgage bankers hand carry loan offerings direct to the lender when possible. They prefer to present and sell their case by making a personal appearance. These visits to the lender may be used for other purposes, including getting updated on current activities, clarifying production goals, and solidifying that personal relationship which is so essential to the correspondent relationship. Some lenders prefer to have the loan submission mailed so that they may review it carefully before talking with the mortgage banker.

The lender may require additional data, more detailed data, or clarifications of the material. There may well be negotiations at this stage, with the mortgage banker as intermediary.

When the commitment is issued, the mortgage banker must read it carefully and be prepared to answer any and all questions which might be raised by the borrower. If securing the loan application was the most difficult part of the process to date, then certainly having the borrower sign the commitment is the second most critical point in the process. Sometimes commitments are issued with changes, and the mortgage banker, armed with the knowledge of the marketplace, current interest rates and terms, and credibility with the borrower, can overcome any and all objections and have the borrower accept the commitment.

Some conditions may be objectionable to the borrower, and a conditional acceptance of the commitment will be obtained. Ultimately, both the borrower and the lender must unconditionally accept the terms and conditions. When this has been accomplished, the mortgage banker must then coordinate the closing activity. Depending on the lender and whether the lender has in-house counsel, the mortgage banker ensures that the lender's attorney receives a copy of the commitment and any other closing instructions which the lender may have. (The loan closing is detailed in Chapter 25.)

In addition to ensuring that the note and the mortgage are proper and that there is title insurance and fire, casualty, and extended coverage, the mortgage banker must ascertain that all the terms of the commitment are met prior to funding.

Some lenders require the mortgage banking firm to close the loan in its own name and deliver the documents for purchase by assignment. Thus the firm must have lines of credit available to accommodate the lender in this aspect of the closing process. Most lenders fund the loan with their own monies, and the mortgage banker is responsible for seeing to it that funds are ordered and transferred properly.

Once the loan has been funded and all documents recorded, the mortgage banker must deliver these executed documents to the lender. At this time, mortgage bankers set up their loan-servicing administration procedures, which include collection of payments and monitoring that taxes are paid and proper insurance coverages are enforced. (Servicing is described in Chapter 27.)

In addition, the mortgage banker must make periodic inspections and usually must obtain annual operating expenses from the borrower, in which case, the mortgage banker should analyze the annual operating statements and report any major differences with the pro forma or with previous years' statements.

During the life of the loan, mortgage bankers may have other duties, for example, fire loss drafts to administer, reevaluations, refinancing, restructuring of the loan, and workouts of various sorts.

In short, the mortgage banker must find the borrower; develop a quality product; analyze, underwrite, and value the transaction; prepare a quality submission; finalize the acceptance of commitments; and service and administer the loan. In all these functions, the mortgage banker serves both the borrower and the lender, paid by the borrower to originate the loan and by the lender to administer the loan. To serve both parties, the mortgage banker must demonstrate that sense of objectivity required to counsel and work with both parties professionally, justifying the respect of both.

3

Parties to the Transaction: The Lender

A. S. Williams, III

Senior Vice President, Protective Life Corporation
Birmingham, Alabama

A variety of lending institutions provide funds for financing income property real estate. These include banks, savings and loan associations, mutual savings banks, insurance companies, pension funds, credit corporations, real estate investment trusts, and others (discussed at the end of this chapter). Although these institutions may evaluate loans in a similar manner, they tend to have investment policies that reflect not only the preferences of the individual companies but also the personalities of the particular lender's real estate decision makers.

Lenders are motivated by the need to invest in instruments that match their liabilities. They try to match their assets (the loans they make) with their liabilities (the funds they owe). The products, such as commercial paper or pension accounts, that lenders offer their customers play a significant role in the type of loans that the lender can make. As products are designed to meet their customer's requirements in a consumer-oriented environment, loan terms change to match the characteristics of these products. Commercial banks tend to have short-term liabilities, pension funds often have long-term liabilities, and life insurance companies have both short- and long-term liabilities. An institution that needs considerable liquidity to meet its obligations will reflect this in its choice of investments. The needs of the investor will greatly influence the mortgage terms which the institution will grant.

Lenders tend to develop preferences for particular types of loans; even the larger financial institutions will often specialize in financing one or more property types. Few institutions readily handle all types of real estate loans. Lender preferences may be motivated by conservative feelings regarding safety, aggressive feelings influenced by the need for high yields, the specific experience of the lender, or simply the prejudices of those involved in the decision-making process. What one lender may consider to be an excellent loan may hold no interest for another lender.

The changing economic environment and the new products offered by lending institutions will change attitudes about the types of loans desired, as well as the terms on which loans will be granted, and the mortgage banker needs to understand what a lender will and will not do. A mortgage banking firm should develop a personal relationship with its lenders to understand their needs and know how to deal with them. It is usually futile to try to sell a loan that does not fit a lender's pattern or to try to change a lender's investment policy. A mortgage banker should understand its lenders, understand the strengths and weaknesses of the loans it offers, and find the proper match.

The first contact with the lender for a particular loan is usually a telephone conversation. When the mortgage banker is armed with the proper knowledge of the lender's lending pattern and the details of the specific loan, the telephone discussion leads to acceptance by the lender if the lender's requirements and the loan match.

The loan application from the owner (discussed in Chapter 2) should be taken by the mortgage banker with one or more particular lenders in mind. It may be based on a preliminary discussion with a lender or with the knowledge of a lender's general lending pattern.

The submission to the lender should be based on an understanding of the lender's preferences for a loan submission. It will be reviewed by an underwriter who will usually complete a form which summarizes the highlights of the loan. It will contain the ratios and underwriting details used by the lender in determining the loan's acceptance. Items covered will include loan terms, information on the borrower, property factors, the lender's estimate of value, tenant information, and a host of ratios and coverage factors. Lenders rely on the real estate or the credit of the borrower or its tenants, or, most often, on both.

What a lender considers of most importance depends on the type of property financed and the characteristics of the particular loan. A lender is always interested in the character, experience, ability, financial capability, and dependability of the borrower or developer, and the developer must be able to complete the building on time and in an acceptable manner. All too often this element is taken for granted.

The property factors are also important on any loan. The importance of location is well known to almost anyone, and there are not nearly as many good locations as there are loans made. Many factors determine a good location, including competitive advantage, convenience, surroundings, visibility, layout, traffic patterns, and the economic environment of the area.

Lenders tend to have their own ideas about determining the appraised value of a property. Some rely on the appraisal of the mortgage banker, and some require an independent third-party appraisal. The mortgage banker needs to know how a lender views certain ingredients of the appraisal, including rental rates, expenses, capitalization rates, and the more advanced appraisal techniques using future income streams. A lender will use its own requirements in underwriting the loan. If the mortgage banker understands the lender's method of financial analysis, the loan has a better chance of approval.

In evaluating the financial aspects of the loan, the lender considers financial ratios, such as loan to value, loan to gross income, breakeven occupancy, value per square foot, loan per square foot, and numerous others relative to the particular type loan, and discussed in later chapters. One of the most important ratios is the coverage of debt service by the net income from the property. Most lenders have basic coverage requirements and frequently determine their preliminary interest in a loan by this factor.

When the loan has been underwritten, it will pass through the particular lender's approval process. That process can take days, or it may take two months or more. Usually the underwriter for the lender will present the loan to a committee which will determine its acceptance.

The Commitment

When a loan is approved and borrower and lender are in tentative agreement, a commitment is issued by the lender. The commitment becomes the binding contract which sets the terms and conditions on which the loan will be made. The major terms of the loan will have been set forth in the application, but many details in the commitment will be covered for the first time. Most commitments will be very detailed and will contain such things as leasing requirements, legal and documentary

requirements, loan-closing expenses, property management requirements, the terms of the commitment itself, and any fee required. Preparing a detailed document will enable the borrower to know what is
involved and what will have to be done for a successful closing. A short
commitment setting forth only the basic terms leaves all parties with insufficient knowledge of what is necessary to ultimately close the loan,
and although a short commitment may be easy for a borrower to accept,
it can lead to misunderstanding when the specific requirements appear.

The commitment will require acceptance within a stated time. The
borrower should have an attorney examine the document to help determine whether the terms and conditions are reasonable based on the
facts of the particular transaction. Circumstances will differ with every
loan, and the borrower should know if the terms and conditions of the
commitment can be met before its acceptance.

The lender's commitment checklist will set forth the information
needed to satisfy acceptance of the commitment. When a commitment is
accepted, it is signed and forwarded to the lender with a commitment
fee. The mortgage banker and the lender then monitor the receipt of
the items necessary to satisfy the commitment. These include some of or
all the following:

- Leases
- Lease amendments
- Construction progress reports
- Appraisal
- Soil tests
- Boundary survey
- Site inspection reports
- Plans and specifications

A commitment may cover an existing property or a property to be
constructed; the commitment may call for an immediate closing or for a
closing at some future date, as in the case of proposed construction.
When the commitment covers existing property and the commitment
terms have been satisfied, the parties simply schedule a closing date and
prepare for closing. On proposed construction, the mortgage banker
and/or the lender should inspect the property during construction and
upon completion. The commitment will require a closing within a stated
time, and the mortgage lender must monitor the construction of the improvements and acquisition of the documents necessary for closing.

The lender schedules funds to be available for disbursement at the commitment closing date. Most lenders expect the loan to be delivered by the mortgage banker; standby or contingent commitments must be negotiated and usually include additional nonrefundable fees. The loan must be delivered, because the lender has given up the opportunity to commit these funds to any other investment and has invested funds to be available at the closing date. A borrower should understand that a commitment is a binding contract and the borrower has no more right to refuse to close than the lender.

Leases

Loans that involve significant leasing often require lease amendments. For example, some lease provisions may give a tenant a right to terminate a lease based on an event the lender cannot control. This makes the lease uncertain for the term required. The borrower and the tenant have usually negotiated the lease before the lender is involved, and the tenant is now being asked to change a lease provision to make it acceptable to the lender. A tenant who does not like the specific amendment language may refuse to grant the change. If the lender will agree to a lease amendment that gives the tenant more of what it has bargained for, while assuring the lender that the lease will continue during its term, the problem may be solved.

Lenders that develop personal relationships with borrowers, tenants, and other interested parties will find completing a transaction much easier than will lenders that are very dogmatic. The mortgage banker should understand the lender's negotiating policy.

The loan closing involves the cooperative effort of the borrower, lender, closing attorney, and often a number of other parties. If everything that should be done in the process up to this time has been done, the closing should be completed without great difficulty. The lender will give closing instructions to the closing attorney, and the attorney will prepare the closing documents for execution. A closing checklist will include such things as the basic legal documents, title insurance, as-built survey, certificate of occupancy, zoning certificate, fire insurance, and other documents depending on the specific transaction. The lender will have specified in the commitment what is expected, and there should be no significant surprises if everyone has taken the time to understand the commitment and remained in the process from the beginning.

After the closing, the lender must follow up to determine that all documentation is received and the permanent loan files are established. The loan is placed on its accounting system, and procedures are implemented for handling taxes, insurance, annual statements, and any other information needed for the specific loan. Lenders may rely on mortgage-servicing relationships, or loans may be serviced directly by the lender. In either case, loans will be monitored for receipt of payment, periodic payment of taxes and insurance, and any other necessary documentation. Property inspections will also be made, usually at least every two years.

It is important to follow the management of any income property to determine that it will continue to provide the income stream required to service the loan. This process often becomes superficial, but proper maintenance and management of a property can be as important as determining the original acceptance of a property to secure the loan.

The servicing relationships with a mortgage banker should be merely an extension of the lender's mortgage operation. The lender relies on the mortgage banker to secure quality loan applications, assist in completing the loan transaction, and assist in servicing the loan during its lifetime. The lender will actually design its staff and establish its operational procedures relying on the mortgage banker to fulfill its obligations assumed under a servicing agreement. If the relationship is to succeed, the parties must work as a team and engage in ongoing activity in all areas covered by the contract. Continuous activity and contact are necessary, and both parties have an obligation to make the relationships work. Each party should understand the other's operation, and if the procedures involved are not mutually satisfactory, it is best not to enter into a servicing relationship.

All parties should understand the terms of the servicing agreement. The basic areas covered by the servicing agreement are:

- The obligation to submit mortgage applications to the lender and the procedures for obtaining commitments
- The responsibilities of the parties for closing documents and completing the loan in keeping with the commitment
- Details of the responsibilities concerning the servicing of the loan during its existence
- The compensation of the mortgage banker
- Terms and conditions for the termination of the servicing contract
- General provisions concerning the rights and duties of the parties to the contract

It would be well for the principals to read their contracts periodically as a reminder of the obligations they have assumed. It is also a good idea for the production personnel to be familiar with the agreement. Lenders prefer that the same people remain involved during the servicing process. It is easier to service a loan if the mortgage banking firm is familiar with its origination. If problems occur, it is best to work as a team to find solutions.

Lenders will continue to evaluate the mortgage loan as a satisfactory investment to meet their specific investment needs relative to other opportunities for investment of their funds. Under the economic conditions in the mid-1980s, lenders are granting a variety of loan terms from 3 to 10 years with longer amortization schedules. Some lenders are again providing long-term amortization without the shorter maturities. Loans are made with adjustable rates, with participations, and with a host of other features. Lenders are also entering joint ventures and outright real estate ownership. Changes in products sold and in the economic environment will continue to influence future mortgage loan trends and the attractiveness of mortgage loans as an investment. If the parties to the mortgage loan transaction are willing to reflect the changing needs and requirements of the respective parties, income property loans will continue to provide a major source of investments for many lenders.

Appendix: Investors in Mortgages

Life insurance companies are the primary lenders for larger commercial and industrial loans. During 1986, $34 billion of loan originations were issued by life insurance companies (statistics are from the Office of Financial Management, U.S. Department of Housing and Urban Development). A relatively small group of life insurance companies hold the majority of income-producing mortgages, both residential and nonresidential. Twenty companies hold 68 percent of the nonfarm mortgages.

Life insurance companies have been attracted to mortgage loans because the yield on commercial mortgages is generally higher than the yield obtained from stocks and bonds of apparently equal quality. Moreover, once a staff has been assembled to evaluate real estate lending and investment, the life insurance company is far better equipped to compete against lenders which have not acquired this capability.

Certain life insurance companies, including Prudential, Metropolitan, and Equitable, operate through branch offices. Other larger life insurance companies, including Aetna and CIGNA, operate with correspondent mortgage bankers. Many of the smaller life insurance companies rely exclusively on correspondent mortgage bankers.

Many life insurance companies seek guaranteed income contracts (GICs) from those who administer pension funds. A GIC is a promise by the life insurance company to pay a specified interest rate over a period to the fund. The life insurance company must then invest the money at the higher rate than that promised to the pension fund to achieve profit and to compensate for risk of loss. Because GICs are generally for a shorter time, such as five years, the life insurance companies tend to invest the money over the same period. This has been a major reason for the prevalence of what is known as "bullet" loans—often only the interest at a fixed rate is to be paid for a period of five to seven years, and refinancing of the entire amount of the principal (the bullet) is required at the end of the term.

Life insurance companies often engage in joint ventures with the developer. Some of their participating mortgages have bonuses related to performance of the project, perhaps in return for the lender giving the developer a larger amount of financing than otherwise might be available. These kinds of mortgages are discussed in greater detail in Chapter 21. Many life insurance companies also purchase properties, and some are involved in the development of real estate directly.

Commercial banks provided about $88 billion in loan originations for multifamily and commercial real estate lending in 1986, primarily in construction loans. Traditionally, banks have been the major construction and development (C&D) lenders, usually requiring a long-term loan as a takeout by which their short-term financing could be repaid. C&D lenders should keep track of the developer's day-to-day business transactions. The rates on such loans often float according to the prime or some other other variable rate, and often the interest is accrued as an obligation to be paid once the long-term loan (often called the "permanent" loan) is applied to the project. In recent years, many commercial banks have extended their C&D loans to continue to finance the project through the rent-up period after construction.

Savings banks have been a major source of mortgage credit since World War II, attracted by the higher yields available on the long-term market. About $8 billion in commercial and multifamily mortgages were originated in 1986. These savings banks are primarily located in the East and Northwest sections of the United States. The designation *FSB* appears after the bank's name to indicate a federal savings bank.

Savings and loan associations (S&Ls) obtained increased powers in the 1970s to invest in income-producing real estate projects. Traditionally the major source of funds for home builders and home refinancings, the S&Ls were initially designed to foster homeownership by encouraging consumers to save. Consequently, they were regulated to keep their investments in mortgage financing and were awarded tax benefits by Congress if they did so.

The largest S&Ls, particularly those in California, have invested heavily in commercial mortgages in the 1980s. S&Ls originated $42 billion in nonresidential and multifamily mortgages in 1986. Certain S&Ls have also established "service company" affiliates to go into the development business directly, often creating income-producing projects.

Pension funds are becoming a major source of long-term mortgage credit for income-producing real estate. Several major state and local government retirement funds originate or buy substantially in commercial real estate, although their investment does not begin to equal the amount invested by the life insurance companies, banks, or thrift institutions.

Because income to a pension fund is not taxed, some of the traditional tax shelter benefits still available through realty have little meaning for pension funds. Reshaping the ownership-lending configuration to account for the lack of tax shelter is often one result of restructuring a loan presentation to a pension fund source.

Real estate investment trusts (REITs) participate actively in financing commercial developments through a combination of equity and lending procedures. Originally formed as trusts after Massachusetts outlawed the ownership of realty by corporations (when the mills owned the workers' housing after the Civil War), these portfolios of income-producing properties are granted conduit tax treatment similar to mutual funds—as long as they do not invest in anything but real estate. REITs (which now can be corporations electing REIT tax status) must be "passive" lenders or investors who do not actually run the businesses in which they invest, so sometimes loans or investments must be structured to meet the unusual REIT tax requirements.

Many trust accounts and other entities are structured to obtain the REIT tax status, but the best-known REITs are publicly held with shares traded on the New York and American Stock Exchanges. A few entities are run by affiliates of major investing companies, such as banks and life insurance companies, but most are operated by real estate entrepreneurs who have tapped the investing public to buy into real estate transactions that otherwise could not be sold in small issues publicly. In general, REITs demand higher yields to compensate for their acceptance of unusual borrower or project attributes.

Federal credit agencies, such as the Federal Housing Administration and the Farmers Home Administration, purchased $2 billion in multifamily or commercial mortgage loans in 1986. The Federal Housing Administration insures multifamily housing loans and has a very limited amount of funds for direct loans for elderly housing. The Farmers Home Administration guarantees or insures multifamily housing but has very limited funds in 1987. A program for guarantees of certain commercial mortgages is no longer active.

State and local credit agencies originated $8 billion in mortgage loans during 1986, mostly multifamily housing mortgages financed through state housing agencies. The investment banking firms that sell the state's credit for such housing agency paper often own a mortgage banking subsidiary which would originate the loans for the agency.

Credit corporations are usually subsidiaries of major industrial corporations which sell debt to the public and trade on the company's name (such as General Electric Credit, Westinghouse Credit, or ITT Credit). They have been attracted to short-term mortgage lending because their funds are raised from the sale of commercial paper or short-term bonds. Loans for construction or interim-term mortgages are made at several percentage points above the cost of raising funds. Such loans often have rates that float by being tied to a moving rate such as the prime or the Treasury Bill rate.

4

Property Analysis: An Introduction

Angelo L. Dentamaro, CMB, MAI

Executive Vice President, Margaretten & Company, Inc.
Perth Amboy, New Jersey

Thomas Z. Minehart, III, CMB

Executive Vice President, Latimer & Buck, Inc.
Philadelphia, Pennsylvania

Each and every piece of income-producing real estate is a separate and distinct entity. Specific types of income-producing properties, including shopping centers, office buildings, apartments, hotels, industrial properties, and medical facilities, are covered in Chapters 14 to 20. However, four broad categories used to describe the various aspects of income property finance provide a general framework for examining any income-producing real estate project.

1. *Location* of the property, the type of improvements at that location, and the surrounding market characteristics affecting its marketability, such as demand and supply for that particular type of facility

2. *Physical attributes* of the project, such as the quality, size, composition, economic efficiency, architectural and structural design (such as external and internal building materials, heating plant, air conditioning, telecommunications), and parking capacities

3. *Tenants* and use of the facility, including the mix of tenants, leasing structures, and management capacities related to the ability to sustain financing

4. *Operating statements* of income and expense and other basic financial data pertaining to the specific project and similar properties

These broad categories pertain to any type of property, from the smallest single-purpose sales outlet to a multipurpose office-retail-residential complex straddling several blocks of a downtown area.

Although the principles of underwriting properties are similar, specific projects differ sufficiently so that the characteristics of the borrower—and especially the manager—are important aspects of any financing. A builder of an office building may not make a good developer of a shopping center. A developer of real estate should not always be expected to manage the property as well.

The mortgage banker's analysis of income-producing real estate is not an exact science. Subjective judgment, experience, and innovative ability all play their part. Each mortgage analysis involves certain fundamentals, however, which create a framework in which the banker's assessments are presented. The fundamental segments of an analysis are:

1. Location
2. Physical property description
3. Sponsorship
4. Appraisal
5. Underwriting
6. Structuring the loan

Location

Perhaps the oldest adage in real estate financing is that the three principles of success are (1) location, (2) location, and (3) location. Obviously this is an exaggeration. A good location can be ruined by poor sponsorship, and some projects in marginal locations can succeed under strong sponsorship. The significant aspect of location is that it must be suitable for the project and property under discussion. Among the location elements to be considered are:

- Proximity to market
- Compatibility with the surrounding environment

- Ingress and egress
- Visibility of the site may be important, particularly for retail
- Transportation to the property
- Work force availability
- Utilities
- Zoning
- Physical characteristics of the particular site

Physical Property Description

The information in the loan submission must determine the exact size of the facility described by legal boundaries, gross and net rentable area, and other specifics, such as parking, amenities, physical and mechanical components, functional and economic utility, and all aspects of physical and economic obsolescence.

Physical property characteristics must be reviewed with respect to the location's designed function and the property's present and future marketability. The mortgage banker must have personal knowledge of or have available professional expertise for such matters as the adequacy of footings and foundations, heating and air conditioning, load-bearing capacities, lighting, and the more apparent elements concerning ceilings, floors, walls, and windows. The analyst is responsible for judging whether the proposed project is adequate to function as intended.

Sponsorship

Mortgage bankers need to know as much as possible about the sponsorship of the project, whether this be an individual developer, a partnership, a corporation, or some other legal development entity. A prospective lender will be interested in the character, experience, ability, financial capability, and dependability of the borrower or developer. Lenders are trained to look beyond the collateral to the capacity of the borrower to succeed. Both the credit standing and the track record of the project sponsor are important. The former indicates whether the development entity is capable of responsibility for its obligations. The latter helps determine if the developer can manage to complete the project and operate it profitably.

Evaluation of the financial stability of the development entity requires a thorough financial investigation and analysis. The credit and financial statements of the corporation or partnership as an entity, as well as the individuals who comprise it, must be scrutinized, so as to determine their capability to carry a project through to completion. And every effort should be made to obtain the best possible financial and credit information. (Financial analysis is covered in Chapter 6.)

Assessment of the track record of the development entity should at the very least entail the following questions: What other properties has this sponsor produced? What other properties of the same type as the subject property has this particular sponsor developed? How much real estate has been or is presently managed by the development entity? What has been the payment record of the development entity?

Appraisal

The economic viability of the project begins with an appraisal, an integral part of any income-producing financing submission. Judgment is required by the mortgage banker in determining exactly how much importance the appraisal should be accorded. Some lending institutions are appraisal-oriented, while others place priority or equal emphasis on other factors such as sponsorship and credit.

There are different methods of determining the appraised value of a property. Some lenders prefer the market approach. Some rely mostly on the cost approach. Some place reliance on the economic value approach (see Chapter 8). Some will rely on the appraisal of the mortgage banker. Others will require an independent, third-party appraisal. The mortgage banker needs to know how a particular lender prefers to analyze certain aspects of the appraisal, such as rental rates, expenses, capitalization rates, or the more advanced appraisal techniques using future income streams.

Notwithstanding the many kinds of appraisals and appraisal techniques (e.g., those for estate purposes, insurance, local taxation, condemnation and sale, or acquisition), the principal consideration of the mortgage banker is that the appraisal should provide a reasonable estimate of value upon which to base the loan amount. This estimate of value must be acceptable to the lender and the many auditors and examiners of the lender. In addition, the information in the appraisal report should be consistent, with no unexplained differences in areas, sizes, room counts, or any other facts.

Underwriting

The next analytical technique employed by the mortgage banker in evaluating income-producing real estate is underwriting. Underwriting is risk analysis and is the aspect of the evaluation process which many lenders consider most important. Various lenders have different underwriting patterns. The mortgage banker should be familiar with the underwriting criteria of a particular lender or a group of lenders. These criteria will vary from property to property and from one geographic location to another.

The mathematics of real estate finance are based on standard equations or ratios which apply to almost all types of income property—for example, loan to value, loan to gross income, breakeven occupancy, value per square foot, and debt service coverage by the net operating income of the property. (See Chapter 11.) Each lender is likely to consider one or several of these ratios to be more important than others in underwriting the loan and may emphasize the importance of one ratio to a particular type of property. Almost all lenders consider debt service coverage a significant criterion; most have basic coverage requirements for each type of property and determine their preliminary interest in a loan by this factor.

Structuring the Loan

The final loan evaluation technique is structuring the loan. In the role of mortgage analyst, the mortgage banker makes a very significant judgment concerning the maximum amount of financing that a particular property can sustain, balancing that figure against loan interest rates and terms and conditions. Based on a thorough analysis of the project's characteristics, this decision will influence the particular lender with whom the mortgage banker is dealing. For example, the mortgage banker must be aware that the expected lender for the project never exceeds a 75 percent loan-to-value ratio for a shopping center when the banker negotiates the application with the sponsor and recommends a particular dollar amount to the lender. However, if the sponsor will accept a lower loan-to-value ratio (therefore less money borrowed) but wants an interest rate lower than that generally offered by the lender for this particular type of project, the mortgage banker engages in negotiating the loan structure with both the borrower and the lender.

The changing environment in the money markets, reflecting changing expectations, will vary these negotiations. Also, the new products offered by lending institutions, such as short-term debt instruments based on the sponsor's credit, debt-equity instruments involving equity participations, and convertible mortgages, will change attitudes about the types of loans desired as well as the terms on which loans will be granted (see Chapters 21 through 23). To help structure the loan, the mortgage banker must be familiar with the changing world of real estate finance.

Although experienced mortgage bankers find futile any effort to sell a loan that does not fit a lender's pattern or to change a lender's investment policy, the mortgage banker, the borrower, and the lender can usually work together to develop creative mortgage financing to meet changing investment needs.

PART 2
Analyzing the Project

5

The Ownership Entity

**Gary S. Smuckler, Esq. and
Howard N. Solodky, Esq.**
*Partners, Melrod, Redman & Gartlan
Washington, D.C.*

Selection of the form of legal entity to own and operate income-producing real estate should be based on a consideration of at least the following three factors: personal exposure to third-party liabilities arising from ownership and operation of the real estate, ease of administration and control of the entity, and federal income tax consequences. Because the two most common forms of ownership, the corporation and the limited partnership, can be structured to insulate individual owners from personal liability, federal income tax concerns often are the most important consideration. An understanding of the nontax features of the various forms of ownership is nonetheless important not only for choosing the appropriate ownership vehicle but also for tailoring that vehicle to meet the needs of the real estate investor or developer.

Direct Individual Ownership

Sole Proprietorship

A single owner of real estate may choose to hold that real estate in her or his own name as a sole proprietor. As the direct owner of the real property, a sole proprietor is personally liable for any losses or claims arising from the property. Under this form of ownership, any income or loss attributable to the real property enters directly into the computation of the owner's taxable income. See Chapter 13 for a discussion of how income and loss are taxed.

Joint Ownership

Real estate is often directly owned by more than one individual. The three principal types of joint ownership are tenancy in common, joint tenancy, and tenancy by the entirety. Frequently, joint ownership of income-producing real estate is treated as a partnership for federal income tax purposes. However, the Internal Revenue Service (IRS) has ruled that under certain limited circumstances, a tenancy in common will be respected without the overlay of the complicated partnership tax provisions of the Internal Revenue Code.[1]

Tenancy in Common. Under this form of ownership, two or more cotenants each own an undivided interest in the entire property. Although all the tenants in common need not have an equal fractional interest in the real property, each must have equal rights of possession and use of the property. This form of ownership does not entail any rights of survivorship; that is, upon the death of a cotenant, the deceased's interest in the real property does not automatically pass to the surviving cotenants but rather is inherited by the heirs or beneficiaries of the deceased cotenant. In most jurisdictions, tenants in common may, without the consent of their cotenants, mortgage, lease, exchange, or otherwise transfer their interest in real property.

Joint Tenancy. Joint tenants own equal and undivided interests in the real property held in joint tenancy. If joint tenants transfer their interest to a third party, the transferee becomes a tenant in common with the remaining joint tenants. The principal characteristic of a joint tenancy is that, unlike a tenant in common, a joint tenant does possess rights of survivorship. Note, however, that in many jurisdictions a presumption operates in favor of treating co-ownership of real property as a tenancy in common rather than a joint tenancy, and some states have abolished the joint tenancy.

Tenancy by the Entirety. A married couple may acquire real property and hold it as tenants by the entirety. Under this form of ownership,

---

[1] Rev. Rul. 75–374, 1975–2 C.B. 261.

each spouse owns an undivided interest in the entire property with rights of survivorship. In most states that still recognize tenancy by the entirety, spouses who own real property as a tenant by the entirety may not encumber or convey their interest in the property without the consent of their spouse. However, a majority of the states have abolished the tenancy by the entirety; therefore, in those states, a conveyance of property to a husband and wife creates a tenancy in common or a joint tenancy. A divorce or annulment will generally terminate a tenancy by the entirety, resulting in the creation of a tenancy in common.

The Corporation

Nontax Characteristics

A *corporation* is a legal entity that is owned by its shareholders. The shareholders control the corporation by electing a board of directors who are responsible for the overall management of the corporation. Officers are selected by the directors to oversee the day-to-day affairs of the corporation. Officers and perhaps directors, but not shareholders, are typically authorized to act on behalf of the corporation.

A corporation is formed by the filing of articles of incorporation or a corporate charter with the appropriate office of the state in which the corporation is organized. In some states, the shareholders must contribute to the corporation a minimum amount of capital as a precondition to the validity of a corporate charter granted by the state. Ordinarily, a corporation, through the passage of a shareholders' resolution, will adopt bylaws that set forth the basic rules governing operation and control of the corporation. For example, the bylaws may contain provisions concerning shareholders and directors meetings, election of officers and directors, and the basic duties to be performed by each of the officers of the corporation.

One advantage to owning property in corporate form is that a corporation has an unlimited life; that is, the corporation continues in existence until its shareholders decide to liquidate and dissolve the corporation. Consequently, a corporation will continue to operate notwithstanding the death or bankruptcy of one of its shareholders, officers, or directors. In addition, in the absence of agreement to the contrary, shareholders may freely transfer their interest in the corporation without the consent of any other shareholder or the corporation. In a closely held corporation, however, the shareholders often enter into an agreement imposing certain restrictions on the transferability of stock in the corporation. For example, the shareholders may agree that upon the receipt by a shareholder of a bona fide third-party offer for that shareholder's stock, the other shareholders and the corporation have a right of first refusal with respect to the stock of the selling shareholder.

Stock ownership of a corporation may be structured to provide different shareholders with different voting, dividend, and liquidation rights. For example, often a corporation will have outstanding both preferred and common stock. Preferred stockholders are ordinarily entitled to receive both dividend and liquidating distributions from the corporation before the common stockholders receive any distributions. However, the amount of dividend and liquidating distributions that preferred stockholders can receive is typically limited to a fixed return on their investment in the corporation. In contrast, corporate earnings remaining after payment of dividends to preferred stockholders may be distributed to common stockholders in as large an amount as the board of directors of the corporation determines. Similarly, common stockholders are entitled to receive a liquidating distribution of all assets remaining after payment to the preferred stockholders of their fixed return. Both common stock and preferred stock may be structured to provide full, limited, or no rights to vote for directors of the corporation.

Perhaps the central nontax attribute of a corporation is that its shareholders are not personally liable for the debts of the corporation. Therefore, if a corporation is sued or becomes bankrupt, any resulting liability may only be satisfied by the corporation's assets and not by the shareholders' personal assets. This characteristic of limited liability obviously distinguishes the corporate form of holding real property from the sole proprietorship and forms of joint ownership discussed above. This distinction is often eroded, however, in the context of a closely held corporation, because creditors of such a corporation may demand that the shareholders personally guarantee the corporation's liabilities.

Federal Income Tax Aspects

"Regular" Corporation. A corporation that does not elect to be taxed as an S corporation under the Internal Revenue Code is a separate taxable entity subject to the imposition of corporate income tax on its earnings. When such a "regular" corporation distributes a dividend to its shareholders, each shareholder is taxable on the amount of the dividend received. This two-tiered system of corporate taxation (taxation at both the corporate and shareholder levels) often discourages the use of a regular corporation as a vehicle for real estate investments. Although the impact of the corporate level tax may be reduced by the payment of deductible salaries to shareholder-employees of the corporation, excessive salaries are subject to recharacterization by the Internal Revenue Service as nondeductible disguised dividends. However, retention of earnings at the corporate level to avoid the shareholder tax on dividends may expose the corporation to an accumulated earnings tax.

If a regular corporation has deductions in excess of taxable income for a particular year, the resulting net operating loss may only be utilized at the corporate level; the shareholders cannot individually benefit from the tax-deductible loss. A net operating loss realized by a regular corporation may be carried back 3 years and carried forward 15 years to offset any taxable income of the corporation in those years.

Subchapter S Corporation. For a corporation to qualify as an S corporation, the following requirements not applicable to a regular corporation must be satisfied: (1) the corporation may have no more than 35 shareholders, all of whom must be individuals or certain types of trusts; (2) the corporation may not own 80 percent or more of the total voting power and total value of the stock of another corporation; (3) the corporation may have only one class of outstanding stock (differences in voting rights among shares of common stock may be ignored); and (4) all persons who are shareholders of the corporation on the date the corporation elects to be taxed as an S corporation must consent to the election.

With certain limited exceptions, a corporation electing to be taxed as an S corporation is not a taxable entity; instead, the shareholders of an S corporation are taxable on their proportionate shares of the taxable income of the corporation. Moreover, the character of any gain (capital gain or ordinary income) realized by an S corporation flows through to its shareholders. In general, the taxation of an S corporation more closely resembles the taxation of a partnership (as discussed below) than a regular corporation.

Each shareholder in an S corporation increases the "basis" in the stock by the amount of the corporation's income on which the shareholder is taxable. A subsequent cash distribution by the corporation to its shareholders, in an amount equal to the income realized by the corporation, is a nontaxable distribution that simply reduces proportionally the basis of each shareholder in stock. As a result, income realized by an S corporation is taxed only once.

Shareholders in an S corporation are also generally entitled to claim their proportionate share of any loss realized by the corporation. Moreover, the character of any corporate loss also passes through to each shareholder. Significantly, however, shareholders may not claim a loss from the corporation in excess of their total investment in the corporation, which consists of their stock basis and the outstanding principal balance of any loans made by the shareholders to the corporation. Borrowings by the corporation, whether recourse or nonrecourse, will not enhance the ability of any shareholder to claim losses. If a shareholder's proportionate share of a corporate loss exceeds his or her total investment in the corporation, the excess loss may be carried forward indefinitely until the shareholder has sufficient basis in corporate stock or debt to absorb the loss. Just as taxable income increases S corporation shareholders' basis in stock, a taxable loss decreases the shareholders' basis (or, if they have no basis in stock, then in any loans made to the corporation).

Partnerships

General Partnership

Ordinarily, two or more parties desiring to organize a general partnership will execute a written partnership or joint venture agreement.[2] No government filing is required to establish that a partnership has been legally created. Moreover, even a written agreement is not a prerequisite if it can be determined from all the facts and circumstances that two or more persons have decided to co-own property or a business for joint profit. Once organized, a general partnership is effectively a mutual agency in which each partner has the authority to act on behalf of, and bind, the partnership and each of the other partners with respect to matters within the scope of the partnership's business. Each partner has equal rights in the management and conduct of the partnership's business unless the partners agree to the contrary.

A general partnership, unlike a corporation, does not possess the characteristic of continuity of life; that is, the death or bankruptcy of a partner does trigger the dissolution of the partnership. A voluntary transfer by a partner of his or her interest in the partnership does not of itself dissolve the partnership. However, the transferee, in the absence of agreement among the partners to the contrary, does not receive any rights to interfere in the management or conduct of the partnership's business other than the right to receive the share of the partnership's profits that the transferring partner was entitled to receive.

Unlike shareholders in a corporation, the partners in a general part-

---

[2]Most of the rules governing partnerships discussed herein are codified in the Uniform Partnership Act and the Uniform Limited Partnership Act, both of which have been adopted in most states with slight variations from state to state.

nership are each personally liable for the debts and liabilities of the partnership. This feature of a general partnership has been a principal force behind the popularity of the *limited* partnership as a real estate development vehicle.

Limited Partnership

A limited partnership is a partnership formed by two or more people, at least one of whom is a general partner and at least one of whom is a limited partner. In virtually every state, a prerequisite to the formation of a limited partnership is the filing of a certificate of limited partnership in the appropriate state or local governmental office. The certificate must contain a variety of details about the limited partnership including (1) the name and location of the principal place of business of the partnership; (2) the name and place of residence of each partner and whether each partner is a general or limited partner; (3) the amount of cash and a description of, and the agreed value of, other property contributed to the partnership by each limited partner; and (4) the share of the partnership profits to which each limited partner is entitled.

The general partner or partners of a limited partnership possess the same rights and obligations as a partner in a general partnership. Thus, a general partner (1) has the authority to act on behalf of, and bind, all of the partners, both limited and general; (2) has equal rights, along with any other general partner, in the management and conduct of the limited partnership's affairs, unless there is a contrary agreement; and (3) is fully liable for all the debts and obligations of the partnership. In contrast, a limited partner is not entitled to act on behalf of the partnership or to participate in the management and control of the partnership's business. A limited partner is not personally liable for any debts or liabilities of the partnership to third parties. A limited partner is liable, however, to the partnership for any unpaid capital contribution to the partnership as required in the certificate of limited partnership.

A limited partner's interest is freely transferable, although the transferee does not automatically become a substituted limited partner. A *substituted* limited partner is a person entitled to all the rights of the limited partner from whom that person received an interest in the partnership. Transferees who do not become substituted limited partners have no right to an accounting of partnership transactions or to inspect the partnership books; they are entitled to receive only the profits or a return of the capital contribution to which their transferor was otherwise entitled. A transferee will become a substituted limited partner if all the partners in the partnership consent or if the certificate of limited partnership automatically confers that status.

The death, bankruptcy, or other withdrawal of a limited partner from a limited partnership does not terminate the partnership. However, the retirement, death, or insanity of a general partner will dissolve the partnership unless the business is continued by the remaining general partners under a right to do so stated in the certificate of limited partnership or with the consent of all remaining partners in the partnership.

The general partner of a limited partnership is often a corporation. Because the limited partners are insulated from the liabilities of the partnership, use of a sole corporate general partner ensures that no individual's assets will be exposed to the debts and obligations of the partnership. To ensure that a limited partnership with a sole corporate general partner is recognized as such, rather than as a corporation, for federal income tax purposes, the corporate general partner must be adequately capitalized. The IRS has prescribed certain tests, including a minimum equity test, that must be satisfied to obtain a ruling from the IRS that a limited partnership with a sole corporate general partner will be treated as a partnership for federal income tax purposes.[3]

Federal Income Tax Aspects

A partnership is not subject to federal income taxation; instead, like shareholders in an S corporation, the partners are taxable on their proportionate shares of the taxable income of the partnership. The character of the gain realized by the partnership flows through to the partners, and the partners' basis is increased by gain recognized and decreased by cash distributed. A distribution of cash to partners in excess of their basis in the partnership interest is generally taxed as capital gains in the amount of the excess.

Each partner in a partnership is entitled to claim a proportionate share of any partnership loss, the character of which passes through to the partners as well. Partners must decrease the basis of their partnership interest by their share of any partnership loss. However, partners may not claim their share of a partnership loss to the extent that the loss exceeds their basis in the partnership interest; such excess loss may be carried forward until the partner has sufficient basis to absorb the loss.

Unlike a shareholder in an S corporation, partners in a partnership are able to increase their partnership interest basis as a result of part-

[3]Rev. Proc. 72–13, 1972–1 C.B. 735.

nership borrowings. In a general partnership, each partner's basis in the partnership interest is automatically increased by her or his share of partnership liabilities. If a recourse loan is made to a general partnership, the partners share the liability in accordance with their loss-sharing ratios. A nonrecourse borrowing is shared by the partners in accordance with their profits interests in the partnership.

Limited and general partners in a limited partnership may increase their basis in the partnership interest by a proportionate share of any partnership nonrecourse indebtedness. Only general partners, however, may automatically increase their partnership interest bases by their shares of partnership recourse borrowings. For purposes of determining the amount of each general partner's basis increase attributable to a limited partnership recourse liability, the general partners are treated as owning the entire partnership in the same relative percentages that they own their general partner interests. Limited partners may also increase their partnership interest bases as a result of a recourse liability to the extent they are obligated to contribute additional capital to the partnership. Here again, nonrecourse loans are shared in accordance with profit-sharing ratios, and recourse borrowings are shared by the partners in accordance with their relative interests in the losses of the partnership.

With the exception of tax credits, all partnership tax items, including losses, may be specially allocated among the partners as provided in the partnership agreement. In other words, one or more tax items may be allocated to partners in a manner different from the percentage interests those partners otherwise are deemed to own in the partnership. A special allocation will not be questioned by the IRS if it has "substantial economic effect," that is, the allocation must actually affect in a corresponding amount the amount of economic profit received, or the amount of economic loss borne, by the partners affected by the allocation.

Real Estate Investment Trusts

The real estate investment trust (REIT) is a creature solely of the Internal Revenue Code. A corporation, association, or trust for state law purposes can qualify as a REIT provided it would otherwise be classified as a corporation for federal income tax purposes. A REIT must be managed by one or more trustees or directors and must be owned by 100 or more persons whose ownership is evidenced by transferable shares or by transferable certificates of beneficial interest. Five or fewer individuals, however, may not own more than 50 percent of the entity.

A REIT must satisfy relatively stringent requirements concerning sources of income, nature of assets, and distributions of income to its beneficial owners. The purpose of these tests is to ensure that a REIT invests primarily in real estate and acts as a conduit to its beneficial owners all or virtually all of its income derived from its real estate investments. Income passed through to the owners of a REIT is taxable to the owners, rather than to the REIT, and the character of the income as capital gain or ordinary income is preserved in the hands of the owner. Losses incurred by a REIT are not, however, passed through to the owners, but may be utilized by the REIT to offset any income retained by the entity. If a REIT fails to satisfy any of the conditions for qualification, it is taxed as a regular corporation as described above.

The mortgage banker should recognize that, although much emphasis is placed on advantages which differing forms of legal ownership afford, equal consideration must also be given to the developer's creditworthiness, experience, and track record with development.

6

Underwriting the Developer: Credit Analysis

Jess S. Lawhorn, CMB
Senior Vice President, Southeast Bank, N.A.
Miami, Florida

This chapter provides an overview, from the perspective of a commercial bank analyzing a larger developer who seeks a construction loan, of the issues involved in analyzing a prospective borrower's financial statements and credit history.

To assess a developer's creditworthiness, three types of information must be analyzed: financial statements, credit reports, and credit references. A complete review of a developer's ability to service and repay debt will be based on both direct and indirect information. The developer's financial statements will provide direct information. There are three kinds of financial statements: the balance sheet, the income statement, and the funds statement. Indirect information is available from a number of sources, including the reports generated by various credit-reporting agencies and references from the developer's existing customers, suppliers, contractors, banks, and previous lenders. Indirect information can reveal material that financial statements obscure or audits do not examine.

Identify the Borrower

The standard credit analysis is usually the first order of business in underwriting an income property development. Before analyzing the potential borrower's financial statements, however, the borrower should be identified, which is not always an easy task. Income property is a form of real estate developed by many different types of business organizations: multinational corporations, individuals, and myriad intermediate forms such as partnerships, limited partnerships, joint ventures, trusts, and subsidiary corporations. Often, the identity of the borrower is not apparent or has been deliberately obscured. There are marked differences in the legal rights and responsibilities of the individuals associated with the project as well as in the legal recourse for the lender from one type of development entity to another. The resource available to repay project financing also depends on the formal structure of the development entity. For example, when a corporation forms to participate in a joint venture, it insulates itself and its assets against claims arising from the project. Unless explicit guarantees are made by the parent corporation, analyzing the parent's financial statements to assess the creditworthiness of the project would be misleading. Instead, the financial statements of the actual participants in the joint venture must be analyzed.

Even when the borrower is a single individual, obtaining accurate information may be difficult. If the individual is married and the spouse is not a party to the project, the financial statements must be adjusted to eliminate the property and income of the spouse.

If the loan is guaranteed, the guarantor should be identified and the nature and extent of the guarantee ascertained. Any guarantee that does not carry the "full faith and credit" of the guarantor may provide only limited recourse to the lender. Many guarantors are willing to issue comfort letters which promise support to a borrower; however, such letters are not legally binding and fall short of a binding guarantee.

Primary Financial Statements

The primary financial statements may be presented on either an accrual or a cash basis. Most corporations use the accrual method, which is designed to match cash flow with the underlying cost of producing a good or delivering a service. In applying the matching principle, revenue is often developed before actual cash payments have been received. Although accrual accounting will more closely reflect the underlying assets and liabilities of an entity, the "bottom-line" entry will not be directly linked to cash flow. The cash basis of accounting simply measures cash flow over a period, with no attempt to tie the cost incurred to the revenue generated by individual transactions. Many partnerships rely on the cash method, and individual income taxes are calculated on a cash basis. At the outset, therefore, an important determination is whether the financial statements have been assembled on a cash or an accrual basis.

There are three major financial descriptions by which to account for an operation. One is static, capturing a glimpse of the operation as of one moment. This is the *balance sheet,* showing assets, liabilities, and owner's equity. The second financial description reflects operations over a period, usually a year. This is the *income statement,* showing revenue, expenses, and profit. The third common descriptive statement is a flow-of-funds or *funds statement,* which traces the source and use of funds. Examples of the three statements for a hypothetical ABC Development Company are shown.

Balance Sheet

The balance sheet describes the financial condition of the borrower on a specific day; it is analogous to a snapshot. The balance sheet shows the net worth of the borrower and, therefore, the total resources available to repay loans.

The standard balance sheet format categorizes assets according to the duration of their economic life. Cash and assets that are expected to be liquidated (converted to cash) within a year are classified as current assets. Beyond actual cash (which includes checking account balances), current assets are comprised of inventory items, accounts receivable, short-term financial investments, and any other asset that can be readily sold. Inventory items and accounts receivable are considered current assets because they will be converted to cash during the normal course of business within the next year. Table 6.1 uses the hypothetical ABC Development Company to illustrate the balance sheet format.

Long-term or fixed assets have an economic life longer than one year and usually cannot be sold on short notice without incurring a significant discount. Fixed assets are permanent and generally include land, buildings, leasehold improvements, equipment, furniture, and fixtures.

Long-term financial assets, such as the investment in a subsidiary, a multiyear loan, or a purchased bond, are all considered fixed assets. Table 6.1 shows that the ABC Development Company has fixed assets of $21 million.

Long-term assets can also include intangible items, such as goodwill, patents, and trademarks. Goodwill arises when a firm purchases an-

Table 6.1. ABC Development Company Balance Sheet
December 31, 1986 (Dollars in Thousands)

Assets	FY 1986	FY 1985	Liabilities and equity	FY 1986	FY 1985
Current assets:			Current liabilities:		
Cash	500	400	Notes payable	1,000	900
Inventory	3,500	3,200	Accounts payable	2,500	2,700
Accounts receiv-			Advances from		
able	2,000	2,100	customers	250	200
			Deferred taxes—		
Treasury bills	1,000	900	current	250	350
			Current portion		
			LTD	1,000	1,000
Total current			Total current		
assets	7,000	6,600	liabilities	5,000	5,150
Long-term assets:			Long-term liabilities:		
Land	3,000	1,980	Mortgage pay-	3,000	3,500
			able		
Buildings	8,500	5,250	Deferred taxes	1,000	1,000
Leasehold					
improvements	3,500	2,300	Bond payable	9,000	9,500
Furniture and			Total long-		
fixtures	1,500	1,400	term liabilities	13,000	14,000
Machinery	2,000	7,370	Total liabilities	18,000	19,150
Investment in					
subsidiary	1,500	1,500			
Goodwill	1,000	1,000			
Total long-					
term assets	21,000	20,800			
			Equity:		
			Capital stock	5,500	4,900
			Retained earn-		
			ings	4,500	3,350
			Total equity	10,000	8,250
Total assets	28,000	27,400			
			Total liabili-		
			ties and equity	28,000	27,400

other entity for a price that exceeds the value of the physical assets owned by the acquired entity. The premium paid by the acquiring firm reflects the economic value of the acquired entity, which has built a customer base and developed technical and marketing expertise. Since the premium measures economic value that cannot be directly attributed to physical assets, it is assigned to the acquiring firm's balance sheet as goodwill. Although goodwill denotes underlying economic value, it cannot be relied upon as a source of repayment for a loan or as collateral because it does not represent an asset that can be sold. Goodwill is an accounting artifice which provides an accurate representation of a firm's assets as long as the firm is a going concern. Should the firm ever fail, the effective liquidation value of goodwill is essentially zero.

Liabilities are also classified according to the duration of their economic life. Current liabilities include all obligations that will be due within one year. Most commonly, current liabilities are comprised of short-term loans or notes payable, accounts payable, deferred taxes, and the principal balance of any long-term debt (LTD) that is scheduled to be repaid within the ensuing year. When customers prepay their bills, the developer cannot recognize the payments as income until the product or service has actually been delivered. In such cases, the advance from the customer must be classified as a liability until the underlying transaction is completed.

Long-term liabilities consist of the principal balances of all obligations that are not due until after the ensuing 12-month period. Term loans, mortgages, and bonds are the most common forms of long-term debt. In general, long-term debt is used to finance the purchase of fixed assets; the borrower then repays the debt from the income generated by the assets. Office building projects, for example, are financed with long-term mortgages, which the developers repay with the rent from the building's tenants. The ABC Development Company has long-term liabilities of $13 million, as shown in Table 6.1.

Income property, in addition to cash flow from rents, also produces significant tax benefits, and is often structured to maximize the tax savings for the developer as well as for the investors. Timing differences between the provision of taxes for financial purposes and the actual payment of those taxes often result in the creation of deferred tax liabilities. Although deferred taxes represent an obligation of the developer, the payment of the tax obligation can often be postponed indefinitely, which gives rise to long-term deferred taxes.

The assets of the ABC Development Company have been created by a combination of liabilities and equity capital. Liabilities, which in this case are mostly long-term loans, have been used to finance $18 million of the firm's total asset base of $28 million. The remaining assets are equity capital. Equity denotes the direct contributions that owners have made to the firm, usually through the purchase of capital stock. Retained earnings are previous profits that have been reinvested in the firm. Retained earnings represent the cumulative net income, earned by the firm since its inception, that has not been paid out in the form of dividends. Equity capital provides a permanent funding base for the developer. Current and long-term liabilities must be repaid, but the equity represents an open-ended contribution to the firm which does not have to be repaid. The capital base of the firm will disappear only if losses deplete the existing capital investment or the owners decide to take the organization out of existence by selling it or filing for bankruptcy. The ABC Development Company has a $10 million capital base.

The size of the capital base is a critical element in credit analysis, because capitalization and creditworthiness tend to be directly related. In general, the larger the relative size of a developer's capital base, the higher the likelihood that development loans will be repaid without incident. The capital base provides resources that can be used to pay obligations as they come due, even if the firm encounters operating losses. The capital base provides lenders with a cushion. Stockholders with a significant investment in a firm have an incentive to avoid bankruptcy, because they are not permitted to receive any proceeds from the liquidation of assets until all creditors have been satisfied. Hence, the larger the stockholders' investment, the greater the motivation to repay borrowings.

Income Statement

Whereas the balance sheet depicts the financial condition of a business at a single moment, the income statement depicts the flow of income over a period, usually a year. The income statement shows the revenue earned and the disposition of that revenue. Table 6.2 illustrates the

Table 6.2. ABC Development Company Income Statement
Year Ended December 31, 1986 (Dollars in Thousands)

	FY 1986	FY 1985
Sale revenue	200,000	187,500
Cost of goods sold	165,000	153,000
Gross profit	35,000	34,500
Selling, general, and administrative expenses:		
Salaries and commissions	11,000	9,500
Depreciation and amortization	4,700	6,600
Rent	4,500	4,500
Utilities	1,500	1,400
Interest	3,100	2,350
Legal	2,000	1,975
Other	3,500	3,650
Operating profit	4,700	4,525
Proceeds from settlement of lawsuit	1,500	0
Casualty loss	1,750	0
Income before taxes	4,450	4,525
Income taxes	1,475	1,850
Net income	2,975	2,675

standard format for the income statement, which delineates fixed and variable costs as well as extraordinary gains and losses.

Since the proceeds from sales are usually the primary source of revenue, sales revenue appears first. The cost of goods sold (CGS) usually appears directly beneath total revenue; CGS shows variable cost, or the cost incurred in purchasing raw materials and assembling those materials into a finished product. The $65 million CGS for the ABC Development Company includes the purchase price of the building materials and the payments made to contractors. The fixed or overhead expenses, which are not directly attributable to production activity, are grouped under the heading of Selling, General, and Administrative (SGA) expenses. SGA expenses include the salaries of management and administrative personnel, rent, utility expense, the cost of legal services, and interest expense. Noncash charges, such as depreciation and amortization, are also categorized as SGA expenses.

Operating profit indicates the revenue remaining after the usual fixed and variable costs have been deducted. The operating profit figure reveals the profitability of the business under normal business conditions. Extraordinary gains or losses are shown separately because they are, by definition, infrequent or random occurrences that are not expected to recur and do not reflect the fundamental profitability of the firm's operations. In the ABC case, the casualty loss from a fire and the proceeds from the settlement of a lawsuit are events unlikely to recur.

Net income provides a summary measure of the firm's performance during the reporting period. Net income shows the net revenue that remains after all expenses, including income tax expense, have been deducted and all gains and loses recognized. Net income is the profit that is available to be either reinvested in the firm as retained earnings or paid out to the owners as a return on their investment in the form of dividends.

Funds Statement

The funds statement, or statement of changes in financial position, is derived from the income statement and the balance sheet. The funds statement indicates the flow of cash through the firm over a period of time. It reveals both the source and the uses of cash, by combining net income with the change that has occurred in the firm's cash balances (see Table 6.3).

Although net income is the primary source of cash inflow, cash can also be generated by issuing common stock or by additional borrowing. Further, any net reduction in assets, such as the sale of inventory items, the collection of accounts receivable, or the sale of fixed assets, pro-

Table 6.3. ABC Development Company Funds Statement
Year Ended December 31, 1986 (Dollars in Thousands)

Sources of Cash	
Operations:	
Net income	2975
Add: Depreciation and amortization	4700
Decrease in accounts receivable	100
Increases in notes payable	100
Increases in advances from customers	50
Subtract: Increase in inventory	300
Increase in Treasury bills	100
Decrease in accounts payable	200
Total cash from operations	7325
Issuance of capital stock	600
Gain on sale of machinery	270
Total sources of cash	8195
Uses of Cash	
Payment of dividends	1525
Purchase of land	1020
Purchase of building	3250
Leasehold improvements	1200
Purchase of furniture, fixtures	100
Reduction of mortgage	500
Reduction of bond	500
Increase in cash	100
Total uses of cash	8195

duces an inflow of cash. In a similar manner, any net increase in current liabilities, such as an increase in accounts payable, a new bank loan, or an addition to deferred taxes, also generates cash.

With respect to cash outflows, a firm uses cash to service or completely repay existing debt, purchase fixed assets, and provide dividends. Cash is also expended when a firm increases current assets, which usually involves stockpiling inventory and the addition of accounts receivable. Similarly, any net reduction in current liabilities represents an outflow of cash. For instance, the payment of a bank loan or an account payable will reduce cash balances.

Since debt can be repaid only with cash, the information contained in the funds statement is invaluable to the credit analysis because the prospective borrower's capacity to repay debt is directly related to the net inflow of cash. In analyzing a prospective borrower, net cash flow from operations can be compared to expected interest payments and the debt amortization schedule to determine whether the borrower will be able to repay current obligations or assume additional debt. If the financial results show net cash outflows or if the borrower can generate positive cash flows only by selling fixed assets or liquidating current assets, experience indicates that the borrower may experience difficulties in the future. In the case of the ABC Development Company, which generated over $7.3 million from operations in FY 1986, the cash flow is sufficient to repay existing debt (see Table 6.3). In fact, if FY 1987 is consistent with previous years, ABC Development Company could safely incur additional debt.

Characteristics of Financial Statements

Accountants place their imprimatur on financial statements, but responsibility for the accuracy of the financial statements remains with the firm. Although financial statements are the firm's self-representation of its financial condition, the accounting profession has developed a series of procedures that enables interested parties, such as investors and lenders, to assign varying levels of reliability to individual financial statements.

Audited Statements

Audited financial statements present the most reliable information. An audited financial statement is prepared under the auspices of a certified public accountant (CPA), an independent third party certified by the state. An audit includes various tests mandated by the accounting profession's supervisory organization, the Financial Accounting Standards Board (FASB). The audit test usually includes the counting and valuation of inventory items, on-site examinations of assets, and evaluations of the actual value of the data that appear in the financial statements. In addition, FASB has established a code which governs the reporting of financial data. This code, entitled Generally Accepted Accounting Principles (GAAP), was designed to provide a uniform system for reporting financial results.

Auditor's Opinion

Audited financial statements are accompanied by the accountant's opinion evaluating the accuracy of the financial statements. An unqualified opinion signifies that the accountant has conducted the requisite test and determined that the data have been reported according to GAAP.

An unqualified opinion indicates that the financial statements accurately represent the financial condition of the firm.

There are four major reasons stated by the accountant in a "qualified" opinion that reflect the CPA's unwillingness to issue an unqualified opinion: (1) The scope of the audit has been constrained. (2) Accounting principles, according to GAAP, have not been consistently applied. (3) Disclosure has been inadequate. (4) There is considerable risk that the firm may fail. Qualified opinions are always justified by detailed explanations.

An opinion is only as reliable as the accountant issuing the opinion. Although the CPA is an independent third party, the developer nonetheless is the CPA's customer, a fact which may have at least some effect on the CPA's capacity to view the developer's information favorably. Therefore, the professional reputation of the CPA may be significant.

If a developer abruptly changes accounting firms, analysts may find evidence that the original accountant was unwilling to accept misleading or faulty accounting practices. Whenever a developer changes accounting firms, the analyst should at least ascertain the reason for the change. Finally, all financial statements should be dated and signed by both the accountant and a representative of the firm.

Footnotes

Financial statements that have been prepared according to GAAP are usually accompanied by footnotes which contain information essential to understanding the various income statement and balance sheet accounts. Since GAAP accounting is done on an accrual rather than a cash basis, numerous methods recognize income, account for expenses, and value assets. The method used to develop financial statements can be critical in assessing the creditworthiness of a borrower. For example, developers do not usually receive cash payments until a project is actually complete, but GAAP allow them to recognize income on a percentage basis. In such cases, the analyst should understand that the revenue figure on the developer's income statement does not represent actual cash payments. Similarly, footnotes will show whether a firm is paying interest on a current basis or capitalizing (and deferring) the interest. A prospective borrower who is forced to capitalize interest may not be able to service additional debt. As a further guide to the creditworthiness of a developer, the footnotes should detail the amortization schedule for long-term debt.

Footnotes also contain important complementary or additional information about developments that may not directly affect the current financial statements but could become important in the future. For instance, if contingent liabilities have been incurred that could affect the future financial condition of a developer, their nature and extent should be indicated. Guarantees, warranties, and lawsuits are the most common contingent liabilities.

Unaudited Statements

Smaller business firms, often unable to afford audited financial statements, will provide compiled financial statements. Compiled statements should have been assembled by the accountant from general ledger data. Since the compilation does not include audit tests, the accountant cannot provide any assurance that the valuations appearing in the general ledger data are reasonable or accurate.

Developers sometimes also save costs by simply assembling their own statements, perhaps reviewed by an accountant. Reviewed financial statements represent an even further step away from certainty. In the review process, the CPA peruses the financial statements prepared by management without examining the general ledger accounts from which the financial statements are constructed. Without an examination of the general ledger, the accountant cannot even confirm that the financial statements have been constructed in compliance with GAAP, let alone verify the valuations that appear in the various income statement and balance sheet accounts.

Consolidated Statements

Business organizations comprised of more than one entity, such as a holding company with subsidiary corporations, should present consolidated financial statements. Since transactions between entities that have common ownership are not arm's-length transactions, transfer prices and the attendant revenue figures may not reflect actual market values. Transactions between affiliated entities can involve significant subsidies which can distort the real profitability of operations. Consolidated financial statements should include a consolidating statement which explicitly eliminates intercompany transactions and provides an accurate measure of the financial results achieved by each of the various entities within a larger organization. Three sets of statements are necessary: the unconsolidated statements of the subsidiaries, the consolidating statement, and the fully consolidated statement for the entire organization.

Interim Statements

Many firms, especially corporations that sell stock to the public, issue interim financial statements, which cover some period less than the full fiscal year. In general, interim financial statements are issued on a quarterly basis. Smaller firms often prepare semiannual statements. Interim financial statements are useful because of their timeliness, but they must be approached with great care for two reasons. First, interim statements are rarely audited, which means there is no assurance that the values assigned within the financial statements have been verified or reported according to GAAP. Second, the results reported in the interim financial statements are not adjusted for seasonal variations, which can be very large. For developers in cold weather climates, income for the spring and summer months is usually significantly higher than during the winter. Any extrapolation of the results from the spring and summer could prove to be misleading, unless the developer has a history of issuing interim financial statements that have been consistent with the final audited results during previous fiscal years.

Current Value Statements

Prospective borrowers, especially those with extensive real estate holdings, often issue current value financial statements. Current value statements restate the value of both assets and liabilities to reflect their current market value. In the inflationary environment of the late 1970s, when the value of assets increased dramatically over nominal debt obligations, current value statements provided a means for recognizing the increase in net wealth that had resulted from rising inflation and high interest rates.

Current value financial statements can often be more accurate for certain purposes than standard financial statements, but they are not sanctioned by GAAP. According to GAAP, assets and liabilities can only be valued when they are sold. Current value accounting anticipates probable market value but does not necessarily accurately reflect market transaction prices. In the absence of market transactions, any method of valuing assets and liabilities will be arbitrary and subject to abuse. Since current value financial statements are not consistent with GAAP, such statements cannot be issued with a CPA's imprimatur.

Techniques for Understanding Financial Statements

Three to five years of historical data allow the analyst to identify trends within each of the financial statement accounts. Without this historical information, the analysis will be static and will not provide an accurate assessment of the prospective borrower's creditworthiness.

Once the raw data have been examined, a series of financial ratios can be calculated to allow the analyst to develop conclusions about the anticipated results of the development entity. The ratios help the analyst detect historical trends. Also, the various ratios can be compared with comparable operations, other industry averages, and general financial expectations to provide additional perspective. The ratios remain, however, only tools for analysis—not the basis for an absolute decision on risk. Thus, even with the "best" set of ratios, lenders still rely on their subjective judgment.

Ratio Analysis

Three ratios derived from the balance sheet accounts are summary measures of a borrower's capacity to repay existing, or assume additional, debt—the leverage ratio, the current ratio, and the quick ratio.

The *leverage ratio,* which compares total liabilities to tangible net worth (tangible net worth is net worth less goodwill), provides a broad measure of riskiness:

$$\text{Leverage} = \frac{\text{total liabilities}}{\text{tangible net worth}}$$

With total liabilities of $18 million and tangible net worth of $9 million, the ABC Development Company has a leverage ratio of 2 ×, which indicates the number of times the capital base of the firm has been multiplied with borrowings in order to purchase assets. The leverage ratio is inversely related to the capitalization rate and, therefore, directly related to risk. When a developer is highly leveraged, the capital base is relatively small. The purchase of assets has been largely funded with debt. One viewpoint sees that the lenders, rather than the developer, own most of the firm's assets. The lack of capital also leaves the developer vulnerable to risk, such as a decline in sales or an unexpected increase in expenses. Further, if the bulk of the firm's borrowings are short-term or carry variable interest rates, an increase in market interest rates could preclude the developer's ability to service debt. At the very least, a highly leveraged developer will incur significant interest expense, which poses a competitive disadvantage in that interest expense introduces a layer of operating costs not incurred by a less heavily leveraged competitor.

The *current ratio* reflects the working capital position of the developer. *Working capital* provides a measure of capacity to meet current debt obligations and is defined as the difference between current assets and current liabilities:

$$\text{Working capital} = \text{current assets} - \text{current liabilities}$$

With current assets of $7 million and current liabilities of $5 million, the ABC Development Company has working capital of $2 million.

The dollar amount of working capital is important, but the relative size of the working capital position is a more telling measure. The current ratio, which provides a measure of liquidity, compares current assets to current liabilities:

$$\text{Current ratio} = \frac{\text{current assets}}{\text{current liabilities}}$$

The current ratio of the ABC Development Company is 1.4 ×, indicating that current assets are 1.4 times current liabilities. In general, the higher the current ratio, the greater the capacity to repay debt and meet all the obligations that are made within the ensuing year, even if unexpected problems arise. For example, if cash flow from earnings for ABC Development Company falls to zero, the company could still meet all its current obligations by selling current assets. On the other hand, if the current ratio were less than 1 × and cash flow from earnings disappeared, ABC would not be able to meet all its current obligations through the sale of current assets. In that case, ABC would be forced to sell fixed assets, which would reduce its productive capacity. The sale of fixed assets is usually a last resort. Companies in danger of bankruptcy will often sell fixed assets to pay current debt obligations.

The *quick ratio* is a lender's additional measuring tool, partly because commercial lenders seek ways to evaluate better business use of inventories. Often, inventory items cannot be readily sold, which means that the current ratio sometimes overstates the actual liquidity of the working capital position. The quick ratio, or acid test, provides a more narrow definition of liquidity because it ignores inventory items and prepaid expenses in comparing cash and near cash items to current liabilities. The quick ratio is the ratio of cash, cash equivalents, accounts receivable, and short-term investments to current liabilities:

$$\text{Quick ratio} = \frac{\text{cash, accounts receivable, investments}}{\text{current liabilities}}$$

In general, the higher the quick ratio, the lower the likelihood that the firm will experience liquidity problems. ABC Development Company's quick ratio can be calculated by eliminating inventory from current assets leaving adjusted current assets of $3.5 million and a current ratio of 0.70 $\times$. In the absence of cash flow from operations, the ABC Development Company would be able to cover 70 percent of its current obligations by selling those assets that are readily marketable.

A number of ratios can be derived from the income statement that provide useful measures of the adequacy of cash flow. The *coverage ratio* compares earnings before interest and taxes (EBIT) to interest expense:

$$\text{Coverage ratio} = \frac{\text{EBIT}}{\text{interest expense}}$$

The coverage ratio shows the ability of a developer to meet interest expenses from the income generated by current operations. A developer who cannot meet debt service obligations from cash flow will be forced to liquidate assets to pay interest expense. ABC Development Company has a coverage ratio of 3.12 $\times$, which means cash flow from operations is approximately three times higher than interest expense.

A prospective borrower's ability to repay longer-term debt obligations is measured by the *current maturity ratio,* relating cash flow to the current portion of long-term debt. In this case, cash flow is defined as net income plus all noncash charges (usually depreciation and amortization):

$$\text{Current maturity coverage ratio} = \frac{\text{cash flow}}{\text{current portion LTD}}$$

The current maturity coverage ratio for the ABC Development Company is 7.68 $\times$. Obviously, the higher the ratio, the greater the likelihood that a developer will be able to meet the amortization schedule for long-term debt.

For a loan to make economic sense, the expected return for the assets purchased with the proceeds of the loan must be greater than the cost of the loan to the borrower. If the return on assets does not exceed the cost of the loan, the profitability of the borrower will decline when the loan is made, which will reduce the borrower's capacity to service and repay debt. The *return on assets* (ROA), which is usually expressed in percentage terms, is the ratio of income before taxes to total assets:

$$\text{Return on assets} = \frac{\text{income before taxes}}{\text{total assets}} \ (100)$$

The return on assets for the ABC Development Company is 15.89 percent. If the cost of a proposed financing is greater than 15.89 percent, the loan should not be made because debt service will reduce the borrower's future earnings.

In a similar manner, the cost of the loan should also be compared to the shareholders' return on equity. The *return on equity* (ROE), which is also calculated in percentage terms, is the ratio of income before taxes to total equity:

$$\text{Return on assets} = \frac{\text{income before taxes}}{\text{total equity}} \ (100)$$

The ABC Development Company has a return on equity of 44.50 percent. If the interest cost of the loan remains below the return on equity, additional asset purchases can be made with borrowed funds. If the ROE falls below the cost of the loan, the firm could issue additional capital stock economically, to purchase new assets.

Common-Size Ratios

When evaluating the changes that have occurred in the balance sheet and income statement over several years, lenders frequently convert the raw data that appear in the financial statements to common-size ratios or percentage terms. Relative changes that have occurred in the various operating margins, as well as shifts in the structure of the balance sheet, can be more easily discerned with common-size ratios.

To convert the balance sheet to common-size form, each balance sheet account is divided by the total asset figure and multiplied by 100. To convert the income statement into the common-size format, each income statement account is divided by the total revenue figure and multiplied by 100.

The use of common-size statements facilitates credit analysis in many ways. Common-size statements present convenient summary measures that can be examined for changes that have occurred over time, and the ratios can also be compared to industry averages. Often potential problems can be seen easily and then a determination reached as to the ability of the borrower to solve the problems. For instance, a decline in net income that is the result of a steady erosion in the gross profit margin may signify a decrease in market share—implying an increase in competition within the industry, a situation beyond the control of the individual firm. In such cases, the individual borrower can do little to reverse the decline in profitability without diversifying into new products. However, a decline in earnings that has been caused by a relative increase in SGA expenses is amenable to corrective action on the part of an individual firm.

Common-size ratios can provide insights into major changes in the structure of the balance sheet. For example, when a firm becomes more highly leveraged, common-size ratios indicate starkly if the firm is using long-term debt or short-term borrowings. If a developer is purchasing additional fixed assets at the same time that current liabilities are increasing, fixed asset purchases are actually being funded with short-term debt. That kind of mismatch between the economic life of the productive assets and the maturity date of the underlying debt increases the likelihood that the loans will be only repaid with difficulty or will not be repaid at all.

More commonly, firms encounter problems when current assets are allowed to grow too rapidly. A large inventory buildup may indicate that a strong increase in sales is expected. However, if the increase in sales does not materialize, the developer will be left holding a high level of inventory that has been purchased with borrowed funds. Ultimately, cash flow from operations may not be sufficient to service the debt that was incurred to build the inventory.

Indirect Information

Although the financial statements contain the basic information to assess the creditworthiness of a developer, there are numerous sources to augment the financial statements. Often, they provide insights that cannot be obtained from the financial statements.

Public companies are required by the Securities and Exchange Commission (SEC) to file numerous reports, including the annual 10-K report, which not only includes the audited financial statements but also contains disclosures that are not always included within the financial statements. A company issuing stock is required by the SEC to prepare a prospectus describing the stock issue and any aspects of the firm's financial condition that will be relevant to prospective investors. Statements issued in response to SEC requirements tend to be highly reliable, because deliberate omissions of required disclosures or intentional misstatements are criminal offenses.

Bank references can provide invaluable information. Prior creditors can describe and document their own experience with a prospective borrower, including any disputes that have occurred. Bank records should indicate if a prospective borrower has ever filed for bankruptcy or been involved in a lawsuit with a previous creditor. Banks can provide information about account balances and history; repeated overdrafts indicate that a borrower often experiences liquidity problems.

Comprehensive credit reports can be obtained from several nationwide credit reporting agencies or bureaus. Narrative credit reports provide information from a variety of sources, including suppliers, court records, newspaper articles, and personal interviews. Credit reports usually provide detailed listings of lien filings, lawsuits, and the history of payments to suppliers.

Interviews with a prospective borrower's suppliers often supplement the information contained in the credit reports. Inaccuracies or inconsistencies that appear in the credit reports can be corrected. In addition, suppliers can provide a firsthand description of a borrower's business practices. The treatment that a prospective borrower accords present suppliers indicates the treatment that the lender can expect.

A development entity's track record is an essential aspect of any assessment of its creditworthiness. Projects that have been built and subsequently sold by the developer should be examined to determine whether they have been successful. Projects that the developer presently manages should be inspected as to their condition as well as the quality of maintenance. Similarly, any projects under construction should be visited to determine whether construction is proceeding according to schedule. Inspections that reveal low occupancy rates, inadequate maintenance, or construction delays may indicate that the developer has already encountered problems critical to the credit decision but which have not yet appeared in the financial statements.

Credit Enhancements

In many instances, a developer will have plans to build a viable project but the lender is reluctant to finance the project because the developer does not meet all the requisite underwriting standards. In cases where the project and the developer both have merit but creditworthiness is marginal, the lending risk can be reduced through various credit enhancements.

Third-party guarantees provide the most direct means of credit enhancement. Whenever third-party guarantees are used, the extent of the guarantee and the creditworthiness of the guarantor must be clear.

Private mortgage insurance policies provide the same kind of enhancement offered by third-party guarantees except that the guarantee is issued by an insurance company. Given the problems experienced by private mortgage insurance firms in recent years, the lender should obtain the financial statements of the private mortgage insurance firm to assess the ability of the insurer to meet the obligations of the policy.

In the absence of third-party support, the borrower can assign collateral to the lender. The more liquid the collateral, the more effective the credit enhancement. Certificates of deposit, treasury securities, and stocks listed on a major stock exchange are the most desirable collateral because they can be readily sold by the lender if the borrower defaults. The assignment of ownership shares in small, closely held companies offers less comfort, because the shares cannot be sold very easily, and the actual value of the shares may be difficult to determine. Whenever collateral is provided, the ownership of the assets assigned by a borrower must be beyond dispute.

Letters of credit can be used to replace the borrower's credit with that of a bank. Letters of credit, which were originally developed to guarantee foreign trade transactions, have been adapted to provide lenders with recourse to a bank if the borrower fails to fulfill the obligations of a contract. Standby letters of credit are most commonly issued during the construction phase of a project. These letters of credit guarantee the project will be completed on time, so that the developer can draw on the permanent financing for the project and pay down the bank loans that financed the construction of the project.

Given the high mortality rate among contracting firms, lenders often require that contractors obtain performance bonds, which provide that a bonding company will advance the funds necessary to complete any work left unfinished by a contractor. When performance bonds are required, it is necessary to assess the capacity of the bonding company to fulfill its obligations.

7

Market Feasibility

Vernon George

Partner, Hammer, Siler & George Associates, Inc.
Silver Spring, Maryland

Many hurdles must be overcome before a project can be deemed feasible and construction and operation are effected. Market feasibility analysis determines the characteristics of the project which will make it most marketable to its intended tenants and then systematically predicts the pace at which the various components will be absorbed in the market and at what price/rent levels. This chapter addresses the market feasibility question in terms of:

- The importance of market feasibility analysis
- The steps in the market feasibility process
- How the mortgage banker should interpret the market feasibility report

The Importance of Market Feasibility Analysis

Market feasibility analysis tells the mortgage banker and other participants in the development process at what pace the proposed project will be absorbed in the market and how the project can be changed to be more successful in capturing a share of the market. Some pertinent terms include the following:

- *Real estate product.* As used here, a real estate product is physically produced in the real estate development process, described and/or measured in the kinds of units users typically perceive themselves buying or renting.
- *Absorption.* As used here, absorption is the calendar pace at which the units could be marketed.
- *Capture.* Capture refers to the share of the total amount of a particular product type marketable in the market area which can be attracted to a particular project.
- *Market area.* Market area is the geographic area in which the proposed project is to be located, where it will compete with similar types of real estate properties.

The most valuable insights derived from a properly prepared market analysis are the following:

1. *Market feasibility analysis identifies the characteristics which are required for success in the market.* There is no discounting the old real estate adage about the importance of location, but there are many other project characteristics of lesser significance—from appearance to types of tenants. One characteristic which has come to dominate the locational quality decisions of the 1970s and 1980s, known as the "entertainment experience," reflects the project's capacity to generate appeal and attraction in its own right. Whether the user is an employee or employer, a hotel patron, a retailer or retail customer, or a resident, customers at newer, larger facilities have come to expect something more than just "a box" for physical facilities. High ceilings and atria, abundant glass, quality materials, plantings and fountains, and, in many cases, programmed entertaining activity have become very important. Other success characteristics relate to the complex of uses, support services and facilities, and interior finishes.

2. *Market feasibility analysis provides reliable estimates of present and future levels of absorption of the real estate product types in the metropolitan area and the market area during the proposed marketing period.* The pace of office construction during 1984–1985 in most suburban and downtown office markets across the country, produced high vacancy rates in 1986–1987. This is an example of the imbalance between space leased and space constructed. This factor affects feasibil-

ity analysis of office buildings, regardless of the quality of the individual project location and characteristics of the building.

3. *Market feasibility analysis provides estimates of the probable capture of each of the real estate product types annually over the proposed development and marketing period.* How much real estate product can be marketed, closed, and occupied and at what price compared to rents in the subject project is a key ingredient to total project feasibility.

4. *Market feasibility is a marketing as well as a research tool.* It can help the developer identify factors which will maximize its market absorption.

The Steps in the Market Feasibility Process

Definition of the Market Area

The criteria and method for definition of the market area relate to the characteristics of the project being proposed. For *retail projects,* the primary market area is often defined as the geographic area of residences within which the subject project is the most convenient location for the particular kind of retail store. The stores that have the greatest appeal, and therefore are most important in determining the market area, are the department stores in regional malls and the supermarkets in community centers. These are called the "anchors." They attract customers who would not otherwise come to shop just at the smaller stores.

For *office projects,* the intended markets of the office tenants usually define the occupancy for the project. For community-serving tenants (such as doctors, lawyers, or real estate agents), the retail community center approach has proven satisfactory, so they are often located near or in community centers.

For office tenants serving the entire city or major sectors of the city, the market area logically includes all those locations which could conveniently serve the residents and employees in the particular area. Major intersections are often the preferred location.

As the economy has shifted toward the service sector as the primary source of jobs, an even larger share of office space has been occupied by firms who serve regional and national markets. These firms can be anywhere in a particular urban area and still serve their customers adequately. Factors affecting their locations include proximity to quality residential areas (for their executives and other employees); proximity to expressways, airports, and other inner-city transportation facilities; image; and, of course, the quality of the space and the project.

For *industrial tenants,* the market area is best defined by locational characteristics in terms of expressway and other major transportation access, existing industrial zoning and use patterns, and employee residential areas. Proximity to common suppliers is often as important as accessibility to customers.

For *hotels,* it is obviously important to be located where there are many travelers. Locations include business headquarters, airports, expressway interchanges, and tourist attractions. The market area for a particular hotel project includes all those locations which would be convenient to the same traveler generators as the subject site.

For *residential projects,* image is extremely important in selling new construction. Image is generalized by neighborhood and community names and then particularized for a project. For example, McLean, Virginia, means something in desirability, price, and school quality—not only to Washingtonians, but to households of similar incomes across the country. To the well-informed or actively house-seeking family, the selectivity of image is even more refined, for example, the Langley neighborhood within McLean has a special quality image. Thus, a group of new homes built in Langley would capitalize on the image of the location. Definition of the market area is being constantly done by the consumer, so the analyst's job is to monitor, record, and then use the data that reflect current thinking.

Evaluation of Existing Projects

The systematic evaluation of the most comparable projects in the market area is often described as "surveying the competition," but it involves much more, including:

1. The characteristics of comparable projects which have been most important to the success (or lack of success) in the market in terms of price, amenity, location, marketing approach, size, or other factors

2. The absorption rate achieved and/or being achieved for comparable projects

3. The amount of product comparable projects still have to market and when it will be exhausted

4. In sum, the total amount of product marketed by new, quality projects in the market area; this total can be related, then, to overall demographic or economic-trend statistics

The sources and methods for evaluating existing projects in the subject market area are derived from such sources as:

1. In-depth personal interviews with developers and marketing personnel at comparable projects

2. Field surveys to examine and record project and locational characteristics (photos are useful)

3. In-depth interviews with development regulatory agencies and use of their project data

4. Interviews with realtors, mortgage bankers, and other informed industry personnel

5. Door-to-door interviews with users to determine what they like and dislike about their projects

6. Use of project data from area real estate data services

This evaluation will provide a good understanding of the product and user characteristics of the extant market area activity for each relevant real estate product type.

Geographic State-of-the-Art Transfer

Developer efforts to meet the specific needs of various user groups are much more creative in some urban areas than in others. User needs are also constantly changing, and some areas are ahead of others in this evolution. Below are some state-of-the-art amenities or improvements which will help to give a project advantage in its market area:

1. The flex industrial/office space, which often features a quality exterior finish, with a wide range of interior finishes within the same multitenant building, all geared to meet the specific needs of a variety of tenants

2. The atrium as the setting for the "entertainment" environment in all types of nonindustrial real estate product

3. The university affiliation and campus design often used to establish instant image and momentum in the market

A comprehensive field trip would be a successful, but expensive, way to learn about innovative building and marketing techniques. Less costly approaches include:

1. Review of periodicals, newsletters, and project files produced in the industry

2. Conference attendance

3. Advice or guidance from consultants with national practice

4. Conversation with regional affiliates

The point here is that maximum absorption will not necessarily come from following closely the most successful projects now in the market when better techniques are being used elsewhere.

The Local Economy

Many market feasibility reports begin with a brief review of past and projected future population and employment growth from local planning agency reports. Frequently, these data are rarely mentioned again, much less incorporated in the analysis, which omits the opportunity to:

1. Examine the trends and evaluate the forecasts for consistency with the trends. Where the forecasts deviate from the trends, identifying the variables which might account for these deviations often provides helpful insights.

2. Determine the dimensions of the economy and population most important to the real estate product type under analysis (industrial employment to industrial land used, or households and total personal income to retail potential). This analysis enables calculation of the relationship between absorption of the real estate product type and any potential change in the "causal" economic or population variable.

3. Use these relationships as a basis for projections of population and economic growth and then credit future absorption rates.

The Role of Trends

Trends can be analyzed and explained in terms of causal factors, and then adjusted, as a projection technique, based upon any perceived changes in these or other causal factors. Trends are useful tools which serve as one basis for market and absorption estimates.

The Project Concept: Be Specific

There is an adage that the answer to any question can never be any more precise than the question itself; this is certainly true of estimates about a project in the feasibility analysis. A detailed description of the characteristics of the project being tested is an essential aspect of analysis. Data about comparable projects are only as valid as defined; comparing rental absorption of a 10-story apartment to the proposed 5-story project is not just an exercise in halving the numbers.

Determination of the Market Share

Determination of the market share is a synthetic task and the culmination of an important part of the feasibility analysis. Market feasibility work must build a strong bridge between analysis of the relevant factors and estimate of specific project capture.

Total Market Area Absorption. The first step in determining the market share (amount of a particular kind of real estate product which can be marketed at the subject property) is to determine the total amount of this type of product which will be marketed by all projects in the market area.

Two approaches are normally used in tandem. First, the trends in total market area absorption of the particular real estate product type are analyzed. The total amount of product absorbed over the last five to seven years is analyzed on both a total average and three-year moving average basis. Those factors which caused the change in absorption are determined, and the extent to which they and/or other factors will be operating in the future is assessed. Based on this analysis, these past absorption trends are adjusted into projections for the future in terms of numbers of physical units (such as floor space) which will be absorbed in each year or small cluster of years.

In the second approach, the relationship between each of the real estate product types and the causal variables that operate at the metropolitan or market area level is established. For retail, the causal variable is households and income in the market area. For most other uses, reliable projections are available only at the metropolitan level, and they have to do with employment by industry type. The relationships between the recent past absorption in each real estate product type and change in the causal variable (such as office land and building with office employment) is calculated. Forecasts made by responsible agencies of those variables are then evaluated and adjusted for reasonableness and the ratios applied to estimate total metropolitan absorptions. The market area share of the metropolitan total is then determined using the trends approach previously described.

Key Absorption Factors. Interviews with developers, industry experts, and tenants or users all include questions on what factors were most important in their selection of the particular project. Analysts combine this information with their previous project experiences, and a set of locational determinants are established and weighted for relative importance.

Each project in the market, or those which will be in the market, is then rated for each of the locational determinants' composite score and then calculated by applying the weightings to the ratings and summing the total. A rating range of 10 and a weighting range of 5 is often used. The multiplication of the rating by the weightings generates total locational quality points for each project.

This model is tested and "calculated" using the following steps:

1. The total locational quality points are calculated for each project using the rating and weighting approach.

2. The total number of quality points for all projects competing in the market area during the recent past test period is tabulated. The percentage share of the total market area quality points generated by each project is tabulated.

3. The actual absorption achieved by each project during the recent period and the total absorption for all projects in the recent period is determined. The share of the market captured by each project is calculated.

4. The share of the total market area absorption captured by each project is compared to its share of total locational quality points. Where there are inconsistencies, the weightings of the factors are adjusted until the locational model fits the actual absorption data.

For instance, a project which had 10 percent of the quality points for projects in the market during 1984 and 1985 should have captured 10 percent of the physical product absorbed during this period. The weightings of the factors are adjusted until the system results are consistent with the actual market performance of the recent past.

Comparable Project Performance. This step involves a direct head-to-head comparison of the subject project, as specifically described, and the other projects which will be competing in the market during the period. Using the matrix of absorption factors, rated and weighted, the subject project as conceptualized is rated for each factor and a cumulative score calculated. Each of the competing projects is likewise rated.

The point score of the subject project is compared to the point score for each of the successful competing projects. The ratio of their point scores is then used as a basis to estimate market share for the subject based on that for projects actually competing in the market. In other words, if a residential project competing in the market area has been marketing 100 units a year and has a locational point score of 80 and another more poorly located and developed project has a point score of 40 and has been marketing 50 units a year, then, if the subject project as conceived has a point score of 60, we could expect an absorption of roughly 75 units a year. In other words, capture is a rational process related to locational quality.

Share of Available Market. The direct comparable project absorption, or "head-to-head," approach is valuable and perhaps the most commonly used systematic market share approach. It is particularly useful in a balanced market.

However, in a market where product production levels are seen to be increasing or overall area and sub-area absorption levels are seen to be decreasing, there may well be too many good projects in the market; that is, the market may be "overbuilt." To test for this possibility in the future market, a share of the market approach must also be used. The steps in this process are as follows:

1. All existing projects are rated according to key absorption measures for each important locational factor.

2. All proposed projects that are judged likely to be in the market during the proposed marketing period for the subject project are also rated.

3. The weightings in terms of the relative importance of the various factors are applied and the locational evaluation point scores totaled. These scores might be called locational quality points.

4. The share of the total locational quality points for all projects earned by the subject project is calculated. These shares change over time as projects enter and leave the active marketing phase.

5. The shares are applied to the previously projected total sub-area potential absorption, and the capture is estimated for the subject project in terms of the appropriate units of that particular kind of real estate product.

By combining the project comparable and share-of-market approaches, each systematically applied, the probability of absorption accuracy is good.

Iteration for Market Optimization

There are two primary purposes for market feasibility analyses. The first is to determine the capture or absorption which can be achieved by the project if built. These steps have been discussed in the preceding paragraphs. Equally important is the role of feasibility analysis in optimizing the market appeal of the project.

1. *Basis for project optimization.* The careful examination of existing projects in the market, the state-of-the-art review, and the experience of the senior analyst, are all important to project optimization.

The design, traffic, engineering, planning, financing, and other team members likewise contribute their experience.

2. *Interdisciplinary sessions.* Each discipline—market feasibility, planning and design, engineering, traffic, finance, and other specialists— makes the greatest contribution to project success not in independent reports but in "over-the-board" work sessions with the client developer and team as a whole.

3. *Optimum project strategy.* Through a series of interdisciplinary sessions with the public or private developer, the optimum project/ marketing strategy evolves.

4. *Testing strategy.* Having devised what appears to be the optimum strategy, all experts must objectively test it and be prepared to justify their results.

5. *Sensitivity analysis.* This analysis tests the impact of different levels of achievement for each of the critical variables, such as a slower or faster absorption pace, lower price/rents, a less preferred zoning category, a more costly sewer solution, or delay in expressway construction.

Sensitivity analysis is often called downside and/or upside analysis. It is important in estimating the risks of the project.

How the Mortgage Banker Should Interpret Market Feasibility Analysis

The mortgage banker needs to know the market feasibility of the project, to understand the assumptions governing the analysis, and to present these findings to the lender.

1. *Timing.* What will be the calendar marketing period, and how does this relate to the competing projects?

2. *Project and facility amenities.* What amenities are recommended and assumed, and what is the impact on absorption if key amenities cannot be fitted in the project budget?

3. *Marketing and promotional strategy.* Will the project marketing be handled by the most successful marketing firm in town with an adequate promotional budget—or by the developer on a shoestring?

4. *Timing of public improvements.* Which roads, sewers, and other

public improvements not now in place are key to the project, and what completion timing is the analyst assuming?

5. *Financing.* Are development, permanent- and end-user interest rates assumed to remain about where they are at the time of the analysis, or are they expected to rise or fall?

6. *Economic trends.* How will economic growth in the region during the marketing period compare with that of the recent past, and why?

7. *Supply/demand balance.* What will the total absorption of the particular real estate product type(s) in the market area be during the proposed marketing period, and how will this compare to projected competitive supply?

The point here is that users are not testing for clairvoyance—they must know what the analyst has assumed so that they may evaluate these assumptions for reasonableness as a part of determining the reliability of the forecasts. Other important assumptions include:

Sensitivity analysis. The mortgage banker or other user must understand not only the probable absorption level but also the reasonable range. The "downside" and what could cause the downside is particularly important.

Project comparables. It is useful for the mortgage banker or other user to compare the actual market absorption of the most successful comparable projects with the projections for the subject property.

Assumptions about competition. The mortgage banker or other user should examine and test for reasonableness assumptions about the number of competing projects that will be in the market and what will happen to their absorption. As an example, if the introduction of the subject property and other new competition into the sub-area requires reducing the capture of existing successful projects, the user should be aware of this and judge whether the reduction is reasonable.

Weaknesses of the subject project. The user and the market analyst should examine the weakness of the subject property and test for overly optimistic assumptions.

Track record of the analyst. Market feasibility analysis is in effect the systematic application of judgment based on experience. The comfort level of the mortgage banker or other user should be very much tied to the reputation of the market feasibility firm as confirmed by its résumé and by contacts with previous clients.

8
Real Estate Appraisals

Harvey P. Jeffers, CRE, MAI, SREA
*Senior Vice President and Chief Appraiser
Landauer Associates, Inc., New York, New York*

General Information

The basis for most underwriting and/or lending decisions is the real estate appraisal, an opinion of the value of a property interest. It is of paramount importance that the interest appraised be specifically defined.

Property interests may be described as a fee simple, leased fee, leasehold, or sandwich lease interest. The fee simple interest may be subject to existing or proposed leases. Therefore, the nature of the property interest and whether any financing restraints or easements (permanent or temporary) exist on the property should be duly noted on the appraisal in order to determine property value.

The date of the value estimate must be stated. This date of appraisal may vary depending on the purpose and function of the appraisal assignment.

Value is typically thought of as value in exchange, that is, dollars are paid in exchange for a parcel of real estate. Another concept on which real estate loans are often made is value in use, as in a manufacturing facility whose value in use to the occupant is typically greater than the value in exchange if the real estate (vacant and available) were put on the market for sale.

From the concept of value in exchange are derived other values such as market value, investment value, assessment value (for real estate tax purposes), inheritance value, and insurable value. In real estate lending the value most commonly sought is market value. One of the most widely used definitions of market value is contained in Proposed Rule dated October 20, 1987 issued by the Federal Home Loan Bank Board, which reads as follows:

> The most probable price which a property should bring in a competitive and open market under all conditions requisite to a fair sale, the buyer and seller, each acting prudently, knowledgeably and assuming the price is not affected by undue stimulus. Implicit in this definition is the consummation of the sale as of a specified date, and the passing of title from seller to buyer under conditions whereby:
>
> a. buyer and seller are typically motivated;
> b. both parties are well-informed or well-advised, and each acting in what he considers his own best interest;
> c. a reasonable time is allowed for exposure in the open market;
> d. payment is made in terms of cash in U.S. dollars or in terms of financial arrangements comparable thereto; and
> e. the price represents the normal consideration for the property sold un-affected by special or creative financing or sales concessions granted by anyone associated with the sale.
>
> Adjustments to the comparables must be made for special or creative financing or sales concessions. No adjustments are necessary for those costs that are normally paid by sellers as a result of tradition or law in a market area; these costs are readily identifiable since the seller pays these costs in virtually all sales transactions. Special or creative financing adjustments can be made to the comparable property by comparisons to financing terms offered by a third party institution lender that is not already involved in the property or transaction. Any adjustment should not be calculated on a mechanical dollar for dollar cost of the financing or concession, but the dollar amount of any adjustment should approximate the market's reaction to the financing or concessions based on the appraiser's judgment.

For ease of analysis and clarity in reporting, the appraiser typically follows the valuation process shown in Figure 8.1. The valuation process is an orderly procedure for estimating value and allows the appraiser to report value in a logical manner.

The valuation of real estate requires the exercise of judgment by the appraiser. For this reason professional appraisers often arrive at a different opinion of the value of the same marketable interest in a particular real property. However, significant differences between appraisals should be reconcilable, based on an analysis of the underlying assumptions and limiting conditions and the judgments made by the appraiser in each appraisal report. This chapter gives the reader an overview of the appraisal process. For a more complete description of the appraisal

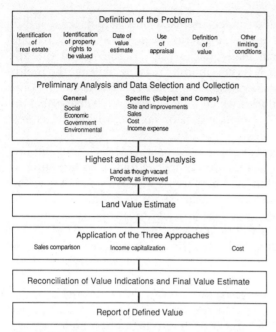

Figure 8.1. The valuation process. (Reprinted with permission from *The Appraisal of Real Estate,* the American Institute of Real Estate Appraisers, Chicago, Ill., 1983, 8th Edition, p. 43.)

process, publications such as *The Appraisal of Real Estate,* published by the American Institute of Real Estate Appraisers, should be consulted.

The Appraisal Process

Real estate appraisal begins with the study of the social, economic, governmental, and environmental conditions of the general area and the specific neighborhood in which the subject property is or will be located. This analysis lays the foundation for the analysis of the supply of the real estate product and demand for that product. The next step in the appraisal process is the analysis of the site, its location, zoning, and physical and economic characteristics.

The site description is followed by a description of the improvements. This requires the appraiser to make a complete and thorough exterior and interior inspection of the improvements. Items noted are foundation walls, exterior walls, framing, floor structures, roof structures, roof covering, windows, interior finishes (floors, walls, ceiling), plumbing, mechanical and electrical systems. In addition, the appraiser comments on items of deferred maintenance, items which would have a life shorter than that of the basic structure, and the actual and effective age of the structure. Functional inadequacies are described, and the appraiser determines whether it is economically feasible to bring the building up to modern standards. Additional comments relate to factors outside of the property boundaries which might have an adverse effect on value. The report should also include data on current real estate assessments and real estate tax rates.

Once the factual data regarding the area, neighborhood, site, and improvements have been completed, appraisers can turn their attention to highest and best use. Highest and best use is a two-part analysis: The first analyzes the site as if vacant and available for development, and the second analyzes the highest and best use of the property (land and buildings) as it exists or as it will be improved.

The concept of highest and best use is based on the economic principle that real estate should be put to the legal use which is most likely to produce the greatest net return to the land or property over a reasonable period. The analysis of highest and best use provides the foundation for the appraiser's market value analysis. Valuation considerations are made in relationship to what is considered the highest and best use.

Highest and best use may be defined as:

> The reasonable and probable use that supports the highest present value, as defined, as of the date of the appraisal.

Alternatively, highest and best use is:

> The use, from among reasonably probable and legal alternative uses, that results in the highest present land value and is found to be physically possible, appropriately supported, financially feasible.

The second definition applies specifically to the highest and best use of the land or site as though vacant. When a site contains improvements, the highest and best use may be different from the existing use. The existing use will continue unless and until land value in its highest and best use exceeds the sum of the value of the entire property in its existing use, and the cost to remove the improvements.[1]

The appraiser reflects the options available to a user of real estate through the use of three approaches to estimating value:

1. The cost approach

[1]"The Appraisal of Real Estate," *American Institute of Real Estate Appraisers*, Eighth edition, 1983, p. 244.

2. The market or direct sales comparison approach

3. The income approach

The Cost Approach

The cost approach requires the appraiser to estimate value of the land as if vacant and available for development. Then, the reproduction cost (new) of existing improvements is estimated. From that is subtracted depreciation, resulting in the depreciated value of the improvements. The estimated land value is then added to the estimated depreciated value of the improvements, and the result is the indication of value by the cost approach.

There are four common ways to estimate land value:

1. The *market data* or *direct sales comparison method* consists of finding sales of similar unimproved parcels of land and relating them to the parcel of land being appraised.

2. The *land residual method* requires a cash flow forecast or pro forma for the optimum building that could be located on the site (in other words, which improves the site to its highest and best use), which would be fully rented. After deducting all operating expenses and a return *on* and *of* the cost of the improvements, the remaining income is said to be the income attributable to the land, which is then capitalized (or discounted to its present value) to reflect the value of the land.

3. The *development method* estimates the gross sales volume which can be achieved from the sale of the property developed to its highest and best use. Development cost, carrying charges, real estate taxes during the construction period, insurance and other costs, and the developer's profit are deducted from this gross sales volume. The resulting net cash flow forecast is then discounted at a rate sufficient to recognize the risk and the time required to complete and market the improvements.

4. The *allocation method* identifies and analyzes sales in similar improved properties with the prices actually paid allocated between land and improvements. The allocated land portion of the sale properties is then used as the comparable for the subject land under appraisal.

Of the above methods, the market or direct sales comparison approach is the most persuasive as an indication of value.

Once the value of the land has been estimated, the appraiser then estimates the "reproduction" or "replacement cost new" of the improvements. The *reproduction cost new* is the current cost of creating an exact replica of the existing improvements by using the same or similar materials. The *replacement cost new* is the current cost of creating an improvement, using current construction technology and modern materials, which has the same utility as the existing improvements. Typically, the replacement cost new estimate eliminates the need to penalize the property for functional inadequacies.

Accrued depreciation is then deducted from the reproduction or replacement cost new. Accrued depreciation is an analysis of the loss in value suffered by a property due to physical deterioration or functional and/or economic (locational) obsolescence.

Appraisers will often estimate accrued depreciation by analyzing the sales of similar comparable properties. Deducting the estimated land value from a comparable improved property sale results in the depreciated value of the improvements. If the depreciated value of the improvements is subtracted from the cost new of the sale property, the result is the dollar amount of the depreciation attributable to the comparable property. The dollar amount of depreciation can be divided by the reproduction cost new which will give the percentage of depreciation suffered by that property. This, in turn, can be reduced to a percentage per year. When this methodology is used, the cost approach typically produces approximately the same result as the direct sales comparison approach based on similar improved properties.

The cost approach is very useful when the property is to be built or has been recently constructed and has suffered little depreciation. The cost approach is often omitted in the valuation of very old and/or functionally obsolete properties.

The Market Approach

The market, or direct sales comparison, approach is used not only to estimate the value of land as if vacant but also to estimate the value of improved properties by the analysis of sales of similar comparable properties which have recently been sold in the marketplace. The market approach concept is based on the principle of substitution, which states that a buyer will not pay more for a property when an equally desirable substitute property is available at a lower price.

The first step in the direct sales comparison approach is to identify, describe, and analyze similar properties which have recently been sold, including physical attributes of the sold properties such as size, location, and improvements. Sales data can be found in recorded sales, contracts of sale, options to purchase, and, of course, in listings. The appraiser verifies the sale prices of properties by interviewing a party to the transaction, by scanning multiple listing sales records, and by examining public records. Discussions with real estate agents, bankers, and knowledgeable individuals and a study of advertisements and listings of properties for sale are useful for obtaining a feel for the marketplace. Often listings of property for sale tend to set the upper limit value.

The next step is to compare each similar comparable sale to the subject property. No two properties are exactly alike, and for this reason adjustments must be made between the comparable sales and the subject property so as to reflect significant differences. Adjustments may be required for such factors as financing, conditions of sale, the difference in time between the date of sale and the date of appraisal, location, and physical characteristics such as the age and condition of the sale as compared to the subject. The final estimate of value by the direct sales comparison approach is made after considering all the sales and the quantity and quality of the adjustments that have been made to those sales and by giving the most weight to the value indicated by the property or properties which are most similar to the subject property.

In an ideal market, the direct sales comparison approach is one of the most persuasive indicators of value, especially in the appraisal of one- to four-family dwellings. However, one of the weaknesses in this approach is that it is valid only if there is a sufficient number of similar sales. Also, this approach must be used with caution because it rests on the assumption that the buyer and seller are fully informed, when in reality many buyers and sellers are novices in the marketplace. Buyer and seller motivations are often affected by tax considerations or below-market interest rates.

The Income Approach

The income approach is the investor's approach to real estate. It is used when the property has an income stream or when an income stream can be reasonably estimated.

The income approach is used in the valuation of income property, that is, multifamily residential properties, office buildings, industrial properties, and shopping centers. The application of the income approach requires an estimate of the gross potential income from the property as of the date of the appraisal.

The gross potential income of a property is based on the quantity, quality, and durability of the income streams. The quantity of the income stream is based on the market rental of the property as of the date of the appraisal. The quality and durability of the income stream are often determined by the length of the lease and the creditworthiness of the tenants who occupy the building.

An allowance is made for the typical loss of income due to vacant units, collection losses, and/or a rental lag (typically caused by leases which prevent the owner from achieving the maximum rental potential from the property, as of the date of the appraisal). This loss of income is typically referred to as "vacancy." Once vacancy has been deducted from the gross potential income of the property, the resulting income is known as the gross effective income.

Once the gross effective income of a property has been estimated, then an analysis of all operating expenses is undertaken. This expense analysis includes a study of real estate taxes past and present; of fire insurance costs; of expenses, such as the cost of water, heat, electricity, gas, labor, elevator maintenance contracts, lawn mower services, snow plowing, building repairs and maintenance, and reserves for replacements of the operating components of a building which will wear out before the end of the building's useful life. Some expense items which are normally shown on an owner's income tax return, such as depreciation and interest on a mortgage, are eliminated from the expense statement.

Once all the expenses have been deducted from the effective gross income, the remainder is known as the net operating income. The net operating income can then be capitalized into an indication of value through the use of a capitalization rate. A capitalization rate is an overall rate of return which expresses the relationship of income to value. It is found in the marketplace by analyzing sales of income-producing property by dividing the net income produced at the time of sale by the sale price. For instance, if a property sells for $1 million and at the time of sale was producing a net income of $90,000, it would reflect an overall capitalization rate of 9 percent. This capitalization rate can then be applied to the net income from the property being appraised to reflect its value.

A capitalization rate is a synthesis of the investors' requirements of a return *on* their capital and a return *of* their capital. The selection of capitalization rate depends on the quantity, quality, and durability of the income stream. The capitalization for a multiple-tenant loft building with "mom and pop" tenants would be expected to be higher than that used on a net leased property to a triple-A-rated corporate entity.

Different capitalization rates will apply to different types of property and within the same class of property will differ depending on market conditions. The capitalization *rate* and the capitalization *methodology* employed to indicate value will depend on how the market views a certain class of property at a given time. If overall value is the desired result, one can use the direct capitalization method simply by dividing the property's net operating income by an overall capitalization rate.

A capitalization rate may also reflect the components of land and building or mortgage debt and equity. In separating the components of land and building, the appraiser uses the land residual or building residual technique. For instance, if land value is known, a return on the land value can be deducted from net operating income, and the residual income to the building can then be capitalized by a rate which would include a return *on* the investment in the building and a provision for the recapture *of* the investment in the building. The capital investment in a building can be recaptured through a return either with a straight-line method or through the use of a sinking fund. Combining the rate of return with a capital recapture rate creates a building capitalization rate, which can then be divided into the property's residual income to reflect the building's value. Once the land is added back to the capitalized building value, an indication of overall property value is achieved.

If the building value is known, the foregoing procedure can be reversed, and the income attributable to a return *on* the building and a return *of* the investment in the building may be deducted from the net operating income; the remaining income is termed the residual income to land. This then may be capitalized at the rate of return to indicate the land value. Adding the two components results in an indication of overall value of the property.

If the property's financing is to figure in its valuation, the mortgage equity method of capitalization may be used. This is achieved by deducting the debt service from the net operating income, which leaves the equity dividend or cash flow, which can then be capitalized at an equity rate of return to indicate the value of the equity. When this is added to the mortgage balance, an indication of the property value is achieved.

Frequently, appraisers will use the *Ellwood Tables*—tables based on a synthesis of mortgage requirements and equity yield requirements. Yield, as used here, includes the cash flow (after debt service) from a property, the buildup of equity through mortgage amortization, and an increase or decrease of the property's value over a projected holding period.

In the valuation of leased fees and leaseholds, the "present worth of $1.00 per period" and the "present worth of $1.00" factors are used from standard compound interest tables at a yield rate sufficient to attract purchase capital to that type of investment. The present worth of $1 per period factors can be used to estimate the value of a level income stream (such as might be generated from a long-term net lease), to which is added the present worth of the property at the end of the lease period. This method is generally used for income-producing property under a long-term net lease with a creditworthy tenant.

The term *net income* signifies the income available after *all* expenses for the operation of the property are deducted. The terms *net-net lease* and *net-net-net lease* indicate to the appraiser a modified gross lease of some form.

In recent years, discounted cash flow methodology has become a widely used tool of appraisers. In this methodology, the net annual cash flows from a property are estimated for each year of a projection period; and the present worth of each of these future cash flows are added, which, when combined with the present worth of the property at the end of the projection period, will yield the value of the property today. This method allows for the recognition of irregular income patterns as well as for the expenses of releasing space during a projected holding period. The methodology can be applied either to net operating income or to cash flow after debt service.

The rate of return in discounted cash flow analysis is a *discount rate* (synonymous with internal rate of return or yield rate). In selecting the discount rate, market factors such as the rate of return demanded by buyers of similar type properties are considered. Lacking this type of information, a reasonable discount rate can be estimated through analysis of bond markets, to which are added components for risk, the management burden, and the lack of liquidity in a real estate investment. In addition, consideration can be given to the reliability of the property's income, its marketability, and tax advantages.

Table 8.1 shows a stabilized income expense statement for a hypothetical professional office building. The table indicates the sources and amounts of the gross income, shows the vacancy factor, itemizes all expenses, and reflects the net operating income from the property upon completion of construction and achievement of projected occupancy. To convert this estimate of net operating income into an indication of value, we will develop a simple capitalization rate through the band of investment technique, assuming that a mortgage loan equal to 75 percent of value will be available at an interest rate of 11.25 percent for a 7-year term (but with 100 percent amortization based on a 30-year monthly payment schedule) and that typical investors would require a 10 percent return on their equity investment. These market parameters indicate an overall capitalization rate of 11.545 percent which, when divided into the net income of $2,690,082, reflects a value of $23,300,840, which would normally be rounded to $23 million.

The use of the income approach requires the appraiser to analyze rental markets, vacancy rates, and expenses in detail to arrive at the net operating income. Relatively minor changes in an expense item or in an assumption of vacancy can radically affect the estimated net income attributable to a specific property. This is also true in the selection of a capitalization rate. A 1 percentage point difference in a capitalization rate can make a significant difference in the estimated value.

Once appraisers have estimated the value of the subject property by the cost approach, direct sales comparison approach, and the income approach, they are in a position to reconcile these three indications of value into a final value estimate. These three approaches rarely indicate the same value. The appraiser's job is to review the three approaches, their assumptions, and the quality and quantity of the data available for

Table 8.1. Stabilized Income Estimate
(On Completion of Construction and Achievement of Normal Occupancy)
Bestway Development Company's Professional Office Building, Midsize City, Somewhere

Gross Income		
First floor		
Le Francoise French Restaurant 4383 ft² @ $25/ft²	$109,575	
First National Bank 10,000 ft² @ $25/ft²	250,000	
Jack's Deli Take-Out 1000 ft² @ $25/ft²	25,000	
Software Whiz (Computer software) 1000 ft² @ $25/ft²	25,000	
Total first floor tenant income	$409,575	$409,575
Floors 2–10 147,450 ft² @ $20/ft²		$2,949,000
Parking income		
Indoor: 360 spaces @ $40/mo × 12	172,800	
Outdoor: 300 spaces @ $15/mo × 12	54,000	226,800
Gross potential income		$3,585,375
Less vacancy 4% (overall)		$143,415
Gross effective income		$3,441,960

Expenses		
Fixed		
Real estate taxes	$101,983	
Insurance	37,994	
Total fixed expenses		$139,977
Variable		
Management/leasing	$169,972	
Building maintenance	101,983	
Utilities	237,961	
Janitorial	33,994	
Common area maintenance	33,994	
Total variable expenses		$577,904
Reserves Replacements/miscellaneous		33,997
Total expenses		$751,878
Estimated net operating income		$2,690,082

Capitalization Rate	
75% mortgage × 0.1206 (mortgage constant)	0.09045
25% equity × 0.10 (rate of return on equity)	0.02500
Indicated overall rate	0.11545

Valuation		
NOI of $2,690,082 capitalized @ 0.11545		$23,300,840
Rounded to	$23,300,000	

analysis in each approach. The appraiser can then review the strengths and weaknesses of each of the approaches and conclude the final value estimate based on that approach which most closely reflects the actions of buyers and sellers in the current marketplace.

The appraiser summarizes the investigation, analysis, and conclusions in the appraisal report. A proper appraisal report must include the date of the appraisal, a complete identification of the property appraised, a definition of the value sought, an appraisal of the property interest, and all the underlying assumptions and limiting conditions affecting the conclusion of value. The report will also contain an area and neighborhood analysis, a description of the site and improvements, assessment and taxes, zoning, highest and best use, the cost approach (including land value), the direct sales comparison approach, the income approach, a reconciliation, the certification of the appraiser, the appraiser's qualifications, and addenda (if the addenda items are not included in the body of the report), which would typically contain area and neighborhood maps, plot plans, floor plans, photographs, detailed sales and rental data.

The highest standard in the appraisal industry has been set by the American Institute of Real Estate Appraisers through its Code of Professional Ethics and Standards of Professional Practice (copyright 1985), obtainable from the American Institute of Real Estate Appraisers of the National Association of Realtors. Appraisers who adhere to AIREA's Code of Ethics minimize the risk of inaccurate appraisals for mortgage lenders.

9

Reviewing an Occupancy Lease from a Prospective Lender's Standpoint

Anita C. Hochstein, Esq.*

Counsel, Aetna Life and Casualty Company
Hartford, Connecticut

Since the income from leases pays debt service and operating expenses and produces investment income, the review and approval of leases are essential to the underwriting of mortgage loans secured by income-producing real property. This chapter briefly describes how to review a lease for a long-term ("permanent") mortgage lender. Any lease, lease certificate, and estoppel certificate should be drafted and reviewed by attorneys.

The scope of reviewing and approving a lease depends on various questions, including: Is the lease final, or is it subject to further negotiation with the tenant? How much space and how much rent are covered by the lease? Is the underwriting of the proposed mortgage loan based on a fully or a partially rented building? In many cases a lease is reviewed only to confirm (1) the business terms (rent, term, etc.) on which the underwriting of the loan is based and (2) the absence of any major

*Assistance in this article was provided by Margaret M. Titolo of Aetna.

legal problems. Lease terms must match those set out in the loan submission package.

The lease is a contract which creates and governs the relationship of landlord and tenant. In general, a lease is a written agreement by which an owner of real estate or an interest in real estate (the lessor or landlord) gives the right to use and possess all or part of that property (the leased premises) to another (the lessee or tenant) for a specified period (the lease term) upon payment of a specific rent.

The following section discusses lease reviews in general, net and gross leases, and ground leases. Leases created by oral agreement (month-to-month tenancies) are not covered in this chapter, since they are terminable on short notice and may not be considered in an analysis of rental income. Sale leasebacks are discussed in Chapter 22.

General

Most mortgage lenders reserve (in each mortgage loan commitment) the right to review and approve all written leases for income-producing properties which secure loans. (For a large project using a form lease, a lender may review a lease form and then accept all leases which follow the standard form and approved business terms.) In issuing its loan commitment, however, the lender's underwriting is based on summary information about the lease terms.

Before beginning a lease review, the reviewer should confirm that the lease to be reviewed has been fully executed (properly signed) and includes all its pages, amendments, exhibits, and side letters. The mortgage loan application and commitment should be checked to verify whether the lender has general and/or specific underwriting requirements for leases at the project and what these are (for example, minimum rent per square foot, minimum term, expense stops). Loan underwriting may involve varying parameters for different tenants at the same project. For example, major or anchor tenant leases may have a longer term than small tenant leases. A lender may also have general requirements which are not specific to a particular mortgage loan or security. For example, a lender may insist that certain insurance provisions be included in each lease. Because a lender may become an owner of the property if and when there is a loan default or foreclosure action, the lender may review leases from both a lender's and a prospective property owner's standpoint. A prospective borrower may be asked to obtain a lease amendment to clarify or correct problems noted by the prospective lender or to meet the lender's requirements.

A lease review includes both business (underwriting) approval of the lease terms and a check for unresolved questions, issues, or problems, both business and legal. The person reviewing the lease generally creates a summary of the lease terms and a lease comment letter or memorandum. The summary form can be used as an outline of the lease summary. It can also serve as a reference description of various lease provisions and commonly held lender policies. Most lenders have their own lease summary form, and the person reviewing a lease should be sure to obtain and use it for that lender's transactions. Table 9.1, at the end of this chapter, lists the titles of some of the important provisions in a lease.

In general, follow-up ensures that comments by the lender on the lease are communicated to the borrower promptly, that the borrower's (and lessee's) questions are answered, and that required changes and clarifications are completed and approved by the lender so that mortgage loan funds can be disbursed within the time indicated by the mortgage loan commitment. This follow-up is a key part of the lease review process. If all of the lender's requirements are not met by the funding date, the lender has several alternatives: to waive some requirements (which it generally is not obligated to do), to insist on strict compliance with the terms of the loan application and commitment (delaying or cancelling the funding), or to negotiate changes in the loan terms (for example, withholding a portion of funds until requirements are met).

The lease summary summarizes the business terms of a lease and assists in identifying issues such as expansion rights given to different tenants for the same space. The lease comment letter or memorandum specifies recommended changes or additions to the lease, addresses unique provisions which should be brought to the attention of the closing attorney or business representative (e.g., rights of first refusal, options to lease space on the roof), and lists both lender requirements which have not been met and items which will be required for closing (e.g., a tenant estoppel certificate, subordination, nondisturbance and attornment agreement, tenant's approval letter regarding layout of shopping center).

A lease which is approved by a prospective lender from a business standpoint is not necessarily acceptable from a legal standpoint (and vice versa.) Typically, different individuals will be involved in deciding the lender's legal and business approvals. Unless the lender specifically agrees otherwise, both business and legal approvals of each lease are needed before a loan is funded.

From a business standpoint, a prospective lender is interested in the continuity of the income stream from a property. Confirming the amount and sources of income from the proposed security, the term of each tenant's lease, and the tenant's credit is of prime importance. A loan underwriting (business) review of each lease focuses particularly on all types of rent payments called for by each lease as well as on the identity, financial standing, and business experience of each tenant and any guarantor of the lease. The location of the tenant's premises and the tenant's type of business may also be important. Approval of insurance provisions is also a business matter, and it is important to understand at the beginning of the lease review process what the lender's insurance requirements are. The business of insurance changes, and many lenders provide detailed insurance language for leases. Either the lessor or the lessee may be responsible for insuring the leased premises.

Certain leases, e.g., retail store leases, require both a minimum (or base) rent payment by a tenant and a percentage rent payment. Percentage rent is based on the amount of business actually done by the tenant. It may be paid in estimated amounts during the lease year, with a final reconciliation and payment (or credit) due after the tenant's business year has ended. In some cases, the entire amount may be due after the tenant's business year ends. Typically, the lease will give the lessor certain rights to audit the lessee's financial statements to confirm the amount of percentage rent due.

Another type of rent payment is a common area maintenance (CAM) charge. Under a CAM provision, a tenant reimburses the landlord for a specified portion of the overall operating costs of the project, e.g., the cost of cleaning and maintaining the lobby and parking area. The amount paid to a landlord under a CAM provision is usually based on the size of the leased premises and the aggregate operating costs of the project. If the tenant so negotiates, the amount can be limited to a set maximum over the lease term or above an agreement upon base amount of the landlord's operating costs (an expense stop.) Frequently, a tenant pays estimated common area fees each month and receives a final bill (or a credit) at the end of the year, when total operating costs are reconciled with payments received.

In addition, many tenants pay the utility costs incurred at the leased premises directly, and shopping center tenants are generally required to contribute to the cost of a merchant's association. The association sponsors advertising and promotions for the center and generally represents tenant interests.

Other issues covered by a business review of a lease include parking rights, rights of first refusal, assignment and subletting, and expansion option. The lease should state whether parking rights are exclusive or nonexclusive, that is, whether specific parking spaces will be set aside for the tenant and, if so, the number and locations of such spaces. Any separate charge for parking should be identified, as well as the tenant's rights, if any, to acquire more parking spaces. In general, a right of first refusal in the case of a lease is an agreement providing the tenant with a first right to accept other or additional space or, in some cases, to purchase the property. A right of first refusal to purchase the property is not acceptable to most mortgage lenders, and a lender will usually require that such a right of first refusal be made subordinate to the lien of its mortgage loan. Where a tenant may desire to expand its leased premises, often a lease provides for the tenant's first right to lease adjacent space which becomes available. This will generally not present problems from a prospective lender's standpoint, as long as the rent provided for is at market rates or at least as much as paid by the prior tenant. When reviewing an expansion option, it is important to check that other tenants do not have similar rights covering all or part of the same space.

Almost all landlords prohibit assignment and subletting without the prior written consent of the landlord. In some states, the landlord has a legal duty not to withhold consent unreasonably; in other states the landlord may withhold consent at its sole (and arbitrary) discretion. Provided that the tenant remains liable under the lease, the lease is not in default, and the assignee assumes the full obligations of the tenant under the lease, a landlord generally should have no objection to an assignment to the lease to a wholly owned subsidiary; an affiliate or the parent company of the corporate tenant; any business entity controlled by, or under common control with, the present tenant or the tenant's parent company; or an entity resulting from a reorganization, merger, or consolidation that succeeds to the business then carried on by the tenant at the leased premises. In other cases, landlords and lenders restrict the tenant's rights to sublease or assign.

From a legal standpoint, a lease review focuses on protecting the continuity of the income stream. More specifically, a lease review should confirm that the lease states a firm commencement date. A lease may provide, for example, that its term begins 30 days after a certain event has occurred, e.g., issuance of a certificate of occupancy or the opening of a major tenant's store in the same shopping center. In general, this is unacceptable, since the exact date may be subject to disagreement later, e.g., when a renewal option is exercised. If a specific date is not stated in the lease, the tenant and the landlord (the prospective borrower) may execute a side letter or other agreement setting out a definite day, month, and year as the lease commencement date.

Similarly, a lease review should confirm the minimum rent payable by the tenant and whether the tenant has a right to occupy the leased premises without paying rent and, if so, far how long. Mortgage lenders often have policies regarding free rent and may not approve a lease if the free rent period is too long or if it has not already passed before the loan is funded. In general, a tenant should not be permitted under the lease to withhold rent or to apply rent to correct landlord defaults or physical problems at the leased premises. (In some instances, a prospective lender will approve such a right of offset if it is limited in amount and/or if the lender is given prior notice of the proposed offset and time to correct the underlying problem.) Any circumstances in which rent can decrease, e.g., upon lease renewal, should be specifically considered by the lender.

Lease provisions dealing with condemnation and destruction should receive both business and legal approval. Many lenders require (in their mortgage or deed of trust form) that any insurance or other payments from condemnation or a casualty loss be used to pay down or reduce the outstanding loan balance at the time these amounts are paid. Lessees, particularly large shopping center tenants, typically require the leased premises to be rebuilt within a specified time after the condemnation or destruction, even if a major loss is involved. If an inconsistency exists, it should be resolved with the lender.

A lender typically requires that a lender protection clause be included in each lease. A lender protection clause gives the lender the right to notice from a tenant if the landlord defaults under the lease. It also gives the lender a right to cure (or begin to cure) any default before the tenant can terminate the lease. Depending on state law, some mortgage lenders may also require that a subordination, nondisturbance, and attornment agreement be executed by each tenant to make the tenant's lease subordinate to the mortgage. Since a recorded mortgage will take priority over a subsequent lease, many tenants do not want to risk termination of the lease upon the foreclosure of the mortgage and so request an agreement with the lender. Many large tenants, particularly anchor tenants, will not agree to subordinate their lease to a lender's lien, and the lender may want such major tenants to continue in occupancy and pay rent after foreclosure (or the lender's receipt of a deed of lieu of foreclosure). The lease may specifically provide for the tenant's acceptance of a new landlord in such circumstances, or a nondisturbance agreement may be negotiated.

Before a loan is fully funded, a lender generally requires that tenants at the property sign tenant estoppel certificates. A tenant estoppel certificate is a statement, signed by the tenant, setting out the major terms of the tenant's lease and certifying that no defaults exist under the lease.

The estoppel certificate may also confirm that the space is occupied by the tenant, and that the tenant has accepted it and the location of any space the tenant has rights to expand into or give back to the landlord. In addition, a lender will often want assurance that the tenant is open for business and has received all rent concessions or other inducements agreed to by the lessor, e.g., reimbursement for the cost of tenant improvements.

A tenant estoppel certificate confirms certain facts about each lease, that is, the term, rent, absence of defaults, and completeness of lease documentation provided to the lender. Each estoppel certificate must be current (dated within an acceptable period determined by the prospective lender, e.g., one month before the funding for which it is required). An estoppel statement generally indicates problems needing the underwriter's attention if it identifies an existing, uncured default in the lease or if information in it (e.g., size of premises, date of the lease, tenant's name) does not match that in the lease. Information in both the estoppel certificate and the lease must match that used in underwriting the loan.

The lender will want a title search to see if a lease certificate or memorandum of lease has been recorded. Such a document summarizes the lease (including as many or as few details as the parties choose, but always addressing the durations of the lease). If it is recorded, the lease will have priority over the lender's lien on the property. Even if there is no such document recorded, in some states leases which predate the loan may have priority over the lender's lien. In such cases, in addition to lease summaries, lease memoranda, and tenant estoppel certificates, a lender often requires a subordination, nondisturbance, and attornment agreement. Such an agreement is a contract between the lender and the tenant to the effect that, upon the landlord's default on the loan, the tenant will recognize the lender as the landlord, and the lender will allow the tenant to continue to occupy the premises, provided that certain conditions are met (e.g., that both parties comply with the lease).

Net Lease versus Gross Lease

In some areas, the terms *net, net-net, net-net-net,* and/or *triple net* refer to occupancy (as opposed to ground) leases. A *net lease* requires the tenant to pay, in addition to a fixed minimum or base rental (and, possibly, percentage rent) a proportionate share of the operating expenses of the property, such as taxes, insurance, and common area maintenance charges. A completely net lease contemplates the landlord receiving the rent free and clear of any expenses relating to the operation of the property; in addition, the tenant is usually responsible for maintaining the property.

Underwriters referring to a net lease usually indicate a triple, or purely, net lease where the tenant picks up all operating expenses on a basis proportionate to the amount of space occupied. A *gross lease* obligates the landlord to pay all or most of the operating expenses of the property.

Ground Leases and Leasehold Mortgages

A builder or developer may decide to lease land for a long term to construct improvements on the property, such as an office building, hotel, shopping center, or industrial plant. For the tenant-developer of the property, the use of a ground lease avoids the expense of purchasing the property. In such a case, the rent paid for the property will reflect the value of the undeveloped property and not the value of the property and improvements that are ultimately to be constructed on it. At the end of the lease term (and any renewals, if exercised), the property will revert back to the fee owner of the property, who will also be ordinarily vested at that time with title to the improvements.

The developer may seek financing secured by the leased property, e.g., for the construction of improvements. As security for its loan, the lender will want a *leasehold mortgage,* which is a security interest in the tenant's rights under the lease and which gives to the lender the right to take over the tenant's position under the lease in the event of default. The tenant's interest in the property (a *leasehold interest*) is valuable because the tenant has the right to use the property for a long time, during which the rental payments are set by the ground lease. Both the ground lessor's and ground lessee's interest in the same property can be mortgageable.

A leasehold mortgage may be either *subordinated* or *unsubordinated.* If a ground lessor (fee owner) agrees (either in the ground lease or otherwise) to join in (subordinate its interest to) the mortgage or deed of trust, the ground lessor's interest can be foreclosed on by the lender, and the lender has what amounts to a fee mortgage, called a subordinated leasehold mortgage. In general, subordination is accomplished by the ground lessor's execution of the mortgage for the express and limited purpose of subordinating its interest; a separate subordination agreement can also be used. The joining of lessors in leasehold mortgages, so that their interest as well as that of the lessees is encumbered, is called subordination of the fee.

In the case of an unsubordinated leasehold loan, the lender will acquire only the interest of the ground lessee upon foreclosure. If the leasehold mortgage is unsubordinated, the lease with the owner of the underlying property (the ground lease) should contain certain provisions which protect the lender. Since the lender's security is the leasehold interest, the lender will want to protect itself against a premature termination of the lease caused by the default of the tenant and will seek to cure any such default. In addition, the lender will want to be able to decide whether to exercise renewal options. The lender will also want to establish its rights to the proceeds of any condemnation award or insurance proceeds policy applicable to the leasehold improvements. In effect, the leasehold lender wants to have rights in the leasehold improvements which are in many ways prior to the rights of the landlord.

Before granting a leasehold mortgage, a prospective leasehold lender can be expected to require a tenant estoppel certificate stating that the lease is in good standing and that all obligations of the landlord and tenant have been met (to date).

Possible Defaults

The leasehold lender is concerned principally about three types of possible tenant defaults under an unsubordinated ground lease.

Defaults Curable by Payment of Money

A default caused by failure to pay rent, real estate taxes, water and sewer rents, insurance obligations, and the like can be cured by paying the requisite amount. The leasehold lender will want the lease to require that it receive notice of such defaults and an opportunity to cure them before the lease may be terminated.

Failure-to-Repair Defaults

If a default results from the tenant's failure to make repairs or perform work necessary to make the premises comply with the law, the leasehold lender cannot cure the default unless it can obtain entry to the premises and time to complete (or at least begin) the necessary repairs. Again, a leasehold lender wants notice of such a default and time to cure (or begin to cure) any default under the lease.

Incurable Defaults

An improper assignment of the lease by the tenant, insolvency, and some other breaches of the lease may not be preventable or curable by the lender. The only real protection for the lender is time to acquire the tenant's rights by foreclosure or otherwise. The leasehold lender can obtain effective protection if the lease provides that in the event of breach by the tenant, the landlord will enter into a new lease, substantially identical to the old one, with the lender as tenant. The lender ordinarily will be obligated to cure any curable default of the tenant as a condition to obtaining the new lease.

The danger to the lender arising from an unexercised renewal option can be avoided by giving the leasehold lender the right to notice of any lease renewal and the right to exercise any renewal right (on behalf of the tenant) which the tenant fails to exercise.

Almost all landlords prohibit assignment and subletting without the prior written consent of the landlord. Provided that the tenant remains liable under the lease, the lease is not in default, and the assignee assumes the full obligations of the tenant under the lease, a landlord generally should have no objection to an assignment of the lease to a wholly-owned subsidiary; an affiliate or the parent company of a corporate tenant; any business entity controlled by, or under common control with, the present tenant or the tenant's parent company; or an entity resulting from a reorganization, merger, or consolidation that succeeds to the business then carried on by the tenant at the leased premises.

Lease Summary

Table 9.1 may be used when reviewing a lease. The reader may take a commercial lease, compare the items covered with the listing of provisions in a lease, and note the items that may be of concern in connection with these lease provisions.

Table 9.1. Reviewing a Lease

Lease provisions	Concerns of the underwriter
Type of lease:	
Name of applicant:	
Date of lease:	If examining a draft lease, be sure to get an executed copy, conforming to the approved draft, before loan funding. Be sure that all exhibits and side letters are reviewed and approved.

Table 9.1. Reviewing a Lease *(Continued)*

Lease provisions	Concerns of the underwriter
Lessor:	If the lessor is other than the loan applicant, look for satisfactory intermediate assignments.
Lessee:	Confirm that the tenant is the one intended (e.g., XYZ Company rather than XYZ Company of California, a subsidiary of the approved tenant).
Guarantor:	The guaranty provision should account for the possibility of lease amendments. Otherwise, the guarantor would have to consent to or join in the amendments. If the guarantor is a corporation, many lenders will want (1) an opinion from the guarantor's counsel to the effect that it can validly give the guarantee and (2) a certified copy of the appropriate corporate resolution.
Lease executed by:	Lessor Lessee
Title of party executing for lessee:	
Insurance:	
Fire and extended coverage:	Lessor Lessee
Control of proceeds:	Lessor Lessee
Protection of mortgagee if lessee providing insurance:	
Liability insurance:	Lessor Lessee
Approval of company:	
General comments:	If the tenant is to provide the insurance, the policy terms and the company should be acceptable to the lender. If the lender cannot have the right to approve the company, the company should have to meet Best's rating or standards acceptable to the lender. Tenant's insurance should include a lender's loss-payable clause.
Real property taxes paid by:	Lessor Lessee Note: If the tenant pays (or reimburses the lessor for) only a portion of the property taxes for its premises, this should be noted.
Repairs:	
Interior of demised premises to be made by:	Lessor Lessee
Exterior-roof-structural to be made by:	Lessor Lessee

Table 9.1. Reviewing a Lease *(Continued)*

Lease provisions	Concerns of the underwriter
Right of lessee to make alterations:	If the tenant can remove its improvements at the end of the lease term, it should agree to do so promptly and carefully and be liable to repair any damage caused by such removal. There should be no rent abatement during any period alterations are being made. Ordinarily, the lessor should have the right to approve the plans for any changes to the leased premises. The tenant should agree to pay promptly for all work done for it at the premises and to keep the building lien-free.

Maintenance:
  Janitorial:
  Utilities:
  Common area:
	
	Lessor Lessee
	Lessor Lessee
	Lessor Lessee

Assignment and subletting:	Lenders are not generally concerned about assignments, as long as the lease doesn't provide for tenant's release from liability.
Subordination provisions:	In states where a subordinate lease is automatically wiped out by foreclosure, lenders want to be sure that most leases, especially major ones, are prior to their lien or, if they are not, that there is an adequate attornment agreement. Without attornment a provision that the subordinated lease could not be wiped out unless in default might be insufficient, since some courts have held that this would give the tenant the option to decide whether there will be cancellation. In states where foreclosure does not wipe out leases automatically, most knowledgeable tenants would want superiority and/or nondisturbance.
Casualty provisions:	If the landlord is obligated to repair, some lenders like at least a 120-day repair period, preferably more. A few lenders dislike provisions that the landlord must, within a certain period, give the tenant notice of election to repair; they substitute a provision that unless the landlord, within that period, gives notice of election not to repair, it shall be deemed to have elected to repair.

Table 9.1. Reviewing a Lease (Continued)

Lease provisions	Concerns of the underwriter
Condemnation:	Most lenders like to see a provision that the tenant can cancel only if a certain percentage of common area is taken. On occasion some accept a provision allowing a tenant to cancel if any part (or a set portion) of the premises is taken, if the premises includes only the building. The condemnation provision is usually a matter of negotiation and should include objective standards rather than subjective. Typically, loan documents call for the proceeds of condemnation and casualty awards to be paid to the lender and used to pay down the loan. Also, a condemnation provision should not allow a tenant to seek an award for the value of its leasehold, since this will reduce the total award payable to the owner of the premises and the lender.
Recording:	Memorandum to be recorded (yes/no). Many lenders prefer that memos for anchor tenants be recorded, especially if the lease is to be superior to the loan. In some jurisdictions, recording is a must. Notarization is generally required for recording.
Use of premises:	The tenant should be allowed to use the premises only for the indicated purposes. If it has broader rights, such as the right to use them for any lawful purpose, there could be a conflict with exclusives given other tenants (in the case of retail space). If the tenant agrees to respect exclusives of which it has been notified in writing, get confirmation that such notice was given. This does not suffice, however, when nuisance uses, rather than competitive uses, are forbidden.
Deposits:	Many lenders prefer not to have more than two months' rent paid in advance. Many lenders also require that security deposits be held in an account designated for that purpose. Some states require an escrow of security deposits, particularly accruing to the tenant.

Table 9.1. Reviewing a Lease *(Continued)*

Lease provisions	Concerns of the underwriter
Option to lessee to purchase and/or right of first refusal:	Any such option must be made clearly subordinate to the lien of the mortgage. If tenant purchases subject to this lien, the lease should not terminate nor merge with the fee as long as the lender or its successors retain an interest in the property.
Parking requirements:	These should be specific as to number, type, and location of spaces; rent; and the lessor's and lessee's rights, if any, to increase or decrease parking availability. A change in parking, e.g., in the event of condemnation, should not lead to a lease termination.
Common area requirements:	The declaration of restrictions should protect the common areas reserved in the lease.
Exhibits:	Copies of all exhibits should be attached to the lease.
Other features:	Lenders are very much interested in any provision for rent offsets or concessions. There should be a severability provision, in the event one or more of the lease provisions is illegal. Unless waived as to smaller tenants, most lenders require a tenant estoppel certificate signed by each tenant immediately prior to funding of the loan. In general, all provisions of the lease must comply with the representations in the loan submission package.

PART 3
Analyzing Income and Expenses

10
The Income-Expense Statement

J. Robert Andrews

Assistant Vice President, Cigna Investments, Inc.
Hartford, Connecticut

The income stream produced by a real estate investment property is the source of funds which will support the mortgage debt or other financing obligations on the property as well as provide a return of, and a return on, the capital invested.

Income Statements

A property's income statement may take one of two forms, depending on the stage of the property's development:

- In the case of a to-be-developed venture, the income is expressed as a pro forma statement, which is an estimate of the property's revenues and expenses as if the property were fully occupied at the current stabilized market rents and expenses. *Fully occupied* is taken to mean less than 100 percent, usually 95 percent, which accounts for some vacancy and collection loss.

- In the case of an operating property, the income statement is developed from actual accounting records, leases, operating expenses, or other sources of actual dollar information.

Many market and other assumptions are made in developing the pro forma statement, but virtually all of an operating property's income statement derives from verifiable financial data. In both cases the underwriter uses a full complement of judgments and factual information to develop, test, and validate the information provided in the property's income statement.

Building Measures

Before starting into a discussion of the income statement, a review of building measurement methods seems advisable, since many income and expense items are determined by building area.

A building's size may be expressed in more than one way, depending on its use and on the conventions of the market in which it resides. There are two basic measures for any building:

- *The overall building size.* This measure is the square foot measurement of each of the floors to the outside surfaces of the building walls (Figure 10.1).

- *The size of the space leased or available to be leased.* This figure is the square foot measurement of each of the floors to the inside surfaces of the building walls (Figure 10.2).

The industry generally calls the first measure *gross building area* (GBA). The second measure, or the amount of space available to be leased to the tenants, can be defined a number of ways, depending on the type of property (retail, office, warehouse, residential), industry standards, and local custom. Some of the most common definitions for the second measure include:

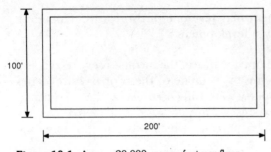

Figure 10.1. Area = 20,000 square feet per floor.

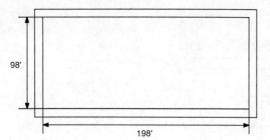

Figure 10.2. Area = 19,404 square feet per floor.

- *Gross leasable area (GLA).* This retail industry measure is the total floor area designed for tenant occupancy and exclusive use, including any basements, mezzanines, or upper floors. In a retail mall, the GLA of the mall shops would be the product of the width of a tenant space measured to the centerline of the demising walls between tenant spaces multiplied by the depth of the tenant space measured from the exterior face of the mall wall to the exterior face of the rear wall (Figure 10.3).

- *Usable area (UA).* This office building industry measure is the area of a structure measured between the finished surface of the outside wall and the finished surface of the office side of the corridor times the width measured to the centerline of partitions that separate one office from another. No deductions are made for columns and projections necessary for the building (Figure 10.4).

- *Rentable area (RA).* Another office building industry measure, RA is the area of a structure measured to the major dominant element of

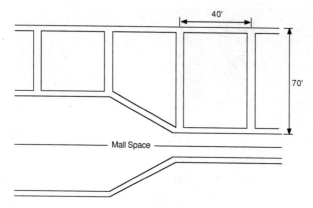

Figure 10.3. GLA (shop) = 2800 square feet.

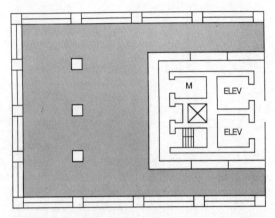

Figure 10.4. Usable area = 16,000 square feet per floor
(approx.).

the outside wall (which is not necessarily the finished surface) excluding any major vertical penetrations of the floor (Figure 10.5).

A building's *R/U ratio* is the ratio of rentable area to usable area. The *R/U* ratio of the building illustrated in Figures 10.4 and 10.5 is approximately 116 percent. A building's *efficiency factor* is the ratio between the total lease measurement (GLA, NRA, UA, etc.) and the gross building area. Thus, the rentable efficiency of the building in Figures 10.4 and 10.5 is approximately 95 percent.

The underwriter should understand how a building is measured or how a market will "allow" a building to be measured, because a misun-

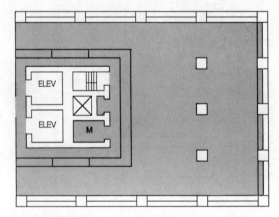

Figure 10.5. Rentable area = 18,500 square feet per
floor (approx.).

derstanding can lead to substantially different measures of space available to lease and hence estimates of potential income. In some markets, considerable concessions are granted or premiums gained by manipulating measurement basis or add-on factors so that leases with comparable face rates have substantially different effective rates.

Lease Income

Leases can be divided in two broad categories[1]:

- *Gross leases* are leases wherein the tenant pays a defined amount, called *base rent,* to the landlord. The landlord is then responsible to pay property operating expenses, taxes, and capital expenditures.
- *Net leases* require that the tenant pay not only base rent but also some or all operating expenses, taxes, and/or property capital expenditures or other obligations directly to the provider of the respective services.

The nomenclature used to describe net leases has varied over the years and from market to market. If a lease has provisions whereby the tenant pays all operating expenses, taxes, and property capital expenditures, the lease is said to be an *absolute triple net lease.* As a caution, it can also be referred to as a *net lease.* In some markets, a net lease requires that the tenant pay a limited group of operating expenses. The lease document determines precisely the tenant or landlord's obligation.

When underwriting a real estate investment, all information provided by third-party sources should be verified. In the case of lease information, best practice is to review and "brief" each lease on a lease-by-lease basis to ensure that all the relevant provisions of the lease are understood. The starting point in the accumulation of lease information is the rent roll, which will typically include the tenant name, term (starting and ending dates), location reference (suite number), base rent, additional rent (escalation income, percentage rent), and other provisions (escalation provisions, renewal, expansion and/or termination options), as shown in Table 10.1. Most of the terms in Table 10.1 are self explanatory—tenant name, term, suite, and base rent. *Escalation provisions* is a general term which describes how or under what circumstances the tenant pays additional sums to the landlord to recover certain operating costs. In general, these additional charges are calculated on a square foot, pro rata share. For example, if a tenant occupies 6000 square feet in a 75,000 square foot building, the tenant's pro rata share is 8 per-

---

[1]See also Chapter 9.

Table 10.1. Rent Roll

Tenant name	Term	Suite	Base rent	1985 Escalations	Other
ABC	10/01/87 09/31/90	101	$15.00	$3.00	1984 Base year, all operating expenses plus taxes (OE&T) 3-year renewal at market

cent—a direct percent based on square footage. In many markets this is a negotiated element of a lease. A tenant's pro rata share may not be based on direct square foot ratios. In some cases, the tenant's share might apply to less than 100 percent of the expenses or at different ratios to different expenses, depending perhaps on other leases in the remainder of the building.

Typical office building leases pay a pro rata share of some or all operating expenses over a defined amount. The defined amount usually is defined in one of two ways:

- *Stop leases* state some minimum operating expense dollar amount. When actual operating expenses are over that amount, the tenant pays a pro rata share of the additional amounts.

- *Base-year leases* carry the obligation to pay a pro rata share of expenses *over* the expenses incurred in a base year.

There are many variations on the theme of stop and base-year leases depending on the general market conditions at the time of writing the lease and depending on what is currently marketable with respect to lease stipulations. Some variations include the choice of base year (the lease year or the prior year) and the method of calculation and payment (in the advance based on an estimate, paid in arrears from actuals). In the case of the stop lease, a dollar amount equal to, greater than, or less than the actual cost may be chosen, depending upon the market. Examples of a stop lease and a base-year lease (assuming one tenant, fully occupied building, on a square-foot basis) are given in Tables 10.2 and 10.3. In the first case, the landlord recovers expenses over $6.50 per square foot. In the second, the landlord recovers all expenses.

As can be determined by the differences in the net income streams in the base-year and stop examples, expense escalation provisions of a lease are very important, completely negotiable, and dependent on marketplace laws of supply and demand.

For an older property with base-year leases, the base-year expense information may not be available to calculate current or future estimates

Table 10.2. Stop Lease (Stop = $6.50 per Square Foot)

	Year 1	Year 2	Year 3	Year 4	Year 5	Assump-tions
Base rents	$15.00	$15.00	$15.00	$15.00	$15.00	
Recovery of operating expenses and taxes	0.00	0.00	0.12	0.45	0.79	
Gross income	$15.00	$15.00	$15.12	$15.45	$15.79	
Operating expenses and taxes	6.00	6.30	6.62	6.95	7.29	5% growth
Net operating income	$ 9.00	$ 8.70	$ 8.50	$ 8.50	$ 8.50	

of recoverable expenses. A property manager's records will always include a record of the most recent escalation charges.

In many markets (although the industry is generally getting away from this type of lease), leases are found with Consumer Price Index (CPI) provisions. These provisions protect the landlord against expense increases by tying the base rent to an index. The index's growth rate almost never exactly equals the growth rate of expenses on an ongoing, regular basis. Since it is applied to a larger number, it tends to provide inflation protection to the landlord. An example (assuming the index growth rate is 3 percent per year) is given in Table 10.4.

Typical shopping center leases work differently with respect to the collection of the tenant's pro rata share of expenses. Common area

Table 10.3. Base-Year Lease (Base Year = Year 1)

	Year 1	Year 2	Year 3	Year 4	Year 5	Assump-tions
Base rents	$15.00	$15.00	$15.00	$15.00	$15.00	
Recovery of operating expenses and taxes	0.00	0.30	0.62	0.95	1.29	
Gross income	$15.00	$15.30	$15.62	$15.95	$16.29	
Operating expenses and taxes	6.00	6.30	6.62	6.95	7.29	5% growth
Net operating income	$ 9.00	$ 9.00	$ 9.00	$ 9.00	$ 9.00	

Table 10.4. Index Lease

	Year 1	Year 2	Year 3	Year 4	Year 5	Assumptions
Base rents	$15.00	$15.00	$15.00	$15.00	$15.00	
Index increases	0.00	0.45	0.91	1.39	1.88	3% index
Recovery of operating expenses and taxes	0.00	0.00	0.00	0.00	0.00	
Gross income	$15.00	$15.45	$15.91	$16.39	$16.88	
Operating expenses and taxes	6.00	6.30	6.62	6.95	7.29	5% growth
Net operating income	$ 9.00	$ 9.15	$ 9.29	$ 9.44	$ 9.59	

maintenance (CAM) expenses are incurred in the maintenance of common facilities in the center (parking lot expenses, snow removal, groundskeeping, mall maintenance, mall utilities, insurance, and cleaning, among others). Unlike stop and base-year leases, 100 percent of these costs are passed on to the tenant. In practice, they are usually passed on at a multiplier (110 percent to 115 percent, depending on the market) to compensate the landlord for certain administrative and other expenses not typically associated with CAM expenses and not recovered through other lease provisions. An example (assuming CAM expense begins at $4 in year 1 and is recovered at 115 percent) is given in Table 10.5.

Typical shopping center leases also provide for additional revenue to be paid to the landlord by tenants under percentage rent clauses. The

Table 10.5. CAM Expense Recovery

	Year 1	Year 2	Year 3	Year 4	Year 5	Assumptions
Base rents	$15.00	$15.00	$15.00	$15.00	$15.00	
CAM recovery	4.60	4.83	5.07	5.32	5.59	115% recovery
Total income	$19.60	$19.83	$20.07	$20.32	$20.59	
Operating expenses and taxes	0.50	0.53	0.55	0.58	0.61	5% growth
CAM expenses	4.00	4.20	4.41	4.63	4.86	5% growth
Total expense	$ 4.50	$ 4.73	$ 4.96	$ 5.21	$ 5.47	
Net operating income	$15.10	$15.10	$15.11	$15.11	$15.12	

additional revenue is expressed as a percentage of gross sales over some base amount, called a *breakpoint*. For example, a retail lease may require a tenant to pay 6 percent of the gross sales, over a base gross sales amount, to the landlord. The *natural breakpoint* is calculated by dividing the annual base rent by the percentage rent rate. Some percentage clauses have offset provisions which allow the breakpoint to increase to offset costs being passed on to the tenant due to increases in certain property operating expenses such as taxes.

In summary, when looking at any real estate investment, a lease-by-lease review is essential. The underwriter should be sensitive to what represents "market" with respect to the secondary provisions of a lease—stops, base-year provisions, CAM provisions and multipliers, among others. Presumably prospective tenants are informed persons; they will look for the best financial arrangement for their own interests if all else is equal. For example, two buildings are offering space at $15 per square foot with $6 per square foot stops. One is an older building with OE&T costing $6.25 per square foot due to operating inefficiencies. The other is a newer building which operates at $6 per square foot. The occupancy cost of the former is $15.25 per square foot versus $15.00 per square foot in the latter. Needless to say, tenants will usually select the least costly alternative, all else being equal.

Other Income

Sources of income in an investment property other than base rent and operating expense reimbursements include the following:

- Parking income, derived from the operation of a parking facility.

- Tenant service income, which is income generated from special tenant services provided to a tenant by the landlord. This income is often in part or wholly offset by corresponding expenses.

- Interest income, which is generated by the investing of excess cash flows from the property prior to distribution. In most instances, interest income is not considered operating income; for the purposes of underwriting, it is not usually included as a source of income.

- Miscellaneous income, such as residential properties deriving income from laundries, vending, furniture rental, and deposit forfeitures.

Like base rent, other sources of income are often both market and occupancy dependent. In the case of parking income, for example, parking charges are subject to supply and demand forces just as any other commodity. Likewise, the proportion of short-term users to long-term monthly users relates to both market and occupancy conditions. Lastly, overall use is directly related to occupancy. If an office property is estimated to be at 95 percent occupancy, the parking facility is not likely to be utilized at 100 percent.

Expenses

A number of general classifications are used to define operating expenses:

- Operating expenses and taxes
- Fixed and variable expenses
- Recoverable and nonrecoverable expenses

These classifications represent a full complement of expenses to which every real estate investment is subject. From an underwriting point of view, not only must the amounts be estimated accurately but also all the expenses which might be incurred must be included in the analysis.

Large bodies of data concerning the expenses have been accumulated by various groups concerning the operating costs of various types of real estate. These groups include trade associations, property-type associations, industry clearinghouses, institutional investors, and owners and operators. Access to these data provide a wealth of resource information and analytical tools to the underwriter. Three such sources of comparative data are:

- *Building Owners and Managers Association International Report.* Published annually, the BOMA report is an income-expense analysis for nearly 3000 office buildings in 79 U.S. and 8 Canadian cities. Separate summaries are presented for various types of special use properties (e.g., all-electric, single-purpose, medical, and government- occupied buildings); operating costs are also summarized by building age and height. Finally, the industry's standard method of floor measurements (i.e., gross, usable, and rentable square feet) is concisely defined.

- *Dollars and Cents of Shopping Centers.* Published every three years by the Urban Land Institute (ULI), this report measures shopping center income and expenses to the point of net operating income. This figure is cross-referenced for four types of centers (super regionals, regionals, community, and neighborhood), five age groups (1–3 years, 4–6 years, 7–9 years, 10–19 years, and 20 years and over), and six U.S. geographic areas (northeast, southeast, midwest, north central, southwest, and far west) as well as Canada. Tenant sales and percentage rent figures are presented for each of the above subcategories.

- *Institute of Real Estate Management Expense Reports.* The IREM reports present median income and expense data for selected metropolitan and regional areas, as well as similar national and Canadian data. Each geographic area is further broken down by the property's size, age group, rental range, and building type. The reports analyze various national income and expense trends and present special reports on current patterns in leasing fees, utilities consumption, and tenant turnover rates. IREM publishes separate reports on apartments, office buildings, condominiums, cooperatives, and planned unit developments (PUDs).

Ratios and rules of thumb can be used to estimate or validate a single number for all expenses or to estimate or validate a line item of an expense statement. For example:

- In the case of a multifamily property, all operating expenses and taxes generally fall in an amount equal to 30 percent to 45 percent of effective gross income (EGI). Expressed another way, a multifamily rental property typically delivers 55 percent to 70 percent of EGI to the bottom line. If a particular property falls outside of this range, knowing these rule-of-thumb targets should prompt the underwriter to identify the cause for the increased expenses.

- Contract cleaning and janitorial services for a typical multitenant suburban office building usually costs about $0.50 to $1.00 per square foot in most markets. If a property is projected to cost more or less than that amount, the underwriter should discover why.

Careful underwriters recognize, however, that this type of information (ratios, rules of thumb, or general average costs) represents averages of many different types of products and many different types of markets over extended periods. For any particular investment, these data may provide a very distorted estimate of expenses. A good example is the rapid rise in property insurance from mid-1985 to 1986 as the insurance industry came to grips with the disproportionate rising cost of claims, settlements, and judgments.

Some estimates of expenses are relatively easy, for example, the real estate tax. Often, a call or visit to the local tax assessment or collection agency is all that's needed to determine the formula necessary to calculate the expected property tax accurately. Good comparable data are available, and, more often than not, the taxation authority will assist the underwriter in the estimating process.

The message to the underwriter is precisely the same message provided in the analysis of income: Develop expense estimates with similar analytical fact-finding methodologies.

Expanded Model

The income statement model can be expanded to include a number of income and expense categories. As determined earlier, various leases and property types operate in different ways; as a result their income statements are different. Typical operating statement categories for various types of real estate investment properties would include the categories shown in Table 10.6.[2]

Reserves

As noted in the expanded model, reserves for replacements are included in the pro forma income statement. The rationale for including this noncash expenditure is that all properties are subject to a number of periodic expenditures for major replacements (roofs, parking lots, HVAC). Rather than deducting 100 percent of expected costs in a pro forma statement (which would severely diminish the amount of funds available to support debt obligations), an apportioned amount is usually included as an acknowledgement that prudent property owners and lenders should not use all available cash flow for the support of debt.

Reserves are most often expressed as a per-square-foot cost and typically range from $0.10 to $0.20 per square foot for most investment types (other than hotels) in most markets. Assuming that nonrecurring expenses happen every 10 years, $1 to $2 per square foot is available over time for one-time expenses. Like all such rules of thumb, this cost varies according to building type, age, and market.

Pitfalls

Several caveats should be mentioned when analyzing income statements from an existing property. Three general types of income statements

---

[2]Hotel operations and descriptions of industry standard accounts are beyond the scope of this chapter. A number of excellent resources exists, however, including material produced by firms which specialize in the lodging industry such as Pannell Kerr Foster (PKF).

Table 10.6. Typical Operating Statement Categories for Various Investment Properties

Office	Retail	Apartment	Warehouse
Revenues			
Base rent + Escalation income + CPI increases + Parking income + Tenant services + Other revenue	Base rent + Percentage rent + CAM recovery + Escalation income + CPI increases + Tenant services + Other revenue	Base rent + Parking income + Late charges + Deposit forfeit + Laundry + Other revenue	Base rent + Escalation income + CPI increases + Parking income + Tenant services + Other revenue
Gross income − Vacancy allowance*	Gross income − Vacancy allowance*	Gross income − Vacancy allowance*	Gross income − Vacancy allowance*
Effective gross income	Effective gross income	Effective gross income	Effective gross income
Operating Expenses and Taxes			
Management fees + Property insurance + Administration + Security + Ads and promotions + Parking expense + Utilities + Maintenance and repair + Cleaning and janitorial work + Real estate tax + Replacement reserves* + Other expense	Management fees + Property insurance + Administration + Security + Ads and promotion + Utilities + Maintenance and repair + CAM expense + Real estate tax + Replacement reserves + Other expense	Management fees + Property insurance + Administration + Security + Ads and promotion + Utilities + Maintenance and repair + Payroll and fringe benefits + Real estate tax + Replacement reserves + Other expense	Management fees + Property insurance + Administration + Security + Ads and promotion + Utilities + Parking expense + Maintenance and repair + Cleaning and janitorial work + Real estate tax + Replacement reserves + Other expense
Total OE&T	Total OE&T	Total OE&T	Total OE&T
Effective gross income − Total OE&T	Effective gross income − Total OE&T	Effective gross income − Total OE&T	Effective gross income − Total OE&T
Net operating income	Net operating income	Net operating income	Net operating income

*Not typically included in actual operating statements. Typically used in pro forma statements.

were identified: property income and cash flow, accounting income (GAAP or statutory), and taxable income. Although this chapter has concentrated on a model of property income and cash flow, other types of statements may be the only source of information available concerning a particular property. The nature of these statements requires modification of techniques based on the overall model.

Generally accepted accounting practices require that rental income from leases which have free rent or step-up provisions be accounted for in a special manner. The free rent is spread out among all the lease years of a tenant. Thus, for example, a 60-month (5-year) lease that provides 6 months of free rent would provide the cash flow rent and GAAP accounting streams shown in Table 10.7. If an underwriter is looking at a GAAP statement in the first year, income is overstated. If it is the fourth year, income is understated.

Table 10.7. Cash Flow Rent and GAAP Accounting Streams

	Year 1	Year 2	Year 3	Year 4	Year 5
Actual rent cash flow stream					
Base rents	$ 8.00	$16.00	$16.00	$16.00	$16.00
GAAP accounting stream					
Base rents	$ 8.00	$16.00	$16.00	$16.00	$16.00
GAAP adjustment	6.40	(1.60)	(1.60)	(1.60)	(1.60)
GAAP income	$14.40	$14.40	$14.40	$14.40	$14.40

Another example that would show up in a GAAP statement or tax statement is the treatment and recording of certain noncash expenses, such as the depreciation of capital expense items or the inclusion of interest expense (debt service interest) as an expense above net operating income. Adjustments should be made by the underwriter to account for them properly.

The common denominator throughout this chapter is the requirement that the underwriter be thoroughly knowledgeable about the property, the market, and the conditions which affect projected income and expenses. An error in judgment or less-than-thorough underwriting can produce estimates of income and expenses which are not readily achievable. This in turn will play havoc with the financial performance of the investment, and investor objectives will not be met. Good underwriting, however, will help ensure that projected results are met.

11

Basic Mathematics of Real Estate Finance

Thomas A. Gauldin, CMB

President, FCR Mortgage Corporation
Raleigh, North Carolina

The actual underwriting of a proposed mortgage loan begins once the income and operating expense statement has been prepared and the tentative values of the real estate have been established. The underwriting of a mortgage loan, as opposed to the appraisal of real estate, deals with the prevention of a default and the anticipation of the benefits, or yield, to be derived from the loan or joint venture. On one hand, the appraiser gives separate attention to the measurement of anticipated income and expenses through comparisons with other properties. On the other hand, an underwriter takes the information supplied by the appraiser and analyzes the property based upon specific types of financing to determine whether (1) the property is capable of safely supporting the debt load and (2) statutory obligations regarding loan-to-value ratios are met.

The first step in underwriting a loan is to calculate how much of the net operating income will be needed to cover the fixed obligations, or debt service, of the requested loan. The three factors necessary to cal-

119

culate this fixed obligation are the loan amount, the interest rate, and the amortization term (if any) of the mortgage. During periods of high interest, lenders may make loans without any provision for regular debt retirement, allowing the borrower to pay only the interest on the loan until the balloon balance is due; consequently, the fixed obligation is merely the interest on the loan without any principal retirement. Such situations will be discussed later in this chapter.

Since interest is paid in *arrears* on the typical mortgage loan (unless it is specifically negotiated otherwise), the amount of interest due during any given period of the loan is calculated by multiplying the loan amount times the periodic rate of interest. For the sake of convenience, a loan is quoted or discussed in terms of its normal annual rate of interest, which is the periodic rate times the number of periods per year. For example, a 12 percent loan could be 3 percent per quarter, 6 percent per semiannual period, or 1 percent per month. The amount of interest due in arrears is therefore calculated by taking the balance at the beginning of the period times the periodic rate of interest.

For income-producing property financing, the mortgage loan constant is the annual amount of mortgage payments that must be made to pay interest on the outstanding principal balance of the loan and provide for principal reduction so that at the end of the amortization period the loan has been fully amortized. The constant is expressed as a percentage of the loan amount.

The algebraic formula is

$$\text{Loan} \times \cfrac{i}{1 - \cfrac{1}{(1 + i)^n}}$$

where i = annual interest rate, expressed as a decimal, divided by the number of payments to be made in the year
  n = total number of *payments* that would be made on the loan
Loan = actual amount loaned

As an example of how a constant is determined, assume a loan request at 11.25 percent interest amortized over 30 years. To determine the constant in percentage terms, use $1.00 as the loan amount. Referring to the algebraic formula above, i is the monthly interest rate or 11.25 percent (0.1125) divided by 12, which equals 0.9375 percent or 0.009375. The figure n is the number of monthly payments to be made over 30 years; 12 × 30 equals 360. The formula is now:

$$\text{Monthly constant} = \$1 \times \cfrac{0.009375}{1 - \cfrac{1}{(1 + 0.009375)^{360}}}$$

It is easiest to use a programmed calculator at this stage:

$$\text{Monthly constant} = \$1 \times \frac{0.009375}{1 - \dfrac{1}{28.764}}$$

$$\text{Monthly constant} = \$1 \times \frac{0.009375}{1 - 0.03476}$$

$$\text{Monthly constant} = \$1 \times \frac{0.009375}{0.96524}$$

$$\text{Monthly constant} = 0.009713$$

$$\text{Annual constant} = 12 \times 0.009713 =$$
$$0.11655 \text{ or } 11.66 \text{ percent (rounded)}$$

This means 11.66 percent of the loan amount must be paid each year in 12 equal monthly installments to satisfy the interest requirement and amortize debt.

To help visualize this calculation, another example might be helpful. Table 11.1 considers a $5000 loan with interest at the rate of 12 percent and a five-year amortization:

Loan amount	$5000
Annual interest rate	12 percent
Loan term	5 years, annual payment
Payment	$1387.05

A loan constant can represent any number of interest rates and amortization periods. Tables have been published to set forth loan constant rates.

Table 11.1. Installment Calculations for a $5000 Loan at 12 Percent over Five Years

Payment number	Interest*	Principal†	Total payment‡	Balance§
0				$5000.00
1	$600.00	$ 787.05	$1387.05	4212.95
2	505.55	881.50	1387.05	3331.45
3	339.77	987.28	1387.05	2344.18
4	281.30	1105.75	1387.05	1238.43
5	148.61	1238.43	1387.04	0.00

*Previous balance × interest rate.
†Payment − interest.
‡Interest + principal.
§Previous balance − principal payment.

Having computed the periodic debt service, which is the monthly payment, the next step is to multiply this by the number of periods in a year to derive the annual debt service. Again, if the loan is made on an interest-only basis, the interest rate is the annual loan constant.

Debt Service Coverage Ratio

Having calculated the annual debt service, the next step is to calculate the debt service coverage ratio. This is one of the most important ratios in underwriting a mortgage loan, since it represents the lender's and borrowers' "security blanket." Simply stated, it is a ratio by which the net operating income in a given year exceeds the amount of debt service. For example, if a property has a net operating income of $120,000 and an annual debt service requirement of $100,000, the debt service coverage ratio is $120,000 divided by $100,000 or 1.2 times. Restated, the net operating income is 1.2 times greater than the debt coverage. As this ratio increases, the likelihood of a technical default on a loan because of changes in occupancy, tenant pattern, or increased expenses decreases. Table 11.2 is a hypothetical calculation of debt service coverage ratios for an office building.

In Table 11.2, clearly the property can satisfy its debt service requirements more easily each year. If the project anticipates many tenants, leases would renew at a higher rate than that being paid at the time of the appraisal. Therefore, the net operating income increased while the debt service remained constant.

The hypothetical illustration in Table 11.2 works out to an initial debt service coverage ratio of 1.149 times, provoking questions about conditions for refinancing the loan at the time of its balloon date (seven years). Since the income is only projected for five years, assume that the balloon will occur at the end of the fifth year rather than the seventh, that the lender will use the fifth year of net operating income for cal-

Table 11.2. Debt Service Coverage Ratio

	Year 1	Year 2	Year 3	Year 4	Year 5
Net operating income	$2,665,567	$2,745,534	$2,827,900	$2,912,737	$3,000,119
Annual debt service ($19,905,166 at 11¼% for 30 years)	$2,319,975	$2,319,975	$2,319,975	$2,319,975	$2,319,975
Debt coverage ratio	1.149	1.183	1.219	1.256	1.293

culating the debt coverage ratio, that interest rates have increased by 2 percent, and that the amount of loan refinanced is $19 million. Adding 2 percent to the 11.25 percent base rate gives a rate of 13.25 percent, with amortization of 30 years and a loan amount of $19 million. Therefore, the monthly payment is $213,897 and the annual payment (debt service) is $2,566,764.

Based on this computation, and deriving from Table 11.2 an anticipated net operating income of $3,000,119, the coverage ratio ($3,000,119 divided by $2,566,764) equals 1.169 times. Since this exceeds the initial debt coverage ratio, the lender could be persuaded that the loan can be safely refinanced even with increased interest rates in the future. (Note that these hypothetical numbers also relate to the equity analysis at the end of the chapter.)

Overall Rate

The relationship between the net operating income of a property and its value or sales price is called the *capitalization rate* or *overall rate*. For a property whose net operating income and value are known, the overall rate can be obtained by dividing the net operating income by the sales price. Mathematically, it is expressed as the following:

$$V = \frac{I}{R}$$

where V = capitalized value of the property
I = net operating income
R = overall capitalization rate

Restating the above, $I = V \times R$ and $R = I/V$. A simple mnemonic called IRV is represented by the following:

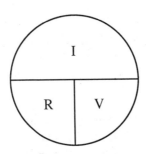

To use this circle, simply cover the variable to be determined and then perform the remaining multiplication or division.

By the time a loan request reaches the underwriting stage, the appraiser has generally selected a capitalization rate either directly from the market or indirectly by a mathematical process. A capitalization rate drawn directly from the market simply compares the net operating income of recent comparable sales with the sales prices. A number of indirect techniques are used to develop a capitalization rate, such as the band of investment theory, with or without residual techniques, and the mortgage equity theory. Regardless of the technique used to derive the number, the capitalization rate pertains to the whole project, recognizing that a part of the money available to purchase a specific property may come from borrowings with the balance coming from equity.

The *cap rate* concept embraces both yield and capital return, often expressed as a return *on* and a return *of* money. One of the fundamental principles in real estate investment is that these two are separate and a change in one will cause a change in the other. The return on money is its yield. The return of money is a return of capital.

In a typical loan, the benefit to the lender is the return of the invested loan proceeds to recoup the investment and the return on the invested loan proceeds. On a loan made on an interest-only basis, the return of the loan is not made by regular payment to principal, but it is nevertheless made at the end of the loan term, when the entire loan proceeds must be repaid. The return on the money, however, should be reasonably expected on a monthly or quarterly basis in the form of interest.

Equity, however, is an investment in the rise or fall of value associated with the income property and benefits primarily from a return on the invested dollar. As described more fully in the next chapter, the internal rate of return is a measurement of the rise and fall of cash flows following an initial investment. No return of equity is computed for ratio purposes, since the entire cash flow subsequent to an equity investment is considered in calculating the internal rate of return.

Cash Flow

Subtracting the debt service, whether interest-only or interest and principal, from the net operating income leaves the cash flow. Cash flow is the return on the invested equity dollar. If the effective gross income and expenses are projected forward, annual net operating income and cash flows can be predicted.

Dividing the cash flow by the invested equity dollar provides what is commonly known as the cash-on-cash return. Table 11.3 simply recog-

Table 11.3. Equity Analysis

	Year 1	Year 2	Year 3	Year 4	Year 5
Net operating income	$ 2,665,567	$ 2,745,534	$ 2,827,900	$ 2,912,737	$ 3,000,119
Less debt service	2,319,975	2,319,975	2,319,975	2,319,975	2,319,975
Cash flow	345,592	425,559	507,925	592,762	680,144
Assuming equity investment of $2.98 million, annual return on initial investment	11.60%	14.28%	17.04%	19.89%	22.82%
Loan balance of $19,905,165	$19,820,231	$19,725,233	$19,618,980	$19,500,137	$19,367,213
Amount amortized each year	$ 84,934	$ 94,998	$ 106,253	$ 118,843	$ 132,924
Cash flow plus amount amortized	$ 430,526	$ 520,557	$ 614,178	$ 711,605	$ 813,068
Revised return on equity*	14.45%	17.47%	20.61%	23.88%	27.28%

*Analyzing the return on the equity provides a basis of comparison with other investments, such as bonds or stocks.

nizes the initial investment divided into the projected cash-on-cash return. The second version uses both the initial investment and amortized principal balance to measure the overall equity return; although the equity investment appears to increase as the loan is amortized, it is merely an opportunity cost until a sale or conveyance takes place and the true equity is realized.

In this chapter we have reviewed basic underwriting computations for income-producing properties. Chapter 12 will continue this discussion with an examination of methods for forecasting future investment benefits.

12

Equity Investment Measurement Techniques

J. Thomas Montgomery, CRE, MAI

Real Estate Consultant, West Hartford, Connecticut

This chapter explains how many institutional investors analyze income-producing properties for the purpose of making equity investments. Since investors do indeed buy "futures," most approaches for estimating equity price and yield involve some prediction of future performance. Equity investment measurement techniques can accordingly be arrayed into two broad categories: those that reflect actual threshold numbers and require no forecasting beyond the first year of ownership and others that require forecasting for the entire investment cycle, however long that is assumed to be.

This chapter is intended as an introductory overview of each of these two broad categories. Inherently more complex, if not necessarily more important, forecasting equity price and yield will receive added attention, as will the matter of the internal rate of return (IRR).

No one technique is perfect nor necessarily better than another. Acquisition specialists may employ several in the same transaction. When comparing investment alternatives and portfolio performance, specialists should be consistent and use the same measurement criteria over time.

A great many equity investment measurement techniques and related software programs are available to convert investors' motivations, objectives, and anticipations into finite numbers. No matter which techniques are employed, singularly or in concert, they must be able to:

- Analyze a specific investment opportunity
- Compare available alternatives within and without real estate (opportunity costs)
- Serve as a decision-making standard
- Subsequently monitor interim and final performance results

Implications and Applications

Some of or all the following considerations figure in every income property type transaction and affect the particular real estate equity investment measurement techniques selected:

- Other non-real-estate investment alternatives available to the equity investor (e.g., common stocks)
- The type and inherent quality of subject property investment relative to other similar, and even dissimilar, real estate opportunities (i.e., location, functional utility, condition)
- Recent market activity and prices of similar property sales and offerings
- The availability and terms of all kinds of financing (leverage)
- Favorable or unfavorable existing leases and the ability (or inability) to "roll" any negative leaseholds, thus improving cash flows over time
- Availability of tax shelter benefits during each of the origination, operation, and termination stages of any investment's life cycle
- Future value considerations concerning real or inflationary appreciation anticipation over the contemplated equity holding period
- The point in time at which the investor recovers its investment

In selecting particular analysis techniques, it is also important to recognize that various classes of investors have different objectives, priorities, and constraints. For example, pension funds typically have longer holding horizons and normally do not incur any income tax consequence. Their investment goals may be radically different from those of a tax-oriented syndicator with a shorter holding expectation.

No Forecasts Beyond
First Year

In introductory fashion, a few of the very important tools and rules of thumb used by acquisition experts when recommending property to their clients are described in this section. These techniques require no forecasts beyond the first year and tend to deal with actual operating numbers in place or ones that can most probably be realized within the first year of ownership.

A *gross income multiplier* (GIM) is the number of times a gross (or effective) income schedule has sold or might sell for. Similar to a stock price/earnings ratio, the multiplier is a model of market and investor reaction to a stream of actual income. It is a universal rule of thumb used by many investors to trigger purchase or sale interest. By using an appropriate operating expense ratio, it is possible to convert an actual GIM into a rough overall capitalization rate.

An *overall capitalization rate* (or "cap" rate) is the relationship between net operating income before debt service and price asked or paid. Using actual income and expense operating figures, this rate is a popular threshold yield bellwether. In making an offer, some investors apply that net operating income figure they feel they can realistically generate during their first year of ownership as their hurdle numerator. When investment property is sold, competitors want to know what the "cap" rate was. It is equally important to know what the net operating income premise was.

A pretax *cash-on-cash rate* is the ratio between actual pretax cash flow after debt service and the original amount of equity investment required. This equity capitalization rate indirectly reflects the overall investment motivations and expectations of a great many real estate equity investors—available financing, tax shelter, appreciation hopes, and anticipations that starting net income can be increased over time. Coupled with quoted mortgage constants, the two rates can be weighted and merged to synthesize a market-related overall capitalization rate.

There is also a reciprocal relationship between cash-on-cash rates and mortgage debt service coverage ratios. Cash-on-cash rates can also be calculated on an after-tax basis incorporating "spillover" benefits.

Forecasts Required for Full
Investment Periods

The following sections describe briefly some better-known and more complex equity investment measurement techniques, and some of these techniques are demonstrated with simple illustrations. All can involve complex forecasting beyond time zero or the date of acquisition.

- Payback
- Present value: capitalization and discounted cash flow analysis
- Net present value (profitability index)
- Real rates of return
- Internal rate of return (three generic variations)

These techniques are executed over an investment cycle or presumed holding period. Any kind of investment, including real estate equity investments, has three stages to its life cycle—origination, operation, and termination. Each stage must first be analyzed separately and then interposed on a time-line from time zero.

Payback Period

All investors are interested in *payback*, that is, return *of* as well as return *on* equity or money invested. In an uncertain world the important questions are: When are the after-tax equity dollars to be returned? How? Who has a prior claim to the investment's income and asset value? Is the equity investor liable to prior claimants?

Payback is perceived as the time required for the cumulative cash flows (return *on* and *of*) from an investment to cover the original and ongoing expenditures to that date of the investment. The concept is simple and easy to understand, but investors use it in different and confusing ways. For example, do the cumulative cash flows include tax benefit spillover or the proceeds of a mortgage refinance?

Payback fails to reflect the time value of money and pays no attention to inflows and outflows beyond the equity investment recapture point. Payback does highlight the liquidity aspects of an investment and gives some clue as to how quickly an investment can generate a positive cash flow. When an investor states that the payback period on investment X was five years, the prudent response is: "Please tell me exactly how you calculated that."

Present Value

Present market value is the most probable estimate, within a reasonable range, which appraisers seek using the three approaches to value. The equity investor should clearly understand the attributes of market value and its difference from investment value. Market value is defined in

Chapter 8. *Investment value* is the value of an investment to a particular investor, based on his or her investment requirements, whereas market value is impersonal and detached.

To an investor buying an equity position, present value analysis should help answer the following questions:

- How many equity dollars should be paid to acquire a property?

- Based on the equity investor's own unique yield and other investment objectives, is that property available in the marketplace at a price (market value) the investor is willing to pay (investment value)?

Because the investor does buy an uncertain future, the present value of any investment is the present worth of all expected future net benefits. In this context, there are two ways to estimate present value—direct capitalization of income, and discounted cash flow analysis.

Capitalization, most often a discounting procedure, is the process that converts an income stream (gross or net) into an indication of capital value. Including better-known mortgage equity methods, there are many ways to analyze or synthesize a capitalization rate, depending in large part on whether the net operating income figure is last year's actual figure, next year's probable figure, a figure representing a number of years into the future averaged, or a figure forecasted each year to the end of the investment cycle. (Appraisal courses can devote several weeks to this one-paragraph synopsis.)

Once the following considerations are taken into account, discounted cash flow analysis is easy to understand; its execution can be complex and tedious:

- Each input and output is treated as a separate reversion.

- Each input and output can be scheduled over the entire investment cycle.

- A user discount rate is selected (i.e., a market rate, a contract rate, the investor's required rate, a hurdle rate, a cost-of-capital rate, a cutoff rate).

- The net benefits are discounted back to present value using appropriate "present worth of 1" factors.

- The objective is to estimate investment cost and/or present value.

For example, assume an equity investment is available at $10,000. The investor's own yield objective is 12 percent. The figures in the following table under "12% rate" are taken from tables showing the "present worth of $1." During the first year, the net equity income is expected to be zero. During the second year, net equity income is expected to be $1000. During the third year, net equity income is expected to be $1500. At the end of the third year, the equity will be sold, and the net equity proceeds from sale are expected to amount to $12,500. The gross cash flow from the income plus the proceeds is $15,000. For purposes of discounted cash flow analysis, the cash flow can be scheduled as follows:

Year	Cash flow	×	12% rate	=	Present value
1	$ 0		0.8929		$ 0.00
2	1,000		0.7972		797.20
3	14,000		0.7118		9,965.20

Present investment value = $10,762.40

Net Present Value

Net present value (NPV) estimates an equity investment value or cost by calculating the dollar difference between the present value (PV) of the outlays and the present value of the receipts at a user-selected discount rate. If the computation yields positive net dollars, the investment opportunity meets the equity investor's threshold yield objective. In terms of opportunity costs, the higher the net present value, the more preferable the investment.

The NPV method should help to rank alternative but similar investments of equivalent risk correctly—as long as all the investments being compared are analyzed using the same rate and the forecasted outlays, receipts, and the timing of each one is correct. Utilizing the same capsule illustration as before:

Year	Cash flow	×	12% rate	=	Present value
0	$(10,000)		1.0000		$(10,000.00)
1	0		0.8929		0.00
2	1,000		0.7972		797.20
3	14,000		0.7118		9,965.20

Net present value = $762.40

NPV's closest relative is called a *profitability index*, alias benefit/cost ratio or present value index. It is computed by dividing the present value of the dollar receipts by the present value of the dollar outflows. Given an equity investor's 12 percent objective, a ratio greater than 1 indicates the opportunity is profitable. The equity investor can then compare this investment with those other alternatives that also jumped the 12 percent "hurdle."

$$\frac{\text{PV inflows}}{\text{PV outflows}} = \frac{\$10,762.40}{\$10,000.00} = 1.08 \text{ profitability index}$$

Real Rates of Return

Funded pension funds are now approaching the $3 trillion mark. These vehicles of capital accumulation tend to be inflation-sensitive and long-term in outlook, and they ordinarily do not require tax benefits from investment. Investment decisions for pension funds therefore entail before-tax techniques. Asset allocation judgments, money management performance, and portfolio results are often converted to real rates of return to standardize comparison and performance.

As with every other kind of yield interpretation, different investors define real rates of return differently. Two common definitions are:

- The nominal interest rate or expected yield less the current inflation rate
- The nominal interest rate or expected yield less a user-prescribed, long-term inflation rate over an assumed investment or portfolio life

Internal Rate of Return

Pretax internal rates of return (IRR) may be the most commonly employed equity investment technique currently used by institutional purchasers of general purpose income property. Because of its almost universal acceptance and complexity, it is examined more thoroughly than other techniques.[1] Some use IRR interchangeably with *discount rate* and *yield*.

An IRR is an annualized time-weighted rate of return which is actually generated (or is capable of being generated) internally within an investment *or* portfolio during the period of ownership.

An IRR can be a before-tax or after-tax calculation. The target, or unknown, is a yield discount rate. IRR and NPV are two aspects of discounted cash flow (DCF) analysis. In the NPV model, the knowns are rate, an investment projection period, benefits, and costs; conversely,

---

[1] See J. Thomas Montgomery, MAI, *Equity Yields and the Reinvestment Issue* and Charles F. Raper, *The Appraisal Journal*, October 1981.

the unknown, or target, is normally (net) present value or investment cost.

For purposes of explanation and differentiation only, the IRR "family" can be arrayed into three generic frameworks:

1. Single-investment IRR (no reinvestment)
2. Portfolio IRR (reinvestment)
3. Single-investment IRR (explicit reinvestment)

$30,000 Real Estate Equity Investment—A Simple Arithmetic Example

A property is purchased for $120,000. A $90,000 first mortgage is arranged for 8.5 percent annual interest, which provides for monthly payments of $724.70 to principal and interest, completely amortizing the loan over a 25-year term; $30,000 cash equity is provided. Average annual net operating income is $11,100 and produces an average overall capitalization rate of 9.25 percent. The property is sold 10 years later for $138,331.85. Some exact calculations provide the following information:

$$\text{Annual mortgage debt service} = \$8,696.40$$

Annual before-tax equity cash flows
$$\text{(cash-on-cash rate of, say, 8\%)} = \$2,403.60$$

Before-tax equity investment reversion
$$\text{at end of tenth year} = \$64,737.52$$

Single-Investment IRR (No Reinvestment)

The internal rate of return has been defined as "the discount rate that equates the present value of the expected cash outflows with the present value of the expected cash inflows"—or, put more simply, that time-weighted before- or after-tax yield rate which produces a net present value of zero.

Because the present market (or investment) value of any investment is the present worth of all rights to future benefits arising from ownership, the IRR in the previous model is 14 percent. The 14 percent return (in this single-asset variation) means that the before-tax future benefit inflows and related present values of this single $30,000 equity investment are:

Ten annual cash flows: $2,403.60 × 5.216116* = $12,537.46

Tenth-year reversion: $64,737.52 × 0.269744**= $17,462.54

Equity investment cost (outflow at time zero): $30,000.00

The actual 14 percent IRR calculation in this instance totally ignores any actual, physical reinvestment of the interim $2,403.60 annual cash flows. Annual cash flows, once credited, simply pass through and out of this one $30,000 investment and 14 percent yield result. The fact that the changes in a series of annual numbers can be explained by a compound interest (or discount) factor does not have to mean that there is any actual reinvestment of funds required to earn the 14 percent. To avoid controversy, the reader should clearly understand the implications of the preceding sentence.

Portfolio IRR (Reinvestment)

A *portfolio IRR* is a measurement of profitability for funds continuously employed for a stated period involving multiple investments. Explicit reinvestment is an integral and critical part of this particular type of yield analysis. Not only does this application measure the cumulative performances of each investment in the portfolio, it also reflects the reinvestment ability and relative efficiency of the portfolio manager.

Portfolio internal rate of return, therefore, is comprised of at least three basic yield elements, not just each investment's before- or after-tax current yield and appreciation components. In order for any portfolio to achieve an internal rate of return over a specified period equal to an individual investment's actual yield to maturity, any intermediate cash flows received must be reinvested immediately at that same yield to maturity. Clearly, a portfolio manager's ability to forecast interest rates and make subsequent investment judgments promptly and wisely are important to portfolio investment success.

For purposes of simple explanation, a two-asset portfolio created by embellishing the model used in the previous example follows on page 136.

---

* Present worth of 1 per period (Inwood coefficient) for 10 years based on a 14 percent annual interest conversion assumption.

**Present worth of 1 for computing the value of a reversion at 14 percent in the tenth year.

Asset 1: $30,000 equity investment and projections used in single-investment IRR calculations. Ten-year IRR is 14 percent.

Asset 2: A money market mutual fund, anticipated 10 percent earning rate, also compounded annually. Asset 1's nine $2,403.60 intermediate cash flows are deposited instantaneously as received at the end of each year into Asset 2.

If all the assumptions, timing, and projections turn out to be 100 percent correct, this specific two-asset portfolio will have an IRR of 13.13 percent over the 10-year horizon.

Single-Investment IRR (Explicit Reinvestment)

In recent years, a series of multirate, reinvestment, single-asset IRR models have been developed. They share a basic conviction that any final single-investment IRR model is a meaningless exercise unless it pays attention to the effects of the reinvestment of intermediate cash flows on future value and wealth maximization. No matter how these models are assembled and refined, proponents of this view are confronted by an IRR school of thought that might be characterized as "purist" and "two-tiered."

An IRR purist might argue that there are only two basic kinds of IRR: single investment (no reinvestment) and portfolio (reinvestment). As soon as the $2,403.60 cash flows are invested into something else, a portfolio is created. Furthermore, single-investment multirate reinvestment models utilize a mathematical portfolio rationalization.

For example, the "embellished" portfolio IRR of 13.13 percent in the model is what some label a *modified internal rate of return* (MIRR). MIRR is used by some investment analysts and decision makers to measure a *single* investment's absolute or relative profitability. Proponents argue that if the single-investment investor could or did reinvest the nine $2,403.60 annual cash flows at a "safe" 10 percent, the 10-year IRR on this single $30,000 equity investment would be more realistically measured as 13.13 percent—not 14 percent. Because some other kind of asset external to the subject investment has been conjured up in this computation, perhaps the professional might better label the 13.13 percent as an external rate of return, which could be explained to the befuddled client as a 14 percent IRR plus an explicit 10 percent reinvestment assumption.

IRR Reinvestment—General Perspectives

If an investor were to use an IRR as a yield measurement to decide on one of two or more mutually exclusive investment alternatives, some contend that a reinvestment assumption would be desirable (if not required) to make a better wealth-maximizing decision. For example, two different investments might offer the same 10-year single-investment IRR (no reinvestment) of 14 percent. However, one might have a late but very large payoff, while the second would have an early larger payoff, followed by some lesser returns.

For reinvestment rates to influence an investment choice significantly, the cash flows of the alternative investments must differ in pattern, timing, duration, or some combination of the three. Practically, such major differences may signal clearly that two fundamentally different alternatives are being compared. This may imply either two entirely different types of property or two very different investment positions (with significantly different risks) in the same type of property. Most prospective real estate investments allow a rational choice between such mutually exclusive alternatives, without resorting to longer-term forecasts of unknown reinvestment yields available on other future, unidentified investments. General investor behavior and market practice seem to support this view.

Whenever a reinvestment assumption is incorporated in choosing between two or more mutually exclusive investments, such an assumption should be *explicit* as to amounts, timing, and reinvestment rate. The amounts reinvested can be all or part of the intermediate cash flows; the timing can reflect the full investment cycle or portions thereof; and the reinvestment rate chosen can be singular or a combination of the IRR, a "safe" rate, a cost of capital rate, an investment hurdle rate, or any other rate that is particular and relevant to the marketplace or to the subjective investor or decision maker.

To avoid misunderstanding, the analyst might avoid the phrase *implicit reinvestment* when discussing IRR concepts and yields.

Overview

If used with care, an IRR approach may produce more benefit in the analysis effort than in the yield result. The technique obviously imposes a discipline on the acquisition expert to abstract leases onto spreadsheets and look to the futurity of such critical variables as lease rollovers, income and operating costs, and improvement outlays over the presumed investment cycle.

However, an IRR analysis abounds in uncertainties, subjective assumptions, and probablistic forecasts. Also, if there are positive and negative cash flows, sometimes a "pure" IRR can produce several different but mathematically correct yields. An IRR also presumes the investment costs and the investment benefits are entitled to the same rate—the IRR. Some real estate investors treat "costs" at their actual cost of borrowed capital while testing "benefits" against a self-imposed "hurdle" or required rate of return on their own equity capital.

A number of other IRR models are equipped to cope with these sorts of rationalizations, including the adjusted internal rate of return and the financial management rate of return (FMRR).

An IRR or NPV software program that includes all the variables is a superb sensitivity drill to run through a computer to simulate future results of a particular project and to test the future reasonableness of entry-level acquisition price and threshold returns. It is effective in establishing a range of most probable investment outcomes. Because a large increment of the IRR may be due to a much higher future value assumption at the end of the holding period, an IRR analysis and printout can delineate what must be done and happen over the holding period to convert an aggressive acquisition price into a future investment winner. If properly constituted, it should also set the stage for subsequent investment budget format and performance accountability.

Conclusions

The real estate acquisition and investment analyst should be adept at, and conversant with, all known value and rate measurement techniques. The professional knows to challenge the quality and direction of others' answers and judgments by pursuing such questions as:

1. Was the most valid yield rate on this illustrated investment 8 percent, 13.13 percent, or 14 percent? Specifically, how was each yield calculated?

2. What are the underlying assumptions and inherent weaknesses in each technique? (None is perfect.)

3. Do the assumptions and calculations accurately reflect how real estate acquisition specialists and equity investors compare investment alternatives, make decisions, and monitor results?

The "appropriate" equity investment measurement techniques used should primarily reflect actual investor-marketplace motivations and objectives, the size of the property, the complexity of the investment, and the requirements and relative sophistication of the client-investor.

13

Taxation of Real Estate

Linda Knell Bumbalo, Esq.
*Associate Legislative Counsel, Mortgage Bankers
Association of America, Washington, D.C.*

Introduction

The U.S. system of taxation, embodied in the Internal Revenue Code, has been designed not only to raise revenue but also to meet certain social and economic objectives that Congress has deemed to be in the public interest. Tax incentives have been created as the tools to implement these public policy decisions.

Numerous major tax revisions have been enacted in recent years, each one expanding or eliminating tax incentives, generally in response to current economic conditions and in accordance with prevailing tax policy. The tax incentives affecting real estate generally reflect congressional decisions to encourage the investment of capital. The Tax Reform Act of 1986 targeted the reduction of various tax provisions which allowed a real estate investor to shelter income from taxation.

Economic versus Tax Benefits

The goal of recent tax reform efforts is to encourage investment in real estate that provides a return to the investor because of the project's economic viability, that is, its ability to produce income from cash flow, rather than its ability to generate tax losses.

The economic income and the taxable income or loss associated from a real estate investment are different amounts. The economic income, or profit, consists of a positive cash flow from operations and residual value in the property. Taxable income or loss reflects adjustments to income that are allowed by the tax code and is the amount used to determine an investor's tax liability.

Positive cash flow from operations is the excess of cash receipts over cash disbursements. For example:

Rental income			$175,000
Less: operating expenses		70,000	
Debt service:			
Interest	78,000		
Amortization	12,000		
		90,000	
		(160,000)	
Cash flow			$15,000

For tax purposes, operating expenses and debt service, to the extent the payments represent interest on the principal amount of the mortgage, are deductible from income. The portion of the debt service that is a payment on the mortgage principal is not deductible from income for tax purposes because it constitutes a return of the investor's capital.

There is a noncash item that is deductible from income and may create a loss for tax purposes even though there is a positive cash flow. This noncash item consists of depreciation expense. The following reflects addition of principal and deduction of depreciation.

Cash flow (from above)	$15,000
Add back: principal payment portion of debt service	12,000
Total:	27,000
Less: depreciation expense	(50,000)
Taxable income (loss)	$(23,000)

The economic income, if it exists, from a property is the first economic benefit from real estate investment. Residual value is the second economic benefit. This consists of the cash flow generated by the sale of the property or by taking the equity out of the property through refinancing the first mortgage or a second mortgage. The third benefit may be tax benefits. These will change from time to time as federal and state governments change the tax laws. The following discussion covers federal laws as they exist in the spring of 1987.

Tax Considerations

In general, the provisions in the Internal Revenue Code that affect income property are passive loss limitations, interest expense deductions, depreciation deductions, capital gains, at-risk rules, rehabilitation tax credits, low-income-housing tax credit, and the alternative minimum tax.

A tax deduction differs from a tax credit. A tax deduction is an "above the line" item. It reduces the amount of income on which tax liability is calculated. A tax credit is a "below the line" item. It is subtracted dollar for dollar from the amount of the tax liability.

Passive Loss Limitation

The Tax Reform Act of 1986 distinguishes between two kinds of trade or business activities. Activities are either *active* or *passive,* and the income and expenses attributable to each activity are placed into separate categories. Income from salaries, wages, and fees is accounted for separately from passive income. Portfolio income is also segregated from passive income and includes income from interest, dividends, or royalties not derived in the ordinary course of business and gain or loss from the disposition of property producing interest, dividends, or royalties or property held for investment.

Rental real estate and limited partnerships are defined as passive activities; therefore, the income and expenses attributable to investments in rental real estate and limited partnerships are treated as passive. Other trade or business activities can qualify as passive activities if the taxpayer does not "materially participate" in the activity, that is, is not involved in its operations on a regular, continuous, and substantial basis.

The expenses attributable to a passive activity can be deducted only from the income from the passive activity. Losses are created when expenses exceed income. Losses from one passive activity can offset income from another passive activity. Passive losses are deductible in a taxable year up to the amount of passive income. Passive losses that exceed passive income can be carried forward and used in succeeding years to offset passive income. Such losses are called suspended losses and are recognized in full when the taxpayer disposes of the entire interest in the passive activity. To trigger the recognition of suspended losses, the transaction disposing of the interest must be treated as fully taxable under general tax rules and must be to an unrelated party.

Active Participant Exception. Losses from rental real estate can be used to offset active income (such as wages) or portfolio income (such as stock dividends) if an individual is an "active participant" in the activity and meets the applicable income test. Taxpayers qualify as active participants if they own at least 10 percent of the rental real estate activity and make decisions about the management of the property. An interest as a limited partner does not qualify. If taxpayers meet these requirements and have an adjusted gross income (AGI) of not more than $100,000, then they can deduct up to $25,000 of rental real estate losses from income from other sources, such as salaries and wages. This provision is phased out and completely disappears when AGI reaches $150,000. For example, if AGI is $130,000, up to $15,000 of passive losses can offset other income. Losses from rental real estate first offset all rental real estate income and then all other passive income before offsetting any active income.

Exception for Rehabilitation Credit and for Low-Income-Housing Credits. The tax law provides tax credits for investments in certain activities, including rehabilitation of historic and pre-1936 buildings and low-income housing. The taxpayer does not have to be an active participant in the activity; an investment in a limited partnership would qualify. These credits can offset tax on up to $25,000 of active income if the taxpayer's AGI is not more than $200,000. The tax credit phases out completely at $250,000 AGI. The two credits are discussed on page 145.

Phase-in of Limitation for Certain Passive Activities. In general, if the taxpayer owned an interest in a passive activity (such as real estate) on or before October 22, 1986, some passive losses from that activity are allowed in the years 1987 through 1990. A percentage of the passive losses can be used to offset income from other sources during those years, as follows:

Year	Losses allowed (%)
1987	65
1988	40
1989	20
1990	10

Disallowed losses from these pre-October 23, 1986 investments can be carried forward and used in a subsequent year if passive income exceeds passive losses for that year or when the interest in the passive activity is disposed of in a fully taxable transaction to a third party.

Construction Interest

Prior to the Tax Reform Act of 1986, most interest was deductible. Interest on construction mortgages and permanent mortgages was fully deductible. In the case of construction period interest, the deduction was amortized over a 10-year period. The deduction for mortgage interest was taken in full in the year in which it was paid (in the case of a cash-basis taxpayer) or the year in which it was incurred (in the case of an accrual method taxpayer).

The Tax Reform Act of 1986 eliminated the deduction for construction period interest. Instead, the interest paid or incurred on debt to finance the construction of real property must be capitalized. It is treated as part of the cost basis of the property and deducted under the depreciation rules as a depreciation expense.

Depreciation

The tax code allows the taxpayer to allocate the cost of a building (not the land) over a period of time. Deductions are taken in each year of this recovery period according to a prescribed depreciation method. These deductions are noncash expenses and offset income in the year in which they are taken.

In the first half of the 1980s, depreciation schedules were changed almost every year. Immediately prior to the Tax Reform Act of 1986, both residential rental and commercial property were depreciated over 19 years using either the straight-line or accelerated method. The Tax Reform Act of 1986 created different recovery periods for residential and commercial real estate and eliminated the use of the accelerated method for calculating deductions. The cost of residential property placed in service on or after January 1, 1987, is recovered over 27.5 years. The cost of commercial real estate placed in service on or after January 1, 1987, is recovered over 31.5 years. The straight-line method must be used for both classes of property. Under the straight-line method, the basis of the property is depreciated by approximately the same percentage in each year of the recovery period. Depreciation deductions reduce the basis of the property by the amount of the deductions—this is called an "adjusted basis." When the property is sold, the difference between the amount realized on the sale and the adjusted basis is treated as capital gains.

When the accelerated method was used, deductions were greater in the earlier years of the recovery period, providing a greater tax benefit up front. When residential property was sold, the difference between the amount that was deducted and the amount that would have been deducted under the straight-line method had to be "recaptured," that is, taxed as ordinary income. The balance of the income from the sale, if any, was treated as capital gains. Commercial real estate generally was depreciated using the straight-line method because when the accelerated method was used all the depreciation deductions—to the extent of gain—had to be recaptured at ordinary income rates.

Under the Tax Reform Act of 1986, there is no recapture of depreciation deductions taken for commercial and residential property.

Depreciation schedules determining the amount of depreciation expense use the mid-month convention. This means that real property is treated as having been placed in service or disposed of in the middle of the month regardless of the actual date of the service or disposition.

Depreciation deductions often produce a loss for the real estate project, but this loss is subject to the passive loss rules which were discussed above.

Capital Gains

Under the Tax Reform Act of 1986, all the gain from the disposition of real property is included in income and taxed at the taxpayer's marginal tax rate. After 1987, incomes, including capital gains, are taxed at marginal rates of 15, 28, and 33 percent.

At-Risk Limitation

In general, the at-risk rules limit the amount of losses from an activity that a taxpayer can take to the amount of funds for which a taxpayer is "at risk." The amount at risk is the sum of cash contributions, the adjusted basis of property contributions, and loans for which the taxpayer is personally liable. Property financed by the seller is subject to at-risk rules. Nonrecourse financing (no personal liability) of real property is not considered an amount at risk if the lender is actively and regularly engaged in the business of lending money. The debt is not at risk even if the lender has an equity interest in the property.

Rehabilitation Tax Credits

The Tax Reform Act of 1986 provides tax credits for expenses attributable to rehabilitating older buildings. Nonhistoric commercial and industrial buildings are eligible for a 10 percent credit if they were first used before 1936. Historic buildings receive a 20 percent credit. There is a procedure, established by the U.S. Department of the Interior, for certifying that a building is historic. The basis used for depreciating the structures must be reduced by the amount of the credit.

Under the passive loss limitations, the credit can be used only to offset tax on income from the rehabilitated building or from other passive activities. As mentioned earlier in this chapter, the credit can offset tax on income from other sources if the taxpayer's adjusted gross income (AGI) does not exceed $200,000. The credit phases out between $200,000 and $250,000 AGI.

Low-Income-Housing
Tax Credit

Investors in low-income housing can receive a tax credit for projects placed in service between January 1, 1987, and December 31, 1989. Projects placed in service by December 31, 1990, are eligible for the credit if 10 percent of the costs are incurred by December 31, 1988.

The costs for new construction and rehabilitation or acquisition of existing low-income rental housing are eligible for the credit. The credit can be used for projects receiving other types of federal assistance under other housing programs.

To qualify for the low-income-housing credit, a project owner must elect irrevocably to meet a set-aside requirement each year for 15 years: At least 20 percent of the units must be occupied by tenants whose income is no more than 50 percent of the area median income, or at least 40 percent of the units must be occupied by tenants whose income is no more than 60 percent of the area median income. These income limits apply to families of four. The income ceiling is reduced for smaller families.

There is also a limit on the amount of rent a low-income tenant can pay. The rent cannot exceed 30 percent of a tenant's income, excluding rental assistance. A low-income unit must meet both the income and rent limits continuously for 15 years.

The amount of the tax credit depends on the purpose of the expenditures and whether there is any federal subsidy. The credits are a "70 percent present value credit" and a "30 percent present value credit."

The 70 percent present value credit could be received for the costs of new construction or rehabilitation of projects that are not federally subsidized. For federally subsidized new construction or rehabilitation, the credit would be the 30 percent present value credit. Acquisition costs of existing projects also would be eligible for the 30 percent present value credit. The present value credits are set by the Treasury and are received over 10 years.

In general, the credit is computed using a specified percentage of the costs of the units in the building. This percentage is the lesser of two ratios: (1) the number of low-income units over the number of all residential units, or (2) the floor space for low-income units over floor space for all residential units. The costs of non-low-income units are included in the cost basis on which the percentage is calculated only if these units meet a comparability standard, which is met if the number of non-low-income units equals the number of low-income units, and the costs for all units are comparable. Federally funded grants are not included in the basis for calculating the credit.

Rehabilitation costs of an existing building must average at least $2000 per low-income unit and must be aggregated within two years after rehabilitation begins to be eligible for the credit. Total rehabilitation costs must be allocated proportionately among all the units, even if only the low-income units were rehabilitated.

Where there is a change of ownership of an existing low-income housing project, acquisition and rehabilitation costs are eligible for the tax credit if a 10-year requirement is met. The building must have been placed in service more than 10 years before change of ownership and must not have been substantially improved within the last 10 years. The 10-year period can be waived under certain circumstances. A transfer of a federally assisted project to a new owner before the end of the 10-year holding period can qualify for the credit if the project is in financial distress and the change of ownership will prevent reversion of the project to the federal government.

Each state has a low-income-housing credit limit of $1.25 per resident to be allocated within the state either wholly to the state housing authority or, alternatively, by either the governor or legislature.

There is a special application of the new rental real estate passive loss rule to the low-income-housing credit. The credits can offset tax on up to $25,000 of income from other sources for investors whose adjusted gross incomes do not exceed $200,000, with complete phaseout at $250,000.

Alternative Minimum Tax

An aim of tax reform in 1986 was to make sure that taxpayers could not use tax shelters to escape paying tax on what was considered to be a "minimum" percentage of their incomes. One tax shelter, or "tax preference" (the term used in the tax law), is depreciation. For computing the alternative minimum tax, the preference item is the difference between depreciation based on a 40-year straight-line method and straight-line write-offs over 27.5 years and 31.5 years, discussed earlier in this chapter. Certain tax-exempt interest and the appreciation on certain donated property are among the many other preference items. Taxpayers must therefore determine if they have preference items and, if so, prepare two forms for tax returns, one based on preparing a regular tax return (with preferences) and another based upon the rates and formulae for the alternative minimum tax. Whichever tax is higher must be paid.

Summary

The tax laws are certain to change. Real estate is particularly complicated insofar as the tax laws and regulations are concerned. Again, the discussion in this chapter is intended only to alert readers to possible tax implications and to persuade them to learn the current tax laws and obtain the advice of a tax counsel or a tax accountant before evaluating the advantages and disadvantages of a real estate investment.

PART 4

Underwriting Properties

14
Office Buildings

Thomas Z. Minehart, III, CMB
Executive Vice President, Latimer & Buck, Inc.
Philadelphia, Pennsylvania

There are three ways to describe and categorize office buildings. Each category overlaps the other two, however, and complexities abound. One yardstick is location or environment surrounding the site. The second is the market analysis. The third is perceived quality, amenities, and internal space.

Describing a project by location reflects popular expectations. The downtown central business district (CBD) usually contains high-rise buildings. The suburbs used to be known for low-rise buildings, but now they may be a mix of both low- and high-rise. Office or industrial parks, usually in the suburbs, but sometimes now downtown, include new projects or ones in rehabilitated industrial buildings or special complexes close to universities. Research parks, which can be downtown, have been mostly located in the suburbs or in exurban areas.

When categorizing office buildings by age, new construction is self-evident. Older buildings used to connote less desirability. However, the recent trend to rehabilitation and energy retrofitting of older buildings has lessened this distinction.

Describing office buildings as class A, B, or C properties is a convenient shorthand, but it can be misused like any other arbitrary stereotype. Class A buildings appeal to prestigious tenants willing to pay high rents. They have prime locations; fine and often luxurious design; the most up-to-date heating, air conditioning, plumbing, energy, security, and telecommunications components; numerous special amenities (atriums, underground parking, restaurants, retail stores, special janitorial

151

and secretarial services); and highly professional management. Class B buildings have a little less of all the above, and class C buildings provide merely adequate or even below-par office space in older and unrehabilitated buildings or basic newer buildings with few amenities. Even this categorization is open to complexity, because a class A building in a central business district will differ considerably from a class A building in a suburban or office park location—and mortgage bankers submitting loan applications for the lender's review seldom describe their client's property as other than a class A project.

Location

Location is critical in any analysis of an office building investment. Although a location suitable for a downtown central city office building is certainly different from one amenable to a suburban office complex, the characteristics of prime location are essentially the same.

Access to transportation is important (railroad terminals, bus terminals, suburban buses, light rail or heavy rail mass transit stations, interstate and state highways, and airports). So is availability of parking (underground or nearby for downtown locations, on site for suburban locations). Also significant is the proximity to shops, restaurants, department stores, quality hotels or motels, government office buildings and courts, and other major office buildings.

Given the tendency of the U.S. city to segregate office functions from industrial or wholesale commercial activity, class A office buildings are not likely to be located near warehouses, special wholesale commercial districts, or industrial shops, plants, or parks. Nor, given the tendency to segregate residential and business functions, are prime office buildings likely to be found in residential areas.

Market Analysis

Market Supply

The demand for different types of office buildings varies with the market for office space. Small businesses neither need nor want the type of offices required of large corporations. Market types need and prefer to cluster together. For example, medical and dental professionals tend to group together near major medical facilities (universities and hospitals). Below is a standard breakdown of the market demand for offices:

- *Major corporations* (financial, manufacturing, service) seek prestigious office space for their management and consumer-oriented (public relations, sales, marketing) functions. Such buildings are typically class A, with the latest in technological and design amenities, high rents, and prime location, either downtown or in suburban locations close to regional or superregional shopping malls (such as Tysons Corner in Fairfax County, Virginia, near Washington, D.C., and Lenox Square Center in Atlanta).

- *Small businesses and commercial tenants,* such as independent lawyers, accountants, and small service businesses (travel agents, employment agencies, mortgage companies, computer software firms), prefer average but adequate office space, either downtown in older buildings which have been rehabilitated or in newer suburban locations, often low-rise and located in office-industrial parks.

- *Medical and dental professionals* seek convenient access to the consumer of health services; proximity to medical facilities; and the sharing of technology, laboratory services, and professional techniques and ideas. The high cost of malpractice insurance, the burden of patient needs, the cost of medical equipment and recordkeeping, and the nature of the tax laws have encouraged medical practitioners to form professional associations in which many doctors or dentists share a large office suite. Professional buildings generally provide adequate office space, but not necessarily class A space with the newest technological amenities and a prime location.

- *Research and development and industrial tenants* cluster in office, industrial, and research parks. Heavy industries usually house certain types of office functions (engineering and design) in close proximity to the factory, although modern technology has rendered this unnecessary. Light industries, certain kinds of computerized and clean warehouse distribution, and "high-tech" research and development activities can be housed together in "smart buildings" with the latest in computerized work stations, flexible office space, telecommunications hookups, and even amenities such as parks, recreational facilities, and nearby hotels and restaurants (e.g., the Forrestal-Scanticon and Carnegie centers in Princeton, New Jersey). Although such research, industrial, and office parks lack the design and architectural amenities of prestigious downtown office locations, they may equal or surpass the downtown buildings in technological advances, overall setting, and convenient access to transportation, shopping, schools, and prime residential housing.

Market Demand

In analyzing a potential office building investment, the current demand for the type of office structure or complex requires documentation. If there is a high absorption rate for new construction, and even for older and rehabilitated buildings, the investment risk may be worthwhile. If the vacancy rate in existing and older buildings is not low and new space is not occupied, the investment risk may not be worthwhile. Office building construction, however, is frequently speculative and cyclical, so professional·lenders know to pay attention to cycles—investing early and withdrawing from investment before the speculative peak crests.

Physical Characteristics

Physical and Structural Design

Almost all modern office buildings, whether class A or class C, and whether rehabilitated or new, require efficient heating and air-conditioning systems, modern and energy-efficient lighting, acoustic ceilings, carpeting, appropriate common area treatment, on-site or underground parking or access to nearby parking for downtown structures, and up-to-date and easily augmented electrical systems.

Physical design characteristics are influenced by market demand. The market for which a particular building is intended will determine its total size, floor size, elevator capacity, design, exterior aesthetics, interior amenities, and parking ratios. Special design amenities may include quality materials, innovative architecture, distinctive appointments, large lobbies and atriums, spacious hallways, and extra-high-speed elevators.

Much more important are structural design elements and amenities which account for present and future technological progress, such as energy efficiency and security (e.g., temperature and security controls administered by a central computer system); auxiliary power sources for elevators, computers, and lighting; fire protection devices; office space that is flexible and which can be easily reconfigured and redesigned; and buildings that incorporate wiring systems that can be modernized and added to so as to handle rapid advances in telecommunications—word processors, computer electronic mailing systems, teleconferencing, satellite communications, laser printers, message switching systems, or optical character readers. The office building of the present is becoming, and the office building of the future will be, an information utility and communications service center.

Other Considerations

Investment analysts and underwriters of existing or proposed office buildings should bear in mind other physical criteria:

Average Square Footage per Office Worker.   This factor generally varies with the age and size of the building. The newer and bigger the buildings, the more square footage per office worker; the older and smaller the building, the less square footage per office. The general range for buildings of all ages and all sizes is 150 to 250 square feet per office worker.

Economic Efficiency.   The economic efficiency of an office building is measured by the relation between the gross building area (GBA) and the net rentable or leasable area (NRA or NLA). A building is generally considered efficient if its NRA is at least 88 percent of its GBA, or, put another way, if its NRA is only 12 percent less than its GBA. Most new high-rise buildings are 90 percent efficient or better. Most buildings constructed between 1920 and 1970 are at least 60 percent to 70 percent efficient. Buildings constructed before 1920 are less than 60 percent efficient, but most of these have either been torn down and replaced by more efficient newer buildings or, given the tax incentives provided for the restoration of older and historic buildings in the 1981 tax law, have been rehabilitated and retrofitted to conform to contemporary standards for economic efficiency.

Parking Ratios.   Some downtown high-rise buildings do not have parking garages. Where such space is provided, one space for every 250 square feet of net rentable office area is considered reasonable. Parking spaces in an underground garage should allow for at least 300–400 square feet each, depending on the size of the cars likely to be parked there and the space available for the garage. Outdoor parking spaces are usually more commodious, only because their construction cost is so much less.

Office Building Leasing Structures

The leasing of office building space is complex and can follow any one of several patterns. Office space is rented monthly and includes all usable square footage plus a floor factor, which is a proportion of the common area on a floor divided by the number of square feet per tenants who occupy the floor. The working definitions of usable area and rentable area for office buildings are discussed in Chapter 10 (see "Building Measures"). In addition to monthly lease payments, tenants are also generally responsible for special tenant improvements over a basic "tenant work letter amount" or initial budget for tenant space improvements.

Leases for office buildings, as with shopping centers, can be divided into two broad categories:

- Gross leases, in which the tenant pays a fixed rent and the owner of the building is responsible for the property's operating expenses, taxes, and capital expenditures
- Net leases, in which, in addition to base rent, the tenant pays a pro rata share (based on the square footage of office space relative to the net leasable area of the building) of some of or all the operating expenses, taxes, and/or property capital expenditures.

In most new office buildings net leases are the rule, but with different kinds of escalation clauses and provisions for tenant payments of operating expenses and capital expenditures. One example, known as a stop lease, requires the tenant to pay a pro rata share of building operating expenses only above a minimum amount stated in the lease. Another example, known as a base-year lease, stipulates that the tenant must pay a pro rata share of the operating expenses incurred above those in a base year (usually the year the lease was signed, or the year prior to signing). Both stop and base-year leases are negotiable and vary considerably. Still another example is the lease which is tied to the consumer price index (CPI). If the inflation index increases, regardless of whether actual costs go up by the same amount, the lease is escalated in accordance with the CPI growth rate, thereby providing both inflation protection and potential extra profit for the landlord.

A more extraordinary example is the "net, net, net lease," in which a tenant will pay all operating expenses, taxes, and insurance. Under the "absolute triple net" lease, the tenant assumes all functions of the landlord except collecting rents, paying the mortgage, and earning income and profit from the investment.

To induce a tenant to lease property, the landlord will usually agree to make certain tenant improvements. These costs, which would often include partitions, electrical work, and occasionally plumbing, are frequently specified in terms of dollars per square foot. Sometimes a number of parking spaces will be provided without charge for the tenant's use.

Rent concessions are frequent in markets where there are high vacancy ratios in office buildings. A concession might consist of rent reduction for a period of time or an agreement to continue a fixed rent over a longer period than initially required. The underwriter for the lender must be able to factor in the cost of tenant improvements and the effect of rent concessions in determining the effective rent for the space leased.

Office Building Rent Rolls, Operating Income, and Expenses

Chapter 10 analyzed rent rolls, setting forth procedures to show the present rental income and rate for each tenant, tenant pro rata contributions to recover operating expenses, and renewal dates and negotiated special provisions and options for each tenant. Even when an existing multitenant building is fully occupied, a rent roll pro forma should always include a realistic vacancy factor based on historical experience and current market conditions.

In addition to rental income, including base rent and operating expense reimbursements, office buildings can yield the following kinds of additional income:

- Tenant service income, which is income from special tenant services which the landlord provides a tenant

- Miscellaneous income from vending machines, sale of utilities to tenants, rental of retail space, rental of advertising space, furniture rental, deposit forfeitures, and other sources

- Parking income, from either underground or attached parking facilities, or on-site spaces

Landlords generally provide the following services to tenants and are responsible for the following operating expenses in whole or part: utility services, cleaning and janitorial services, elevator operation, and building security. In the newer so-called high-tech or smart buildings, landlords may also be expected to maintain telecommunication services and replace and upgrade telecommunications equipment. Other typical operating expenses which may be shared by tenants are the following: staff payroll, maintenance contracts, supplies and uniforms, repairs, real estate taxes, insurance fees, management fees, reserves for mechanical replacements, lease commissions, and expenses for supplies.

15
Shopping Centers

Thomas Z. Minehart, III, CMB

Executive Vice President, Latimer & Buck, Inc.
Philadelphia, Pennsylvania

Categories

There are many types of retail properties, ranging from the local hot dog stand to the freestanding store; from the local McDonald's restaurant to the trilevel downtown mall. For the evaluation and review of retail facilities, a convenient and accepted practice is to discuss the properties in terms of six categories. The size of the center and store type most often suggest which of the following categories is appropriate:

- The freestanding building
- The neighborhood convenience shopping center
- The community shopping center
- The regional mall
- The superregional mall
- The specialty center

The *freestanding retail* building comes in a variety of shapes and sizes, some of which are so distinctive as to be relatively worthless for a second use upon foreclosure. Often intentionally surrounded by parking to attract fast-service customers, these structures can be anything from a 2000 square foot convenience chain store to a 100,000 square foot furniture warehouse outlet store.

Location of the property, as always, is paramount. The nature of the structure is usually dictated by the operator, often a chain or franchise operation.

The *neighborhood* or *convenience center* specializes in goods and services required for daily living, mainly foodstuffs, drugs and toiletries, cleaning and laundering services, and perhaps a liquor store, a barber shop, or a coffee shop. The gross leaseable area of a neighborhood center can be as little as 50,000 square feet but usually is not more than 100,000 square feet. Its principal stores or "anchors" are generally a supermarket and a drug store. Competitive supermarkets are larger—often as large as 40,000 square feet—than they were 10 or 15 years ago, when 20,000 to 25,000 square feet was normal. Super drug stores, which often anchor the convenience center at the opposite end from the supermarket, may range from 7500 square feet up, which is why most neighborhood centers are today in the range of 75,000 to 100,000 square feet.

The *community center* is a somewhat larger shopping center. Whereas the neighborhood center is oriented for necessary and everyday shopping, the community center is more specialized and subject to retail fashions and fads. It will usually include a supermarket and a drug store, but its anchors are likely to be a variety store (five and ten); a discount store such as Walmart, Roses, or Marshall's; and a junior department store such as Jamesway. In recent years several community centers have been anchored by discount hardware chains or home improvement stores carrying lumber, building materials, and most home decorating needs.

Besides the anchors, the supermarket, and the drug store, the community center may include one or two restaurants; stores selling clothing for men, women, and children; dry goods stores; appliance (large and small) and electronics stores (e.g., Radio Shack); a bookstore; a record or video store; and an auto supply store, all amounting to as much as 75,000 to 100,000 square feet of specialty stores. A bank, a fast-food restaurant, and a cinema may be located on the site but may be housed in an independent structure separate from the shopping center. Such businesses usually build their own facility and pay land rent to the shopping center owner.

The *regional mall* is a large shopping center. It is a major operation and may contain as many as 50 tenants in addition to its anchors, which usually include two or more full-scale department stores. Regional malls may be anchored by local department stores, but nowadays a chain department store such as Sears or J.C. Penney usually provides the regional mall with its drawing power. The regional mall contains every type and description of retail and service store, including home furnishings and major appliance stores; large national chain apparel stores for men and women, e.g., The Limited, Casual Corner, The Gap, Brooks Brothers, Ann Taylor; plus several restaurants, banks, and, recently, medical clinics, small health spas, and multiplex cinemas. Like the community center, the regional mall will contain stores which are franchises or branches of national chains and stores—called satellites—which are locally owned and operated. The anchor or department stores in the regional mall are usually about 100,000 square feet or more in size, and several of the large apparel and home furnishing stores may be as large as 25,000 to 40,000 square feet. Stores in both regional and superregional malls, however, have tended to shrink in size in recent years, primarily because there is a tendency to downsize department stores and home furnishing and appliance stores and increase gross sales per square foot. As rents for local and nationally franchised specialty stores in regional malls have risen, the satellite stores have followed suit and reduced their size while attempting to increase their sales.

The *superregional mall* or *shopping center* is a special breed of retail facility which is typically found in primary or secondary cities; and which is centered around three, four, or more full-line department stores of 100,000 square feet or more. The superregional center is sited on 85 acres or more and generally contains no less than 750,000 square feet. This center may contain as much as 2 million square feet, and it serves a population of 1 million or more within a radius of 1 to as many as 50 miles. The superregional mall will include every kind of shop and class of restaurant; also found at this mall will be a mix of high-, medium-, and low-priced merchandise, services, recreational facilities, and food courts clustering as many as 15 to 25 small purveyors of food, entertainment, and special events. The market area for the superregional is everything from residences and other businesses in close proximity to people and businesses from the extent of the metropolitan area.

The *specialty center* is exactly what its name implies: a shopping mall which specializes in one or two particular kinds of merchandise or services (food, entertainment, specialty boutiques). The specialty center aims for a special market and is characterized by a theme or singular design, site, or environment. They have neither anchor stores nor basic merchandise and services. Some specialty centers are housed in historic buildings such as the Union Stations in St. Louis and (forthcoming) Washington, D.C., and Station Square in Pittsburgh; others are sited dramatically on harbor sites such as Harborplace in Baltimore and

South Street Seaport in New York; still others, like the Yamhill Market in Portland, Oregon, profit from the ambiance of historic districts. Specialty centers can be relatively small, such as the 75,000 square foot Waterside Mall in Norfolk, Virginia; the Pavilion in Washington, D.C.; or the Dayton Arcade in Dayton, Ohio. They can also be relatively large, such as Georgetown Court in Washington, D.C., the Pike Place Market in Seattle, and the Quincy Market–Faneuil Hall Marketplace in Boston.

A variation on the specialty mall concept, often a regional mall, is the so-called outlet or off-price mall. Although not a traditional shopping center that attempts to provide a broad variety of high-traffic stores, the outlet mall attracts tenant-discounters to gather together in one mall setting, so that shoppers may look for bargains in one locations.

Location of Shopping Centers

Shopping centers should be located near their markets, within the appropriate radius of their primary market and with access to major highways. The shopping center has become the child of the interstate highway system, and almost all centers—from the smallest neighborhood center to the vast superregional mall—are located on major state or county roads where they intersect one or several interstate highways. Very often malls are located directly across from each other or in close proximity, on the theory that each stimulates the business of the other and that the cluster of shopping centers recreates something which the shopping center itself displaced: a central shopping district.

Physical Characteristics of Shopping Centers

Some shopping centers are enclosed malls, replete with large and well-decorated common areas and both indoor or sheltered and outdoor parking. Other shopping centers are merely a collection of attached stores on a common site with a communal parking lot. An important physical consideration is the placement of anchors where they can best attract customers not only for themselves but for the other stores in the center. In neighborhood and community centers, the anchors are usually at opposite ends of the center. In regional and superregional malls, the anchor stores may be at both ends and also in the center.

Perhaps the most important aspect of the physical design of a shopping center is parking. The Urban Land Institute (ULI) stipulates the following standards for shopping center parking:

- Four spaces per 1000 square feet of gross leaseable area (GLA) for malls of 25,000 to 400,000 square feet
- From 4 to 5 spaces in linear progression with an average of 4.5 spaces per 1000 square feet of GLA for centers of 400,000 to 600,000 square feet
- Five spaces per 1000 square feet of GLA for centers with over 600,000 square feet.[1]

The ULI also advises that centers with cinemas of more than 750 seats should allot three additional parking spaces for every 100 seats.

Valuing Shopping Centers

The value of a shopping center, much as the value of an office building, depends on the quantity, quality, and durability of its rent roll. The larger the net income from rentals generated, the greater the capitalized value of the center. Rents derived from a shopping center are directly related to the sales generated by each retailer; if sales are down, tenants cannot pay aggressive rents, the shopping center income is less, and the center's value is correspondingly lower.

The Importance of Anchor Stores

Anchor stores are essential to shopping centers. Anchors are the attractions which draw the market and generate sales. For this reason, anchor store operators tend to dominate negotiations with shopping center developers. Most lenders or equity investors are reluctant to put money into a shopping center without a firm letter of commitment from an anchor or anchors. Very often banks will refuse to consider short-term development loans until the anchors are signed on. Anchors receive favorable lease terms. For example, they may not have to pay percentage rents but only bare minimum base rent. They generally receive long-term fixed-rate leases (10 to 20 years is not uncommon) and may not be subject to escalation or inflation indexing. In some cases, they are allowed to lease the property beneath their store or use it for free. They may also build their own store and pay no rent at all. Sometimes they are provided all these privileges and are also included as limited or joint venture partners in the shopping center development.

Of course, anchor store operators are always looking for good loca-

---

[1]*Development Review and Outlook 1983–1984*, The Urban Land Institute, Washington, D.C., 1983, p. 25.

tions for their stores. Projects which will locate them in the right market area to generate healthy sales and allow for the expansion of their business may negotiate better leases. Developers often have special relationships with department stores and supermarkets. Anchor retailers may often cultivate partnerships and special arrangements with selected and proven developers. Indeed, in what may be described as a trend in the retailing business, some prominent developers have recently taken to acquiring department store chains and, conversely, some large department store chains have become shopping center developers or joint venture partners.

Satellites, Locals, and Chain and Franchise Specialty Shops

Since the anchor stores provide the draw and take up much of the square footage of the shopping center (e.g., in a superregional mall of 1 million square feet, four department stores will occupy anywhere from 40 to 50 percent of the total GLA), the shopping center developer or investor depends on the satellite or small shops which cluster around the anchor to generate the major part of the income stream and most of the profit from the investment. The better the sales in the small shops, the more valuable the shopping center, particularly if the square footage of the shops is down, and both sales per square foot and rents are up. Put another way, the developer's interest is to get the maximum rent and the maximum sales per square foot from each satellite or specialty store. This is why the small shops, which pay much higher base rents per square foot than the anchor, also pay a percentage of their gross sales as rent to the owner and have short-term leases that are raised to what the current market will bear once they expire. (See Chapter 9.)

Merchants' Associations

"Either we survive together, or we all hang separately" is an appropriate motto for both the developer-owner and the retail merchants in a shopping center. Signage, snow removal, common area maintenance, security, trash removal, advertising, special events, entertainment, and common policies with respect to customers, sales representatives, and distributors are all handled more effectively on a collective basis, as is the relation between merchants and the owner of the center. For this reason most shopping centers have merchants' associations. They are a necessity in a superregional and regional mall, and most community centers also have these associations. They can be found in many neighborhood centers.

Shopping Center Management

Shopping center management requires more than simple maintenance of the center, since the manager or manager-owner is responsible for negotiating the terms of new or expired leases and for recordkeeping concerning monthly sales data (sales per square foot) for each store in the center. Thus when leases expire, management can assess minimum or base rents in relation both to market criteria and to sales per square foot generated by each store and can calculate percentage rents or overages for each store.

Lease Structures

Retail leases are usually very complex and include clauses relating to tenant responsibilities for store improvements, to a pro rata share of operating expenses such as utilities, to common area maintenance, to merchant association dues, to hourly operating covenants, to strict merchant quality requirements, to sign requirements, to advertising, and to other special assessments at various holiday sale times. All these clauses are ways to ensure that the center generates the maximum sales per square foot.

Most tenants pay a base net rent for the space they occupy. Before accepting a tenant, a landlord will take care to see that the tenant is likely to generate sales which will allow for the payment of the base net rent per square foot plus all tenant operating costs and a common area maintenance (CAM) contribution. In addition, the landlord will want to know that the tenant can generate sales per square foot that will allow for the payment of a percentage rent, based on gross sales per square foot.

The percentage rent is usually established on the following basis: The tenant pays the landlord the greater of two amounts—a minimum base rent or a negotiated percentage of gross sales. The minimum base rent is usually the highest rent for a particular kind of retail store of a certain square footage which the market will bear in any particular locale. The percentage rent is established by negotiation, but typical percentage rent ranges are established for each type of retail trade and can easily be found in such publications as *Dollars and Cents of Shopping Centers,* published by the Urban Land Institute in Washington, D.C. If a lease calls for a rent of $1400 per month or 7 percent of gross sales, whichever is greater, $20,000 gross sales per month would be the point at which percentage rent would come into play. The minimum base rent–percentage rent structure is the principal reason that shopping center leases are subject to intense negotiation, especially since both parties have so much to gain or lose either way. If landlords accept a low base and a high percentage rent, they take on the risk of the tenant; if landlords require a high base rent, the tenant accepts the responsibility for generating sales sufficient to pay the rent.

As with office buildings, most shopping center tenants have net leases and pay a pro rata share of the operating expenses of the center, with either a stop or base-year provision. Some leases include clauses which allow for payment of pro rata share of expenses from the overage or percentage rents, when they exist.

Tenants also pay a CAM charge, which can be assessed in several different ways:

- A pro rata charge based on the percentage of tenant's gross square footage to the GLA of the center
- A stipulated fixed charge
- A charge based on the percentage of gross sales per square foot

Shopping Center Income and Operating Expenses

Dollars and Cents of Shopping Centers will provide anyone who is interested with a typical index of income categories and operating expense categories for shopping centers and will indicate the standard ratio between income and expenses for different types of centers. Income usually includes all minimum and percentage or overage rents, common area charges, any income from rent escalation clauses, income from the tenant's share of operating expenses such as utilities, and miscellaneous items such as vending machine income. Operating expenses generally include building maintenance, common area maintenance, utilities, office area services, advertising and promotion, property taxes, insurance, and management fees.

16

Rental Apartments: Underwriting

Gaye G. Beasley

President, The Patrician Mortgage Company
Washington, D.C.

General Information

The basic underwriting of apartment loans is a commonsense methodology used to project and analyze the future income stream of a given apartment property and is very similar to the underwriting of other types of commercial properties. In fact, the underwriting for an office building, shopping center, warehouse, or hotel is similar to an apartment underwriting in more respects than it is dissimilar. In all types of commercial loan underwriting, the lender endeavors to analyze the present net operating income and to project the future income stream of the property. Then, after allowing a certain margin for safety, the lender capitalizes that net income to produce the maximum mortgage supported by the debt service on the property.

In many ways, the underwriting of an apartment property involves less guesswork than does the underwriting of other types of commercial real estate because there is a wealth of comparable data from similar properties in most markets. Although a given community or neighborhood is likely to have a limited number of hotels or shopping centers, for example, almost every community has a reasonable supply of apartment properties. In addition, most communities have a number of properties targeted toward each of the various submarkets for rental apartments. Therefore, an appraiser usually does not have to make many large adjustments in projecting the rental income stream for the property or in estimating the project's operating expenses.

One of the disadvantages in underwriting apartment properties, however, is that many apartment properties experience substantial turnover. Particularly in cycles of overbuilding, tenants often vacate their current apartments and flee to the newest unit offering the greatest rent concessions. Whereas leases in a shopping center or office building are relatively difficult to terminate, many apartment tenants have only a month-to-month lease after their first year of occupancy in a given project.

Most apartment lenders calculate the mortgage amount based on (1) a ratio of the property's value, (2) a percentage of the property's replacement cost, and (3) the debt service coverage that the property will attain in a specified year, generally the first stabilized year of operations. Of course, the value of the property and the amount of debt service that the property can sustain are closely connected. Most lenders put primary emphasis upon the debt service coverage ratios and use the other mortgage calculations as guidelines. Many lenders will not loan more than a certain percentage of the project's replacement cost, and many lenders require that a developer put a certain amount of hard-cash equity into a project. Some lenders will allow builder-developers to donate the builder's profit in lieu of part of the equity. However, since all lenders rely heavily on the debt service approach to financing calculations in determining the maximum loan amount, the remainder of this chapter will focus on determining the debt service approach to financing.

Rent Calculations

A market study and/or an appraisal, using comparables, can establish what rents should be used for a given project. After gathering and reviewing such comparables, the underwriter must use discretion in applying a trend factor to the rents.

There are basically five different types of multifamily properties available for first mortgage loans, each of which requires a slightly different technique in establishing rent projections and in arriving at a trend factor:

- *The refinancing of an existing property for the present owner.* This usually involves collecting and analyzing the property's operating statements for the past two or three years. Standard refinancing loans are generally underwritten based on the "as is" rents of the property, although some lenders allow a modest trend to show in anticipating future rents.

- *An acquisition loan.* If the seller provides operating statements to the buyer, the lender can use rental information gathered from those statements as well as rental comparables in the area. Usually buyers plan to implement some sort of renovation program or to make management or marketing changes once they acquire the property. Therefore, the rents and expenses used for acquisition loans are often adjusted significantly from the project's operating statements for the period before the sale.

- *New construction properties.* This type of underwriting always involves rents and expenses which are estimated using comparable projects in the area. Most lenders will allow an upward trend projection of the rents and expenses until the end of the construction period or, in some cases, through the first year of stabilized occupancy.

- *Substantial rehab.* These properties are generally underwritten using rent and expense comparables for projects that are similar in amenities and marketability to the subject property after it is rehabilitated. In general, the developer is planning to make changes which will make management of the property more efficient, frequently including a changeover from centrally metered utilities to an individually metered utility combination. In addition, the developer may be targeting the renovated units to a higher-income tenancy than the property had previously served.

- *Special-use projects, such as retirement service centers.* The underwriting for this type of property involves gathering comparable rents from other special-use properties which provide similar special services. Also involved is a very extensive process of estimating the cost of the special services to be rendered to the project's tenants. For example, if meals are to be served, the cost of food and the hourly wages of each of the kitchen and dining room workers has to be estimated and added to the operating expenses. A total rent is derived by estimating the rent that could be obtained for the unit without any extra services and then adding the additional rent increment which is obtainable because such services are available (albeit at an extra cost) to the tenants. This rent level will be higher than rents charged at standard rental apartments in the area but should be comparable to rents in other special facilities with similar services. Lastly, the total expense of the extra services needs to be added to determine the total rent charge to the tenant. For special service properties such as retirement service centers, the absorption rate may be extremely slow, probably not more than five or six units per month. Therefore, this type of property almost always has a large operating deficit guarantee.

Once the rental information is assembled, the per-unit rent is adjusted to reflect any utilities which are included in the rent, and further adjustments are made depending on the unit sizes and on the amenities offered in the property. In addition, the projected rents are analyzed on a rent per square foot basis. To the projected gross rent, the underwriter should then add additional income such as that obtained for laundry facilities and/or for commercial space within the property.

Vacancy and Absorption

Other important steps in calculating the debt service mortgage amount are an estimate of effective gross income (after a deduction for vacancy allowance) and completion of an absorption analysis. An appraisal or market study should accurately determine the vacancy factor in the specific neighborhood in which the project is located, as well as the vacancy factor in the general area. If possible, this study should establish which types of units are incurring the highest vacancies. The appraisal or market study should consider not only apartments currently existing in the market but all those under construction or planned to begin construction which might compete with the subject property. Once this calculation is done, the underwriter can determine what vacancy factor to apply against the total gross rent.

Once the underwriting for the apartment project is complete, the underwriter should perform an absorption analysis to determine how many units can reasonably be expected to lease each month once the first units are brought on line. Frequently, this calculation will show a substantial operating deficit for the project. Depending on the developer's financial strength and ability to cover such deficits, the lender may require a letter of credit or special guarantee to cover such anticipated shortfall.

Operating Expenses

Comparables for operating expenses are gathered along with rent comparables, as outlined above. In addition to checking the projected operating expenses for the subject property against comparable expenses, the underwriter must develop a complete breakdown of projected operating expenses under the following categories:

- Administrative expenses (management fees, advertising, etc.)
- Utility expenses (for all common area space and for centrally metered utilities)

- Operating and maintenance expenses (including all payroll and payroll taxes, decorating, repairs, and maintenance)
- Taxes and insurance (the underwriter should obtain quotes for hazard insurance and check with the local real estate assessor's office to determine what the assessment of the property might be and what millage rate will be applied against that assessment)

If the expense budget varies greatly from the expense comparables, the underwriter needs to check further and perhaps make appropriate adjustments to arrive at the proper estimate.

In addition to calculating the per-unit operating expenses, most lenders are concerned with the ratio of the total operating expenses to the effective gross income. Generally this ratio will vary by geographic location and services provided by the owner.

Debt Service Constant

One of the last calculations the underwriter must make in determining the debt service of the mortgage is the constant. The constant is usually built up by adding the loan interest rate plus the mortgage insurance premium, if any, plus amortization for the term of the loan.

Most lenders underwrite the loan by dividing the projected net operating income (NOI) by the constant and then dividing the result by the appropriate debt service coverage ratio. Other lenders choose a capitalization rate which may reflect the pay rate rather than the actual interest rate on the loan. Many lenders are willing to allow for a lower interest rate during the early years of a project loan and accrue interest to be added to the debt service in the later years. In such instances, the mortgage may be obtained using the pay rate, and the maximum mortgage derived from such a calculation would then be adjusted based on the appropriate loan-to-value ratio which is supported by an appraisal. Some lenders do not require any amortization on the loan in the first few years or calculate amortization based on a 30-year loan even if the loan has a 10- or 15-year balloon. These lenders make similar adjustments in the maximum mortgage amount based on loan to value.

Debt Service Coverage

When the projected net operating income is determined, debt service coverage can be computed. Many lenders require a debt service coverage of 1.2 to 1, and others will accept a lower coverage of 1.10 or 1.15 to 1. For example, the Department of Housing and Urban Development's (HUD) insurance program for new construction allows a debt service coverage of 1.1 to 1, but the Federal National Mortgage Association (FNMA) prefers to see a 1.2-to-1 coverage.

Obviously the difference between the debt service and the projected NOI is the lender's cushion. Presumably, the higher the debt service coverage, the safer the loan. Another ratio that is of equal importance to the debt service coverage is the breakeven point, which illustrates what percentage of the project's units must be occupied at the projected rents in order for the project to pay all operating expenses and debt service. The breakeven point is determined by annual expenses plus debt service divided by gross income. Remember that the ratio is only a guide and will vary with each particular project.

Establishing the Maximum Mortgage Amount

Based on the debt service coverage at projected rents, a maximum mortgage amount can be determined. It should be adjusted by the lender's requirement for equity contribution and/or by the lender's limit on loan to value. The result establishes the final mortgage amount. After the loan amount is established, the underwriter must then calculate the operating deficit during the start-up period and decide what guarantees and/or deposits will be required from the developer and at what point in the project's operating history those reserves or guarantees should be released.

Summary

There are many different types of loan products in the market today. The developer may select from a wide variety of options and terms ranging from a 3- to 5-year "miniterm" to a federally insured or coinsured loan offering a term of 40 years plus the construction period. Frequently, developers arrange a construction loan and then place the permanent loan once the project has reached sustaining occupancy and has a successful operating history. Lenders can make graduated payment mortgages for apartments by offering an initially lower pay rate and then stepping up the debt service constant each year until the loan is paid off. Many also have the flexibility to set a long amortization period with a balloon on the loan in 10 or 15 years. Frequently, a balloon carries with it a personal guarantee from the developer or a guarantee that the lender will be able to maintain a certain yield should the loan not be paid off when called.

Finally, many lenders will enter into joint ventures with developers and provide 100 percent of the replacement costs, including a developer's fee in exchange for a negotiated interest in the project. Other lenders will grant developers a low fixed return on the loan and then participate in the cash flow and residual value above that fixed rate.

Underwriting Example

In the example that follows on pages 174 and 175, the NOI shown in Table 16.1 assumes that, when the apartment has rented up, the rents shown will be the rents received and there will be a 4 percent vacancy. That NOI is used in Table 16.2 to determine the value of the property. The value should always be higher than the estimated project costs, shown in Table 16.3, or the project will probably not be economically feasible.

The lender has set 1.18, shown in Table 16.4, as the debt service coverage. Dividing this figure into the NOI gives an amount available for debt service that is approximately that shown in Table 16.5 as first-year debt service at 9.5 percent on a loan of $6.8 million. Note on Table 16.1 that the interest rate changes.

There are almost as many types of loan structures as there are lenders with cash to loan on apartments. This chapter is not intended to cover all of them. Its purpose, and the purpose of the sample loan underwriting shown in Tables 16.1 through 16.5, is to instruct the loan underwriter on how to ensure a successful loan through careful analysis before the issuance of the loan commitment.

Table 16.1. 161-Unit Garden Apartment Project Sample Underwriting:
Pro Forma

Number of units	Unit type	Monthly rent	Monthly income
1	0BR/1BA	$495	$ 495
147	1BR/1BA	575	84,525
11	2BR/1BA	675	7,425
2	3BR/1BA	750	1,500
161		Monthly rental income	$ 93,945
		Months	× 12
		Annual rental income	$1,127,340
		Laundry income @ $5 PUPM	9,660
		Gross annual income	$1,137,000
		4 percent vacancy	(45,480)
		Effective gross income	$1,091,520
		Annual operating expense	(331,200)
		Net operating income	$ 760,320

Table 16.2. 161-Unit Garden Apartment Project Sample
Underwriting Computation of Economic Value

Assuming that a typical lender would accept a capitalization rate of 9 percent
for the subject property, economic value is calculated as follows:

Net income divided by cap rate = value
$760,320 divided by 0.09 = $8,448,000

To arrive at a final rounded *indicated economic value* of $8,450,000.

Table 16.3. 161-Unit Garden Apartment Project Sample
Underwriting Estimated Project Costs

	Total	Per unit
Rehabilitation costs	$2,415,000	$15,000
Architectural and engineering fees	75,000	466
Marketing and rent-up	96,600	600
Interest during construction		
(8 months, 9.5% pay rate, 75% out)	323,000	2,006
Financing fees @ 2.5%	170,000	1,056
Legal and organizational fees	35,000	217
Relocation	40,000	248
Taxes and insurance	75,000	466
Title and recording	30,000	186
Total development cost	$3,259,600	$19,345
Acquisition and cost to carry	4,278,000	26,571
Total replacement cost	$7,537,600	$45,917

Table 16.4. 161-Unit Garden Apartment Project Sample
Underwriting Loan Summary

Amount:	$6,800,000
Security:	First mortgage secured by a substantially reha-bilitated 161-unit garden apartment complex. The project is located on a 50-acre site on the southwest corner of the intersection of
	in _____
Borrower:	A _____ limited partnership to be formed with _____ and its general partners.
Term:	Fixed for five years with an option to extend for an additional five years.
Rate:	Accrual rate to be fixed prior to construction.* Pay rate at 9.5 percent through construction plus one year, increasing at 0.5 percent per year to the accrual rate.
Closing:	Estimated to be _____ Construction to be completed in phases, with completion of the first units anticipated in
	Total construction and rent-up period esti-mated to be 18 months.
Debt service coverage:	1.18

*Note: The accrual rate will be fixed for five years at 225 basis points above the Federal Home Loan Bank's rate for the Atlanta region.

Table 16.5. 161-Unit Garden Apartment Project Sample
Underwriting Loan Analysis

Loan amount:	$6,800,000
Valuation:	$8,450,000
Loan gross rent multiplier:	5.98×
Loan/value:	80%
Total development cost:	$7,537,600
Loan/cost:	90%
Number of units:	161
Loan/unit:	$42,236
Effective gross income:	$1,091,520
Expenses:	$ 331,200
Expenses per unit:	$ 2,057
Expenses per income:	30.3%
Net income:	$ 760,320
Debt service—first year @9.50 percent interest only:	$ 646,000
Net income coverage of debt service:	1.18×
Breakeven point:	85.9%

17
Rental Apartments: Financing

Kenneth Lore, Esq.

Partner, Brownstein, Zeidman and Schomer
Washington, D.C.

Multifamily housing takes many forms in the United States, from rental to cooperatives and, to a lesser degree, condominiums (which are generally viewed and financed as single-family structures). The variety of project types is matched or exceeded by the available financing alternatives, both debt and equity, and by the types of lending and investment institutions willing to consider multifamily housing financing.

Chapter 16 discussed underwriting apartments for a loan from a savings and loan association or other traditional source. This chapter covers those sources and then describes the federal insurance programs and the secondary market for multifamily rental properties.

Traditional Sources of Multifamily Finance

For much of this century, federal assistance centered on single-family housing, although as early as 1934 the Federal Housing Administration (FHA) provided a program for long-term financing of multifamily housing. Until recently, multifamily loans were almost exclusively made as whole loans (which were sometimes sold as participations), either as FHA-insured loans or on a conventional basis by large insurance companies, savings and loan associations, and, to a lesser degree, banks and pension funds.

At present multifamily financing, like its single-family counterpart, has changed dramatically as a result of such innovations as tax-exempt financing, private credit enhancement, and securitization in the form of various kinds of mortgage-backed securities.

Insurance Companies

Given their predilection for long-term, large denomination investment, the major U.S. insurance companies have historically been involved in real estate development and in real estate financing.

At times the major insurance companies lent money for real estate development, and at other times and for briefer periods—after World War II, for instance, and currently, to some degree—they became equity investors. After World War II, for example, Metropolitan Life developed Parkfairfax in Arlington, Virginia, and Parkchester and Stuyvesant Town in New York. Prudential began large-scale real estate development on its own account and in the mid-1980s announced its decision to sell a significant portion of its commercial equity portfolio. Other companies have also created equity investment funds to purchase or act as joint venturers in real estate projects. In 1985 life insurance companies ranked third among all sources of credit for all mortgage originations, with their percentage of holdings in multifamily mortgages at about 11 percent of their total portfolios, as compared with only about 1 percent of total assets in single-family holdings.

Banks, Thrifts, and Other Financial Institutions

Although threatened by competition from larger and more diverse financial institutions, savings and loans and commercial banks came to be major players in multifamily finance. Statutory requirements for housing investment define and distinguish savings and loan associations from the commercial banks, and thrifts continue to dominate in the origination of multifamily mortgages.

Federal National Mortgage Association Direct Loans

The Federal National Mortgage Association (FNMA) is a privately owned association chartered by the Congress in 1938. Mortgage bankers are particularly active among the FNMA network of lenders, with 43 percent of FNMA's business with lenders coming from mortgage banking firms in 1985. Although the bulk of FNMA's purchases are single-family mortgages, it also purchases multifamily mortgages.

FNMA has purchased FHA-insured multifamily housing, but, in the 1980s, it has limited its multifamily mortgages to those that are conventionally financed. These are restricted to those apartments designed for moderate- and middle-income families.

Details of standard multifamily programs, including cooperative mortgages, rehabilitation mortgages, and FNMA's credit enhancement program, appear in *FNMA Guides*.

The Federal Home Loan Mortgage Corporation Purchase Programs

The Congress established the Federal Home Loan Mortgage Corporation (FHLMC) in 1970 to provide additional liquidity and flexibility to the mortgage market. FHLMC links the mortgage and capital market by purchasing mortgages from lenders, securitizing them, and selling the securities in the capital markets. FHLMC purchases fixed rate, conventional multifamily mortgages from eligible sellers, i.e., institutions insured by the Federal Deposit Insurance Corporation (FDIC) or the Federal Savings and Loan Insurance Corporation (FSLIC), or approved FHA mortgages.

FHLMC has been purchasing multifamily mortgages since 1972 and packaging some as part of offerings of FHLMC Participation Certificates (PCs). These are sold with the guarantee of FHLMC, which has a Triple A credit rating. In 1986, FHLMC purchased over $3 billion in existing multifamily loans, each with a 15-year term and a clause preventing prepayments for at least 54 months.

Pension Funds

According to analysts, domestic pension funds will be the fastest growing pool of institutional assets for the rest of the century. Although to date these funds invest only a miniscule portion of their assets in real estate, their activity is more varied than one might have envisioned 10 years ago.

The passage of the Employee Retirement Income Security Act of 1974 (ERISA) posed formidable obstacles to those private pension plan managers with the authority to make substantial investments in mortgages and mortgage-related securities. ERISA requires plan fiduciaries to satisfy "prudent" standards of conduct in the choice and management of plan assets. For example, conflict-of-interest provisions in the law and the government regulations may prevent mortgage bankers, acting for the sellers, from selling commercial mortgages to private pension plans while acting for the buyers as servicing agents of those mortgages. There is considerable personal liability to fiduciaries under ERISA standards, sufficient to encourage extremely conservative investment policies. ERISA does not apply to pension plans of state and local governments.

Notwithstanding these constraints and pension plan managers' relative unfamiliarity with housing, pension funds have invested in multifamily housing. Regulatory changes and educational efforts by the Department of Housing and Urban Development (HUD) and investment bankers have improved housing's stake in pension fund assets, although HUD estimates that less than 6 percent of private pension fund assets were in mortgage-related assets as of September 1985.

Public Debt Markets

Multifamily housing financing increasingly relies on the public debt markets. There is an accelerated pace of financial innovation within that market, both in the United States and abroad. This rapid pace of innovation has been spurred by high price and interest volatility, general economic uncertainty, and tax and regulatory changes, both current and prospective. Wall Street investment firms have pushed aggressively into territory previously acceded to FNMA, FHLMC, and Government National Mortgage Association (GNMA). The degree to which real estate, particularly multifamily and commercial real estate, will compete for capital is likely to depend directly on the strength of mortgage-backed securities and variations on that form.[1]

Real Estate Investment Trusts

Similar in some respects to mutual funds, real estate investment trusts (REITs) are financial vehicles which use pooled funds raised by selling shares to investors to acquire and finance real estate debt or equity. Their principal attractiveness is that they pay no tax at the corporate

---

[1]See generally, Kenneth Lore, *Mortgage-Backed Securities: Developments and Trends in the Secondary Mortgage Market,* Clark Boardman Company, New York, 1986.

level, as long as they distribute 95 percent of their reported earnings as income and meet other statutory requirements.

REITs offer publicly traded, highly liquid shares in corporations that own real estate ranging from multifamily housing to hotels, commercial buildings, industrial, health care, and other properties. Depending on the investment emphasis of their portfolio, REITs focus on property ownership (equity trusts), on real estate lending activities (mortgage trusts), or on both equity and mortgage-related activities (hybrid trusts).

REITs, essentially dead for a decade after a burnout in the 1970s, are benefiting from an enhanced image (abetted by some recent block-buster transactions) and the diminution of other investment alternatives.

Public Limited Partnerships

Public limited partnerships are structured to provide the opportunities of a REIT and to allow the pooling of funds for large-scale real estate debt and/or equity positions. The advantages of such pools are significant liquidity and tax benefits, in many cases more advantageous than the REITs.

Public limited partnerships have recently been formed for the purpose of investing in taxable and tax-exempt mortgage-related instruments, often with contingent interest features. In general, such partnerships are structured to provide investors an opportunity to receive a base level of interest along with a percentage of cash flow and residual value in the form of contingent interest payments. The mortgages and base interest payments may also be insured. The investor is promised a safe return at the base level, with inflation protection in the form of contingent interest.

A simplified partnership profile might appear as follows:

- A partnership is formed to acquire a portfolio of participating loans on multifamily residential projects insured, coinsured, or guaranteed in part or whole by FHA and GNMA.

- Yield is below the market, in exchange for perhaps 25 percent of the "upside" in a project, which is attractive to a developer or owner currently unable to raise equity in tax-sheltered syndications.

- The partnership objectives are (1) to preserve capital, (2) to provide quarterly cash distributions, and (3) to provide appreciation and liquidity to holders of the units.

- The partnership is directed by a managing general partner whose responsibilities include the origination of many of the mortgages, handling normal management responsibilities, as well as the final selection of project mortgages.

- A reinvestment plan is a possible option, although this feature adds considerable complexity to the structure of such partnerships.

Federal Programs

The Insurance Programs of the Federal Housing Administration

FHA multifamily mortgage insurance programs insure certain mortgage loans for FHA-approved lenders, including mortgage bankers, to finance the construction, purchase, and rehabilitation, or the refinancing of rental housing, cooperatives, and condominiums. More targeted programs insure multifamily housing designed for the elderly and the handicapped, hospitals, health care and nursing home facilities, and group practice facilities. The standard multifamily programs of the National Housing Act are designated by their section numbers under the National Housing Act of 1937, as amended.

Section 207. The basic FHA insurance program insures mortgages for multifamily projects. No specific tenant or income limitations are imposed. Underwriting criteria are a maximum limit on total project mortgage and a maximum mortgage amount, under the regulations, to be the lesser of 90 percent of project value or statutory per-unit amounts. These limits may be increased in high-cost areas or on approval of the secretary of HUD.

This section has served as a model for most subsequent FHA multifamily programs, but Section 207 never has been a major force for multifamily production. From 1934 through September 1983, FHA insured close to 2400 projects with nearly 305,000 units. By comparison, more than twice as many units have been insured under Section 221(d)(4) of the National Housing Act since its passage in 1954.

Section 213. Loans insured under this section cover mortgages made by private lending institutions on cooperative housing projects of five or more units. The units are to be occupied by members of nonprofit cooperative ownership housing corporations. The loans may be used for new construction, rehabilitation, acquisition, or the improvement of an already owned project as well as the resale of individual memberships.

The loans also may cover construction of projects of individual dwellings having separate mortgages to be purchased by cooperative members and the construction or rehabilitation of projects that owners plan to sell to nonprofit cooperatives.

Sections 221(d)(3) and 221(d)(4). Both programs support the construction or substantial rehabilitation of rental and cooperative housing for low- and moderate-income families and are sometimes used for upscale projects. They are the principal programs used in conjunction with Section 8 housing assistance payments (defunct in the mid-1980s). Up to 100 percent of Section 221(d)(3) projects could be available to tenants receiving rent supplement assistance (also no longer available for new projects). Projects insured under Section 221(d)(4) are eligible for public housing projects financed with tax-exempt obligations.

Eligible lenders under these programs are HUD/FHA-approved mortgages. Underwriting criteria are as follows: For Section 221(d)(3), the full amount of the mortgage may be insured for nonprofit rental or cooperative housing. For Section 221(d)(4), up to 90 percent of the estimated replacement cost (which includes a builders' and sponsors' profit allowance) may be insured, regardless of the type of mortgagor.

HUD and FHA are presently authorized to enter into coinsurance contracts with approved multifamily lenders for the Section 221(d)(3) and 221(d)(4) new construction and substantial rehab projects. In a co-insurance program, the mortgage banking firm takes the initial risk of loss in case of default, and the government takes the loss after the share taken by the mortgage banking firm (see Section 244). Under Section 221(d)(4), the department also will insure retirement service centers, requiring a 90 percent loan-to-replacement-cost ratio, 90 percent debt service ratio and statutory cost limitations.

Section 223(f). Mortgage insurance may be provided under Section 223(f) for the purchase or refinancing of existing multifamily projects. The apartments must have five or more units, be at least three years old, and not require substantial rehabilitation. The mortgage cannot exceed 85 percent of the FHA-estimated value of the project, although this can be raised to 90 percent in certain instances. Statutory per-unit cost limits may be raised in high-cost areas up to 75 percent and up to 90 percent on a project-by-project basis with the secretary of HUD's approval.

Sections 231 and 232. Section 231 provides mortgage insurance for the construction or rehabilitation of rental housing for the elderly or handicapped. Projects must have eight units or more. FHA will insure up to 100 percent of costs for non-profit and public mortgagors, but up to only 90 percent for private mortgagors. As of September 1983, FHA had insured 513 projects with 67,936 units.

Under Section 232, FHA insures mortgages for nursing homes, board, and care, and other related facilities that meet statutory eligibility criteria. The projects insured under this section are unsubsidized. This program covers construction or renovation of facilities for 20 or more patients requiring skilled nursing care or intermediate—continuous but minimal—care provided by licensed or trained staff. Equipment and day-care facilities may be included in the mortgage.

Qualified mortgagors may be investors, builders, developers, and private, nonprofit corporations or associations. The loan-to-value limitation is generally 90 percent, and the program permits mortgages of up to 40 years. Through 1985 there has been increasing activity under the basic program, although the number of projects under Section 232(e), which insures projects in areas or neighborhoods defined as "declining," has decreased.

The FHA Coinsurance Programs

Under Section 244 of the National Housing Act, HUD may coinsure mortgage loans with approved coinsured lenders to expedite the financing of multifamily rental housing. State agencies may qualify as coinsured lenders. Approved lenders assume many of the responsibilities previously handled by the HUD field office. In exchange for the authority to perform underwriting, servicing, management, and property disposition functions, approved mortgagees accept a percentage of the risk for any loss on the insured mortgage. The mortgagee also receives a part of the mortgage insurance premium. Both Section 221(d) and Section 223(f) projects are eligible for the coinsurance program.

The program has grown very rapidly in 1986-1987. In 1986, more coinsured loans were made than FHA-insured loans were underwritten by FHA offices.

The GNMA Mortgage-Backed Securities Program

The Government National Mortgage Association (GNMA), a government corporation within HUD, facilitates the channeling of funds from the capital markets into the residential mortgage market, primarily through its guarantees on securities issued by private lenders and backed by pools of federally insured mortgages. Although GNMA does not itself issue securities, the application of the "full faith and credit" of the U.S. government guarantee to a private issuer's debt does enable regulated institutions to treat the investment as highest-grade paper— thus making GNMAs preeminent in the secondary mortgage market. GNMA mortgage-backed securities are the most widely held and traded in the world. There are two active GNMA programs: GNMA I, the original program, and GNMA II, which in 1983 began to offer new issues that took advantage of many of the technological developments that had become available.

Mortgage bankers are active participants in the GNMA market, along with savings institutions and commercial banks. Eligible issuers must meet certain net worth requirements, be FHA-approved mortgagees, and be able to demonstrate experience appropriate to participation in the program. GNMA receives a fee from the issuer as guarantor of the multifamily securities.

The pools that collateralized GNMA securities, all under GNMA I only, include the following types of FHA-insured multifamily mortgages: construction loans; project loans; buydown loans; and FHA-insured loans for nursing homes, hospitals, and group practice facilities.

The Secondary Market in Multifamily Loans

The FNMA Secondary Market Programs

FNMA, whose purchase program is mentioned earlier in this chapter, is an issuer of mortgage-backed securities (MBSs). Most of the securities are issued through swap transactions, in which an approved lender delivers a pool of loans in exchange for a like quantity of FNMA MBSs. These represent an undivided interest in the collateral; the lender may sell or hold them. Principal and interest at the pass-through rate are distributed to the holder of the security. FNMA guarantees full and timely payment of interest and principal.

FNMA also issues securities for cash through public offerings or private placements and uses the cash to purchase conventional multifamily mortgages, which it holds in portfolio. FNMA also swaps mortgage pass-through certificates for pools of multifamily loans and purchases fixed-rate mortgages with varying maturities of up to 15 years.

The FHLMC Secondary Mortgage Market Programs

FHLMC has been the seller of conventional mortgage securities in the form of Participation Certificates (PCs). Funds to purchase mortgage loans and participations and securitize them come primarily from the sale of PCs. Although for many years FHLMC has included multifamily mortgages in the pool of mortgages collateralizing its obligation, it was only in 1985 that it issued its first securities backed entirely by multifamily mortgages. In 1985 and the first half of 1986, FHLMC sold $1.7 billion of multifamily PCs and then began a weekly auction of these certificates. Although the thrifts are far and away the corporation's best customer, mortgage bankers are the second largest sector of FHLMC's customer base.

Tax-Exempt and Taxable Bonds

Tax-Exempt Bonds. It is and has been possible to finance multifamily rental housing with tax-exempt industrial development bonds issued under Section 103(b)(4)(A) of the Internal Revenue Code. A state or local agent may issue bonds to finance building rehabilitation and acquisition of multifamily housing. The mortgage financing produces comparatively low interest rates, reflecting the rates on the bonds.

Beginning with New York in 1961, state housing finance agencies used the state's authority to issue bonds to finance subsidized multifamily housing. The 41 other states which have housing agencies followed New York in issuing bonds to build apartments for rental to low- and moderate-income families. Over the years these agencies added single-family housing to their objectives; by 1979 the escalating volume of issues to finance single-family housing precipitated a fierce policy debate, culminating in additional constraints under successive tax bills and, finally, in the Draconian constraints of the Tax Reform Act of 1986.

The Tax Reform Act of 1986 severely limits the use of tax-exempt bonds for multifamily rental housing. Requirements which target loans to low-income families, caps on the volume of bonds that may be issued, continuous compliance requirements, arbitrage restrictions, alternative minimum tax treatment, and a myriad of additional restrictions adopted by Congress limit, and in some areas eliminate, the use of tax-exempt bonds for multifamily housing, particularly for the middle-income sector.

Taxable Bonds. After the restrictions were imposed on tax-exempt bonds in 1986, interest surfaced in the market concerning taxable

bonds to finance multifamily housing. Many state and local governments have had the option to issue taxable securities but did not do so
because they carried a higher interest rate than tax-exempt bonds. In
some areas new authorizing legislation is required to issue taxable bonds
for housing by state or local agencies.

There has also been discussion of a taxable bond program with federal assistance, to take the place of what many said was an inefficient
program of assistance through tax-exempt bonds. In fact, a program to
provide such assistance to qualified agencies was included in Section
802 of the Housing and Community Development Act of 1974. None of
the 37 eligible state agencies applied for such assistance, and the funds
were eventually rescinded. In this area, as in federal insurance, coinsurance, and tax-exempt bonds, financing multifamily rental housing is
such a complicated field that a number of mortgage banking firms specialize exclusively in that subject.

18

Hotels and Motels

President, McG Real Estate Company
Los Angeles, California

Of all the income-producing property types, hotels (in this chapter, *hotel* is generic for all types of lodging facilities unless otherwise noted) are the most complex and therefore the most interesting to underwrite. Hotels have operating ratios, debt service coverage requirements, stabilized occupancy levels, and expense categories that differ from those of office buildings, apartments, industrial parks, and shopping centers. For this reason, most developers, investors, and lenders are not overly familiar with hotels as an investment property.

A lack of working knowledge in any business setting breeds discomfort, and unfortunately ignorance is often mistaken for risk. However, with solid, prudent underwriting standards and an in-depth understanding of how the lodging industry operates, the risk factor can be mitigated to an acceptable level that need not be any greater than for other commercial real estate investments.

Distinctive Nature of Hotels

Listed below are some of the major dissimilarities that can provide a challenge when analyzing a hotel investment.

- Hotels are the truest form of speculative buildings. There are no leases. Therefore, by traditional thinking, they are 100 percent speculative, with no guarantees that any guest will walk through the front door on any given day. (The only exception is prebooking for group and convention business.)

- The lodging industry is extremely dependent on management. It is a labor-intensive, retail type of service-oriented business. A hotel sells hospitality 24 hours a day. According to Horst Osterkamp, president of U.S. Hotel Properties, "There is probably no other business that is more dependent on professional hands-on management for its success than the hospitality industry."[1] In the final analysis, no matter how great a location the hotel might have, regardless of how strong the sponsorship is, and independent of the quality of the product being offered the public, it cannot succeed without experienced, professional managers to implement a well-planned sales and marketing program. For all other property types, when given the right location, strong sponsorship, and superior quality, success is virtually guaranteed in the marketplace eventually, at least, if not immediately due to prevailing economic conditions. Hotels need more than location, sponsorship, and quality; hotels need proper, competent management!

- Hotels are both an operating business and a piece of real estate. It is the "ongoing business concern" of hotels that eliminates many investors from financing this property type. Although hotels *are* real estate deals, attempts to separate the real estate value from the hotel's value as a growing concern are generally unsatisfactory and a somewhat meaningless exercise for investment purposes.

- Hotels are labor-intensive, with the emphasis on personal service. Employees must be trained, motivated, and supervised properly. The impressions made by the hotel staff, whether positive or negative, will have an impact on the guest's perception of the facility and could influence whether the guest will return. Repeat business is critical to the successful operation of a hotel. Proper staff training is an ongoing challenge to management and is complicated by two factors: extremely high turnover of personnel, and the fact that many hotel positions are filled by minimum wage employees who generally have limited education.[2]

---

[1]"Hotel Development and Investment," *National Real Estate Investor*, December 1985, p. 84.

[2]Laventhol & Horwath, *Hotel/Motel Development*, The Urban Land Institute, Washington, D. C., 1984, p. 304.

- In general, hotels are more capital-intensive than other property types for three reasons: First, it is extremely difficult for developers to obtain 100 percent financing due to tougher underwriting standards imposed by the lenders. Today it is not uncommon for the developer to have 15 percent to 25 percent of the total project cost committed in the form of an equity contribution. Second, hotels typically do not generate enough cash flow in their early years of operation to carry debt service obligations. The operating deficits for the first two to three years of operation, until the hotel achieves stabilization, are difficult to predict accurately when short-term and long-term financing is being arranged. Third, unlike other real estate investments, hotels need a working capital account to replace furniture, fixtures, and equipment (FF&E) as they become worn or outdated in order to maintain the hotel's total value, which is not a small capital expenditure item.

- Many outside influences that affect a hotel's performance are beyond the control of competent management. Hotels are directly affected by the health of the national economy. When a recession is followed in cyclical fashion by economic recovery, hotel occupancy lags behind recovery by six to nine months. A substantial proportion of the hospitality industry's business depends on discretionary versus essential spending. During recessionary periods, when corporate profits are down, business travel and convention attendance are among the first things cut back. When the personal income of customers is eroded during inflationary periods, vacation travel is cancelled. Lacking the long-term leases which stabilize other property types, hotel occupancy will immediately decrease because of national and international events. For example, the oil embargo and energy crisis of the early 1970s devastated occupancy rates at highway motels. When Seattle's major employer, Boeing, curtailed its operations in the late 1960s, the city's hotel business was hit harder than any other type of business.

- On the positive side, because they lack leases, hotels are almost the perfect inflation hedge. Historically, for any given 10-year period during the past four decades, the annual compounded growth rate in average daily room rates (ADRs) has outpaced the annual compounded inflation rate, as measured by the Consumer Price Index (CPI) for the same period. This has been true both nationally and locally. According to some skeptics, this trend is now temporarily being reversed due to the overbuilding in some market areas. Most likely, however, there will be a net spread of 2 to 3 percent annually in ADR increases, resulting in an annual net real growth.

- Hotels, more than other income-producing properties, can have a major impact on a given municipality's economy. A hotel usually is one of the major employers in the area. It generates substantial revenue for the local community in the form of bed tax revenues. It brings outside dollars in the local area, both from expenditures within the hotel and outside the hotel at neighboring restaurants, nightclubs, and retail outlets. Its real estate taxes are generally substantial. And it can often serve as the impetus for the redevelopment of a given area.

Types and Marketing Classification of Hotels

The classification of hotels runs the entire gamut, depending on pricing, location, amenities, specific markets served, and style. Table 18.1 summarizes the various types of lodging facilities by category.

Table 18.1. Types of Hotels, by Selected Development Criteria
(Generically Described)

Price	Amenities	Location	Specific markets served	Distinctiveness of style or offerings
Budget-Economy Hotels	*Convention Hotels*	*Downtown Hotels*	*Executive Conference Centers*	*All Suite Hotels*
Rooms-only operation with little or no public space, no on-premise food and beverage facilities and room rates 20 to 50 percent below the average for the market area.	Large hotels with 500 or more guest rooms, extensive meeting space, several restaurants and lounges; sometimes adjacent to convention centers.	High-rise buildings with attached or covered parking; varying numbers of guest rooms and varying ranges of facilities and amenities, according to pricing and to market orientation of the property.	Facilities sited in secluded, country-like settings with fewer than 300 rooms, a variety of well-planned small meeting rooms and classrooms, and modern audiovisual equipment. Meals and the use of athletic facilities are included in the quoted daily room rate.	Facilities characterized by larger-than-normal room size, a living/parlor area separated from the sleeping area, cooking and refrigeration equipment, residential-looking public space, and the aim of catering to long-term guests.

Table 18.1 . Types of Hotels, by Selected Development Criteria
(Generically Described) *(Continued)*

Price	Amenities	Location	Specific markets served	Distinctiveness of style or offerings
Middle-Market Hotels	*Commercial Hotels*	*Suburban Hotels*	*Health Spas*	*Renovated or Converted Hotels*
Operations offering a wide range of facilities and amenities, with room rates equal to or slightly above market-area averages.	Operations emphasizing comfortable, functional guest rooms with ample work area, smaller meeting and conference rooms, and limited recreational amenities.	Low- to mid-rise buildings with surface parking, interior corridors, recreational amenities, and meeting and banquet facilities.	Specialized hotels catering to specific needs such as to spend a concentrated, secluded period of time losing weight, reducing stress, or breaking a habit. These facilities usually have professional staffs including dietitians, therapists, physicians, and/or counselors.	Old, historic structures that were once grand hotels or other older facilities, refurbished to the original era's splendor and elegance. Most of these are considered classic hotels. An example of an unusual conversion is the Quaker Hilton Inn in Akron, Ohio, which was converted from an old Quaker Oats grain elevator.
Luxury Hotels	*Resort Hotels*	*Highway-Interstate Hotels*	*Resort Hotels*	*Mixed-Use Focal-Point Hotels*
Hotels providing upscale decor and furnishings, concierge service, a limited amount of high-quality public space, a high ratio of employees to rooms available, and room rates substantially above market-area averages.	Hotels that emphasize recreational amenities, food and beverage outlets, and meeting and banquet space; typically located in a picturesque setting.	Low-rise structures having surface parking, exterior corridors, some food and beverage space, minimal banquet space, and an outdoor swimming pool.	Hotels that emphasize recreational amenities, food and beverage outlets, and meeting and banquet space; typically located in a picturesque setting.	Components of large multi-use developments, serving to focus the other uses or to complement them. Architecturally significant and designed to be inward-facing.

SOURCE: Laventhol & Horwath, *Hotel/Motel Development*, The Urban Land Institute, Washington, D. C., 1984, p. 13.

The airport hotel is an important location-oriented classification that is not listed in the table. Transportation improvements have always had a major bearing on the hotel industry—seaport villages and stagecoach rails in colonial days, the railroad network in the 1880s, the highways since the 1920s, the airports since the 1950s. Airport facilities cater to commercial travelers and small groups. Demand is also generated from airline crews and delayed passengers. Typically these accommodations have several small meeting rooms, a three-meals-a-day restaurant, and a cocktail or lounge area. With few exceptions, these properties rarely accommodate larger convention groups or resort travelers.

Hotels are designed and located to attract one or more specific market segments. The hotel developer (and investors) must analyze fully which market segments the particular product will attract and why, the characteristics of the traveler within that market segment, and how the proposed hotel can best capitalize on this knowledge and enhance its share of its particular market niche.

There are three categories of hotel patronage—commercial, convention or group, and tourist. Ideally, a healthy market mix from all three categories enables a hotel to minimize the fluctuations in conditions from any one segment. Full-service hotels, regardless of location, will generally capture a portion of each market segment.

Market segmentation, primarily by pricing, has been the "buzzword" in the 1980s for the national chains. Faced with the dilemma of having saturated their primary market areas over the previous three decades (even in second-tier cities), the national lodging companies sought to continue their growth and expansion plans by offering the traveling population a new product type. As the Real Estate Research Corporation (RERC) stated in its publication, *Emerging Trends in Real Estate: 1983*, "Major hotel/motel chains, attempting to be 'all things to all people,' continue to create subsidiaries that cater to other than their primary segments of the market." As examples:

- Holiday Inn Corporation developed the budget-priced Hampton Inns, mid-priced Holiday Inns, luxury-priced Crowne Plazas, and the all-suite hotel property, Embassy Suites.

- The Marriott Corporation has the economy-priced Courtyards, the high-end priced Marriotts, and the luxury-priced Marriott Marquis. On Marriott's drawing boards are upper-middle-priced Marriotts with construction costs budgeted at $65,000 to $85,000 per room.

- Quality Inns and Ramada Inns have come out with upscale products, known respectively as Quality Royale and Ramada Renaissance. In addition, Quality Inns introduced their economy motel—Comfort Inns.

- In 1985, Doubletree introduced the mid-priced Compri Hotel.

The above list is not inclusive, but it represents a five-year market-place trend. The variety of choices offered the public is likely to cause confusion, although the experimentation with market segmentation has produced identifiable winners and losers.

Hotel Management

During the 1950s a significant development occurred that altered the basic structure of the U.S. lodging industry: the formation of national chains as hotel operators. This concept has grown steadily during the past 30 years to a point where the vast majority of existing hotel rooms in the United States (estimated to be 70 + percent) have national chain affiliation, under either a franchise agreement or a management contract. The importance of having a national chain today can best be demonstrated by the fact that it is extremely difficult—not impossible, but tough!—to obtain financing (both debt and equity) without it.

National Chain, by Contract or Franchise

By Management Contract.   A management contract is a written, legal document between the hotel's owner-developer and a national hotel company (such as Sheraton, Hyatt, or Marriott) specifying the terms under which the hotel operator assumes total managerial responsibility for the hotel's operation. For this service, the hotel operator receives a fee based on a negotiated formula. The hotel owner has no say in the day-to-day decision-making process of the hotel nor in the staffing of its employees. The owner does assume all financial responsibility for the hotel, including the replacement of chattels (FF&E) as required; the provision of adequate fire and liability insurance; the payment of annual real estate taxes; and the responsibility for covering the operating losses during the initial start-up years, if necessary. The owner does actively participate in the preparation of the operating budget with the operator for the forthcoming fiscal year.

During the management contract negotiations, several issues always seem to surface between the parties: fees, responsibility, and termination. First, the hotel company's fees are a critical item. There are always two components to the contract—a base fee and an incentive fee. Other than that, there is no other uniformity among contract provisions. The fee structures vary from operator to operator, and they vary from deal to deal with the same operator—truly an issue resolved only through negotiation. Some management contracts have been signed with a base fee of 3 percent of gross revenues versus an incentive fee of 15 percent of income before fixed charges (formerly known as gross operating profit—GOP). Others have been negotiated with a base fee of 4 percent of gross revenues *plus* 20 percent of the GOP line as an incentive fee. With respect to the incentive fee, the developer is always trying to negotiate this fee as far down on the pro forma as possible, preferably basing it on a percentage of annual net cash flow (after debt service). The operator always wants the base fee predicated on the GOP line with the argument that only the operator has complete control over how much income is brought to the bottom line before fixed charges. After that, to reach the annual cash flow, expenses to be subtracted are real estate taxes, insurance, chattels, reserves, ground rent (if any), and annual debt service over which the operator has no operational control. Regardless of how the incentive fee is determined, it is normally subordinate to the debt, since the lender is in no position to understand why the operator should be paid an incentive fee when the hotel's operating results are generating insufficient income to pay the mortgage loan.

Who is the employer—the operator or the owner? With the exception of the general manager and perhaps one or two key employees (e.g., director of food and beverage), most employees are paid by the owner. Although the owners have no control over these employees, the owners are held responsible for the employees' actions.

Another important issue is the performance clause. The owner wants the ability to fire the current operator and bring in new management if hotel profits are not where, in the owner's view, they should be.

In today's market the hotel operator should have a financial commitment to the project; risk is a motivation for success. There is a movement within the lodging industry to end the days of the straight management contract, whereby the operator collected its base fee off the top and was not overly concerned about hotel profitability. Lenders prefer a deal in which the operator has a "piece of the action." The operator's financial commitment can take on many different forms, such as:

- A percentage of the ownership in the form of a joint venture with the developer
- A loan of a specified amount to the developer, to defray some of the initial operating deficits; the loan is paid back with interest out of future cash flows
- Provision of credit to the project, so that the developer may borrow against it to defray losses in the start-up years

By Franchise Agreement. A franchise agreement is a written legal document between the owner-developer of a hotel and a national hotel company (such as Holiday Inns, Hilton, or Ramada Inns). Unlike a management contract, the independent owner manages and operates the hotel on a day-to-day basis. The national chain allows the owner to use its name, logo, reservation system, national advertising, and operating manuals. For this service the owner pays the national chain an initial franchise fee plus a monthly royalty fee. Depending on the hotel company, additional fees may be charged for advertising, reservations, training, and signage. The fees vary from operator to operator, and the industry is currently experiencing a wide range of changes.

Under a franchise agreement, the owner (franchisee) is required to adhere to certain standards with respect to construction, design, operation, and maintenance. These standards are enforced through a quality control established by the national chain (franchisor). The obvious benefits to the owner are instant recognition in the marketplace and a central reservation system. For the hotel company, franchising is an inexpensive method of growth and public recognition.

In analyzing franchise labels, the underwriter's first task is to examine the experience of the owner. Since there is no professional hotel management company overseeing the hotel's operation, the owner is the operator; the project's ability to obtain financing often depends on the hotel manager's capacity to succeed.

Nonaffiliated Hotels

An independent hotel operation is a truly entrepreneurial endeavor by an independent operator; there is no national chain of affiliation, no management contract, no franchise. In general, the hotels in this category are either the small mom-and-pop motels, built during the 1950s and 1960s and gradually becoming obsolete as they are replaced by the newer chain-affiliated hotels and motels, and some of the older prestigious hotels that enjoy a significant amount of repeat business, are highly visible, have convenient locations, and offer service of superior quality, such as the Standford Court in San Francisco, The Beverly Hills Hotel, The Drake in Chicago, and The Pierre in New York. An exception to these two classifications would be the better known resort hotels: The Broadmoor in Colorado, The Pointes in Phoenix, The Kapalua Bay Hotel in Hawaii, and Hotel Del Coronado in San Diego.

An existing independent hotel with an outstanding track record can be readily financed, but a to-be-built independent is difficult to finance. At the very least, such independents must have access to a national or international reservation system.

Hotel Lenders and Financing Methods

Hotel financing in the 1980s can be categorized as complex, dynamic, challenging, and different. The uniformity that prevailed in the 1970s is gone. Each type of lender offers different types of financing. Even within the same lender classification, the variety of deals is great. In this volatile and unstable environment, the role of the mortgage banker-broker becomes more important, for the developers who attempt to keep pace with all the available financing alternatives will waste their businesses' time.

Summarized below are the major sources of financing for debt and equity, as well as the methods by which each finances hotels.

Life Insurance Companies

Life insurance companies were the dominant force in lodging industry financing until the early 1980s. Although they still play a major shorter-term financing role on existing hotels, with loan terms of from 3 to 10 years, fewer lenders will offer 15-, 20-, or even 30-year money without engaging in joint ventures with developers. Often the companies will provide 100 percent of the project costs in the form of both debt and equity dollars, and in return they will demand at least a 50 percent ownership position and a preferential return on their equity investment. They also provide second mortgages for existing hotels which are profitable and well-run. Life insurance companies prefer medium to large deals; they will not consider anything under $5 or $10 million. Although they have been reluctant to issue 24- to 36-month forward commitments on to-be-built hotels, this opinion may change.

Pension Funds (Private and Public)

In recent years, pension funds have become a major source of funds for commercial real estate including hotels. As growth in the hotel industry is high, this trend is likely to continue for the next several decades. Presently less than 3 percent of pension fund assets are invested in real estate, compared to 30 to 35 percent for the life insurance industry. Most pension fund managers see the need for portfolio diversification, so funds invested in real estate may gradually increase over the decade to 5 to 10 percent. At 10 percent, the dollar amount of pension funds committed to real estate would double that of the entire life insurance industry.

Commercial Banks

The commercial bank's role has traditionally been to provide short-term construction lending for commercial real estate, including hotels, with a strong preference for a takeout (long-term financing) in place. The loan pricing is structured as a floating rate over a specified index (e.g., the prime rate), the London Interbank offered rate (LIBOR), the T-bill rate, or the 90-day certificate of deposit (CD) rate. Depending on the competition, some banks will offer fixed-rate options and interest rate ceilings. Hotel construction loans usually carry with them 1 to 2 points of nonrefundable commitment fees.

In recent years, as the traditional long-term lenders shortened their loan terms and began requiring equity participations, the banks seized the opportunity to offer a package deal combining construction loans with floating-rate intermediate loans (miniperms) for five to seven years. Although the miniperms' rates are correlated to an index, the banks are willing to allow for accruals by fixing the "pay rate," or having a stepped-up pay rate. This new financing tool has been successful, enabling the banks to capture a growing share of the real estate financing market. However, the competition has encouraged some of the life insurance companies (particularly those with REITs) to enter the hotel construction lending business.

Savings and Loan Associations

Savings and loan associations (S&Ls) are now permitted more involvement in commercial realty lending, joint ventures, development, and syndication and have become extremely active in hotel financing. Loan structures vary greatly but are usually variable-rate mortgages, the "coupon rate" floating over the cost of funds, with the borrower paying at a fixed pay rate and accruing the difference until maturity.

S&Ls have also become a major source of construction lending for hotels. Rates typically float at 2 percent over prime, with an additional 1 to 3 points in origination fees. Some will provide takeout financing, for another 2 to 3 points in fees, whereas others want to be out of the deal as soon as the construction is done. S&Ls are strong in small- to medium-size deals. However, they also are willing to participate in large transactions, as evidenced by the $350 million commitment made in 1985 by a consortium of S&Ls to finance Marriott's New York Marquis Hotel.

Credit Companies

The nonregulated lenders have recently become more active in hotel financing, providing construction loans, with or without a takeout;

miniperm loans; and standby loans that can be rolled into a miniperm loan. Their pricing typically floats over prime or their commercial paper rate, from as little as 1 percent to as high as 3 to 4 percent over prime. Nonrefundable fees vary from ½ point to 2 points. Their standby loans are considered sound or "bankable" and enable the developer to obtain construction money to build the hotel. Most credit companies' fees are usually 2 points for the first 12 to 18 months, and 1 point for every 6 to 9 months thereafter. Since many banks are reluctant to give uncovered construction loans for hotels, a credit company's standby loan is attractive to some developers. When the hotel opens or when it achieves a track record in the marketplace, the developer will roll over the project's debt with the life companies to obtain a 10-year fixed-rate bullet loan. Credit companies also provide second mortgages and wraparound loans.

Syndicators

Syndicators became the major source of equity financing for hotels in the 1980s, thanks to the tax shelter attributes of hotel development. This is because the hotel industry has shorter depreciation periods for FF&E, with a greater appreciation potential during the period after start-up (years 7 through 10). However, these tax attributes attracted more money than understanding, so much of the equity raised as joint venture capital was overvalued. This has created concern about an unhealthy situation in the real estate market, including overspeculation and crisis, which was resolved in part by the reduced fervor caused by the 1986 tax changes.

Distinctive Aspects of Hotel Underwriting

Hotel underwriting is as different from other types of real estate underwriting as hotels are from other types of income property. Below are several pointers for hotel underwriting.

1. Lenders have always charged higher rates for hotels to compensate for the increased risk involved in financing them.

2. Because of the risks associated with hotel deals, lenders used a higher debt service coverage factor in determining their loan amounts. Typically in 1986, on existing hotels with fixed-rate bullet financing, the debt service coverage (DSC) requirement is between 1.20 and 1.25. Given the following equation used to determine loan amounts,

$$\text{Loan amount} = \frac{\text{net operating income}}{(\text{debt service coverage}) \, (\text{mortgage constant})}$$

hotels with the same net operating income (NOI) as an office building will be financed with a lower loan amount and therefore require more equity. Both the DSC factor and the pricing factor are in the denominator of the equation. These two factors for any given lender are higher for hotels than they are for other property types.

3. Since hotels do not reach their stabilized operating ratios until the third or fourth year of operation, sophisticated hotel lenders use the third year's "numbers" for loan determination purposes.

4. Hotels have a higher stabilized vacancy factor than any other income-producing property type. It is the only property type that does not try to maximize its occupancy level at 100 percent or as close to 100 percent as possible. Ironically, a hotel which consistently operates at 90 + percent occupancy year after year does not maximize profit, experiences wear and tear on the physical plant, and provides less than good guest service. Such an operator should raise the room rates (since room revenue is extremely lucrative) until occupancy slips back down to the 84 to 86 percent level. For underwriting purposes, lenders use a hypothetical stabilized 75 percent occupancy level, which is 5 percent more than the typical 70 percent stabilization level of a decade ago. This increase was needed in order for deals to "pencil out," as structuring loans based on 75 percent occupancy, even if comparable hotels in the market area are consistently experiencing 80 + percent occupancy.

5. Since hotels are underwritten on the third operating year's numbers, and since approximately two years are needed to build a 500-room full service hotel, the average daily room rates (ADRs) for the proposed hotel may have to be projected as much as five years in the future.

6. Hotels are unique in that they have a heavy capital investment in chattels (furniture, fixtures, and equipment). These items must be replaced on a regular basis in order for the hotel to maintain its image and remain competitive in the marketplace. When making 10-year financial projections on a hotel operation, a chattel reserve allowance must be included before arriving at the annual projected NOIs.

In analyzing a hotel's financial projections, lenders will accept the following criteria for chattel reserves: first year—1 percent of total gross revenues; second year—2 percent of total gross revenues; third year and each year thereafter—3 percent of total gross revenues. Some lenders and hotel operators will require the hotel owner-developer to establish an annual active sinking fund account for chattel replacements.

Other lenders feel comfortable with the "deep pockets" of the borrower and will not require a reserve account but will monitor the property through inspections to ensure that it is properly maintained.. All lenders require a first lien position on chattels. A hotel without its FF&E is like a hospital without beds. This keeps the lender informed of all changes (or lack thereof), and in the unlikely event of foreclosure, the borrower will not be able to walk off with the chattels.

7. There is no one standard solution for the industry's common problem. Hotel lenders are concerned about the operating deficits during the hotel's first two to three years of performance and how the borrower is going to make the debt service payments during this period. Some lenders may require the borrower to post a letter of credit to cover the shortfalls in order to protect themselves. Other structure the deal with a floor-ceiling loan amount arrangement in order to minimize their exposure. Still others require that the borrower obtain gap financing or bring in equity partners.

8. Although hotels are not the only property type that requires an independent feasibility study to attract debt and equity financing, such studies are commonplace and useful as decision-making tools for all parties concerned: developer, mortgage banker, and lender. Since the developer pays for the report, there is the misconception that negative attributes or aspects are seldom included. Quite the contrary: A senior partner from a large accounting and hotel consulting firm has stated that over 50 percent of their assignments end with a negative feasibility report. However, because the negative factors generally become apparent early in the analysis, a meeting is set up with the developer, a decision is reached not to proceed, and the report never goes to print. Invaluable information can be obtained from these studies, however, and the quality of the content has improved dramatically over the past 10 years.

Hotel Pro Forma

All hotel financial statements are categorized in accordance with the Uniform System of Accounts for Hotels. This system, which was established by the Hotel Association of New York City in 1926 and later adopted by the American Hotel and Motel Association, provides a simple line item summary for classifying the accounts used by lodging facilities of all types and sizes.

Table 18.2 is a typical pro forma for a hotel, showing representative

Table 18.2. First-Class Hotel

	Amount (thousands of dollars)	Ratio (%)
Revenues		
Rooms	15,841	56.2
Food	7,779	27.6
Beverage	3,509	12.4
Telephone	640	2.3
Other operated departments	141	0.5
Rentals and other income	274	1.0
Total revenues	28,184	100.0
Departmental costs and expenses		
Rooms	3,960	14.0
Food and beverage	8,819	31.3
Telephone	608	2.1
Other operated departments	106	0.4
Total costs and expenses	13,493	47.8
Total operated departmental income	14,691	52.2
Undistributed operating expenses		
Administrative and general	1,692	6.0
Management fees	846	3.0
Marketing	1,015	3.6
Property operation and maintenance	1,035	3.7
Energy	1,185	4.2
Total undistributed expenses	5,773	20.5
Income before fixed charges	8,918	31.7
Fixed charges		
Real estate and property taxes	631	2.2
Insurance on building and contents	56	0.2
Replacement of fixed assets	846	3.0
Total fixed charges	1,533	5.4
Income before other fixed charges (net operating income)	7,385	26.3

dollar amounts and operating ratios for a first-class, full-service facility. Here are key operating ratios in analyzing a hotel's financial statement:

- The percentage of room revenue to total gross revenue for a full-service hotel generally falls between 50 and 65 percent. The combined total of room revenue and food and beverage usually is between 93 and 97 percent of the total gross revenues.

- The percentage of income before fixed charges (formerly known as gross operating profit) should fall between 30 and 35 percent.

- The percentage of income before other fixed charges (NOI) is typically 25 to 29 percent (i.e., net-to-gross ratio). Since the rooms department is extremely lucrative (for every $1 the hotel generates in room revenue, the operator can typically bring 75 to 80 cents to the bottom line on a departmental profit basis), the higher the room revenue is to total gross revenue, the higher the net-to-gross ratio can be demonstrated to the lender. For example, since cheaper motels have very little food and beverage revenue, the percentage of room revenue to total gross usually represents greater than 90 percent of total revenues. Hence, the GOP line for these properties is normally 48 to 51 percent and the net/gross ratio is 43 to 46 percent.

Hotel Underwriting Made Easy

The following example is a simplified five-step approach to hotel underwriting, based on an actual hotel project. It is intended to enable the underwriter to determine the approximate loan amount that can be generated in the marketplace, to determine whether the numbers support what the developer needs to build the project. It is not intended to be a format to be used in a formal, written presentation to a lender.

1. *Determine the stabilized average daily room rate (ADR) for the proposed hotel based on operating years—not on calendar years.* The rack rates of the competition in the subject's market area can be obtained by calling the front desk of the hotels and asking for them. However, because of widespread discounting (for corporations, groups, or other regular customer segments) the average daily rate (ADR) is actually quite difficult to find, since discounting is confidential information. The ADR also acknowledges the market mix that the hotel is experiencing. The following are some sources that have this information:

- The management of comparable hotels seldom reveal this information, but they might wish to pass along deceptive figures. If the hotel's employees are interviewed, the night manager (not the general manager), who is often inexperienced, might slip up and provide some accurate information.

- Lending industry contacts often may share data. For example, the lenders for the hotel properties receive annual financial statements and know the ADRs for their loans. Other operators know, so if the comparable is a Marriott and someone is available as a source at Marriott, comparable numbers can be computed.

- The hotel accounting firms know their clients' statistics as well as comparables for an area. Most likely these are the same firms that provided the feasibility for the subject property. Due to the client confidentiality relationship, this information cannot be passed along on a specific basis. However, they can provide you with the composite ADRs for three or four comparable hotels, which may be just as good as knowing one individual hotel.

As an example, assume that the 1985 results for the competition showed a composite ADR of $63.83. Therefore, at a 6 percent annual inflation rate, this would imply the following projected ADRs (rounded to the nearest 5 cents):

1985: $63.83

1986: $67.75

1987: $71.70 (commence construction in April)

1988: $76.00

1989: $80.55 (hotel opens in April)

1990: $85.40

1991: $90.50 (third calendar year)

However, the $90.50 ADR will not generate the maximum loan for the developer. To do so, first convert the ADRs from calendar years to operational years—which is always different for a proposed hotel, unless it is scheduled to open January 1. In the example, the first operational year has nine months in 1989 and three months in 1990. Hence the ADR for the hotel's first full operating year is:

$$0.75 \times \$80.55 = \$60.41$$
$$0.25 \times \$85.40 = \underline{21.35}$$
$$\overline{\$81.76}$$

Say, $81.75. A 6 percent inflationary factor to determine the third year's stabilized ADR will yield the following:

Year 1: $81.75

Year 2: $86.65

Year 3: $91.85 (not $90.50)

2. *Determine the total gross room revenue.*

      Gross room revenue = Number of hotel rooms × stabilized
                        ADR × stabilized occupancy × 365
                        days/year

     Assume the hotel has 365 rooms, then the

      Gross room revenue = 365 rooms × $91.85 × 0.75 × 365
                      days/year = $9,177,535

3. *Obtain the stabilized percentage of room revenue to total gross revenue.* This is the only ratio not available from the marketplace. No two hotels have the same ratio, even if they are next to each other and have the same number of rooms, since no two hotels are exactly alike. The composition of this ratio depends on too many variables, such as the number of restaurants, or the seating capacity of the restaurants, or the square footage of meeting space, or the size of the ballroom, or whether there is a lobby bar, or whether there is 24-hour room service. Hence, the most likely place to obtain this ratio is from financial projections of the hotel operator or the consultant who completed the feasibility study. In the earlier example, assume that this ratio stabilized at 60.65 percent. Therefore, if the total gross room revenue determined above was $9,177,535, then,

$$\text{Total gross revenue} = \frac{\$9,177,535}{0.6065}$$
$$= \$15,131,960$$

4. *Determine the net operating income by using net-gross ratios that are acceptable to the lending community.* Assume that a 25 percent rate is prevalent. Therefore,

$$\text{Stabilized NOI} = \$15,131,960 \times 0.25$$
$$= \$3,782,990$$

5. *Calculate the loan amount based on the lender's current underwriting criteria regarding pricing and debt service coverage requirements.* Assume that a pension fund is willing to lend a participating mortgage at 11 percent, 35 years. Also assume it will accept hotel deals at 1.30 debt service coverage:

$$\text{Loan amount} = \frac{\text{net operating income}}{(\text{debt service coverage}) (\text{mortgage constant})}$$
$$= \frac{\$3,782,990}{(1.3) (0.11)}$$
$$= \$26,454,476$$

Say, $26,450,000. The loan amount would be $26,450,000.

The hotel is a specialized and unique form of income-producing property which has been regarded by developers, investors, and lenders as complex and risky. However, when specific underwriting guidelines are followed carefully, financing hotels and motels can prove to be very profitable.

19
Industrial Properties

Robert F. Plymate, CMB
Houston, Texas

General Information

Industrial properties are a highly specialized type of real estate. They include warehouses, industrial parks, certain research and development facilities, and buildings used for industrial production.

An invaluable aid to any mortgage loan underwriting process is the development of a checklist. In using an industrial property checklist, be sure to update the list continually. An example of an industrial property checklist, with general categories to which the lender should give attention, is included at the end of this chapter.

Types of industrial buildings would certainly include manufacturing of all kinds, as well as public warehousing facilities, printing and publishing plants, and storage and distribution facilities for foods and beverages. The transportation industry also uses maintenance facilities and, in some cases, actual terminal space.

A relatively new type of industrial building is the light industrial, also referred to as a "high-tech building." These structures contain a combination of research and development, office, showrooms, and distribution areas.

Location

In the Surrounding Area

In the underwriting process of industrial building loans, the primary consideration is physical location. Location is more than the building site, for it includes the geographic location of the industrial area. This is one of the most critical aspects of the initial underwriting process. Pay particular attention to the types of operations that are already in the area. If the subject property does not conform, or if the industrial park or area is not anchored by a regional or national operation, then the underwriting will concentrate on the financial ability of the borrower-developer, as well as the tenant.

In discussing location, an item not to be overlooked is the general aspect of access and visibility of the industrial park or area. Interstate highway access, as well as local feeder routes, is very important to the success of the park. Rail availability, although not as important to the light industrial or high-tech operations, should be a major concern.

The proximity to the local labor supply and to related industries is another factor to be considered in the analysis of location. High on the list of any industrial building user is the availability of an adequate labor force in the general area. With this in mind, the tenant and borrower should note the nearness of public transportation, if any, and the planned or existing parking areas. The high-tech building user generally is interested in the educational facilities within driving distance of the industrial park.

Within the Industrial Park

Second in importance to the location of the industrial park is the location of the subject building within the park. Depending on the intended use of the subject building, the site is particularly critical. The size and configuration, as well as the access within the park, should be given careful consideration. The building will have to conform to the general restrictions and requirements of the planned industrial district.

Zoning and Development Controls

The use of and compliance with restrictions and zoning controls such as setbacks, architectural design, and landscaping are very important. The more restrictive of these covenants generally falls into the area of ecological concerns. Equally important is the local governing authority's overall philosophy as far as industrial development is concerned. The taxing entities can certainly be a determining factor in the progress of any area of industrial development.

Building Design and Construction

The third consideration is the design and construction specifications of the subject building. These specifications will vary from one geographical location to another, as well as within the particular industrial park. As an example, the requirements for heating, ventilating, and air conditioning (HVAC) in Rochester, New York, will be considerably different from those in Brownsville, Texas. The insulation and the roofing materials are also greatly affected by the differences in climate. Industrial buildings generally fall into three categories:

1. *General purpose.* This category mainly describes the building that is constructed on a speculative basis—speculative in that there is no specific user at the time of construction. The building is designed to accommodate a broad range of tenants from simple storage to assembly and light manufacturing operations.

2. *Single purpose.* As the name implies, the building is designed for a particular purpose and would not be easily adapted to any other use. As a rule, these buildings are built from the user's plans and specifications.

3. *Special purpose.* These buildings are generally designed to accommodate a particular tenant; however, the adaptability to all types of product handling and storage is possible. In general, these buildings can be physically altered at a minimum cost. This is desirable in the event the tenant falls on hard times. A good example of this is the use of knock-out loading door sections along the loading dock wall.

Builder-Developer's Past Record

After consideration of the physical and geographical characteristics of the industrial park in general and of the subject site and the subject building in particular, comes the all-important issue of the builder-developer's track record. This aspect of underwriting is vitally important in any real estate development project, despite a tendency to downplay this factor in so-called warehouse building. The industrial builder-developer must be as experienced and as well-informed as any other. The knowledge of the market and the ability to lease and promote the subject property is an absolute must.

A thorough check of the builder-developer's projects, both past and under construction, must be made. Present banking relationships must be investigated, and all financial information verified.

Another factor to check carefully is the relationship between the builder-developer and the local governing bodies. The taxing authority and its eventual impact on the whole industrial activity in the area (as well as on the subject property) cannot be overemphasized.

Leasing Considerations

As in any property that is to be leased, close consideration must be given to the relationship between the physical layout of the building and the provisions in the lease itself. For example, in a multitenant industrial building, the exact statements as to tenant responsibilities should be clear and concise. The term for a multitenant lease is normally no longer than five years and should contain provisions for expense stops.

Building Management

The overall management of the industrial building, either single-tenant or multitenant, is extremely critical. Unless the borrower-developer is large enough to have in-house management and leasing capabilities, outside firms should be engaged. Any outside firm should be checked as to experience and reliability.

Regardless of the manner in which management and leasing is carried out, the two functions must interact. The leasing of the space is primarily a selling or merchandising activity, and the management consists of the maintenance work and collection of the rents. Although the two are separate, they should work very closely with each other.

Types of Leases

There are four general types of industrial leases in use today:

1. *Straight lease.* This lease is used in the case of an improvement that is existing or to be built as a general purpose building.

2. *Built-to-suit lease.*   Under this arrangement, the builder-developer executes an agreement that outlines the physical aspects of the building dictated by the tenant—generally, a special purpose building.

3. *Sale-leaseback.*   This lease outlines the conditions under which a third party or the tenant will buy the property at a given time for a given price sometime in the future.

4. *Leased ground.*   The tenant leases the improvements and the lease is subject to a long-term ground lease. The ground rent is an obligation of the lessor on the improvements.

Redevelopment

As land values and costs in general have escalated, especially in the planned industrial parks, more attention has been given to redeveloped land. Redevelopment has generally occurred in the older, centrally located industrial areas within a city. Although the surrounding improvements may not be as attractive in suburban locations, one of the major attractions is the availability of the nearby labor supply. Urban renewal programs have aided in the redevelopment of this kind of location. All the industrial loan underwriting criteria should apply on these projects, and particular emphasis should be given to the creditworthiness of the tenant and/or borrower.

Tenant Creditworthiness and Responsibilities

As a general rule, the financial strength of the borrower is of primary consideration in any mortgage loan transaction; however, in the loan underwriting process on industrial buildings, the tenant's creditworthiness is also very important. This is especially true in the case of a single-tenant building. Very often the assignment of the lease and rentals from a Triple A tenant will allow a lender to consider a loan of a larger size than would be practical if the only credit was from the builder-developer. Because of the reliance of the lease itself, in this illustration it should be obvious that all aspects of the lease—from the actual dollar rental to who pays for what—should be clearly set out in the lease. As an example: Who pays for major repairs and expenses? The one major item of expense on any industrial building is the roof. Structural maintenance, as well as exterior and interior expenses, are of primary importance, and who is responsible for each item should be clearly defined in the lease.

Industrial Properties
Checklist

Figure 19.1 is an industrial properties checklist. It includes only those aspects that are peculiar to an industrial-type project. In addition, all the general underwriting techniques covered in the text should be used in the analysis.

Figure 19.1. Industrial properties checklist.

  I. Market Analysis
   A. Demand factors
     1. Competition
     2. Size of market area
     3. Availability of land
     4. Local governmental attitudes
     5. Costs
 II. Location Analysis
   A. Supply factors
     1. Future land requirements
     2. Uses—present and future
   B. Location factors
     1. Highway access
     2. Labor supply
     3. Rail availability
     4. Utilities
     5. Nearby educational facilities
     6. Size of industrial area
III. Specific Site Analysis
   A. Type of area
     1. Planned industrial park
     2. Suburban location
     3. Redeveloped land
   B. Site configuration
     1. Land-to-building ratio
     2. Access within the park
   C. Use restrictions
     1. Zoning
     2. Local government
   D. Utilities to site
IV. Building Analysis
   A. General types (described herein)
     1. Special purpose
     2. General purpose
     3. Single purpose
   B. Specifications
     1. Roof

(Continued)

Figure 19.1. Industrial properties checklist. (*Continued*)

```
        2. Clear span
        3. Floor loads
        4. Loading docks
        5. Loading doors
        6. Office space
        7. Utilities
        8. Sprinkler system
        9. General floor plan
 V. Developer Analysis
    A. Financial condition
    B. Track record
        1. Projects in progress
        2. Projects completed
    C. Management
        1. Developer's involvement
        2. Contracted management
        3. Outside leasing
    D. Leases
        1. Terms
        2. Expense stops
        3. Maintenance responsibilities
```

20
Nursing Home and Retirement Housing Facilities

Stephen F. Wood, CMB

President, Woodmark, Inc., Brentwood, Tennessee

Every day, some 5500 Americans celebrate their sixty-fifth birthdays. Twenty-eight million people—11 percent of the U.S. population—are over 65, and the proportion of senior citizens is expected to double over the next 40 years. The "graying of America" comes in the midst of other social changes. Because families are smaller and more mobile, and houses less roomy and more expensive than a generation ago, often aging parents cannot live with grown children. Many spouses have jobs or careers and cannot stay at home to care for aging parents or in-laws. The aging also have more financial independence because of pension and retirement plans, more liberal social security payments, and the fact that inflation may have significantly increased the value of their fixed assets, such as their homes.

The U.S. Bureau of the Census estimates that real population growth from 1980 to 2000 will average 16.5 percent. The 75 to 84 age group, however, will increase at a rate of 47.9 percent, and the 85 + age group will increase by 60.9 percent. Although medical science is extending the average life span, it has not resolved all the ills that are associated with aging. There has been a consequent demand for various forms of housing that include medical care facilities.

Facilities for housing and caring for the elderly can be categorized broadly into two groups: nursing homes and retirement housing facilities. Because of skilled medical services provided to patients, operations of nursing homes must be licensed. Retirement or congregate housing (also called retirement centers or elderly housing facilities) provides various levels of care not requiring medical supervision and must meet strict code requirements, but licensing usually is not required.

Nursing Home Operations

Types of Care

Nursing homes vary widely in their operations depending on the types of services provided for patients. In general, they provide two levels of care—intermediate and skilled.

1. *Intermediate-care facilities.* These facilities provide for the daily needs of infirm patients, including the availability of nursing services when required, dispensing of medications, dietary service, assistance with social services, and physical therapy. The market for such services is primarily the elderly—generally those over age 75—who may be afflicted with the normal maladies of the elderly but are not considered totally infirm. They may be ambulatory or require the assistance of walkers or wheelchairs. Most are not totally bedridden and require some social interaction with others. Most are considered long-term patients since, once admitted, they usually remain in the facility until they die or become so ill that they require the acute care of a hospital.

2. *Skilled-care facilities.* These facilities provide a higher level of nursing care for patients who are, generally, bedridden and may require such sophisticated services involving respirators, catheters, or other tools which monitor bodily functions. Such patients may be elderly and/or may have been previously hospitalized and need convalescent care before returning to their home environment. A skilled-care patient typically will not stay for as long as an intermediate-care patient, and the costs of maintaining a skilled-care patient are greater.

State licensing requirements usually dictate the nature and extent of a facility's intermediate or skilled care. In some states, a dual certification is provided so that the facility is licensed to provide either level of care, depending on the patient's needs. In some facilities, one wing or a certain group of beds in the facility will be dedicated to skilled-care patients, and the remainder of the facility may provide services only at the intermediate level.

A third level of care sometimes found in nursing homes is known as "personal care" or "custodial care." This service may consist of a number of rooms which are not actually licensed for nursing care but are available to provide assisted living and custodial care for those elderly and infirm patients who do not require specific medical or nursing care, but who nevertheless require assistance from the nonmedical staff in day-to-day living. Such custodial services also may be found in the various types of retirement housing facilities, where restrictive licensing generally is not required.

Sources of Income

Nursing home operations generally account for income on a daily basis, utilizing daily rates for their various types of services. Funding for the patients' daily services may come from the patients' private resources ("private pay patients") or from various government programs. Private insurance also is beginning to cover long-term care; a small number of patients may have resources derived from private insurance companies.

Three current government programs which pay for nursing home costs are Medicaid, Medicare, and Veterans Administration (VA) benefits.

1. *Medicaid.* Medicaid is funded on a joint federal and state basis but is administered by the states. For this reason, the Medicaid program varies significantly from one state to another—an important factor in underwriting loans on nursing home facilities. Medicaid assistance is available only to indigent patients—those who have exhausted their personal assets and do not have sufficient income to pay for their care. In general, Medicaid payments by the state are provided on a retrospective basis, that is, the nursing home providers are reimbursed according to some formula based on their actual cost of providing the services, plus a specified profit or return on investment. Such reimbursements usually provide for a maximum daily rate based on the average cost in the area. Some states provide incentives for efficient operators by allowing a greater profit margin for those who are most cost efficient. Frequently, patients entering the facility as private pay patients will ultimately exhaust their resources and convert to a Medicaid patient. Medicaid payments may provide for those requiring either intermediate or skilled care, with the formula for reimbursement of each depending on the particular state in which the facility is located. For the purposes of fi-

nancial reporting, Medicaid patients are billed at the private pay rate, although Medicaid reimburses only a portion of the charges (thus the debit item "contractual adjustment for Medicaid" is often found on the statement). Medicaid is the broadest form of government-provided payments to the nursing home industry.

2. *Medicare.* Medicare is part of the Social Security program and is, therefore, available to anyone eligible for Social Security benefits regardless of alternative financial resources. Medicare was developed primarily to provide acute medical care rather than long-term nursing care. Patients receiving Medicare reimbursement, therefore, must be transferred to the nursing facility from a hospital, and the patients then are limited to a certain number of days of convalescent care in the nursing facility before the Medicare payments are exhausted. Because the patients must be admitted directly from a hospital, Medicare patients usually require the services of a skilled-care facility rather than intermediate care.

3. *Veterans Administration.* The VA contracts with some nursing homes to admit VA nursing home patients for a set daily rate which includes all services necessary for the particular patient, such as medicines and laundry. Nursing homes which admit VA patients will usually screen such patients to ensure that the nature of services required by the patient will not cost more than the flat daily rate provided by the VA.

Another source of income for most nursing homes is classified as ancillary income and includes any income from patient services which is not normally included in the daily rate. This might include charges for special services such as physical therapy or other counseling; billing for personal laundry services; and revenue from vending and snacks, guest meals, and pharmacy.

Loan Underwriting Considerations for Nursing Homes

Because of the management-intensive nature of nursing homes, the underwriter must examine not only the real estate but also the business management aspects of the project.

Location. Although most types of real estate require a location offering high visibility, ease of access, and proximity to population centers, these are not necessarily the most important considerations for a nursing home loan. A nursing home does not require a highly visible location and need not be located on a major thoroughfare. Rather, the environment can be pleasant and quiet; often a residential neighborhood is preferred. A nursing home is usually located near at least one hospital, and a transfer agreement usually exists between the nursing home and the nearby hospital for ease of entry of patients from the nursing home to the hospital, as well as discharges from the hospital to the nursing home when appropriate. Also, doctors prefer to have patients near their hospital for the convenience of visiting such patients while in the neighborhood. Although physician referrals may not be as crucial to nursing homes as they are in hospitals, they are certainly an important factor. Appropriate favorable relationships should be fostered and maintained between the nursing home management and the medical community.

Design. The design of a facility reflects the nature of the services to be provided and, particularly important, the type of patient that may be attracted to the facility. A quality facility with a large percentage of private rooms along with such amenities as carpeting, decorator furniture, and landscaping is likely to attract a goodly proportion of private pay patients.

In a suburban or low-density area, a nursing home normally is a one-story structure consisting of one or more wings with central corridors branching from a highly visible nursing station. Normally, one nursing station can accommodate 50 to 60 beds, but it is important that all corridor areas serving such rooms be within sight of the nursing station. Total floor area, including common area, usually averages 250 to 300 square feet per bed. On-site parking for employees, along with adequate visitor parking and physician parking, is sufficient. Safety is extremely important in nursing home design and is supervised by the licensing authorities.

Management. Because operation of the facility is highly management-intensive, the experience and qualifications of the management usually represent the most important factor in underwriting a nursing home loan. Single-facility ownership and multifacility, or chain ownership, are common. Each has advantages and disadvantages.

In general, single-facility management indicates an owner-managed facility. There is frequently a genuine and deep commitment on the part of the owner-managers to provide the best possible care for their residents, often including a personal pride that might not be evident in multifacility management operation. Analysis of owner-managed facilities reveals, however, that staffing usually is greater than required for efficient operation and that the cost of purchases and supplies is greater than in multifacility operations. Such cost inefficiencies may be offset, though, by the absence of an independent management fee charged to support the corporate overhead of a multifacility operation.

Multifacility operations may be classified either as chain (group) operations containing a number of nursing homes under a single ownership or as nursing homes under individual ownership which are leased to or are under long-term management contract to experienced multifacility operators. Usually, there is security in dealing with an established chain staffed with experienced corporate personnel who have a successful track record in nursing home acquisition, development, and management. Also, certain efficiencies of scale in purchasing, training, and bookkeeping derive from chain operation.

Valuation.   As with other types of real estate, the underwriting of a nursing home requires a detailed appraisal of the facility best accomplished by someone experienced in nursing homes. An appraiser who is not familiar with the nursing home industry is not likely to be familiar with all the nuances—objective and subjective—for valuation of a nursing home project.

Because of the significance of management to a nursing home, the cost approach does *not* necessarily set the upper limit of value. There is a considerable expense in the initial staffing, rent-up, and marketing of a facility that may be included in the cost approach. Additional value also may result from the limitation of new facilities in most jurisdictions by the certificate of need process, which creates a virtual franchise by the jurisdiction to a particular facility.

Consequently, the income approach and the related market approach may be preferable in setting the valuation of a nursing home. Typically, nursing homes are valued on a per-bed basis, but this valuation may vary significantly from location to location and with the nature of operations. An intermediate-care facility, for example, located in a small town and catering primarily to Medicaid patients, may be profitable but may be valued at a considerable lower amount per bed than an upscale facility in a major metropolitan area which caters exclusively or primarily to the private pay market. Market comparisons, therefore, should include details of the nature of the operations. In addition to per-bed comparison, gross income multipliers also might be compared.

Land value usually is a relatively insignificant portion of the overall value of a nursing home. Many nursing homes are located in less-traveled areas or in semirural areas where land values are quite low, but the locations still are satisfactory for use as nursing homes.

As for other types of real estate investments, the net operating income (NOI) is the key figure—the remaining cash flow available to service the proposed debt on the property after all other cash expenses and reserves. In the case of a nursing home, a reasonable vacancy allowance is appropriate, depending on the experience in the area with the particular facility (or with competing facilities in the area). Despite the presence of waiting lists, because of reasonably high turnover which may occur in nursing homes, a vacancy factor of at least 5 percent generally is imputed by prudent lenders. Expenses used in determining the NOI should include a liberal reserve for replacements and supplies. A professional management fee in the range of 5 percent to 7 percent of gross receipts should be imputed in the expense category even if the facility is owner-managed, since professional management could become necessary in the event of default. As a rule of thumb, most nursing home operations at full occupancy will have operating expenses ranging between 70 percent and 80 percent of gross income.

In analyzing the loan, most lenders will require that the projected net operating income cover the initial debt service requirements by as much as 1.3 to 1.5 times. Although this coverage ratio is higher than that generally required in other real estate investments, a nursing home generally trades at a higher capitalization rate because of the intensity of management required.

Loan Security Considerations. In addition to a mortgage on the real estate involved, the lender on a nursing home operation should also have a security interest in all nonrealty: furniture, fixtures, and equipment (FF&E). This includes extensive kitchen equipment as well as patient room furniture, common area furniture, and office equipment. Such fixtures and equipment comprise a significant portion of the initial cost of the facility and, of course, are essential to its operation. The usual Uniform Commercial Code financing statements (UCC-1) are applicable for nursing home personalty.

If the property is leased to an operator, the lender should receive a conditional assignment of the lease and examine the credentials of the lessee. A due-on-sale clause in the mortgage provides the lender with some measure of control over who manages the facility. Consideration should also be given to a specific acceleration clause in the loan instrument, in the event of a change in the management entity without the lender's prior approval, whether or not a sale of contract is involved. If the loan is underwritten on the strength of a management contract with an established, well-regarded operator, any change must be approved by the lender.

Management contracts with related or unrelated parties are common in the nursing home industry. In cases where the management fee is paid to an entity related to the ownership, the management entity is frequently required to subordinate all or a portion of its management fee to the debt service.

To monitor nursing home operations, operating statements must be submitted to the lender at least annually, perhaps more often in the early stages of operation. These statements should be analyzed carefully and compared with prior years' statements, as well as with other nursing home operations, with particular attention to such items as overall occupancy levels, percentage of private pay versus government-assisted patients, changes in daily rate schedules, and inordinate increases in any expense categories. Such data are essential for spotting adverse trends that may need to be addressed, because, although real estate secures the loan, the business is highly dependent on cash flow management. Such statements also can be very helpful reference material in the underwriting of future nursing home loan applications.

Other Underwriting Considerations. The management of nursing home services provides income more than the inherent value of the real estate itself. Because the management of the facilities is so critical, most lenders require personal guarantees of individuals or small partnerships who own nursing homes. Chain facilities generally provide significant corporate guarantees, either on the mortgage note directly or by way of a lease of the facility from an investor group.

Nursing homes are required to be licensed in their appropriate jurisdiction, and such licensing generally carries with it some level of monitoring by the licensing authorities. Most states require that a developer be granted a certificate of need (CON) before construction of a new or expanded facility may begin. The application for a CON must include a great deal of demographic data demonstrating the absolute need of additional beds in the appropriate jurisdiction, and the commission which grants the certificate has absolute control over the amount of new beds that may be constructed as well as which applicant may be granted a CON for new construction. Because a large proportion of nursing home beds are funded through Medicaid, and the Medicaid program is administered by and partially funded by the states, one measure of cost containment of Medicaid expenses is simply to limit the number of beds available. This is accomplished through very restrictive requirements for the granting of new CONs. In effect, therefore, competition among nursing homes is severely limited by regulation in most states. If significant vacancies exist in the marketplace, a new CON will not be easily granted. This virtually ensures, over the long term, a reasonably high occupancy level of all properly managed nursing homes in such jurisdictions. The fact that the nursing home market is regulated is a very significant factor in the underwriting of loans, particularly when compared to other types of income property lending, where success breeds strong competition.

Funding Sources for Nursing Home Loans

Funds are available for financing nursing homes on both a conventional and a HUD-insured basis. The HUD programs require more processing time and are available only for new construction projects. The HUD insurance protects the lender and may make the loan available for refinancing through mortgage-backed securities. The HUD insurance also may provide the necessary credit enhancement for marketing tax-exempt or taxable bond issues for the financing.

Conventional financing of nursing homes is available from various institutional investors, including a number of life insurance companies, thrifts, and real estate investment trusts (REITs). Many institutions, however, refrain from investing in nursing homes because of the specialized nature of the operations.

Retirement Housing Facility Operations

Retirement housing facilities generally provide fewer services than nursing homes. Some facilities may dedicate themselves totally to one specific market niche, and others may attempt to provide a continuum of care for residents ranging from the active retirement type to those requiring custodial care or even nursing care where such licensing is available. There are three categories of retirement housing: personal-care facilities, congregate-care facilities, and retirement apartments.

1. *Personal-care facilities.* Sometimes known as custodial-care or residential-care facilities or homes for the aged, these facilities may be part of nursing homes or may be independent operations. Residents

generally reside in a bedroom which may be private or semiprivate in nature, with an adjoining bath. They are ambulatory (with or without assistance) and do not require continuous medical treatment or care but do need help with grooming, diet, exercise therapy, or similar services. Their rooms do not contain kitchen facilities; meals may be served in a central dining room or brought to the patient's room. Rate structure is customarily on a per diem basis.

2. *Congregate care facilities.*   Also called "adult congregate living facilities," these generally provide a protective environment for moderately active retired persons. Residents live in apartments which may be studio, one-bedroom, or two-bedroom units with private baths. Some units may be furnished with small kitchens; usually a small refrigerator and microwave oven is sufficient and reduces the risk of cooking accidents. The rent usually includes at least one meal per day, provided from a central dietary source, which may be taken in the main dining room or delivered to the resident's room. The residents may use their own furniture and maintain a fairly independent daily routine. Transportation is provided for residents to attend such functions as church services, shopping trips, and entertainment events. Rate structure is monthly, and nursing or other medical services, although not routinely included, are available on a call or as-needed basis. Apartments typically will include emergency call systems with 24-hour monitoring, all handicap facilities, and periodic "checking up" on the resident by the staff to make sure everything is in order.

3. *Retirement living apartments.*   Also known as elderly housing, these facilities are marketed to a broad range of retirement-age individuals. Such apartments usually include handicap facilities, and they may also provide amenities such as swimming pools, shuffle board, and various other recreational facilities for the residents. Residents maintain a relatively independent lifestyle with an added measure of security and freedom from maintenance responsibilities. Such facilities may be marketed on a rental or condominium basis and usually include one- and two-bedroom apartments with complete kitchens with optional on-site dietary service available.

As with nursing homes, the ownership and management structure of any such facility must be examined carefully to determine the qualifications and the experience of the management. In the case of existing facilities, where ongoing operations may be observed, trends from past operations can be projected. Care should be taken, however, not to assume that past high occupancy levels can be maintained. Since there is a relative ease of entry into this area, as compared to nursing homes where certificates of need are required, new and competitive facilities may be built in many markets, adversely affecting the occupancy rate of existing operations.

Continuing-Care Living Facilities

The financing for a continuing care living facility (CCLF) is somewhat special. A CCLF typically includes all the elements outlined above (retirement apartments, congregate-care facilities, and personal-care facilities) along with intermediate-care and, often, skilled-nursing facilities. The concept behind CCLF is to provide a living environment for the remainder of the inhabitant's years with assurance that the necessary services will be available, regardless of the infirmities of age. Theoretically, an individual or couple may enter the CCLF through a retirement apartment and progress, as necessary, through the congregate care area, to the personal care area, and ultimately, if necessary, to the skilled nursing facility. The CCLF concept is appealing to the market not only for its "completeness" but also because married couples may enter with the assurance of remaining in close proximity even if one member of the couple should become ill or incapacitated.

A typical continuing-care community may contain 200 to 250 congregate and independent retirement living apartments, coupled with 20 personal care or custodial care units, and perhaps, a 60-bed skilled- and intermediate-care nursing facility. All this would be contained in a campus setting exhibiting residential rather than institutional characteristics.

Such facilities originated, primarily, through sponsorship by nonprofit organizations—principally religious organizations. Known as living care or life care communities, the marketing usually involved a substantial "entrance" fee or "endowment" fee paid by the resident, presumably from the sale of a home. Such a use-for-life fee helped cover the capital cost of the facility and provided an insurance component to make available the higher level of care for the resident, including nursing home care, if necessary, usually at little or no additional cost. Many of the first projects depended for continuing income upon resales of residents' units after their deaths. Not surprisingly, persons in such facilities tended to live longer than the average according to actuarial tables, so early endowments to cover future contingencies were found inadequate. With spiralling health care costs, a number of facilities experienced difficulty in fulfilling their obligation to residents. Although a number of life care communities remain in existence, few new facilities are employing the life care concept. CCLF differs from life care principally in that it is organized on a fee-for-services basis.

A second generation of such facilities being developed on a proprietary (as opposed to nonprofit) basis are founded with a fully or partially refundable entrance fee and with services provided on a purely rental basis with provision for more intensive services on a fee-for-service basis. In the following description of financing, only rental facilities are considered, which produce a stream of income to cover operating expenses and retire capital indebtedness.

Loan Underwriting Considerations for Continuing-Care Living Facilities

In underwriting a CCLF loan, the housing operation is usually analyzed separately from the nursing home operation. Although housed on the same campus, the facilities are operated separately although they may share a common kitchen. The nursing home component of a CCLF is underwritten like any other nursing home, as described above.

Location.   As with nursing homes, a pleasant and quiet setting for the CCLF is preferred to a high-activity location. Because of the usual nursing home component, proximity to a hospital is desirable. Because many of the retirement housing residents are moderately active and independent, the development should be convenient also to grocery stores and perhaps to a shopping mall.

Design.   The design qualities, the setting, and the amenities of a CCLF play an even more significant role in determining the type of income level of a resident than for regular nursing homes. Because virtually all residents of the housing components are private pay, and because typically they are younger and in better health than those directly entering a nursing home, the housing component of a CCLF will exhibit more strongly the characteristics of rental real estate. Although service remains very important, the overall quality level of the real estate itself plays a substantial role.

The layout of a typical CCLF will reflect the range of service levels provided. Often, two- or three-story apartment wings are attached to a common area which may adjoin the nursing facility. Although housing residents should be able to visit spouses and friends in the nursing area, the facilities should be designed such that housing residents and nursing patients do not interact regularly. Each component should have its own common area, for example. Although the nursing and housing facilities usually share a common food service kitchen, separate dining areas should be provided for the housing residents and for those nursing patients who do not take their meals in their rooms.

Many CCLFs include one or two private dining areas seating 8 to 12 people to accommodate both visiting families and other special occasions when small groups of residents wish to dine separately. Another amenity commonly found in CCLFs is a beauty parlor and barber shop. In many locations local hairdressers and barbers, because of the captive market, will rent space and provide equipment to set up a small salon in the CCLF. Residents enjoy being able to maintain this ritual, and it provides a good marketing point. Many CCLFs also have set aside a small space for a "general store," sometimes managed by the residents themselves, which sells grocery staples and convenience items. Again, the key aspect is that the residents are active.

Of course, safety is quite important in CCLFs, as it is in nursing homes. In most locales, though, the housing component of the facility will be considered as apartments for purposes of fire safety regulations, and sprinklers often will not be required. Installation of sprinkler systems may be necessary for market leasability, however, as many retirement center residents report that the potential for fire is a primary concern in seeking a retirement housing facility.

Another consideration in the layout of a CCLF is the configuration of the residential units with respect to the common area. Corridor length should be kept reasonably short, since the residents usually will make at least one walk each day to and from the dining area. Facilities are often arranged so most of the smaller units (which generally house the less capable residents) are located closer to the common areas.

In evaluating the design of a CCLF, the number and proportion of studio, one-bedroom, and two-bedroom units are important, as is the relative square footage of the respective units. Types and sizes of units vary in accordance with differing markets and income levels. For a CCLF, a market feasibility study and an architectural plan are indispensable underwriting tools.

Management. Although setting and design aspects play a more important role in the success of CCLFs than is the case with nursing homes, the experience and qualifications of the management still represent the key factor in underwriting a loan on a CCLF. The advantages and disadvantages of single-facility versus multifacility management, as discussed under the nursing home section above, apply to CCLFs as well.

Valuation. As with nursing homes, valuation of a CCLF requires an appraiser experienced in this specialized type of real estate. Although an existing operation might be analyzed primarily on its operating history and trends, a proposed new facility is much more challenging to the underwriter. Most lenders require that developers produce a marketing study and a feasibility study, although the two may be combined. Various major accounting firms and others provide such studies. The marketing study will deal primarily with the potential demand in the local community, competition, and the nature of facilities and services desired by the elderly and aging components within the community. The feasibility study will make income projections for a facility similar to the one indicated by the market study and will apply anticipated rental income availability and operating expenses to determine economic feasibility. The time estimated to reach full stabilized occupancy is perhaps the most important aspect of this report; 18 months is the usual period necessary to achieve this level of occupancy, but in many CCLFs full occupancy took two years or more. Some lenders double the number of months estimated in the feasibility study to provide a margin of contingency.

Another item of importance in the feasibility study is the marketing cost. Unlike conventional apartments, continuing-care living facilities require much more intense marketing, generally beginning prior to or during the construction phase. A budget of $2000 to $3000 per unit for marketing is not uncommon, so if a significant allowance is not provided in the developer's budget for marketing, a caution may be appropriate.

Operating expenses in the housing component of a CCLF typically will run 50 percent to 60 percent of effective gross income, although this percentage can vary widely depending on the nature of the facility and how food costs are allocated between the nursing and housing components. Such a facility may have 60 percent to 65 percent of its space in net rentable area, with the remainder in common area. Marketing emphasis is placed generally in the common area, with attention directed to the activities areas, the dining area, and social areas, rather than the individual living units, which typically are quite small.

From an operating standpoint, although continuing-care facilities are not as intensely service-oriented as nursing homes, intensive management is still required on a 24-hour basis, involving security, dietary, and activities management. The operating budget presented, therefore, should reflect the developer's understanding of the staffing needs. The fixed costs of such facilities are high, and most of the staff must be on board from the opening day. Significant reserves for start-up losses are required.

In determining an appropriate loan value for a CCLF, based on net operating income after reserves, different debt service coverage ratios may be applied to the income attributable to the housing component and to that of the nursing home component. Some lenders will underwrite the apartment operation on a coverage ratio of approximately 1.25 to 1, while requiring a ratio of 1.4 to 1 for the nursing home operation.

Loan Security Considerations.   Although equipment and furniture cost are not as significant to the housing component of a CCLF as to the nursing component or to a pure nursing home, FF&E costs nonetheless are substantial, and the personalty should be secured. As with a nursing home, any lease or management contract should be conditionally assignable to the lender. Other considerations outlined under the nursing home section above also will apply to financing of CCLFs.

Financing Sources for Loans on Continuing-Care Living Facilities

Except for the nursing home component, continuing-care living facilities usually are considered residential facilities and are, therefore, qualified for tax-exempt housing bonds in many jurisdictions, subject to availability under current federal laws. This has been a popular method of financing such facilities in the past. Some lenders will make direct portfolio tax-exempt loans, but when the facilities are financed with bond issues, often a credit enhancement must be provided, either through HUD insurance or through surety companies or bank letters of credit.

Conventional financing of CCLFs is available from the same sources as for nursing homes, namely various life insurance companies, thrifts, and REITs. Like some nursing homes, a few life care communities have experienced adverse publicity because of financial problems, and many institutions are hesitant to consider financing. For this reason, loans on CCLFs also usually require a premium in yield over that for more traditional property types.

Summary

The range of facilities for the elderly can be outlined:

1. Nursing homes
   a. Intermediate-care facilities
   b. Skilled-care facilities
2. Retirement housing facilities
   a. Personal care or custodial care or homes for the aged

   b. Congregate care facilities
   c. Retirement living apartments, elderly housing
3. Continuous-care living facilities

With growth of the elderly population, there is probably no area of development which promises more opportunities for innovation.

PART 5

Structuring the Loan

21
Construction Lending

Henry S. Kesler, CMB, MAI

Senior Vice President, CrossLand Mortgage Corporation
Salt Lake City, Utah

R. Lynn Tucker
Vice President, CrossLand Mortgage Corporation
Salt Lake City, Utah

Construction lending has become very attractive to real estate lenders, not only to the commercial banks, but also to traditionally longer-term investors, such as savings and loan associations and certain life insurance companies. Though risky, it provides the lender with the opportunity to generate large fees and interest income. Construction lending is also attractive because it is creative: A new project is built; the landscape is changed; a community is transformed.

In construction lending many factors affect the underwriting decision. Underwriting is the analysis of the risks inherent in the investment; the subsequent loan reflects these risks. The underwriting analysis includes a complete review of the project's development entity; its experience and creditworthiness; the project's economic value and future market viability; and a complete check of plans, specifications, and costs.

The construction lender is making a short-term investment decision and must be concerned about repayment, which usually takes place when the property is purchased or its permanent financing by a long-term lender is provided. The construction lender must be attentive not only to the construction aspects of a project but also to current trends in the long-term mortgage market. If there is no "takeout" on the loan and a permanent lender cannot be found when the project is completed, the construction lender will have to retain the loan or assume management of the completed property.

The four aspects of income property construction lending reviewed in this chapter are risk, policy, pricing, and documentation.

Construction Lending Risks

Each income property project, and hence each construction loan, has unique assets and risks. All parties to the construction process face different types of risks and have varying degrees of liability. Not all risks can be controlled by the construction loan administration department. The risks faced in construction lending can be subsumed under four categories:

- Incomplete construction
- Legal problems
- Unforeseen risk
- End loan failure

Incomplete Construction

Incomplete construction is probably the greatest risk associated with construction lending. During the construction process, the security for the loan is the land with a partially completed building. If the loan budget does not allow for completion of the construction, or the loan goes into default for some other reason prior to completion, the lender's security will be greatly reduced.

The lender's security during the construction period is usually much less than the value of money loaned until the completion of the building. Figure 21.1 diagrams the created value in relation to funds outstanding on a typical construction loan.

A lender who, for whatever reason, has to finish an incomplete project, will find that delays raise costs above original projections. Since the economic value of the project is not related to its cost but to net cash flow over time, increases in construction costs do not necessarily result in an increase of the project's value. This reasoning also applies to

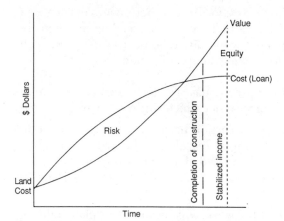

Figure 21.1. Construction—cost to value.

downgrades and decreased costs. Reduced costs can reduce value more than the sum saved.

The following are examples of problems that can lead to *insufficient funds available for construction* and therefore an incomplete construction project:

1. Original project costs underestimated

2. Poorly capitalized borrower

3. Poorly negotiated subcontracts which failed to limit overruns or adequately cover scope of work

4. Costs increased after the loan budget was established and during the course of construction

5. The failure of early rentals or sales to develop as anticipated

6. Financial problems faced by the borrower unrelated to this project or loan—for example, a financial overextension on other construction projects

7. Fraudulent diversion of funds

8. Insufficient contingency reserve budgeted and underestimated interest reserve requirements—the estimation of interest rate reserve during periods of fluctuating interest rates may be difficult at best

9. Use of originally budgeted funds for unauthorized change orders or upgrades

10. Pilferage and theft

11. Uninsured losses

Poor management and/or business failure is another major concern, usually caused by lack of experience and incompetence. The problems resulting from poor management would apply to borrowers, prime contractors, and subcontractors. Some examples include:

1. *Increased complexity* of the project has created a need for specialization beyond the general competency which sufficed for past projects.
2. *Personal risks,* including construction hazards, are increased under poor management. For example, the already hazardous nature of construction work can be increased if the construction site is not clean and orderly. Accidents can result in delays, lawsuits, and increased insurance costs.
3. *Inadequate coordination* of the work, which can cause delays, add significant costs to the project, and create payment and performance problems. For example, a poor manager may have a roof system delivered for payment several months prior to the point at which the walls are scheduled to be completed.
4. *Subgrade quality* work through inadequate or improper supervision is often a reflection of poor management.
5. *Delay of payments* because of poor or inadequate management can cause liens and other legal complications as well as divert attention and energy from the job.
6. *Front-end loading* is often attempted by less experienced contractors and/or developers. In their attempts to recover funds spent during the development stages of the project, they may hamper the project's success and temporize the lender's security during construction.

Incomplete and inadequate plans and specifications can lead to construction and structural problems. Work contracts may not be clear to both parties, resulting in cost overruns, delays, legal problems, and, finally, incomplete construction. Additional risks and problems to be considered are:

1. The qualification of the design architect
2. The adequacy and appropriateness of specifications
3. Inadequate correlation between structural, electrical, and mechanical drawings
4. Code violations or design requirements that have been overlooked
5. Lack of ongoing review and supervision by the design architect—de-

velopers sometimes limit the ongoing responsibilities of the design architect in an effort to save money

6. Inadequate control of the scope of the project and inadequate follow-up concerning deletions, additions, and change orders

Legal Problems

Many parties are involved in bringing an income property to completion. From start to finish, each group is expected to perform its required duties in accord with its contract. If all parties fulfilled their duties as required, there would be no legal problems.

Legal disputes can hamper a construction project with delays, additional costs, and liens that prevent title transfer. Potential risks in this area are:

▪ *Breach of contract.* Any party associated with the project could be involved in a breach of contract which would excuse inadequate or incomplete performance and release parties from execution of their responsibilities. For example, breach of contract would release a surety who had underwritten bonds, negate a takeout commitment, or belie a firm price to which a contractor had agreed.

▪ *Liens.* These relate to failure to pay for previous work.

▪ *Conflicts.* Conflicts may arise between the contract requirements of the various parties. An example might be a 10 percent retention requirement between the lender and the borrower and a 5 percent retention requirement between the borrower and the contractor.

▪ *Encroachment.* Encroachment involves foundations and even complete structures have been built which encroach on another's property.

▪ *Zoning.* Failure to adhere to zoning and building requirements can cause problems.

Unforeseen Risks

Unforeseen risks, such as the following examples, most often occur during the course of construction.

▪ *Site.* Projects can run into unknown site conditions such as changed subsoil conditions or problems not uncovered by soils reports. It is impossible for an engineer or contractor to have all the information on subsoil conditions.

- *Hazardous substances.* The determination of hazardous waste problems on a site can have enormous impact on project values and liability to potentially responsible parties. Lenders may be held liable for cleanup costs when taking title through foreclosure actions. Hazardous waste issues require that lenders be thoroughly familiar with site history or perform professional site evaluations to identify the risks in this area.

- *Weather.* Poor weather conditions can exceed estimates that were incorporated into the underwriting. A spell of poor weather often creates a "ripple" effect in that subcontractors cannot complete another job to show up on time for this one.

- *Business conditions.* Some economic and supply considerations include inflation, strikes, labor disputes, supply shortages, bankruptcy, or defaults.

- *Management.* Death, injury, or incapacity of a key individual will cause problems for the many contractors who rely on the ability of one leader who was unable to share authority and whose absence may threaten stability.

Unforeseen risks can create additional expenses and delays, some of which could preclude project completion.

End Loan Failure

A construction loan is by definition a short-term loan. The usual source of repayment derives from a takeout loan of permanent financing. Since the permanent loan is the primary source of repayment, the C&D lender wants to be assured of repayment on completion of the project prior to committing on the construction loan. The mortgage that repays the construction loan is called the "takeout" or "end loan."

Even with a firm commitment from the permanent lender to make the end loan, there is still the risk that certain eventualities will release the takeout lender from the obligation. It is important to understand the risks and obligations which might result in takeout failure:

- *Failure to start or to complete construction.* This includes all required approvals, within a prearranged time period.

- *Improperly completed construction.* This may occur when approved plans and specifications are ignored or completion is accomplished according to approved plans but not in conformance with required results of the loan commitment, e.g., a soundproofing standard may not have been met even though plans and specifications were followed.

- *Violations of laws, codes, or any ordinances and environmental rules.* The takeout commitment may be invalidated regardless of completion according to specifications.

- *Borrower financial problems.* The borrower suffers changes in financial condition. An adverse material change, such as an adverse judgment on a lawsuit unrelated to the financed project, could release the permanent lender from its commitment.

- *Valuation.* Failure to meet appraised value may occur.

- *Cost overruns.* The construction lender may have loaned more than the permanent lender has committed to loan.

- *Inadequate leasing.* The project may not achieve leasing at an agreed upon level (e.g., 50 percent) by the time of takeout, thereby reducing the amount the permanent lender is willing to lend or invalidating the takeout commitment entirely.

- *Interest rate changes.* These might reduce the desirability of a precommitted loan to a permanent lender—this development can increase the takeout lender's desire to find reason to invalidate a commitment, but unless a clause has been negotiated into the takeout regarding rate levels, the mere change in market rates is usually not a reason for invalidation per se.

- *Lender liquidity.* The possibility that the takeout lender may lack the financial capacity to fund the loan on completion may serve as the reason behind technical objections to findings.

The risk associated with end loan failure may depend to some degree upon the various requirements of each project and commitment. However, experience has shown a permanent lender can usually find sufficient reasons to decline the purchase of a loan if necessary. In fact, most loan agreements are in technical default the minute the ink is dry.

Construction Lending Policy

With the volatility of the marketplace, the increasing dollar magnitude of individual projects, and the risks inherent in construction lending, a formal written statement of C&D lending policy and procedure has been demonstrated to be vital. Mortgage bankers undertaking C&D loans should first recognize and define the overall corporate philosophy and commitment to real estate lending. For example, how much of a company's total assets will be committed to real estate, more particularly, how much to income-producing property construction lending? What ratio of loans with or without takeout commitments does the lender desire? What geographic area does the company choose to be active in—local, statewide, regional, or national? Does the lender intend to rely on outside experts or an internal staff for appraisers, supervising architects, and attorneys? What part of the market will be sought by the lender?

A number of considerations should be addressed in establishing credit policy. It is important to determine what constitutes an acceptable borrower. That is, should the borrower be restricted to an experienced professional, or is the lender willing to work with a less experienced developer without a long track record? The lender should determine the extent of credit support expected from the borrower and whether personal guarantees will be required. Separate criteria for higher-risk borrowers, such as syndicators or Subchapter S corporations, may be appropriate.

The selection of acceptable property types is also important. Any property financed should, of course, be of perceived benefit to its community, but what about original, risky, or controversial projects? What about projects that are management intensive, low cost, special use, or that have strictly local appeal? Sometimes it is useful to establish a list of less desirable property types.

Other credit policy decisions are required of the lender. For example, qualifications and information standards required of the general contractor need to be established, since it is the contractor upon whom the construction lender and the developer are relying to create the physical improvements. Often the developer is also acting as general contractor. The risks inherent in this combining of functions should be reviewed. The lender should also review and approve all the construction contracts, including those with the project architect and engineer.

Acceptable loan types and loan-to-value ratios should be determined. This sounds simple enough, but different lenders have widely divergent comfort levels, as well as differing approaches to value. One of the risks unique to construction lending is that the value of the property upon which the loan is made is being created only as the project is constructed. In fact, the value of a project is typically less than the loan and its cost until near completion. The acceptable relationships of loan to cost and loan to value must be established. These may vary based upon the presence or lack of a takeout commitment. The acceptable loan ratios will also change with the type of property financed.

The marketability of any project is always of vital concern. In this regard a construction lender may choose to establish minimum requirements for preleasing or presales for certain types of projects. If so, how should these be verified? Many a lender has committed on what it thought was a 100 percent preleased property, only to find it significantly empty upon completion.

Construction lenders should also consider a policy regarding the holdback of retainage from construction draw amounts. The magnitude of the retainage as a percentage of each draw of labor or material, how and when it will be released, and whether the retainage is more or less than that required by the contracts are all appropriate matters for discussion.

The lender must develop a policy concerning the requirement of payment and performance bonds. Here the lender must clearly understand its responsibilities to the surety company. When are bonds to be required? They might be based upon the size of contracts, the type of property being constructed, or the lender's previous experience with the contractor or borrower.

All lenders require title insurance, but both the underwriting title insurance company and the local issuing company should be approved by the lender. Minimum standards for the financial strength of the title company should be considered, along with the acceptable terms for the policy. Allowable exceptions to the title insurance should be determined in advance.

The lender should also approve the builder's risk insurance coverage policy, as well as the issuing insurance company. The lender's policy should determine in advance whether the amount of insurance is to equal the loan amount or the insurable replacement cost of the improvements. And worker's compensation insurance should not be overlooked.

The lender must determine whether to use in-house staff appraisers or outside independent appraisers. If independent appraisers are used, the lender needs to decide whether they must have a nationally recognized designation and by what procedures the lenders will review and approve appraisers.

Few lenders have licensed engineers on staff, but the review of plans, specifications, soil reports, and surveys are commonly required. The criteria and instructions for review and acceptance of these reports need to be established. The construction lender deals in many different geographic locations, and, because local building codes may vary, a lender may want to establish its own minimum building standards or adopt the current Uniform Building Code. Local building codes simply may not be enough to ensure investor-quality construction.

Finally, the construction lender needs to establish its policy regarding the pricing structure of a loan. This policy should consider the matter of fees, the basis for calculation and payment of interest, and all other changes and aspects of the loan structure that will affect the expected yield on the lender's investment.

Construction Lending Pricing

Income property construction lending is one of many investment alternatives available to an institution's investment portfolio manager. Because of its relative short-term nature, typically one to two years, construction lending allows the manager to match assets with short-term liabilities. A good "match" can be measured at maturity, when the term of the investment reflects the term of the source of funds, and by the cost of funds, where the interest charged on a loan is directly related to the cost of the funds used for the investment. Because of the need to match assets to liabilities, the construction loan portfolio is sensitive to interest rate changes and will, over time, make adjustments to changes in the money market.

It is the marketplace which sets the yield that a lender can obtain, rather than the lender's investment. Pricing of a loan, therefore, is the technique by which a loan is structured so that it both is acceptable to the marketplace and provides the lender with its expected return. The lender must decide whether the expected yield, as dictated by the market, is acceptable given what underwriting analysis reveals about the risks inherent to the investment.

A lender should be fully aware of the pricing components which constitute the yield on investment. In its simplest sense this is no more than a discounted cash flow analysis of the expected return on the lender's investment. These components include, of course, the interest rate to be charged on the loan. The interest rate may be a fixed percentage rate, or it may vary during the life of the loan according to a predetermined formula. Usually a variable rate is some increment over a fluctuating index, such as the prime rate, Treasury bills, certificates of deposit, or some other verifiable index. The first objective in choosing an index is to match the fluctuations in the lender's cost of funds, thereby assuring the lender a stable margin over cost for the duration of the investment. Lenders should also consider the possibility of setting a minimum "floor" and a maximum "ceiling" rate to be charged on the loan.

Fees paid by the borrower are an important aspect of the yield to the lender. These fees may include a fee charged when the loan is committed, a fee charged when disbursement of funds commences, and a fee to extend the term of the loan, but there are many variations in pricing. The timing of the payment of these fees has a significant impact on their contribution to overall yield, and the lender should charge fees based on its expectation for the investment. The yield from a fee is directly related to the maturity or repayment term of the investment. Again the term of a loan is dictated more by the type of project and extant market conditions than by the lender's profit criteria.

A lender should also consider increasing its yield by means of participation with the borrower in the profits from the project. This may take many forms, including an outright joint venture with the borrower, loans convertible to equity, and contingent interest agreements.

The construction lender can reduce its amount of risk in an investment and increase its yield by bringing other lenders in as participants on the loan. The participation may be pari passu, or the lead lender (the one that originated the loan) may be able to negotiate more favorable pricing of its interest rate and fees to increase its yield. This pricing differential may reflect an administrative overage due the lead lender because of the costs of administering the loan. It may reflect an agreement whereby the lead lender allows the participant or participants to recover funds before the lead lender recovers its funds, in case of loss. The participant has what is known as a "first out" protection, but its yield is less than that of the lender taking the greater risk.

Sometimes the market will allow pricing that will render the success of the project difficult. The lender should put the long-term success of the project before short-term expectation of gain. Because construction loans typically fund their own interest charges, it is tempting for lenders to estimate the interest reserve conservatively. If this estimation is incorrect, other estimated costs may be affected to a point that the loan contains insufficient funds or is out of balance from the outset. The lender must be prepared to evaluate the terms of the loan and to make changes if necessary.

Construction Loan Documentation

The documentation requirements for an income property construction loan reflect the unique characteristics of this type of lending. The construction loan is a hybrid of unsecured commercial lending and term mortgage lending. As such, the documentation requirements include both credit and real estate collateral considerations. As with any loan transaction, it is the documents themselves that delineate the covenants, conditions, and expectations of the transactions for the parties involved. A construction loan is uniquely "future tense," that is, the loan is alive, creating its own security and relying on future performance by the borrower. When that performance is complete, the construction nature of the loan ceases.

As with other types of real estate financing, the loan commitment is the primary document of construction lending. The loan commitment is a preliminary and summary document and may not contain every term or condition of the loan transaction, but it should be understood as a blueprint for the loan, and it is therefore important to negotiate and spell out all significant terms of the loan at the commitment stage.

The following is a sample documentation checklist for construction loans. The basic required loan documents are:

1. Loan application

2. Loan commitment

3. Promissory note

4. Deed of trust or mortgage

5. Construction loan agreement

6. Security agreement

7. Assignment of leases

8. Architect, engineer, and general contractor contracts

9. Continuation Letters from architect, engineer, and contractor

10. Guaranty of principals

11. Takeout commitment

12. Buy-sell or triparty agreement

13. Borrower's attorney's opinion letter

14. Corporate borrowing resolution

15. Real estate appraisal

16. Title insurance binder or commitment

17. Survey

18. Necessary building, zoning, or environment permits

19. Builder's risk insurance policy

20. Itemized cost breakdown

The construction loan agreement, or building loan agreement, is the master document for the construction loan. This document specifically sets forth the requirements the borrower will have to fulfill to obtain disbursement of loan proceeds, affirmative and negative convenants, default clauses, remedies provisions, and more.

The typical conditions found in the construction loan agreement are outlined below, with appropriate comments as to their importance for the construction lender.

1. *Definitions.* All parties involved with the transaction (guarantors, contractor, architect, title insurance, etc.) are identified, the required loan documents are specified and defined, and unique terms or requirements are spelled out.

2. *The terms of the loan.* Rate, fees, maturity, and so on are defined.

3. *Requirements for title insurance, hazard insurance, and bonding.* Normally coverage in these areas will be stipulated by the lender, as well as approval of the issuing companies. The required form of policy will be indicated.

4. *Borrower representations and warranties.* This regards the borrowers' legal status and legal ability to enter into the transaction, the equity which they will contribute, and any financial information required by the lender.

5. *Provisions regarding a permanent loan commitment.* This may include incorporating the permanent loan commitment by reference into the construction loans, so that a default by the borrower on the commitment will also be a default on the construction loan. The loan documentation may be altered to create a combined construction-permanent loan, a triparty agreement (the borrower, the construction lender, and the takeout lender), or a buy-sell agreement. Procedures for funding or conversion to a permanent loan are necessary.

6. *Definition of expected loan expenses.* These costs (e.g., inspecting architects fees and legal expenses) and the responsibility for paying them will be established.

7. *Disbursement procedures.* These will include specific requirements for the initial loan disbursement at closing, continued periodic disbursements during the life of the loan, and the final loan disbursement upon completion of the improvements. Dates for specific performance should be identified as well as the exact documentation and procedures to be required in processing a draw request. This area is the one of greatest potential contention between the borrower, lender, and contractor and must be clearly and thoroughly spelled out. Do not leave this area to the subjective discretion of the lender. The specific construction requirements must be identified.

8. *Identification of reserves or deposits for expected but unpaid expenses.* These would include reserves for interest, tenant improve-

ments, real estate taxes, insurance premiums, unpaid lender commitment fees, leasing commissions, and contingency. The disbursement prerequisites on these monies should be clearly defined.

9. *The "loan balance" provision.* One of a construction lender's greatest concerns is insufficiency of loan funds to complete the proposed improvements. The loan balance provision requires the borrower to deposit funds to balance the loan if there are insufficient funds in the loan, less reserve plus equity to complete construction.

10. *The general agreements of the borrower.* The borrower agrees to complete construction according to plans and specifications, to make no changes without the lender's approval, and to pay all mechanics liens and taxes

11. *The lender's rights and permissible actions for its protection.* The lender specifies its right to foreclose in case of default and, where applicable, take assignment of rents. The lender has the right to pay liens and to charge the borrower.

12. *Additional collateral in the form of letters of credit or certificates of deposit.* The conditions of their use and the specific options for their use by the lender and/or borrower need to be defined.

13. *Schedules.* These should be attached and incorporated as a part of the construction loan agreement. They should include: note, trust deed, detailed cost breakdown, documentation checklist, sample draw request package, additional terms, insurance and survey forms, leases, loan commitments, and so on.

Poor administration can undermine even the best underwritten loan. However, the best construction administration cannot save a poorly underwritten loan.

22

Permanent Debt Financing and Land Sale-Leasebacks

Helen I. Daniel*
Associate, Giegerich & Associates
Rockville, Maryland

John Oharenko*
Vice President, Cushman and Wakefield Financial Services
Chicago, Illinois

Jane D. Endres*
Analyst, Cushman and Wakefield Financial Services
Chicago, Illinois

When equity investors in income property survey the financial marketplace for debt financing, a number of options are available. This chapter takes a close look at three types of permanent debt financing widely offered in the marketplace today: the fixed-rate loan, the accrual loan, and the minipermanent loan. Which lending institutions offer which types of debt-financing alternatives, loan terms, and conditions, and why will also be covered. The chapter then discusses how the developer-

*Ms. Daniel is the author of the section on permanent debt financing. Mr. Oharenko and Ms. Endres authored the section on land sale-leasebacks.

owner may obtain additional funds by selling the land underneath the building and leasing it back.

For the purposes of permanent debt financing, the leading lenders are life insurance companies, commercial banks, and savings and loan associations. Pension funds (primarily those of state and local government agencies) and savings banks are also active as lenders. Although financial institutions are briefly described in Chapter 3, it is important to understand how each of these lenders operates under different regulatory constraints and obtains its funds from different customer and client sources for different periods. Because of differing regulatory requirements and the need to match liabilities, or the funds obtained from customers, with its assets or the loan investments made with these funds, the types of debt financing, loan terms, and conditions will differ among each of these three institutional lenders.

The largest group of permanent mortgage lenders, the life insurance companies, receive the funds they invest from either their own account (i.e., the premiums paid in on insurance policies) or now more commonly from pension fund guaranteed income contracts (GICs). GICs are pension fund money that the life insurance companies purchase for a fixed period and guarantee a specific interest rate return to the fund. Using their real estate investment expertise, the life companies then lend the funds at rates of ½ percent to 1 percent above the guaranteed interest rate on the contract.

Life insurance companies are regulated in the states in which they are chartered, and pension fund investments are regulated under federal Employee Retirement Income Security Act (ERISA) legislation.

Banks, in contrast to life companies, have liabilities with much shorter periods to maturity. Their sources of funds are more dependent on short-term deposits from their customers. Bank operations and investment activities are under the supervision of several federal agencies—the Federal Deposit Insurance Corporation, the Federal Reserve, and the Comptroller of the Currency in the Treasury Department.

Savings and loan institutions obtain their funds from customer savings account deposits and are regulated by the Federal Home Loan Bank. Since the name of the game is to match liabilities and assets, the difference between what a lender pays to attract customer and client money and what it earns when these funds are invested will determine the profit or loss for the institution.

Permanent Fixed-Rate Loans

With this larger picture in mind, consider the first of the three widely offered debt-financing options, the permanent fixed-rate loan. This loan is also known as the bullet loan. Here both the rate and term are fixed (e.g., 10 years at 9 percent). In today's market, these bullet loans are offered from periods as short as 3 years to periods as long as 20. They can be for interest only, amortized over 15, 20, or 30 years, or use a combination of interest only for the first several years and then an amortization of principal. But whatever the variations, at the end of the term, a balloon payment of the remaining principal is due the lender.

A bullet loan is for immediate funding on existing property—"immediate" may mean that, after commitment, the loan is to be disbursed (funded) within the following six months or less.

The life insurance companies are today the primary lenders offering permanent fixed-rate loans. Since their largest source of money is from pension fund GICs, life companies will usually have prepayment restrictions as part of their loan conditions. These restrictions either allow no prepayment during the term of the loan or require a yield maintenance penalty from the borrower to insulate the lender from any income lost in reinvesting the loan proceeds at lower interest rates.

Savings and loan institutions in the permanent fixed-rate loan market frequently offer debt financing that matches loan rate and terms to the Federal Home Loan Bank's advance rate for 5- to 10-year money. Savings institutions will offer rates at 100 to 200 basis points, or 1 to 2 percent over the cost of these funds. In 1987, comparing the fixed-rate permanent loan product offered by these two lenders, life companies generally offer lower rates and smaller up-front fees than do savings institutions. However, the life insurance companies usually underwrite their loans on higher debt service coverage and lower loan-to-value ratios.

Accrual Loans

Two types of accrual loans are offered in the permanent loan market today: the fixed-rate accrual loan and the floating-rate accrual loan. Both products have been favored by the savings and loan industry.

For the fixed-rate accrual loan, the contract or coupon rate may be set at, say, 10.5 percent with a pay rate at 50 to 150 basis points (0.5 percent to 1.5 percent) below the contract rate. The lower pay rate differential of 0.5 percent to 1.5 percent is added to the principal balance. This formula gives the borrower a low fixed monthly debt service payment below the contract rate. However, it also gives an increasing principal balance on the loan, known as negative amortization.

A floating-rate accrual loan works the same as the fixed-rate accrual loan except the contract or coupon rate is tied to a suitable index such as the prime rate, Treasury bill rate, rate on certificates of deposit, or Federal Home Loan Bank cost of funds. Accrual loans are usually for shorter periods than the permanent fixed-rate loan. These are generally three- to seven-year interest-only loans with no or small prepayment penalties, low debt service coverage, and high loan-to-value ratios.

Minipermanent Loans

The minipermanent, or miniperm, loan market has been popular with both banks and savings and loan associations. These loans are short-term, usually three- to five-year, interest-only loans often given to developers whose construction projects are basically completed but the leasing has not reached the breakeven point, so a longer-term permanent loan is still not supportable by the property's cash flow. Here the lender, often the same one who has given the construction loan, will provide a miniperm to allow the project more time to achieve its pro forma income level.

A miniperm can be tied, like the variable-rate accrual loan, to any one of several interest rate indexes—the prime rate, certificates of deposit, the London Inter-Bank Offering Rate (LIBOR), Treasury bills—at so many basis points above the rate. Also, like accrual loans, a fixed pay rate can be arranged with the additional interest added to the principal owed. Caps and floors on the interest rate are also possible, as well as hedging and swap programs that essentially fix the rate for the short term of the loan while leasing proceeds to the point where the property can either be sold or more permanent debt financing can be obtained.

Borrower Considerations on Loan Alternatives

With the variety of debt financing available, equity investors in commercial property must make several important decisions about their real estate investment before a loan package is submitted to a lender. Investors must first decide what their anticipated holding period will be on the property. Is it a short-term investment to be sold when all space is occupied at peak rents, or is it a property the owners want to keep in their portfolios over the long term? If the first option is chosen, a fixed-rate permanent loan may initially be cheaper, but with prepayment restrictions on these loans, the owner loses flexibility to sell the property at the most favorable time. So in the end this may be the most costly type of financing.

A second important decision for the investor is how much financing leverage or debt to put on the property. Remember, a longer-term fixed-rate permanent mortgage will usually carry a lower loan-to-value ratio and higher debt service coverage, so more equity is needed for this type of loan. To a large extent the net operating income the property generates and its appraised value will determine the debt service coverage and the loan-to-value parameters for the real estate. But even with enough cash flow to service debt easily, owners still need to decide whether to leave their equity in the property to obtain lower rates and longer loan terms.

In making these decisions, the equity investor must have accurate figures for current year's net operating income and realistic projections for anticipated cash flows during the holding period. These projections should also take in all possible fluctuations in cash flow in future years. Then various financing alternatives can be applied to the projected income stream to see which loan offers the best fit.

In review, the steps to follow are: first, take the current year's net operating income; next, project income into the future holding period; third, consider each debt-financing alternative and the terms and conditions that go along with each; then analyze the fit between the projected performance of the property and the debt service from each of the loan alternatives.

The Land Sale-Leaseback

The land sale-leaseback is a hybrid joint venture that involves two real estate transactions. These two transactions involve a separate land transaction along with leasehold mortgage transactions on the building improvements. In a land sale-leaseback transaction, the borrower will sell the land to an investor (lender), and the investor then leases the land back to the borrower. The borrower then proceeds to obtain a leasehold mortgage from the investor on the building improvements. Note that this type of transaction can include from two to four separate parties. The transaction can simply involve the borrower who is both the seller of the land he or she owns and the builder of the improvements, or a separate seller of the land and a separate owner and builder of the improvements. The lender can also be "the buyer" and the mortgagee, or there can be a separate investor who purchases the land and a separate lender who places a mortgage on the building improvements.

Typically, the term of the land lease will at least equal the term of the mortgage; in most cases the term of the land lease is much greater than the term of the mortgage. As mentioned before, the lender can be both the entity which invests in the land and the mortgagee of the mortgage on the building improvements. This would be called the land sale-leaseback leasehold mortgage. However, if the land investor is separate from the lender of the improvements, the ground rent payments on the land may take the form of first lien, and the lender then only funds the borrower's building improvements if the land owner agrees to subordinate the land to the first mortgage. This arrangement is known as a subordinated land sale-leaseback with a traditional mortgage. In the event that the lender agrees to subordinate the leasehold mortgage to the land investor, we have what is known as an unsubordinated land sale-leaseback mortgage with subordinated leasehold mortgage. As one can observe, there are several variations of the land sale-leaseback.

The key behind the land sale-leaseback transactions is that the borrower receives 100 percent financing, because the investor (lender) can provide all this money up front through equity capital from the purchase of the land and debt capital from the funding of the building improvements. The land sale-leaseback is used for new construction, refinancing of existing properties, and land banking.

Land sale-leaseback financing is most common with new construction projects. Borrowers are typically owners of prime land and are seeking 100 percent financing. The borrowers sell the land to the investors and lenders, and when the project begins to generate cash flow, the borrower pays ground rent and debt service to the investor and lender. For these types of new construction projects, lenders receive attractive long-term yields and, in many cases, a large participation in the form of the preferred return after ground rent payments and debt service payments.

In the case of an existing piece of real estate that requires refinancing, a land sale-leaseback structure may transform the land into working capital as well as generate tax losses in the form of ground rent payments. In this situation the borrower achieves full financing, and ground rent payments can be deducted as an operating expense. This scenario works well for investors (lenders), because they obtain aggressive yields from the long-term lease of the land while receiving mortgage payments on building improvements that already have a proven track record and developer. Note that an investor (lender) has no qualms in investing in a nondepreciable asset such as land, because in such cases the lender is typically a tax-free institution such as a pension fund, life insurance company, bank, or local government.

Land sale-leaseback financing requires careful tax and legal advice to ascertain the proper tax benefits of both the borrower and the lender. Also, the borrower's options to repurchase the land includes provisions to buy the land at a market formula that coincides with market conditions, otherwise the tax authorities may recognize the land sale-leaseback transaction as a tax avoidance scheme designed to use the land as a depreciable asset.

Land sale-leaseback financing can also be used for a land banking transaction where a borrower needs to purchase land that will be developed over a long period. In this situation, the land will be developed in segments over a period of time. However, equity is needed immediately to tie up all the land. In this situation, a land investor or lender has to be willing to take control of all the land immediately, including the parcels of land that will be developed only over a period of several years. When the land investor purchases and leases back the land to the borrower, the borrower can then obtain financing for each separate segment of the total project.

Land sale-leaseback financing can be very creative and very complicated, with various benefits and risks allocated to each unique land sale-leaseback project. In addition to the basic benefit of full financing, the borrower also receives a maximum depreciation allocation as a result of land rent being classified as a tax-deductible expense. By employing the method of land sale-leaseback financing, borrowers also add to their capital through land sale proceeds. These proceeds can be invested in either real estate or other investments. Although the borrower often has to cede cash flow participation to the lender, these participation payments are not set payments, but payments based on project performance.

The drawbacks of a land sale-leaseback financing structure to the borrower are as numerous as the benefits. Foremost, the borrower sacrifices possession of the land and, therefore, sacrifices land appreciation. In addition to this, fixed land rental payments, mortgage payments on improvements, and lender's cash flow participation erode a large portion of a project's profitability. This is especially true if a new project gets off to a slow start.

The borrower also loses substantial control of the project in terms of transfer of ownership if the mortgage becomes due and the ground lease is not financed, or if there is a sale, when transfer of ownership must be approved by the investor and lender. Many land investors also stipulate that building improvements revert to them at the end of the land lease term.

The investor (lender) benefits of the land sale-leaseback structure are also varied but start out from the basic benefit of owning land along with its value appreciation. The investor also receives guaranteed land rent payments along with participating cash flows that provide attractive yields and long-term inflation protection.

As an illustration, suppose that ABC, a developer, sells land to XYZ insurance company at its present market value of $2.5 million. XYZ leases it back to ABC for 50 years at 10 percent, being $250,000 plus 50 percent as additional ground rents, of all net income after debt service payments on the leasehold mortgage.

XYZ makes a leasehold on a office building mortgage for $19.9 million (80 percent of its cost) for 10 years at 11.25 percent, amortized over 30 years (11.655 constant), to ABC.

At the end of the 10-year holding period, XYZ expects the property to sell for $35 million. ABC has to repay the leasehold mortgage balance, which is then $18,425,549. The lender, XYZ, shares in 50 percent of the sales price after adjusting for the original land purchase price, remaining mortgage balance, and ABC's equity contribution. In this way, ABC finances about 93 percent of the cost at a sacrifice of 50 percent of the cash flow and appreciation.

23

Participating Mortgages and Joint Ventures

Robert H. Gidel

President, Alex. Brown Realty Advisors
Baltimore, Maryland

Philip D. Morse

Senior Vice President, Heller Financial, Inc.
Washington, D.C.

A joint venture is an agreement between a real estate entrepreneur and a money partner to accomplish specific goals. The documentation outlines the duties, obligations, and responsibilities of each venturer to reach the project's objectives. A participating mortgage is a form of financing in which the lender seeks a return, in addition to interest on the loan, in the form of participation in the cash flow and, usually, in any appreciation of the property upon sale or refinancing.

Although there are numerous variations of joint venture and participating mortgage arrangements, this discussion will center on the most common: A real estate developer or owner, the borrower, provides the expertise and staffing, and a money partner supplies the capital. The money partner may be referred to as a lender, investor, or venture partner. To understand joint ventures, several basic concepts are necessary:

- A joint venture is not a partnership, it is an agreement by each party to undertake certain obligations to attain specific objectives. Without clear definition of the performance expected from each venturer, the relationship will deteriorate as unexpected problems arise.

- Although a common goal is established at the outset of the venture, over time, as circumstances and performance change, the individual goals of the participants may conflict. A good venture agreement will anticipate and provide for changes involved.

- Real estate value will be affected by economic, social, and political changes. Even if a project achieves its pro forma objectives, subsequent circumstances may dictate an alteration in strategy. Although real estate is viewed primarily as a fixed asset, equity values will rise and decline based on market particulars. Both parties to a joint venture must be aware of this situation and deal with situations beyond the control of the venture.

The many variations of joint ventures can all be subsumed within two categories. In the first category of joint venture, at least part of the capital has been invested as equity. In the second category, funds are participated, invested, and structured as debt.

Motives of the Parties

Joint venture and participating debt structures provide attractive advantages for both the developer and the lender. For the structure to be successful, however, both parties must have sufficient stake in the project to see it through, in spite of risk and difficulty, to completion.

Developer Objectives

The developer's aims in seeking a joint venture are, of course, needed funds and the ability to limit the developer's liability. The developer also enters into joint ventures because of the following:

1. *Deep pockets partner.* Money partners are quite frequently major financial institutions, who have "deep pockets" to offset unanticipated cost increases that may occur during the development of a project. In a competitive market, interest and tenant improvement costs can escalate rapidly. The institutional investor is usually responsible for its share of cost increases and may be persuaded to fund the developer's share for an increased economic interest in the project.

2. *Large capitalization projects.* Larger, multiphase projects often

require a significant initial equity investment to purchase land or develop property infrastructure (streets, utilities, etc.). These funds can be obtained from an institutional investor as equity instead of debt. These "patient" dollars do not strap the developer with required debt service payments until the property is generating income.

3. *Fix financing costs in advance.* It is difficult to obtain permanent financing prior to the start of construction. Permanent lenders, who are typically matching funds (assets to liabilities), are unwilling to commit funds at a specified rate for funding in the future when the cost of raising the money is unknown. With joint ventures and participating debt, the lender is hedging this rate risk by participating in income and value increases and therefore is willing to fix the base interest cost of the permanent loan well in advance of funding. The joint venture enables the developer to deal effectively with a critical variable in the development process—the cost of long-term financing.

4. *Term and rate.* Joint venture financing is usually available for longer terms and at lower coupon rates than nonparticipating fixed-rate loans. In recent years, few nonparticipating loans carry terms in excess of 10 years. On the contrary, most participating loans carry terms of 15 to 25 years and interest rates of 50 to 150 basis points below nonparticipating loans. In periods of high interest rates, as was experienced in 1982 and 1983, a rate differential as high as 200 to 300 basis points was not uncommon.

5. *Leverage.* Due to the lower cost of debt in joint venture financing, more dollars can be obtained than in a conventional loan. The ability to leverage the project's cost through debt may increase the return to the developer as the income grows.

6. *Retention of ownership and tax benefits.* With a participating loan, the borrower retains title to the property and 100 percent ownership and therefore keeps all the tax benefits associated with the property. Further, the lender's kicker is quite often structured as additional or contingent interest, which may be treated as a deductible tax expense for the developer.

7. *Managerial control.* With a participating loan, the developer can often maintain managerial control over the property, although the mortgage or deed of trust will often specify more operational requirements on the part of the developer than what is normally found in a nonparticipating mortgage document.

The joint venture structure may also be disadvantageous for the developer. For example, the developer sacrifices a portion of the cash flow and equity appreciation in the property in exchange for the capital.

Many developers are accustomed to retaining 100 percent of the appreciation of the property and cannot see allowing the investor to participate in 50 percent or more of the value increase in the property over the holding period. Many joint venture structures also allocate a portion of the tax benefits to the investor partner.

The joint venture structure often calls for dual control and authority over policy and management decisions by developer and investor, both of whom may not always agree about overall strategies or chose to handle problems in the same way.

Once a participating loan or joint venture structure is in place, there will be prohibitions against the refinancing or sale of the property until the coventurer agrees to the sale or refinancing or until a certain period has passed. The developer is quite often locked into the structure for a longer period of time than is typical for most nonparticipating loan structures.

Joint ventures are often complicated transactions. It may take a long time to negotiate a joint venture agreement properly. This time up front can delay construction in excess of six months and, more important, may mean that, given the volatility of the marketplace and the short-term exigencies that determine project success or failure, the project will face a less favorable market situation than when it was first conceived.

The lender's overriding goal is to obtain more than minimum return on its investment through participation in cash flow, tax benefits, and appreciation of the property on sale or refinancing. During the 1970s, many lenders, particularly life insurance companies, saw their returns on long-term fixed-rate mortgages eroded by high inflation. Since real estate has always been considered an excellent hedge against inflation, lenders began to see this concept of additional compensation as an excellent way to invest in real estate. The joint venture structure, in particular, seemed an excellent means for the lender to participate in the benefits of real estate ownership while using the experience and expertise of the developer.

Since most joint ventures are structured prior to start of construction, the lender can participate in the value created by real estate development. This is particularly true of larger multiphase projects where the value of each subsequent phase is enhanced by the success of each previous phase of development.

Participating in ownership and appreciation also enables the lender to justify making loans on higher-risk properties such as co-op conversions, commercial condominium developments, and hotels.

Not all lenders feel comfortable with joint ventures or participating loan structures, because the overall yield to the lender very much depends on property yield and economic conditions, neither of which are within the lender's control. Further, additional time and effort by experienced personnel is required to negotiate and monitor these types of transactions.

It is true that the developer assumes the risk of primary loss, but after the 1973–1974 real estate crunch, which involved many unfavorable judicial decisions, lenders have become less certain about which party bears the loss when projects do not perform to expectations. Consequently, many investors now prefer to acquire a 100 percent equity interest without a developer partner.

Roles and Responsibilities

The motives of each party in a joint venture or participating loan structure are frequently quite different. These motives condition the roles and responsibilities of each party to determine the joint venture's financial structure.

Several issues are related to the structure of the joint venture which must be addressed at the outset of the negotiations. Significant compromise is often required to complete these transactions. The developers' typical negotiating position is that they are the experts and therefore should control all development decisions. The lender, however, is likely to believe that whoever has the gold should rule. The lender will view the transaction from the perspective of a secured creditor adhering to business judgments and guidelines that it has developed over the years as a lender.

There must be a meeting of the minds between developer and lender for a joint venture structure to be successful. Each party must perceive that the scales are in balance, i.e., its contribution c plus risk undertaken r equals its perceived benefit b: $c + r = b$. If either party does not perceive this equation to be in balance for itself and its partner, the venture will not run smoothly. Therefore, it is critical that each party feel comfortable with both sides of the equation prior to accepting a joint venture agreement.

In a joint venture with a participating debt structure, the lender takes the role of a creditor and will require the typical mortgage clauses found in any nonparticipating loan structure. The lender does not fund until the base building is completed and until a certain minimum percentage of the leases has been signed. The lender will insist on leasing requirements, since it is concerned not only with maintaining the present value of the property but also with ensuring that the future rents and income escalate to provide the opportunity for the lender to share in cash flow. Participating debt lenders will generally veto a 10-

year fixed-rate lease, even if it is with a Triple A tenant, because this form of lease structure does not allow the project's income to keep pace with inflation and market conditions and thereby limits the interim value of the lender's participation.

The shared responsibility of the parties for policy and management is often the source of problems. The developer thinks and makes decisions extemporaneously, while institutional investors tend to be cautious and require committees to approve certain decisions. Further, in many situations, the institutional investor is both the lender and a joint venture partner, and therefore, active in both the debtor and ownership aspects of the venture. Often what is good for the joint venture may not be good for the lender. Consequently, the institutional investor must carefully evaluate its investment goals in the venture.

Whether or not the joint venture is set up in a general partnership form, the institutional investor will want to exercise some measure of control over the affairs of the venture. Often the institutional investor will not have the experience or personnel to manage the daily operation of the property, and, therefore, these functions are typically delegated to the developer. But the institutional investor will require either unanimous consent or majority consent with respect to major decisions including selling or mortgaging joint venture assets, making substantial capital improvements, borrowing funds, settling insurance or condemnation claims, taking legal action on behalf of the venture, and hiring or firing the manager of the property.

The mortgage and joint venture agreement should be carefully written and negotiated to define and limit what the institutional investor's fiduciary responsibilities are to its coventurer so that if the venture fails, the institution will not be precluded from exercising its rights as mortgagee as defined in the mortgage documents.

Forms of Joint Ventures and Participating Debt

Participating mortgages are debt instruments that feature additional yield provisions to the lender in the form of equity and/or cash flow participation. The basic structure involves a below-market interest rate, usually 50 to 200 basis points below nonparticipating, fixed-rate debt, and a participation by the lender, sometimes referred to as a "kicker" or "additional interest." There are basically three types of participation: percentage of cash flow, percentage of effective gross income, and percentage of appreciation of the property.

The participation as percentage of cash flow allows the lender to share in profits only when net income exceeds all expenses and debt service. Most participating mortgages with cash flow participation will allow a lender to share in 25 to 50 percent of net cash flow. There is a practical problem with this form of kicker—difficulty to administer, particularly in ascertaining actual expenses. Most lenders will insist upon annual audited statements and detailed language within the loan documents that define which expenses are to be included or excluded in the calculation of additional compensation.

The alternative is to tie the kicker into a percentage of effective gross income, which may or may not exclude charges for common area maintenance, utilities charges and other pass-through income items not directly related to charges for occupancy of space. The percentage of effective gross income available to the lender typically ranges between 3 and 7 percent. Unfortunately, this structure does not always enable the developer to retain enough income to pay debt service prior to allocation of a kicker to the lender. Consequently, many effective gross income kickers are structured with participation over a floor or base amount of income to ensure coverage of expenses and debt service and a minimum return to the developer prior to participation by the lender. This form typically allows the lender to participate in anywhere from 15 to 40 percent of the increases in effective gross income over first-year effective gross income or a base amount.

Lenders prefer that the kicker be applied to gross rather than net income, because this permits the lender to share directly in any increases in revenues irrespective of changes in operating expenses. Further, this form of participation is simpler to calculate and administer. Borrowers, however, prefer to deduct operating expenses prior to calculating the lender's income participation, because operating expenses may be more volatile than revenues.

Both lender and borrower will be indifferent to the type of income kicker when the property exhibits a relatively fixed operating expense ratio or the lender's participation in effective gross income is above a stated minimum amount and takes into account offsets for leasing and refit expenses and pass-through expenses.

The third kind of kicker is a participation in the appreciation of the property upon repayment of the loan or sale of the property. Typically, the lender will receive a percentage of the net sales price, which is the total sales price less the cost of sale, less one of the following: (1) the unpaid principal balance of the mortgage, (2) the original mortgage amount, (3) the original investment, (4) the original appraised value, or (5) some other number agreed upon between lender and borrower. Depending on which structure is used, the lender will receive a percentage of appreciation in property value, original equity, and equity buildup.

The interest rate, percentage of cash flow, and percentage of appreciation are all negotiable. But the lower the interest rate that the lender is willing to offer, the higher percentage of participation the lender will require in compensation for the lower rate.

Effective Gross Income Kicker

Effective gross income, net operating income, operating expenses, and net sales proceeds need to be well defined in the loan documents so that neither lender nor borrower will disagree as to how the kicker is calculated. The participation structure is delineated in the promissory note and may appear as follows:

> The Lender shall receive as contingent interest an amount equal to the product of both: (i) 50 percent and (ii) the amount equal to the excess of Gross Income (as hereinafter defined) over $4,000,000 (the Floor Amount), on the date (the Determination Date) when not less than 200,000 net rentable square feet of space in the Building have been leased.
>
> Gross Income shall mean (i) total rental receipts and all other revenue from the Premises attributable to the Development less only (a) rental increases to the extent provided for in occupancy leases, based on increases in operating expenses and taxes over those in effect during the first full year of operation after completion, and (b) an annual amount equal to any payment or payments that would be required to provide level amortization, at your cost of funds (but not to exceed the prime rate of National Bank, N.A.) as of the commencement of use of each approved improvement over the useful life thereof, of the cost of any capital improvement approved by Lender; (ii) excess funds generated from any refinancing of the Mortgage (as hereinafter defined); and, (iii) net sales proceeds from the sale or transfer of the Premises.
>
> Contingent Interest will be payable with respect to the first calendar year in which it is determined that Gross Income exceeds the Floor Amount, as adjusted (if any), within 120 days after the end of such year.
>
> Thereafter, Contingent Interest will be payable in advance in estimated monthly installments subject to adjustment within 120 days after the end of each such year based on statements prepared by the accountant.

Net Cash Flow Kicker Structure

> The Lender shall receive as Contingent Interest, 50 percent of the Net Cash Flow, as hereinafter defined, from operation of the land and the improvements (to be built) thereon ("Demised Premises"). Contingent Interest shall be payable quarterly on or before the 20th day of the month following the end of the quarter and shall be based on the Net Cash Flow for the previous quarter. There will be an annual reconciliation of the quarterly statements based upon an annual audit prepared by a nationally recognized certified public accounting firm satisfactory to Lender.

For purpose of computing Contingent Interest, Net Cash Flow shall be defined as follows:

Total annual cash receipts from operations of the Demised Premises from which there shall be deducted:

(1). Annual debt service which is paid on any permanent first mortgage loan permitted by the Lender;

(2). Actual annual charges paid in connection with the operating of the Demised Premises which shall consist of real estate taxes and assessments; premiums for insurance coverage approved by Lender; utility costs; elevator maintenance charges; cost of repairs and maintenance; charge for the independent audit required above; and charges for cleaning and cleaning supplies;

(3). Actual annual costs associated with the management of the Demised Premises, said management costs to consist of salaries, benefits, and payroll taxes of all supervisory and "in-house" personnel, rents paid for office space, supplies and telephone costs; but said total management costs not to exceed 3 percent of total annual cash receipts;

(4). A deposit to be placed in a reserve fund in form and content satisfactory to Lender and as defined below in the amount of 5 percent of the total annual cash receipts not to exceed $500,000 at any one time to be used to pay tenant improvement costs for space released, outside broker releasing commissions, and capital replacement items. With the exceptions of those included in contracts to arm's-length third-party contractors, any payroll and/or salary expenses associated with the operations of the Demised Premises are to be included under Management and/or Payroll and are not to be allocated to the other expense categories listed above. In addition, no debt service except for that referred to in (1) of this provision is to be recognized as an expense of the Demised Premises.

A reserve fund shall be established into which 5 percent of the total cash receipts not to exceed $500,000 at any one time shall be deposited quarterly. Funds may be withdrawn from this account to cover the cost of capital expenditures for rehabilitation of tenant improvements and leasing commissions incurred with new and/or renewal subleases or for major capital replacements and/or necessary improvements to the Demised Premises. Said reserve fund shall be maintained in an interest bearing account at a local bank satisfactory to Lender. Withdrawals from the account may be made by Borrower without Lender's consent, provided the amount of any single expenditure specified above does not exceed $10,000.

In the event the property is sold, the proceeds of sale will be distributed as follows: First, to retire the existing Loan, with prepayment penalty, if applicable; Second, to pay brokerage costs, if any, incurred on such sale and usually paid by seller; Third, to pay title policy costs and other incidental costs of the sale usually paid by the seller; Fourth, the remaining net proceeds 50 percent to Lender and 50 percent to the Borrower.

Life insurance companies and pension funds are the most active participating debt lenders. There lenders are looking not only to protect their investment against inflation eroding a fixed rate of return but also to share in the excellent returns that are available from the ownership of commercial real estate.

Convertible Debt

The convertible debt instrument has recently become an attractive investment vehicle, particularly for pension funds. Convertible debt features a conversion option allowing the lender to convert its mortgage balance into equity ownership some years in the future. The lender offers the borrower an attractive mortgage with a high loan-to-value ratio, and a below-market interest rate, in exchange for the privilege of buying into the future ownership of the property.

The typical structure involves a participation or kicker feature whereby the lender receives a percentage of cash flow (50 to 90 percent) and the right to convert the loan balance into an ownership position (anywhere from 50 to 90 percent) between the third and tenth year of the loan. Often, the lender will combine the conversion option with an option to buy the borrower's remaining equity interest at a predetermined price or price based on a formula. This way, the lender is in the position to acquire 100 percent ownership. As an alternative to the conversion option, the lender frequently is given the right to call the loan at conversion time or renew the loan on specified terms.

The convertible loan structure gives the lender the element of both debt and equity positions in real estate investment. Prior to conversion, the lender's investment is in a primary collateral position, receiving a fixed rate of return and a participation feature providing an inflation hedge and interest in the appreciation of the property. The lender has several years to observe the performance of the property and the managerial ability of the borrower, prior to making the decision regarding ownership of the property.

This structure nevertheless entails several disadvantages for the lender. If the property does not perform up to standards, the lender will receive only a minimal rate of return, which can be 200 or more basis points below fixed-rate, nonparticipating yields. Further, the lender is in a riskier position with a loan-to-value ratio as high as 80 to 90 percent. Although borrowers are limiting their share of the appreciation of the property, they retain all tax benefits until conversion, since this is a debt structure until that time.

A word of caution with respect to the convertible debt structure. Significant legal and tax problems may arise if the IRS deems this structure to be a partnership and not a loan. The borrower may be limited from deducting interest and taking full advantage of the tax benefits. Most developers who choose this loan structure believe the tax risk is offset by the fact that the current market value of the percentage of ownership available to the lender upon conversion equals the lender's initial investment.

Land Sale-Leaseback and Leasehold Mortgage Loans

The land sale-leaseback transaction is a multitiered real estate transaction that involves segregating land and improvements into separate elements of financing. The parties involved in this structure include an investor who purchases the land and leases it back to the developer; the lender who places a mortgage on the improvements; and the borrower who intends to develop the property or owns the existing improvements on the land. It is explained in Chapter 22 as a form of permanent financing and is also briefly discussed in Chapter 9.

Joint Ventures

A true joint venture involves a money partner putting up the entire cost of development either in the form of all equity or combination of debt and equity. In return, the money partner receives a percentage ownership interest in the development. This ownership interest usually includes a percentage of all the benefits of real estate ownership including cash flow, appreciation and tax benefits. The all-cash equity joint venture involves a money partner putting up all the dollars in the form of equity and, in return, obtaining a general partnership position. The developer receives a partnership interest equal to the increase in market value as a result of construction and development of the project ("value created"). Typically, the split is 80 percent to the money partner and 20 percent to the developer. Each partner receives a preferred return on equity invested, with the developer's preferred return related to the equity realized from the development of the improvements.

A second type of joint venture can be structured with the lender-investor providing a first mortgage loan equal to 75 percent to 85 percent of the cost of the improvements and a rate that is 100 to 200 basis points below nonparticipating, fixed-rate yields. The rest of the construction cost is provided in the form of equity with the investor receiving a preferred return of 8 to 10 percent on the equity invested. With this format, the lender-investor receives 50 to 60 percent interest in the development. The reason for the reduced percentage, as opposed to the all-equity joint venture, is the fact that the lender has a primary collateral position with the first mortgage loan, and the interest rate on the first mortgage loan is typically 50 to 100 basis points higher than the preferred return on equity. Both structures reduce the developer's risk by providing a "deep pockets" money partner who will be responsible for contributing its share of any cost increases. Further, this deal structure may provide for the investor partner to come up with all the cost increases if the developer is unable to contribute its share.

The third type of joint venture structure is similar to both of the aforementioned joint venture structures but has a shorter or interim time frame. This financing transaction between a real estate developer and a lender is intended to last fewer than five years. The lender puts up the required funds, and the developer supplies the staffing and expertise necessary to build a project. Institutions such as savings and loans, commercial banks, syndicators, and credit companies receive 25 to 60 percent of the financial benefit of the real estate development in exchange for providing this interim structuring.

Although most interim ventures are structured for speculative construction projects, they also finance existing property in need of renovation or retrofitting for new tenants. Regardless of property type, developers who choose this type of financing are generally more risk oriented than those who would prefer longer and more permanent equity funds; at the same time, they are more conservative than those developers who speculate on interest and rental rates.

In an *interim joint venture* structure, the lender will provide up to 100 percent of the cost in the form of an 18- to 24-month construction loan that converts into a three-year miniperm loan. The interest rate is a floating rate at market with 1 to 2 points in fees. Thus developers not only receive 100 percent financing, but they limit their risk of leasing the project since these loans typically become nonrecourse at completion of shell construction. Cash flow generally is meaningless in these ventures because the lender is already getting most of the cash flow in its debt service requirement. Therefore, the lender's main return is in the form of a kicker or a percentage of the appreciation of the property.

There are several variations to this structure, including one in which the lender takes a kicker as a "back-end fee" or a fixed dollar amount, instead of outright ownership benefits. Another variation is the standby equity structure, which is a two-tiered loan structure. Here a construction lender is willing to advance all the costs if the borrower provides that lender with a letter of credit for the top 10 to 20 percent of the loan amount. Savings institutions as well as syndicators, credit corporations, and banks have agreed to provide this "letter of credit" for either fees, kickers, or ownership. The compensation is based on the risk involved; however, it is usually in the form of fees plus a 25 to 50 percent of the ownership if the letter of credit is funded. This is exactly the same as an interim debt joint venture structure, except that two separate institutional investors are involved in the deal.

Credit Enhancement

Credit enhancement is used more often in bond financing than in conventional transactions. Banks and insurance companies will agree to add their credit in the form of a direct repayment obligation to a third-party lender in order to facilitate 100 percent financing. In return, the institution gets an ownership position for its role. Life insurance companies use this vehicle often for tax free bond financing. The financial strength of the life insurance company guarantees a tax free bond. This allows the borrower to go to the capital markets and sell the bonds at attractive tax-free rates. In return, the guarantor typically receives up to a 50 percent ownership position in the project.

Banks typically use letters of credit to enhance the credit of the bonds. Thus, the bond holders look to the letter of credit and financial strength of the bank to secure repayment. The bank takes the real estate risk and secures its obligation with a first mortgage lien on the property.

The use of credit enhancement has also been expanded to conventional loans, primarily in the securitization of commercial real estate mortgages. With these transactions the credit enhancer usually receives fees, 1 to 2 percent per year, and not an equity position in the transaction.

As one can see, joint ventures and participation loans can take various forms. The form chosen depends greatly upon the objectives of both the developer-borrower and lender-investor. The developer-borrower must establish clear objectives before embarking on and structuring a joint venture structure.

Figure 23.1 (pages 268 and 269) shows a checklist of joint venture issues, and Figure 23.2 (pages 270 and 271) is an outline of a joint venture agreement.

Figure 23.1. Joint venture issues checklist.

QUALIFICATIONS

1. How much development experience is required?
2. What properties are eligible?
3. Can existing properties qualify?
4. What information is necessary for presentation?
5. Is there a minimum dollar amount?
6. Can a developer also be the contractor?
7. How do lenders calculate desired return rates?
8. What is the minimum cash-on-cash rate required?
9. Do lenders want long-term partnerships?

COSTS

1. Do lenders put up all the money?
2. Can a developer charge a fee for services?
3. How much rent-up expense can be included?
4. How should interest be calculated?
5. Can excess tenant work be included?
6. Do lenders usually charge a loan fee?
7. Should a contingency reserve be included?

PROCEDURES

1. How fast can a lender act and fund?
2. What documentation is involved?
3. What form of ownership is used?
4. Is the money advanced as debt or equity?
5. When is the money funded?
6. Do lenders require audited statements?
7. Can individuals get separate ownership interest?
8. Is there a development agreement?
9. Can construction be fast-tracked?
10. Can land be purchased prior to completion of construction drawings?

COMPENSATION

1. Do lenders want ownership or kickers?
2. Who gets the tax benefits?

(Continued)

Figure 23.1. Joint ventures issues checklist. (*Continued*)

3. How is the lender's share of cash flow calculated?
4. Are preferred returns cumulative?
5. Can a developer charge a leasing fee?
6. How are resale procedures split?
7. Can a partner charge a sale fee?
8. Who gets the excess refinancing proceeds?
9. Can a developer get a property management fee?

CONTROL

1. How are leases approved?
2. Who can approve change orders?
3. Which party can arrange the sale?
4. Who handles subsequent financing?
5. Which party determines the tax strategy?
6. Are there any performance standards?
7. Who handles construction issues?
8. Who manages the property when completed?
9. Do lenders require an independent consultant?
10. Who handles the publicity?

NEGOTIABLE

1. Which party is responsible for overrun?
2. How is a dilution handled?
3. What if one party wants to sell?
4. Can an early buyout provision be negotiated?
5. Can the loan be prepaid without penalty?
6. Who gets the cost savings?
7. Does the developer have to guarantee cash flow, costs, or repayment?
8. How are interests valued at time of sale?
9. Are disputes handled by arbitration?
10. Can a developer get a below-market rate?
11. Who obtains the construction loan?
12. Do lenders guarantee performance to third parties?

Figure 23.2. Outline of a joint venture agreement.

ARTICLE	1	CREATION AND PURPOSE: DURATION
SECTION	1.01	Creation and Purpose
	1.02	Options of Counsel: Corporate Authorizations
	1.03	Designation of Representatives
	1.04	Assumed Names; Name of Project
	1.05	Principal Place of Business
	1.06	Duration
	1.07	Memorandum of Joint-Venture Agreement
ARTICLE	2	ACQUISITION OF THE PROJECT
SECTION	2.01	Completion of the Project
	2.02	Acquisition of the Project
	2.03	Conditions Precedent to the Acquisition of the Project
	2.04	Payment for the Project
ARTICLE	3	SOURCES AND APPLICATION OF JOINT-VENTURES FUNDS; DEPOSITORIES: ACCOUNTING PROCEDURES AND AUDITS
SECTION	3.01	Permanent Financing of Project
	3.02	Initial Capital Contributions
	3.03	Liabilities of Venturers: Additional Capital Contributions
	3.04	Accounting Procedures
	3.05	Auditors: Reports
ARTICLE	4	DECISIONS REGARDING VENTURE
SECTION	4.01	Decisions Regarding Venture
	4.02	Limitations on Authority of Venturers
	4.03	Disputes
	4.04	Consummation of Sale
ARTICLE	5	MANAGEMENT OF PROJECT
SECTION	5.01	Developer as Manager
	5.02	Compensation of Project Manager

(Continued)

Figure 23.2. Outline of a joint venture agreement. (*Continued*)

ARTICLE	6	TRANSFERABILITY RESTRICTIONS ON TRANSFER
SECTION	6.01	Right of Transfer Restricted
	6.02	Permissable Transfers
	6.03	Right of First Refusal
	6.04	Buy-Sell
	6.05	Indemnification of Selling Venturer
	6.06	Sale in Violation of Joint Venture Agreement
ARTICLE	7	BANKRUPTCY
SECTION	7.01	Bankruptcy or Insolvency of a Venturer
	7.02	Right to Purchase Interest of an Inactive Venturer
ARTICLE	8	EVENTS OF DEFAULTS: REMEDIES
ARTICLE	9	WINDING UP : LIQUIDATION DISTRIBUTION
SECTION	9.01	Winding up
	9.02	Liquidation Distribution
	9.03	Distribution of Project
ARTICLE	10	MISCELLANEOUS
SECTION	10.01	Further Assurances
	10.02	Notices
	10.03	Equitable Remedies
	10.04	Remedies Cumulative
	10.05	No Partnership
	10.06	Brokerage
	10.07	Indemnities
	10.08	Legal Disabilities
	10.09	Captions; Partial Invalidity
	10.10	Entire Agreement
	10.11	Applicable Law
	10.12	Counterparts, Complete Agreement
	10.13	Successors

PART 6

Submitting, Negotiating, Closing, and Administering the Loan

24

The Mortgage Financing Submission

Donald H. Schefmeyer, CMB, SRPA

President, Action Mortgage Corporation
South Bend, Indiana

The mortgage financing submission, or "loan package," may be defined as an analytical report which presents information about a particular income property project including data and reasoning to support the requested loan.

The purpose of the loan package is to underwrite a deal. Its function is to sell an investor on the deal. Functionally, at least, the submission is a sales tool. It should be tailored to the specific investor or lender targeted as the most likely source of funds for the transaction. Most life insurance companies, as well as large thrift institutions, have specific criteria to govern the underwriting of a particular type of income-producing property. If possible, a set of current underwriting guidelines should have been obtained from the proposed lender prior to preparing the submission.

This chapter reviews the critical path to be followed in the preparation and presentation of loan submissions for income properties, focusing on the general items that should be included in all loan submissions as well as some of the specific exhibits necessary for several of the major property types.

The Loan Application

After a developer or project sponsor has been contacted and a preliminary evaluation has indicated that the project warrants financing, the mortgage banker must determine which of the available sources are the most likely candidates to provide the funds. Mortgage bankers know in advance the general terms and conditions under which a particular investor will make a loan. This knowledge, coupled with an analysis of the requirements for the project, will enable the mortgage banker to select the appropriate application format for the particular project.

A formal application should always be taken even when the mortgage banker and sponsor (borrower) have a long-term established business relationship. Most applications take the form of a unilateral contract that specifies both general and specific terms and conditions governing both the mortgage banker's employment by the sponsor and the type of financing being sought. The application will cover the following items:

- Mortgage banker's authority from the potential borrower to arrange financing
- Exclusivity of authorization—the borrower usually makes one mortgage banking firm its exclusive agent but may limit the exclusive agency to particular sources of financing
- Consideration—covers the fee to be received for placing the loan
- Application period and cancellation provisions—the mortgage banker is the authorized agent for a specified period, and terms of cancellation are specified
- Sponsor's agreement to provide necessary exhibits and information to be included in the loan application
- Authority of sponsor to contract (e.g., corporate authorization)
- Applicable governing law (regarding application)
- Assignment provisions of application

The foregoing items clarify the employment of the mortgage banker. The remainder of the application recites the general terms and conditions under which the lender will extend credit.

Since the mortgage banker's fees are earned at the point at which a commitment for financing has been obtained (1) in accordance "with the terms and conditions enumerated in the application" or (2) upon the sponsor's acceptance of a commitment, the application should be as specific as possible. Just how detailed an application should be depends on the following criteria:

1. The mortgage banker's knowledge of a particular lender's program and commitment format

2. The complexity of the financing being sought

3. The sponsor's level of sophistication

On balance, an extremely detailed and specific application is a two-edged sword. It will eliminate many misunderstandings and provide a large measure of comfort about the sponsor's and mortgage banker's responsibilities to each other. However, in the likely event that the lender changes a term or condition from that which is specified in the application, the mortgage banker's fee may be at risk until the application is amended.

At an absolute minimum, the application should address the following items:

- Loan amount
- Interest rate
- Term of loan
- Amortization schedule and payment frequency
- Escrow requirements (tax and insurance)
- Description of collateral offered as security
- Loan delivery date
- Guarantees (personal endorsement)
- Legal style of borrower; capacity, authority
- Transfer/alienation rights of mortgagor
- Copies of leases
- Prepayment privilege
- Adverse change provisions
- Utilities and services available
- Roads and access
- Plans and specifications
- Construction contracts/mechanics liens
- Inspections
- Equity kickers (if any)
- Documents required

The documents required include:

- Survey
- Title insurance

- Operating and financial statements
- Insurance (hazard, liability, flood)
- Appraisal report
- Soils report

Having signed up the sponsor and having obtained a good faith deposit, the mortgage banker is now in a position to place the loan with an investor.

The Loan Submission

A good loan submission is one which is *effective*. Depending on the complexity of the deal and the credibility of the mortgage banker, a loan submission can be as brief as a cover letter with a photograph or as complicated as a full-blown analytical report with all ancillary exhibits. The extent of detail in a submission depends on the complexity of the financing and the length of time available to the mortgage banker to arrange it. In recent years, submission packages have begun to grow in weight and sophistication. The use of computers to develop projections, inexpensive graphics, and quality copier service have all contributed to a product which is much more impressive to look at than the nondescript Acco-bound reports of previous years. However, quality, not quantity, is the touchstone of a good submission. A well-developed neighborhood analysis with supporting rental, sales, and tax comparables is far more valuable to a lender than 10 pages of projections leading to an internal rate of return (IRR) of questionable validity. As in a well-researched appraisal report, the best submission will concentrate on the basics.

A standard loan submission package consists of the following sections, each of which is discussed hereafter:

- Cover letter (letter of transmission)
- Cover page (with photo)
- Project summary
- Appraisal or feasibility analysis
- Borrower analysis
- Rental
- Underwriting
- Supporting exhibits and addenda

In a normal economy, the mortgage investment personnel in the income property departments of life companies and thrifts constantly review requests from mortgage bankers, developers, and affiliates. The mortgage banker's job is to get the "deal" reviewed as early as possible. Several things motivate a lender to pick a particular loan submission from the stack of those received: First is the credibility of the company making the submission and that of the particular mortgage banker, and second is the loan application package that is well-organized, well-written, and complete. Nothing is more frustrating for a lender than an incomplete package or one which looks as if it has been written by an illiterate. Write concisely and grammatically, or hire someone who can.

Whenever possible, be brief. Most reports should not exceed 20 written pages (not counting exhibits) with emphasis on the supporting assumptions used in accurately calculating income and expenses. This support should include rent comparables, improved property sale comparables, land sale comparables, subject land acquisition history, and a project cost review. Existing properties should provide documentation such as three to five years' operating statements, with accompanying analyses.

The Letter of Transmittal

The letter of transmittal, or cover letter, is a key part of the submission package. It is the first item to be read. A well-crafted cover letter sets the stage for a financing request and can prejudice a lender for or against a project. The purpose of the letter is to excite the investor's curiosity to read further. It is also an excellent place to call attention to the project's strong points and, conversely, to finesse any perceived weakness.

The cover letter should be written immediately prior to submission to a particular lender, to reflect the lender's preferences and idiosyncrasies. It should rarely exceed 2 pages and should be kept separate from the bound report. It should address the following items:

- Basic loan terms
- Fee structure and servicing rate
- Estimated delivery date
- Mortgage banker's recommendation

The Cover Page

The cover page of the bound report should include the project's name, location, and the name of the mortgage banking firm. If available, a 5-

inch by 7-inch color photograph should be mounted in the center. This format establishes an early visual identity with the project.

The Project Summary

The project summary is to a financial submission what a "Summary of Salient Facts and Conclusions" is to an appraisal report. It is a *1-page* recitation of the project: Description of improvements, loan request, sponsorship, tenancy, statistics regarding the costs, income characteristics and underwriting ratios. (See Figure 24.1.) The summary is the single most important page in the report. It is easily reproduced for loan committee distribution and allows a busy lender to get the facts "at a glance."

Figure 24.1. Mortgage Loan Summary.

<table>
<tr><td colspan="3" align="center">NOTTINGHAM APARTMENTS
INDIANAPOLIS, INDIANA</td></tr>
<tr><td>PROJECT:</td><td colspan="2">Contemporary styled, 102–unit garden apartment and townhouse project currently under construction.</td></tr>
<tr><td>LOAN REQUEST:</td><td colspan="2">AMOUNT: $3,400,000   TYPE: Construction/Permanent
RATE: 10%   YIELD: 13%   TERM: 10 YEARS</td></tr>
<tr><td></td><td colspan="2">PAYMENTS: Payments to interest-only for the first 2 years; 28-year annotation thereafter.</td></tr>
<tr><td></td><td colspan="2">EQUITY KICKER: Participation in the Before Tax Cash Flow and the Reversion in an amount sufficient to yield 13% IRR.</td></tr>
<tr><td></td><td colspan="2">GUARANTY: Both the debt and the yield of 13% are guaranteed by the Sponsor.</td></tr>
<tr><td></td><td colspan="2">FEE: 2% ($68,000)   Delivery: Immediate</td></tr>
<tr><td>SPONSOR:</td><td colspan="2">*Nottingham Associates*, an Indiana Limited Partnership.</td></tr>
<tr><td></td><td>General partner</td><td>% owner   Net worth</td></tr>
<tr><td></td><td>Bob Smith</td><td>33⅓ $1,013,661</td></tr>
<tr><td></td><td>John Jones</td><td>33⅓   556,300</td></tr>
<tr><td></td><td>Bill White</td><td>33⅓   923,500</td></tr>
<tr><td></td><td colspan="2">The partners are also limited partners in the project. Their combined annual income exceeds $500,000 annually.</td></tr>
<tr><td>UNDERWRITING DATA:</td><td colspan="2"></td></tr>
<tr><td></td><td>Site Area: 6.4 acres</td><td>Cost: $280,000</td></tr>
<tr><td></td><td>Parking: 215 cars</td><td>Parking Ratio: 2:11 units</td></tr>
<tr><td></td><td>No. of units: 102</td><td>Land Cost/Unit: $2,745</td></tr>
</table>

(Continued)

Figure 24.1. Mortgage Loan Summary. *(Continued)*

No. of Garages: 104		Garage Area: 27,456 sq. ft.	
GBA: 122,910 sq. ft.		NRA: 103,673 sq. ft.	
% Efficiency: 84%		No. of Buildings: 6	
			Rent per
Unit mix	Rental	NRA	square foot
48 2BR	@ $506	1012 sq.ft.	$.50
6 2BR	@ 526	2012	.52
36 2BNR	@ 536	1071	.50
12 3BRTH	@ 666	1332	.50
Community Building: 1080 sq. ft.			
GROSS POTENTIAL INCOME		$681,264	
Vacancy Allowance (5%):		(34,064)	
EFFECTIVE GROSS INCOME:		647,200	
Annual Expense:		(213,040)	
NET OPERATING INCOME:		$434,160	

Appraisal and Feasibility Analysis

This analysis is the research section of the report. It essentially follows the format of a narrative appraisal but typically will not include the superfluous rhetoric normally found in appraisals, such as certifications, limiting conditions, the appraiser's life history, numerous pages of Chamber of Commerce data, description of the three approaches to value, or other such material.

In recent years it has become the fashion among mortgage bankers to include a separate appraisal report prepared by an MAI or SRPA appraiser in lieu of presenting their own field work. The excuse most often heard is that since a mortgage banking firm's fee is based on a percentage of the loan obtained it cannot be objective when it comes to estimating value. Although the uninitiated might find this logic compelling, it is in fact nonsense. There is no excuse for not doing one's own field work.

Economy of language should be stressed in this section. The standard report framework is outlined as follows:

Site Analysis. The site analysis should emphasize that the site is adequate to support the intended use. The following items should be addressed:

- Brief description of specific location in area

- Size (dimensions and square footage)
- Topography and drainage
- Frontage and access
- Utilities available
- Services available: police, fire, and transportation
- Parking available on-site
- Landscaping
- Reference to site plan, photo, aerial photo

Improvements Analysis. Improvements analysis should focus on the quality and cost-effectiveness of the improvements. Other important aspects would include the salable nature of the real estate and its potential for conversion to another use. Lenders prefer functional, general-purpose properties.

1. Basic, brief description of buildings
   a. Type of construction
   b. Gross building area and net rentable area
   c. Motif
   d. Layout and special features
2. Major building components
   a. Foundation
   b. Floors (and coverings)
   c. Walls (and coverings)
   d. Ceiling
   e. Roof (and cover)
   f. Interior design (partitioning)
   g. Windows and doors
   h. Mechanical systems: electrical, plumbing, HVAC, sprinkler, alarm
3. Reference to plans, specifications, and photos

Neighborhood Analysis. Neighborhood analysis is far more important than overall area analysis, since it calls for specific knowledge from the mortgage banker. This analysis should proceed from general to specific observations. The lender will rely on the mortgage banker's assessment of the local market and any observable environmental obsolescence or special benefits in close proximity to the subject, e.g., medical building near a hospital.

- Describe the neighborhood in detail: its position in the city; its general boundaries; its developed uses (commercial, retail, industrial); and its position in the life cycle (established, transitional).

- Describe traffic arteries: the distance to the central business district, the distance to major interchanges, and the traffic count.

- Tie in site and building sections by discussing the subject property's impact on the neighborhood (and vice versa).

- Give a mortgage banker's view of future neighborhood trends and their possible effect on the subject property.

Area Analysis.   The area analysis should be brief, especially if the project is located in a primary or secondary urban area well known to the investment community at large. Presentation of all data should focus on data's effect on the subject:

1. Location
2. Population and trends
3. Demographics
4. Industrial classifications
5. Retail sales
6. Type of local government
7. Major employers and characteristics of labor force
8. New construction (permits and special developments)
9. Reference to community profile, Chamber of Commerce data, Department of Labor data, census
10. Local newspaper articles of interest

Real Estate Tax Analysis.   Real estate tax analysis is an important part of the overall income and expense analysis, since real estate taxes are typically the single highest item of annual expense. The analysis should not be overlooked, even in the case of an absolutely net lease. The discussion should reflect that the existing tax or proposed burden on the property is similar to other competitive properties:

1. Assessment—assessment methodology for land and buildings
2. Ad valorem tax rates (breakdown)

3. Special charges and flat rates: flushing, snow removal, water purification, etc.

4. Tax calculations

5. Tax trend discussions and whether the subject's tax burden is similar to those of competitive properties

Economic Analysis.   Economic analysis is the most important section of the submission. It is also known as the "income approach" and entails an accurate and clearly developed stabilized income statement. All income-producing property is valued primarily on the basis of its capacity to generate rental income. In this section of the report the mortgage banker takes the estimated net operating income and capitalizes it into a value estimate by any one of a number of conceptually defensible methods. (An analysis of the income and expense statement is contained in Chapter 10.)

Stabilized Income and Expenses

1. Calculate gross income

2. Calculate vacancy allowance

3. Calculate expenses

4. Calculate net operating income

5. Develop capitalization rate

6. Capitalize net operating income into value estimate

These calculations *must* show support for the following:

1. Income used
2. Vacancy projected
3. Expense items
    a. Real estate taxes
    b. Insurance
    c. Management
    d. Utilities
    e. Maintenance and repair
    f. Decorating
    g. Reserves for replacement
    h. Lawn, snow, trash, exterminator
    i. Supplies and janitorial
    j. Advertising
    k. Payroll
    l. Miscellaneous

Physical Analysis. Physical analysis deals with the costs associated with the development of the project. It can be a valuable check for the economic analysis, particularly in cases where the project is recently completed or yet to be constructed. Older properties typically have varying amounts of curable and incurable obsolescence, which is extremely difficult to estimate.

Physical (Cost Approach) Analysis

1. Land value
    a. Acquisition cost
    b. Entrepreneurial cost
    c. Land sale comparables
        (1) Date of sale
        (2) Size of parcel
        (3) Sales price per square foot, per front foot, and per acre
        (4) Grantor and grantee
        (5) Liber (book) and page number (from land records)
        (6) Zoning and restrictions
        (7) Motivation for or type of improvements
        (8) Verification
2. Improvements cost (direct or hard)
    a. Contractor's sworn statement or engineer's cost estimate
    b. Copies of bids
    c. Check with Marshall-Swift, Dow, Boeck (services that provide construction costs)
3. Soft (indirect) costs
    a. Architect
    b. Engineer
    c. Legal and accounting
    d. Appraisal
    e. Financing fees
    f. Interest during construction

Sponsor (Borrower) Analysis

The mortgage banker's recommendation should be based on verified facts, not hearsay:

Describe the borrowing entity and its principals—is it a corporation, a partnership, or individuals?

Discuss the borrower's track record, management capabilities, financial strength, reputation.

Refer to financial statements, retail credit reports, Dun & Bradstreet reports, and the 10-K report (filed by certain corporations with the Securities and Exchange Commission).

Discuss personal endorsement, call provisions, transfer with assumption rights, prepayment privilege, special requests of borrower.

Rental Analysis

The rental section deals with each tenant or occupant of the property and its ability to pay the rent. The lease is analyzed with particular attention to those aspects which are rent payment restrictive, i.e., "who pays what," cancellation rights, subordination, eminent domain, assignment, and other topics. Figure 24.2 shows a sample lease analysis form.

Underwriting

In the underwriting part of the report, the mortgage banker analyzes the net operating income in its relationship to the annual debt service projected for the proposed loan:

1. Calculate annual debt service
2. Calculate cash throw-off
3. Debt service coverage ratio
4. Calculate breakeven point
5. Loan per square foot
6. Loan-to-value ratio
7. Balloon payment
8. Five-to-ten-year cash flow projections
9. Discounted cash flow analysis
   a. Before-tax cash flow
   b. After-tax cash flow
10. Sensitivity analysis

Exhibits

The following list of necessary exhibits is reasonably complete but will not be adequate in every case:

1. Legal description
2. Leases and lease analysis forms
3. Financial statements
4. Credit reports and Dun & Bradstreet reports

Figure 24-2. Lease analysis—data sheet.

```
                              Date: _____    Analyst _____
LESSOR:
LESSEE:
LOCATION AND/OR DESCRIPTION:
AREA LEASED:
LEASE TERM & RENEWALS:
LEASE COMMENCEMENT & EXPIRATION:
ANNUAL RENT:                  RENT/SQ. FT. _____
PERCENTAGE RENT:
USE OF PREMISES AND RESTRICTIONS:
TAXES PAID BY:                INSURANCE: Fire _____
                                         Liability _____

TAS ESCALATION CLAUSE ___ YES ___ No  BASE YEAR _____

OPERATING EXPENSE ESCALATION CLAUSE YES No BY:_____

EXPENSES PAID BY:      HEAT _____    REPAIR AND MAINTENANCE
                       WATER _____   INTERIOR _____
(T-Tenant)           ELECTRIC _____  EXTERIOR _____
                         A/C _____   ROOF _____
(L-Landlord)        JANITORIAL _____ GLASS _____
                  SNOW REMOVAL _____ STRUCTURAL _____
                 TRASH REMOVAL _____ DECORATING _____
                                     PLUMBING SYSTEM _____
PARKING LOT:          repair _____   ELEC. SYSTEM _____
                    striping _____   OTHER _____
                    lighting _____   _____
                    cleaning _____   _____

TENANT CONTRIBUTION TO PUBLIC AREAS:

CONDEMNATION CLAUSE:

CANCELLATION RIGHTS:

ASSIGNMENT AND SUBLETTING:

SUBORDINATION:        nondisturbance clause? _____

PURCHASE OPTION:

DATE SIGNED:

COMMENTS AND NOTES:

This analysis is for basic information only and is not to be considered a legal
option.
                              ACTION MORTGAGE CORPORATION

                              BY: _____
```

5. Photographs (35 mm, color)

6. Aerial photo

7. Maps—use graphics, *original map or photocopy*

8. Site plan (survey)

9. Building plans (schematics)

10. Sponsor résumé

11. Operating statements, pro forma

12. Application

13. Title policy commitment

14. Appraisal report

Some Final Thoughts

The first order of business for a mortgage submission is to sell a deal. Never send a lender a package that could be personally delivered. Never send a submission by regular mail. The cost of using one of the overnight express services is negligible in relation to the time saved and fees involved.

Try not to send a submission package to more than one lender at a time. When time constraints make this impossible, inform the lender that other people are looking at the project. No lender wants a "shopped deal."

Remember, each submission package is a direct reflection of the mortgage banker's personal professionalism, and by extension, the professionalism of the firm. A professional package enhances not only personal credibility but also the credibility of the mortgage banking firm and that of the profession as a whole.

25

Closing the Permanent Loan and Understanding the Loan Documents

Margaret V. Hathaway, Esq.

Director, Income Property Department
Mortgage Bankers Association of America, Washington, D.C.

Introduction

To a person unfamiliar with loan closing, the procedure may seem as mysterious as an initiation rite into a medieval cult. If mishandled, it can be a frustrating and costly experience for all the parties, especially when the problems cause delays in disbursement of the large sums of money involved. Unless the loan closer keeps the process smooth and well organized, the borrowers and/or lenders may take their next deal elsewhere.

Chapter 25 aims to demystify the loan-closing process by explaining how to move from the loan commitment to the actual disbursement of loan proceeds. This chapter includes a sample Commitment Letter and illustrates how a loan closer can develop a checklist from a Commitment Letter. It also explains, for those new to the real estate field, the importance of the documents to the loan transaction.

Role of the Loan Closer

The loan closer is responsible for taking the loan step by step from the commitment through to the actual disbursement of funds. The loan closer's goal is to close the loan. Perfect documents in perfect order serve no purpose if the process causes one too many requests for extension of the loan commitment and kills the deal.

If the loan is arranged through a mortgage banker, the loan closer is usually an employee of the mortgage banker or the mortgage banker's attorney. If no mortgage banker is involved in the transaction, the lender usually designates someone in its internal loan-closing department or its attorney (whether in-house or outside counsel) as the loan closer. If the loan closer is an attorney, much of the reponsibility is often delegated to a legal assistant.

The role of the loan closer is to orchestrate the entire loan-closing process. The loan closer must understand the transaction, who the parties are, and who the decision maker is for each party. The loan closer must know all steps required prior to closing the loan and deadlines for each step and must communicate all these tasks to the parties and remind them to complete the tasks on time. The parties often fail to understand all their responsibilities at the outset of the transaction (even though they should do so), and the loan closer often must educate parties about the consequences of failing to fulfill certain responsibilities.

Loan closers must not assume roles beyond their authority. Points of contention on business issues always arise before a loan is closed. The loan closer should not try to become a deal negotiator but should direct the business problems to the appropriate decision makers. If not an attorney, the loan closer should not draft loan documents or give legal advice.

Loan closers who are mortgage bankers are responsible to both the borrower and the lender. If the loan closer is an employee or attorney of the lender, the borrower will be wise to remember that the loan closer is not its representative. The borrower should protect its own interests accordingly.

Basic Assumptions

Several assumptions are basic to the role of the loan closer. For instance, it is assumed that the loan closer understands the basics of real estate law and loan documentation. A loan closer who is inexperienced in real estate transactions must become educated by reading, taking courses, observing other transactions, and talking with more experienced loan closers.

A corollary to this assumption is that the loan closer understands local customs with regard to real estate transactions. Such customs vary from state to state, and even within states, on such matters as who pays for which closing costs and arrangements for recording documents. The parties will rely on the loan closer to know these local customs, especially where the lender is an institutional investor headquartered in another area of the country.

It is also assumed that the loan closer will know and understand the various parties. Each investor functions differently from other investors and has different policies and priorities. Each person has a different negotiating style. The loan closer who is sensitive to these issues will effectively promote the cooperation of all parties toward the goal of closing the loan.

It is assumed that the loan closer will work with the attorneys for all parties and will have access to competent legal counsel of its own throughout the transaction. Good attorneys, like good loan closers, will not nitpick but will keep in mind that the goal is to make the loan and will advise their client accordingly. The loan closer should realize that although the common goal of all parties is to close the loan, it is also the goal of the attorney for each party that the loan be made on terms most advantageous to the attorney's client. Attorneys must advise their clients of provisions which create risks and potentially adverse legal consequences. Thus, the roles of attorneys for the lender, borrower, and other participants are partially adversarial. The loan closer should understand that the documents will be reviewed by attorneys, allow time for such review and for resolution of any problems which arise, and keep close watch on the process to make sure that all problems are resolved in time for documents to be completed before the loan closing.

Here the closer's knowledge of the various parties is crucial. Although all decisions are ultimately business decisions of the client rather than the attorney, some clients take risks not recommended by their attorneys. If the loan closer understands who ultimately make the decisions, the loan closer will not waste time talking to the wrong person about a decision or wrongly anticipate that a decision will be reversed.

Establishing Case Control

It is assumed that the loan closer will immediately establish control over the file. The loan closer does so by two means: holding a preclosing meeting and developing a critical path or checklist of what is necessary to close the loan.

Preclosing Meeting

As soon as the loan commitment is made, the loan closer needs to meet with the appropriate people. When the loan closer is not the same person as the loan officer who originated and underwrote the loan, the meeting must include the loan officer. When there is a closing department, the head of the loan-closing department should attend to help identify problem areas. If the loan closer is an in-house loan closer of the lender, the attorney (and legal assistant, if any) handling the loan should also attend.

The purpose of the meeting is to transfer responsibility for the transaction from the loan officer to the loan closer. Prior to the meeting, the loan closer should have read the loan officer's file. The loan officer needs to explain the basic business agreement and any transaction points which have been previously negotiated between the parties and to identify the persons who make decisions for each of the parties. The loan closer should ask questions which will help anticipate problems, so that they may be solved early in the process.

Critical Path

The loan closer must establish a critical path or checklist of all steps which are necessary to close the transaction. The checklist will consist largely of documents which must be submitted and approved and should specify who prepares each document, who reviews and approves it, whether approvals have been completed, what are deadlines for receipt of final documents, who has the authority to sign each document, and whether the document needs to be notarized and recorded.

Because commercial real property loans are negotiated and have provisions unique to each transaction, the loan closer must develop a separate critical path for each loan. A standardized checklist may remind the loan closer what to include but cannot be relied on from one transaction to another.

Timing

The critical path must address timing. Not only should each item on the checklist be assigned a deadline, but the loan closer should have an understanding of overall duration of the process from commitment to closing. Normally from the time the loan closer receives the file until the loan is closed will be at least 30 days. Many commercial loans require longer periods, especially when issues are negotiated after the loan commitment is signed.

It is possible to close the loan within 10 days or even a week if all parties are committed to doing so, will refrain from negotiating all but the most crucial issues, and are willing to work long hours. Such closings are common at the end of the calendar year, when people rush to complete transactions in time to capture tax advantages before the year expires.

The parties, especially borrowers (who almost always need funds), are usually anxious to close a loan and will exert pressure on the loan closer to work quickly. The loan closer should remember that, after a loan is closed, people will conveniently forget how fast the transaction was completed but will remember mistakes that may have unpleasant consequences. However, the loan closer should not insist on perfection which may threaten the deal. In cases when the loan closer has been instructed by the parties to proceed even though certain conditions have not been met, the loan closer should be satisfied that the persons have the authority to waive conditions and would be wise to put a memo in the file regarding who made and concurred in the instruction.

In developing deadlines for the critical path, the loan closer should always allow for the unexpected. It is inevitable that something will cause a delay. On a loan for an existing office building or shopping center, one of the most common causes for delay is that estoppel certificates have not been obtained from all existing tenants.

Some loan closers find that it is useful to group the tasks on the list into categories of those which must be dealt with immediately, those which must be dealt with periodically until the loan closes, and those which must be handled at the time of the loan closing.

The Commitment Letter

Both novice and experienced loan closers have a document to assist them in preparing a checklist: the Commitment Letter. The Commitment Letter is a letter from the lender to the borrower which, when signed by the borrower, becomes a contract for a loan which binds both parties. It specifies the terms and conditions on which the loan is to be made. To the loan closer, the Commitment Letter serves as a blueprint of the transaction which, if followed, will result in the closed loan.

Unwritten Requirements

There are always unwritten requirements which are so basic to any real estate transaction that they are not addressed in the Commitment Letter but must be included in the closing process. The appraisal of the value of the property is one of the most important of these unwritten requirements. Another example is the closing statement prorations. When a lender is funding the purchase of property (rather than funding a permanent loan following a construction loan), expenses such as taxes, insurance, and utilities are prorated between the buyer and seller as of the close. Although the purchase and sale agreement between the borrower and seller may refer to the prorations, the Commitment Letter is not likely to do so. Nevertheless, someone (usually the escrow officer or loan closer) must draw up a statement of these exact costs and who bears which portions of each cost. Unless the borrower and seller agree on the prorations, the loan cannot close.

The Tax Reform Act of 1986 imposes a duty on loan closers to report certain information to the Internal Revenue Service. Because responsible parties who fail to do so are subject to fines, all loan closers should consult their own attorneys about who is required to comply with this reporting requirement and how to do so.

Follow-up

Once loan closers have developed a checklist, they should send or give the list to all parties and make sure that each party understands its responsibilities and deadlines. Thereafter, until the closing, the loan closer should remind the parties of deadlines, keep a close watch on all the proceedings, and communicate problems to business decision makers so that they may be solved in timely manner.

Sample Commitment Letter

The following sample Commitment Letter is based on the Southbury-port Community Shopping Center. This commitment is for a permanent or takeout loan to be used to pay off the construction loan and other costs incurred in constructing, developing, and leasing the shopping center. It has been arbitrarily assumed that the property is located in California. The left side of the page is the text of the Commitment Letter. The right margin isolates closing items required by the Commitment Letter which must be included in the checklist. After the Commitment Letter, each item is discussed, and unwritten requirements are addressed. No time lines have been set out in the discussion of the various documents, as it is impossible to assign deadlines except in the context of a specific loan, but the discussion does address some of the concerns with regard to timing.

The loan amount is set at $10,500,000 to absorb cost overruns which may occur in construction. In the example, a great deal of the shopping center has already been leased and there is a favorable loan-to-value ratio. Thus it is safe to make a loan of this size.

The sample Commitment Letter which follows does not illustrate the far more complex arrangements necessary if the loan were any of the following: a construction loan rather than a permanent loan; a tripartite agreement involving the borrower, construction lender, and permanent lender; an equity transaction in which the lender both lent funds and held an equity interest in the project (such as a joint venture interest); or a transaction involving public funding (using, for example, industrial revenue bonds). Also, because the subject of this chapter is the loan-closing process, the example uses simple loan terms. These loan terms are unrealistic in the 1986 commercial real property loan market. It would be much more likely to have a fixed rate of interest at approximately 10 percent, maturing in 10 to 12 years, or a variable rate of interest tied to a common index, adjusted semiannually over a term of 7 to 15 years.

Southburyport Community Shopping Center Associates
ATTN: John Moran and Paul Birnie
123 Main Street
Southburyport, California

RE: Loan for Southburyport Community Shopping Center

Ladies and Gentlemen:

Century Puritan Life Insurance Company ("Lender") has received your loan application and hereby offers to make a loan (the "Loan") evidenced by a promissory note (the "Note") secured by a first deed trust (the "Deed of Trust") on the Secured Property (as hereinafter defined) in the form satisfactory to Lender's Counsel and subject to the terms and conditions provided in this letter (the "Commitment").

1. *Borrower:* The borrower shall be Southburyport Community Shopping Center Associates, a California limited partnership (the "Borrower"), the General Partners of which shall include John Moran and Paul Birnie. — Partnership Agreement / Certificate of Limited Partnership

2. *Loan amount:* Ten million five hundred thousand dollars ($10,500,000). — Note

3. *Interest rate:* Twelve percent (12%) per annum (the "Note Rate").

4 *Term:* All unpaid principal and interest and other charges shall be due and payable fifteen (15) years from the date of the Note.

5. *Amortization schedule:* Thirty (30) years.

6. *Secured property:* The Note will be secured by a first Deed of Trust on:

Deed of Trust

(a) that certain real property consisting of no less than fifteen (15) acres located at the northwest corner of Stafford Street and Morris Avenue (State Route 221) in the City of Southburyport, County of Seaside, State of California, which is more particularly described in Exhibit A attached hereto and incorporated herein by reference, and all rights and easements appurtenant thereto (the "Real Property"); and

Legal Description of Real Property

(b) improvements on said Real Property consisting of a shopping center with no less than eighty thousand (80,000) rentable square feet of premises opening onto an enclosed mall, plus the following: one premises consisting of at least forty-five thousand (45,000) rentable square feet, one premises consisting of at least sixteen thousand (16,000) rentable square feet, one premises consisting of at least twelve thousand (12,000) rentable square feet, one premises consisting of at least eight thousand (8000) rentable square feet, and no fewer than 4.5 automobile parking spaces for each one thousand square feet of rentable area in the shopping center, and other appropriate improvement (the "Improvements"). The Real Property and Improvements are sometimes hereinafter referred to collectively as the "Secured Property." The Improvements are sometimes hereinafter referred to as the "Shopping Center."

7. *Personal property:* The Note will be additionally secured by a first lien in favor of Lender on all personal property and fixtures owned by Borrower, any of the General Partners thereof or Southbury Properties, Inc. or other manager of the Shopping Center and located on

Security Agreement
Financing Statement

and/or used in connection with the Secured Property (the "Personal Property"). In this regard, Borrower shall execute a security agreement (the "Security Agreement") and all documents as may be necessary or appropriate to perfect and record a security interest in said personal property pursuant to the California Uniform Commercial Code. The Security Agreement and any or all such documents described in this Section 7 are hereinafter referred to collectively as the "Personal Property Security Documents."

8. *Assignment of leases and assignment of rents:* The Note shall be additionally secured by an assignment of leases (the "Assignment of Leases") by which Borrower assigns to Lender any and all leases (written or oral) affecting the Secured Property and by an assignment of rents (the "Assignment of Rents") by which Borrower assigns to Lender all of Borrower's right, title and interest in any and all rents related to use of the Secured Property.

Assignment of Leases

Assignment of Rents

9. *Loan documents:* The Note, Deed of Trust, the Personal Property Security Documents, the Assignment of Leases, and the Assignment of Rents, are hereinafter referred to collectively as the "Loan Documents."

10. *Payments:* Payments shall be one hundred eight thousand four dollars ($108,004.00) per month and shall be due and payable on the first day of each month.

11. *Prepayment:* Except as provided in this Section 11, no principal may be paid in advance of the payment schedule specified in Section 10 hereof. Borrower may prepay the full amounts remaining on the Note at the end of the thirty-sixth (36th) month of the Loan or at the end of the seventy-second (72nd) month of the Loan (whichever respective date

is applicable is hereinafter referred to as the "Prepayment Date"), provided that:

(a) Borrower notifies Lender in writing of its intention to prepay the Loan (the "Prepayment Notice") no earlier than twelve (12) full months and not later than six (6) full months before the Prepayment Date (whichever respective date is applicable is hereinafter referred to as the "Prepayment Notice Date"); and

(b) Borrower pays all amounts owed pursuant to the Note on or before the Prepayment Date; and

(c) Borrower pays to Lender a prepayment fee of one percent of the outstanding principal balance due at the time of the Prepayment Date (the "Prepayment Fee").

Upon the giving of such Prepayment Notice, all amounts owed pursuant to the Note and the Prepayment Fee shall become due and payable on or before the Prepayment Date, and it shall be a default under the Note and Deed of Trust if Borrower fails to pay all such amounts by the Prepayment Date.

12. *Impounds:* In addition to the payments of principal and interest, Borrower shall pay to Lender on the first day of each month a sum equal to one-twelfth ($\frac{1}{12}$) of the annual real estate taxes and assessments levied against the Secured Property and one-twelfth ($\frac{1}{12}$) of the annual premiums for insurance required by Lender, both as estimated by Lender. Said payments are hereinafter referred to as the "Impounds." The Impounds shall be held by Lender in an escrow account to be used for payment of such taxes, assessments, and insurance premiums. No interest shall be payable by Lender to Borrower upon such Impounds. At the time of funding of the Loan, additional

Tax Bills

Insurance Bills

funds will be excrowed from the proceeds of the Loan to assure that sufficient funds are available for the first year's taxes, assessments, and insurance premiums. Provided that there have been no late payments or defaults under the Loan, during periods when at least ninety-five percent (95%) of the number of rentable square feet in the Shopping Center is leased and occupied by tenants having leases approved by Lender, Borrower will not be required to pay Impounds.

13. *Due on sale or encumbrance:* Lender would not make this Loan on the terms and conditions provided herein were it not for the financial strength and management and leasing capabilities of Borrower and the General Partners of Borrower. The Loan Documents shall provide that Lender may, in its sole discretion, accelerate the indebtedness and declare the entire outstanding balance due and payable without notice if, without prior written consent of Lender:

(a) there is a sale, transfer, or other disposition of all or any part or interest in the Secured Property or Personal Property, or

(b) any lien, including but not limited to a second Deed of Trust, attaches to all or any part or interest in the Secured Property or Personal Property.

The General Partners of Borrower shall at all times consist of at least John Moran and Paul Birnie, who shall collectively own at least fifty-one percent (51%) of the interests in Borrower and who each individually shall own at least twenty percent (20%) of the interests in Borrower. Any transfer of any interest in Borrower or any withdrawal by either John Moran or Paul Birnie shall be deemed a transfer pursuant to this Section 13 if, as a result of such transfer or withdrawal, both John Moran and Paul Birnie are not General Partners of Borrower, or John Moran and Paul Birnie do not collectively own at least fifty-one percent (51%) of the interests in Borrower, or John Moran does not own at least twenty percent (20%) of the interest in Borrower, or Paul Birnie does not own at least twenty percent (20%) of the interests in Borrower.

At the time of such acceleration, there will be a Prepayment Fee of one percent (1%) of the outstanding principal balance owing on the Note at the time of such acceleration.

14. *Management:* The Secured Property shall at all times be managed by a corporation in which John Moran and Paul Birnie collectively own at least a fifty-one percent (51%) interest and in which John Moran and Paul Birnie are General Partners and collectively own at least a fifty-one percent (51%) interest and in which John Moran and Paul Birnie each individually own at least a twenty percent (20%) interest. Said corporation or partnership is herein referred to as the "Manager." As of this date, it is anticipated that the Manager shall be Southbury Properties, Inc., a California corporation. The Secured Property shall be managed pursuant to a written Management Agreement approved by Lender (the "Management Agreement").

Articles of Incorporation By-Laws, Shareholder List of Southbury Properties, Inc.

Management Agreement

15. *Plans and specifications:* Final and complete plans and specifications for Improvements on the Real Property, including but not limited to architectural, structural, mechanical, plumbing, and electrical improvements, a soils report, and landscaping plans (hereinafter referred to collectively as the "Plans and Specifications") shall be submitted to and approved by Lender prior

Plans and Specifications

Soils Report
Landscaping Plans

to loan closing. Lender shall have the right to make such inspections of Secured Property as it deems appropriate to determine that all Improvements have been completed to its satisfaction and in accordance with the approved Plans and Specifications and the terms of this Commitment, and this Loan is subject to Lender's approval of the Plans and Specifications and Lender's approval upon such inspection prior to loan closing. Lender shall also have the right to make such other inspections of the Secured Property and Personal Property as it deems appropriate, whether before or after the loan closing. Neither Lender's approval of Plans and Specifications, nor any inspection or approval of the Improvements will constitute a warranty or representation by Lender or any of its agents or employees as to the technical sufficiency, adequacy, or safety of the Improvements.

Should Lender determine in its sole discretion that the Real Property and/or Improvements are not suitable security for the Loan, the Borrower's commitments fee shall be refunded to the Borrower, and this commitment shall be deemed terminated.

16. *Environmental hazards:* Prior to Loan closing, Borrower shall submit to Lender reports from licensed engineers, acceptable to Lender, who have inspected and tested the Real Property and Improvements, including but not limited to soils, for hazardous and/or toxic wastes. This Loan is conditioned upon Lender's approval of said reports prior to loan closing and fulfillment of any conditions Lender may impose as a result of the content of such reports.

Environmental Engineers' Report

17. *Permits:* Prior to the loan closing, Lender is to be furnished with copies of all required building and oc-

Building permits

cupancy permits, variances (and
evidence of compliance with conditions therefor), evidence of the issuance of all appropriate federal,
state, and local environmental protection permits, utility availability
letters, certificates of compliance
with all zoning and building laws,
ordinances and regulations, and all
other evidence which Lender might
reasonably require to ensure that
the Improvements have been properly constructed and may be occupied and used as intended, all of
which are hereinafter referred to
collectively as "Permits." Permits
shall include but are not limited to
certificates of occupancy for all tenants for whom Tenant Improvements (as hereinafter defined) have
been completed.

Evidence that Utilities are
Adequately Supplied

Certificates of Occupancy
for Each Existing Tenant

18. *Survey:* As a condition of funding, the Borrower shall furnish
Lender with an ALTA survey (as
built) of the Real Property and Improvements, made by a licensed
surveyor satisfactory to Lender and
the title insuror, prepared after the
completion of the Improvements
and dated not more than thirty (30)
days prior to closing. The as-built
survey shall delineate:

Survey

(a) all lot lines;

(b) the dimensions and location of
the Real Property and Improvements;

(c) means of access and location of
all adjoining streets;

(d) all easements and parking areas
including the number and location
of parking stalls (all recorded easements must be identified by document number);

(e) provisions reflected in the Reciprocal Easement Agreement referred to in Section 24 (b) of this
Commitment;

(f) other physical and title matters
affecting the Real Property or Im-

provements and/or their use and affecting the title as may be requested by Lender.

The Survey shall contain a certificate setting forth the street address of the premises along with the legal description and the dimensions and total square foot area of both the Real Property and the Improvements within said description. The legal description of the survey shall be identical with the description in the Deed of Trust and title policy. The surveyor shall certify to Lender and the Title Insuror that the survey is accurate, that there are not encroachments on or from the Real Property and Improvements, except as approved by Lender, that the survey accurately shows all visible or recorded easements or rights of way affecting the Real Property and Improvements, and that access is provided by Stafford Street and Morris Avenue (State Route 221), publicly dedicated streets. The survey shall further certify that, except as approved by Lender, the Secured Property does not, to the best of the surveyor's knowledge, serve any adjoining property for drainage, ingress, egress, or any other purpose.

19. *Title insurance:* At the time of loan expense and in a form satisfactory to Lender's counsel, an ALTA Mortgagee Title Policy from a Title insurance company acceptable to closing, Borrower shall provide, at its own expense and in a form satisfactory to Lender's counsel, an ALTA Mortgagee Title Policy from a Title insurance company acceptable to Lender (the "Title Insuror"). The title policy shall:

(a) insure Lender that Borrower holds a good and marketable fee simple title to the Secured Property and that the Deed of Trust constitutes a valid first lien on Borrower's good and marketable fee simple ti-

Preliminary Title Report and Documents Underlying All Exceptions to Title

ALTA Title Policy

tle to the Secured Property, subject only to such liens, exceptions, and encumbrances as shall have previously been approved by Lender in writing, and

(b) shall contain such endorsements as Lender may require.

Title Endorsements

20. *Insurance:* Borrower shall provide evidence of the following required insurance on the Secured Property prior to funding and shall maintain these coverages during the life of the loan: (1) fire and all risk coverage, (2) six months' rent loss insurance, (3) flood insurance (if available pursuant to the Flood Disaster Protection Act of 1973), (4) earthquake insurance, and (5) comprehensive general liability insurance, in amounts acceptable to Lender, protecting Borrower and Lender against claims arising from any insurable incident in, on, or about the Secured Property, and (6) other appropriate insurance as Lender may require from time to time. Fire and all risk coverage and flood insurance shall be in the amount of the full replacement value of the Improvements [less a deductible not to exceed five thousand dollars ($5000)], and the policy shall contain a full replacement cost endorsement. All insurance policies shall be in form acceptable to Lender's counsel, shall be written by companies acceptable to Lender, and shall have loss payable provisions in favor of Lender in accordance with a standard mortgagee clause (except for comprehensive general liability insurance on which Lender will be named as a named insured).

Casualty Policy or Policies

Liability Policy

21. *Operating and financial statements:* The Loan documents shall require that Lender shall be furnished, prior to the close of the Loan and within ninety (90) days following the expiration of each fiscal year, a copy of

Borrower's current annual operating statement for the Secured Property and current financial statements of all General Partners of Borrower. The operating statement and financial statements shall be in such detail as Lender may reasonably' require, and the operating statement shall indicate all income and expenses which were projected or budgeted at the beginning of the fiscal year, together with the actual income and expenses for the year. These statements are to be prepared by a Certified Public Accountant in accordance with generally accepted accounting principles consistently applied and certified by Borrower and the General Partners of Borrower as being correct. Lender will have the right to audit Borrower's records and the records of the General Partners to verify the accuracy of the statements. The Loan Documents shall also require Borrower to furnish Lender with such financial information as it may reasonably require to satisfy other institutional investors in connection with their purchase or proposed purchase of all or any interest in the Loan.

Operating Statements
Financial Statements

22. *Attorney's opinion letter:* Prior to loan closing, Borrower shall submit to Lender an opinion of counsel that the Loan and the making thereof shall be in all respects legal and shall not violate any applicable law or other requirements of any governmental authority, including but not limited to usury laws, and that the documents evidencing such Loan and security interests are valid and enforceable in accordance with their terms.

Opinion Letter from
Borrower's Counsel

23. *Tenant improvements:* Tenant Improvements are defined as follows: floor coverings; window coverings; partitioning appropriate for each tenant area; ceilings with lighting installed and operable; plumbing

and all electrical work fully completed; air conditioning and heating systems installed and operable with zone controls; finished painted walls; and all other improvements necessary and appropriate to finish space for use by Tenants.

24. *Leases:* Prior to loan closing, Borrower shall provide Lender with the following, all of which are subject to Lender's approval:

(a) a Ground Lease to Southburyport Citizens Bank (the "Bank") for a pad consisting of not more than 2000 square feet (the "Bank Pad"), which will yield an annual rental to Borrower of at least thirty-five thousand dollars ($35,000) per year and which Bank Pad shall be used as an operating branch of Southburyport Citizens Bank,

Ground Lease to Bank Pad

(b) a Reciprocal Easement Agreement ("REA") by and between Borrower and the Bank governing the allocation of costs and responsibilities with regard to insurance, taxes, repair, maintenance, and capital improvements to the common areas of the Shopping Center and ingress to and egress from the Bank Pad and the remainder of the Shopping Center,

Reciprocal Easement Agreement

(c) a lease to Giant World, Inc., for the premises consisting of at least forty-five thousand (45,000) square feet (the "Supermarket Premises") which will yield an annual rental of at least seven dollars and fifty cents ($7.50) per square foot per year, plus two percent (2%) of gross sales in excess of nine million dollars ($9,000,000) per year, over a term of at least ten (10) years,

Lease to Giant World, Inc.

(d) a rent roll listing all tenants with whom leases have been signed ("Existing Tenants") and the dates of their leases, duration of the terms of their leases, and rents currently payable,

Rent Roll

(e) leases for Existing Tenants show-

Leases

ing that at least seventy-five percent (75%) of the number of square feet in the Shopping Center (excluding both the Bank Pad and the Supermarket Premises) is leased to tenants acceptable to Lender on terms and conditions acceptable to Lender. All leases of Existing Tenants shall be subject to the review and approval of Lender,

(f) a lease form to be used for all rentable areas not yet leased,

Form Lease

(g) estoppel certificates from all Existing Tenants certifying such items as Lender may require, including but not limited to certification that the tenant is occupying the premises and open for business, that the lease is valid and in full force and effect, that no rent has been or will be paid more than thirty (30) days in advance, that Borrower has fulfilled all obligations with regard to Tenant Improvements and that there are no defaults under the lease,

Estoppel Certificates

(h) subordination and attornment agreements from all Existing Tenants showing that the leases of Existing Tenants shall be subordinate to Lender's interest in the Secured Property and that, in the event of Borrower's default on the loan, the Existing Tenants shall attorn to the Lender.

Subordination and Attornment Agreements

25. *Future leases:* The Loan Documents shall provide that all future lease for all or any portion of the Secured Property, in addition to leases of Existing Tenants, shall be subject to Lender's approval.

26. *Tenant improvement escrow:* At the time of loan closing, to secure completion of Tenant Improvements for future tenants, a sum equal to eighteen dollars ($18) per square foot of all leasable areas of the Shopping Center which are not yet leased shall be held in an escrow account with an escrow company

Escrow Agreement

and under an escrow agreement (the "Escrow Agreement") reasonably satisfactory to both Lender and Borrower and expiring not later than three hundred sixty-five (365) days following the date of the loan closing. Funds shall be released from escrow as space is completed, leased, and occupied under leases satisfactory to Lender and for which a certificate of occupancy has been issued by the local governmental authority. Funds shall be released at the lesser of the actual costs per square foot of Tenant Improvements or eighteen dollars ($18) per square foot of Tenant Improvements. At the expiration of the Escrow Agreement, any unreleased funds shall be returned to lender and shall be applied, at the option of Lender, to reduce the principal amount owing on the Loan or to premises not yet completed (if any).

27. *Commitment fee:* This Commitment is contingent upon Borrower's written acceptance hereof on or before _____, 19 __, together with payment to Lender of the sum of two hundred ten thousand dollars ($210,000) (the "Commitment Fee"). One hundred five thousand ($105,000) of the Commitment Fee is nonrefundable in consideration of the issuance of this Commitment and Lender's obligation to hold the Loan Proceeds available to Borrower. Lender is issuing this Commitment with the understanding that Borrower will borrow the funds from Lender. Should Borrower fail to do so in accordance with the provisions hereof, Lender shall have no further obligation to Borrower. In such event, it is agreed that the damages to Lender are difficult to ascertain and one hundred five thousand dollars ($105,000) of the Commitment Fee paid by Borrower will be retained by Lender as liquidated damages, and is

Payment of $210,000— Commitment Fee

a reasonable estimate of Lender's damages and has been negotiated by the parties hereto, provided however that Lender may alternatively elect specific performance of Borrower's obligations and agreements hereunder or to exercise such other rights and remedies as are available at law or in equity for the enforcement of this Commitment. Notwithstanding the foregoing, Lender shall refund the Borrower's Commitment Fee in the event that Lender does not fund the Loan as a result of Lender's nonapproval under any of the following Sections of this Commitment Letter: 15, 16, 17, 18, 19 or 24. None of the Commitment Fee shall be returned to Borrower in the event that the Loan is funded in accordance with the terms of this Commitment.

28. *Assignability:* Lender may assign all or a part of the Commitment or the Loan to another institutional investor. The Commitment may not be assigned by Borrower. Any assignment or attempted assignment of the Commitment by the Borrower will be void and will terminate Lender's obligations under this Commitment.

29. *Costs:* Whether or not the Loan is funded, Borrower shall pay all costs, fees, and charges in connection with the processing of this Loan, including but not limited to appraisal fees, survey fees, recording fees, title insurance and other insurance premiums, escrow costs, any taxes required to be paid, and attorneys' fees for outside counsel hired by Lender.

30. *Approvals:* All documents and submissions pursuant to this Commitment shall be in form satisfactory to Lender and Lender's counsel.

31. *Condemnation or damage to improvements:* At the time of closing, the Secured Property shall not be damaged or destroyed from any cause, and no condemnation proceedings shall have commenced or

be threatened against the Secured Property or any part thereof.

32. *Applicable law:* This Commitment shall be construed and enforced in accordance with the laws of the State of California.

33. *Lender's inability fund:* In the event of Lender's incapacity to comply with any law or governmental regulation which in any way might be applicable to this loan, the full Commitment Fee paid by Borrower will be returned to Borrower, and this Commitment will become void. Lender has no knowledge of any present law or governmental regulation which would prevent it from issuing this Commitment or funding the Loan.

34. *Borrower's statements:* The Commitment is subject to the accuracy of all information, representations, exhibits, and other materials submitted in connection with the Loan application. Prior to the closing of the Loan, there shall have been no material adverse change in the assets, liabilities, financial condition, or other condition of the Borrower or any general Partner of Borrower.

35. *Commitment expiration date:* Time is of the essence of this Commitment. Borrower agrees that Lender shall not be required to close the Loan or make any disbursements under this Commitment until all conditions have been satisfied. Funding shall be conditioned upon the continuing accuracy of the facts and representations in the Loan application and submissions upon which this Commitment is based. If the Loan is not closed by _____, 19 __(the "Expiration Date"), Lender shall have no further obligation, and this Commitment shall terminate.

Borrower's Affidavit

Century Puritan Life Insurance Company

By: _____
John Q. Lender
Vice President

The undersigned hereby accepts the foregoing Commitment and agrees that it will comply with all of the terms and conditions herein.

Dated: _____ Southburyport Community Shopping Center Associates

By: _____
John Moran
General Partner

By: _____
Paul Birnie
General Partner

Checklist and Explanation of Loan Documents

The following portion of this chapter is based on the sample Commitment Letter and documents needed to close the loan. The discussion often refers to what issues may give rise to negotiation. It should be clarified that most of the negotiations take place prior to the acceptance of the Commitment Letter. It is often difficult or impossible to negotiate issues after the Commitment Letter is finalized.

Partnership Agreement and Certificate of Limited Partnership. This sample Commitment Letter assumes that the partnership entitled Southburyport Community Shopping Center Associates has been formed prior to the date of the Commitment Letter. If it had not yet been formed, legal issues would arise as to whom the commitment is made and who is required to fulfill the obligations of Borrower pursuant to the partnership and assignment of the Borrower's obligations to the partnership. Whether the partnership is formed before or after the date of the Commitment Letter, the Partnership Agreement must show the general partnership interests specified by the Lender (in this case by Section 13 in addition to Section 1 of the Commitment Letter). The Partnership Agreement is drafted by counsel for the partnership and must be submitted by the Borrower to the Lender for Lender's approval. In California, limited partnerships formed after the effective date of the Revised California Limited Partnership Act must be registered with the California Secretary of State in a way similar to the registration of corporations; the document evidencing such registration is a Certificate of Limited Partnership. Whenever the state where the property is located has similar registration requirements for limited partnerships, the documents must show proper registration prior to the loan closing.

Note. The Note is the basic loan document, the written promise by the Borrower to pay the Lender the money loaned plus interest. The Note is drafted by Lender's counsel and submitted to Borrower and Borrower's counsel for review. The terms are always negotiated before the commitment letter is signed. It is common for amortization to take place over a longer period than the payment rate; in our example, payments are calculated as if the loan were to be paid off over 30 years, but all principal and interest are due at the end of 15 years, which means that there will be a large balloon payment due at the end of the 15-year term. Borrowers almost always anticipate selling the property before maturity or obtaining another loan before or on the maturity date.

Whether the Note will be due and payable upon sale of the property or further encumbrance of the property (taking out a second loan) is always a matter for discussion prior to signing the commitment letter. As in the example (see Section 13), lenders generally insist that the loan will become due on sale or further encumbrance. Section 13 also restricts reduction of the General Partners' interests in the partnership; such provisions are common because lenders rely on the talents and reputations of the particular individuals involved in developing property. If the due-on-sale clause is not negotiated prior to completion of the commitment, it is rare for the borrower to obtain any important concessions from the lender on this issue.

It is also common to negotiate whether the loan may be prepaid prior to the maturity date and, if so, if there is a prepayment fee. Again, the example specifically addresses this problem in Section 11; it allows prepayment at two times during the term of the loan upon payment of a specified prepayment fee.

Other items commonly negotiated in connection with the Note revolve around late payments: Will a grace period be allowed (5 to 10 days is common), will a late charge apply, and will a late charge depend upon the lender's having given the borrower notice and opportunity to cure? Our example does not specifically address this problem, which will require these items to be negotiated in the process of reviewing the Note.

Deed of Trust or Mortgage.   The Deed of Trust provides that the property is the security for the loan. The most important provision in the Deed of Trust is the lender's right to foreclose on the loan by selling the property if the borrower defaults. All states have laws which govern the procedures by which lenders may exercise their right to foreclose. Although procedures vary from state to state, such laws generally give some notice and opportunity to the borrower to cure the default before the sale. States also vary in the degree to which the law will override provisions in the Deed of Trust.

Although there are legal differences between a mortgage and a Deed of Trust, the subtleties are beyond our scope here. For purposes of loan closing, a Deed of Trust is the same as a mortgage. State laws govern whether a Deed of Trust or a mortgage is used. The borrower is called a trustor under a Deed of Trust and mortgagor under a mortgage. The lender is called a beneficiary under a Deed of Trust and mortgagee under a mortgage. With a Deed of Trust, there is also a trustee who technically holds the right to sell the property but whose responsibilities are merely administrative if the lender decides to foreclose.

The Deed of Trust is always on a form provided by the lender or is drafted by lender's counsel. It is often negotiated between counsel for lender and borrower and always contains a long list of affirmative obligations which the borrower must fulfill, the breach of which will constitute a default, such as a duty to maintain the property in good condition and to repair and to insure the property, and a prohibition against waste.

Among the items negotiated are the insurance and condemnation clauses. In the event of an insured casualty, both parties want to control insurance proceeds, and the lender wants the discretion to apply the proceeds to the loan or to repairs. If a public authority condemns all the property, there is little argument that condemnation proceeds should go to the lender to pay off the loan. However, it is much more common for a public authority to condemn a portion of the property, in which case both parties again want to control the condemnation award, and the lender again wants to decide, in its sole discretion, whether to apply the condemnation award to the loan or to the repairs. The condemnation clause may be a particularly difficult problem in shopping centers, where portions of the shopping center may be owned by different owners or anchor tenants have leases giving them powers in instances of condemnation.

The Deed of Trust is always notarized and recorded with the appropriate public official, which varies from state to state but is usually such an official as a County Recorder or a County Clerk. The purpose of the recording is to put the public on notice of the information recorded. Upon recordation, anyone purchasing the property or putting another lien on the property is deemed to know about the recorded document, whether or not such person actually knows about it. Another purpose of recording the Deed of Trust is to establish the priority of the Deed of Trust with regard to other liens. After the loan closes, if the borrower were to find another lender who would make a second loan secured by the same property, the recording would inform the second lender that there is already a first lien on the property.

Legal Description.   Whenever a parcel of real property is referred to in a recorded document, it is mandatory to describe the property by legal description rather than by street address. A street address may change over time, but a legal description indicates actual boundaries of the property on the land. A legal description most often is derived from a survey of the property by a licensed surveyor and consists of a description by metes and bounds. In some states, it is legally sufficient to describe a property by reference to a recorded map. This practice should be avoided because a description by reference to a map is not easily understood, and if there is a discrepancy between a legal description by metes and bounds and a legal description by reference to a map, the metes and bounds description will be given precedence.

Legal descriptions are esoteric and difficult to read. Because they are so detailed, it is easy to make mistakes in transcribing them, yet they must be incorporated into all the recorded loan documents and are often incorporated into unrecorded loan documents. Thus, legal descriptions are often incorporated by reference to an exhibit and the exhibits are photocopied from one original rather than retyped into the body of each document. In such cases, the loan closer will need to make sure that the correct exhibit has been properly attached to each document. However, some people feel that it is too easy for exhibits to become detached from documents and insist that the legal description be retyped into the body of each document; in such cases, all legal descriptions will need to be carefully proofread.

Security Agreement and Financing Statement.   Loans on real property are almost always secured by any personal property of the borrower in addition to the real property and improvements. In buildings which have large investments in furnishings, such as hotels and furnished apartments, the personal property comprises a significant part of the security for the loan. In buildings such as office buildings and shopping centers, the personal property is a minor part of the security for the loan because it probably consists primarily of cleaning, maintenance, and landscaping equipment, and furniture and equipment in the property manager's office.

In any case, a separate security agreement always governs the personal property or chattel. A description of the personal property is often overlooked and must be included in the security agreement. The lender's security interest in the personal property is perfected and enforced through procedures provided in each state's version of the Uniform Commercial Code (UCC) (except in Louisiana, which has not adopted a version of the UCC as it pertains to security interests in personal property). Again, procedures vary from state to state, but essentially all require the filing of some form of financing statement or other document with a designated public official. In California, the financing statement is called a UCC-1 and is filed with the California Secretary of State. The filing of such a financing statement serves the same purpose as recording the Deed of Trust serves for the real property: It puts the entire world on constructive notice of the lender's lien and establishes priority of liens on the personal property.

The security agreement is always on a form provided by the lender or is drafted by lender's counsel, and the financing statement is usually on a standard form prescribed by the public official with whom the financing statement will be filed.

Both the security agreement and the financing statement will be reviewed by borrower's counsel, but the documents are not usually the subject of intense negotiations. Our sample Commitment Letter imposes a lien not only on the personal property of the borrower but also on the personal property of the property manager; thus, the property manager must be a party to the security agreement, and a separate financing statement must be signed and filed for the personal property of the property manager.

Assignment of Leases and Assignment of Rents. If the borrower defaults on the loan, the lender wants the option of collecting the rents from the property, in addition to the power to sell the property at a foreclosure sale, and it is the assignment of rents and leases which empowers the lender to do so. Although counsel for some lenders feel that the lender is best protected by separate documents, often the assignments of rents and leases are incorporated into one document and sometimes are incorporated into the Deed of Trust.

These documents are always on forms provided by the lender or are drafted by lender's counsel, and are usually notarized and recorded. Although they are reviewed by borrower's counsel, they do not require as much negotiation as the Note and Deed of Trust.

Tax Bills. Whether and under what circumstances amounts will be impounded for taxes and insurance and, if so, whether interest will be paid to the borrower are often the subjects of negotiation. Accounts for payments for insurance and taxes are often referred to as escrows or escrow accounts; as these accounts are ongoing during the term of the loan, they should not be confused with the initial escrow procedure used to close the loan.

If impounds are agreed upon, to estimate the amounts to be impounded for taxes reasonably, the lender needs to see the most recent tax bill for the property. One of the loan closer's unwritten tasks is to obtain the amount and date of the tax assessor's latest assessment of the property. It is especially important to do so with new construction or rehabilitation, which triggers a reassessment of the property. In California under Proposition 13, any change in ownership triggers a reassessment of the property. Unless it has been ascertained whether the tax bill reflects such anticipated reassessments, it is impossible to know how much to impound for taxes. The borrower is usually required to contact the tax assessor and provide this information to the lender.

Insurance Bills, Casualty Policy or Policies, Liability Policy. Determining the proper amounts to be impounded is much more complex for insurance than for taxes. It is not merely a matter of obtaining copies of the old policies and bills for the premiums for such policies. If the improvements are newly constructed, as in our example, the insurance requirements for a completed project differ from those for a project under construction. Even if the loan is for an existing building, the lender may require insurance which is different from that previously carried. The lender often requires insurors to have certain minimum ratings in *Best's Insurance Guide.*

Because the borrower may wish to keep insurance costs to a minimum and the lender wants maximum insurance coverage, insurance requirements are often negotiated. Because negotiations sometimes involve disagreements over the meanings of esoteric terms (such as whether the lender should be an additional or a named insured under the liability insurance policy), negotiations may on rare occasions involve the borrower's insurance broker and lender's insurance broker or risk manager. If the loan closer has an insurance expert available, that expert should be consulted when the insurance negotiations lead to serious disagreements.

With casualty insurance, the lender wants to be sure that its security interest in the property is protected and that it will have control over the insurance proceeds after the occurrence of a casualty. That is why Section 20 of the sample Commitment Letter requires a standard mortgagee clause (other terms for this same protection are sometimes used). The casualty insurance policy will generally include insurance for rents lost during periods of repair. Flood and earthquake insurance (if required) may be combined in the main casualty policy or may be the subject of separate policies. Flood and earthquake insurance are generally not required in areas not prone to such disasters, and earthquake insurance is so expensive that it is not always required even in areas prone to earthquakes.

In the past, lenders were not as concerned with liability insurance as they have become since litigation has burgeoned in our society. The lender wants both itself and the borrower to be adequately protected by liability insurance to ensure that a judgment for an accident on the property will not threaten the financial resources necessary to pay off the loan and operate the property properly. Although borrowers usually want to specify a reasonable cap on the amount of liability insurance, lenders usually do not want to do so because what seems like sufficient coverage today may seem inadequate several years into the loan term.

Commitment Letters almost always call for submission of actual insurance policies by the borrower to the lender. In practice, the borrower often contacts its insurance broker and the insurance broker issues a 1-page certificate of insurance or insurance binder for each policy. The loan closer needs to know if the lender will close upon receipt of such a document in lieu of the actual policies.

Articles of Incorporation, Bylaws, Shareholder List of Southbury Properties, Inc. The lender wants to know that the property manager meets the ownership requirements specified in the Commitment Letter. In the example, because the property is being managed by a corporation, the lender wants to see the Articles of Incorporation, Bylaws, and Shareholder List of the Corporation. These documents should already exist prior to the Loan Commitment, are provided by the borrower to the lender, and are not generally negotiated by the borrower and lender.

Management Agreement. The management agreement governs the relationship between the borrower and the property manager. In the example, both the borrower and the property manager are controlled by the same two individuals; thus it is not likely that the management agreement will be lengthy or negotiated. Where the property manager is not controlled by the same person or entity as the borrower, as is often the case especially with hotels, the management agreement is usually detailed and the subject of negotiation between the borrower and the manager. After the management agreement is completed, the borrower should provide it to the lender for the lender's review and approval.

Plans and Specifications, Soils Report, Landscaping Plans. These documents are especially important with regard to newly constructed projects. Of course, some projects have little or no landscaping, but in shopping centers and many suburban developments landscaping is frequently an important part of the construction review process. In the underwriting process, working plans and specifications will have been provided to the lender. There are always changes from working plans and specifications, and some provision must be made for obtaining the lender's approval of change orders. After completion of the project, the borrower's architect will indicate changes on the plans or will provide final plans and specifications of what was actually constructed ("as-built plans"). An appropriate engineer must review the soils report on behalf of the lender. All these documents are drawn up by the borrower's architect and engineers, and the borrower should submit these documents to the lender for review and approval.

Even when lending on existing buildings, the lender will want a copy of the as-built plans to be reviewed by its construction experts. With both newly constructed and existing projects, before the loan can close, a representative (usually a construction expert) of the lender must inspect the property and indicate approval thereof.

A requirement which is not always written into the Commitment Letter but which is almost universally required of newly constructed projects is a certificate from the architect of the borrower addressed to the lender and certifying that construction has been completed in compliance with designated plans and specifications. This certificate of completion is an important document which can expose the architect to liability if inaccurate.

Environmental Engineers' Report. In the past, hazardous wastes seldom concerned lenders. In the 1980s, environmental hazards have come to be perceived as a threat to the security of the lender's lien on many kinds of real property, including those used for gas stations or manufacturing computer components. Hazardous waste problems can affect both soils and underground water supplies.

Asbestos was often used in buildings built in this century, especially between the mid-1950s and mid-1970s; now that asbestos fibers in high concentrations have been found to cause health problems, it may be necessary to remove asbestos or otherwise treat it, and the costs may be so high as to jeopardize the lender's lien.

Under federal law, the owner of real property can become liable for costly cleanup even if it was the previous owner or user whose use caused the toxic waste problem. If the borrower cannot afford to pay the cleanup cost, the borrower may simply abandon the property, leaving the lender with the dilemma of foreclosing on the loan, thus becoming an owner responsible for the same costly cleanup, or writing the entire loan off as a loss.

Some states have enacted superlien laws which provide that the government may clean up hazardous wastes when the property owner fails to do so and impose a lien on the property for the cleanup costs which has a higher priority than the lender's lien. If the cleanup costs are significant, the lender's lien may erode or become worthless.

Thus, it is increasingly common for lenders to evaluate environmental hazards before they agree to make loans. When borrowers are unable to persuade lenders not to require environmental experts, the borrower usually identifies the environmental experts, obtains the lender's approval thereof, arranges for the particular reports required by the lender, and submits them to the lender's representative for review and approval.

Permits.   The lender wants to know that the project has been built pursuant to appropriate building permits and that the use of the property complies with zoning laws. Sometimes the lender asks the borrower's attorney to render opinions about or the borrower's architect to certify compliance with such permits and laws, which is usually resisted. Other times, lenders will accept copies of the applicable building permits (there are often several) and certified copies of the local zoning laws and maps showing the location of the property within a particular zone.

In some areas, the local government or other utility supplier provides a letter certifying which utilities are supplied to the property; lenders usually accept this or any other reasonable evidence that adequate utilities are provided to the property.

Certificates of occupancy (which are known by different terms in different areas) are documents issued by the local government stating that the property meets the requirements of the local government for occupancy. In shopping centers, usually the certificates of occupancy are issued for each premises as they are finished for individual tenants. Although it is always necessary to check compliance with zoning, obviously building permits, utility availability letters, and certificates of occupancy are far more important for newly constructed property than for existing and operating properties.

The borrower provides these documents to the lender, either directly or through the loan closer, for the review and approval of the lender.

Survey, Preliminary Title Report and Underlying Documents, ALTA Title Policy, Endorsements.   A survey of the property by a licensed surveyor is always required in connection with obtaining an ALTA (American Land Title Association) title insurance policy. A title insurance policy is an insurance policy that shows all recorded matters affecting title or ownership to the property and the dates and priority of such recorded matters. A borrower wants assurance that no one else has an ownership interest in the property, and the lender wants assurance that no one else has a lien on the property of higher priority than the lender's (except, of course, when a lender makes a second or third loan on the property in which case the lender expects the liens of the previous lenders to have priority). If there are recorded items affecting the property which are not shown on the title policy, the title insurer is liable to both the property owner and the lender in whose favor the title insurance policies have been issued.

In general, a preliminary title report or title commitment is requested from the title insuror as soon as the loan commitment is accepted. The preliminary title report or title commitment lists all the existing recorded matters (known as exceptions to title) including: liens for unpaid property taxes, if any (which always have a higher priority than any lender's lien); liens of existing lenders, if any (if so, the lender will require that the loans be paid and the liens released prior to the loan closing); mechanics' or material suppliers' liens if any of the contractors or subcontractors have not been paid for construction work (if so, the lender will require that the matter be resolved and the lien released prior to the loan closing); any easements (such as easements for sewer lines or underground utilities or the right of an adjacent land owner to use part of the property for access to its own property); mineral rights of others in the property; and leases which have been recorded. The report lists the exceptions, but to understand the exceptions fully it is necessary to see copies of the documents which, when recorded, created the exceptions. The title insurer will obtain these underlying documents upon request. Usually the loan closer or escrow officer orders copies of the preliminary title report for all parties, and it is reviewed by both borrower and lender and their respective counsel; the underlying documents are generally reviewed only by the attorneys.

An ALTA policy is a title insurance policy in form approved by the American Land Title Association. A survey of the property is required before the issuance of the ALTA policy because the survey will indicate the boundaries of the property (and hence any discrepancies between the existing legal description and the boundaries shown by the survey), footprints of all buildings on the property, encroachments of other buildings, and many other matters. The survey gives the title insurer extra assurance that the exceptions are properly listed or highlights problems which must be resolved before the title policy will issue.

If the lender requires a survey to reflect material not usually included in the ALTA survey, the lender should so specify at the outset.

In addition to the standard ALTA policy it is possible to insure for additional risks by requests for special endorsements. For example, it is possible to have a zoning endorsement which, when available, ensures that there is a particular zone applicable to the property that permits certain listed uses. If a lender wants any of the additional endorsements, it should so specify early in the process.

Once the preliminary title report has been reviewed, the parties will specify which exceptions are acceptable and which must be removed prior to the loan closing.

Ordinarily, the exceptions which must be removed are liens of prior lenders, liens for overdue taxes and assessments (if any), and mechanics' and/or workers' liens. Assuming that instructions of the parties are reasonable and acceptable, the title insurer will issue title insurance policies to the borrower and lender dated as of the date of the closing listing the acceptable exceptions to title.

Operating Statement and Financial Statements.   In general, an operating statement for the property and financial statements of the general partners have been obtained and reviewed during the underwriting process. Nevertheless, the lender will want updates of these statements prior to the loan closing. If the project is newly constructed, the lender will generally require an accounting of the construction costs and other costs incurred in development of the property. It is the responsibility of the borrower to provide these statements to the lender for the lender's review and approval prior to the loan closing.

Opinion Letter from Borrower's Counsel.   Lenders want assurances about a number of items which they often seek in an opinion letter from borrower's counsel. Opinion letters are costly for the borrower because if the attorney renders an opinion that turns out to be mistaken or has a fatal omission, and if the borrower defaults on the loan, the attorney may be directly liable to the lender. The attorney will not write such a letter without investigating with due diligence all the matters on which the attorney is requested to opine. Such letters have been the subject of considerable discussion in legal circles; they are often (but not always) negotiated between borrower's and lender's counsel, and rarely give the broad assurances lenders would ideally prefer. There are many items for which the lender requests opinions. A few examples are: that the loan is not usurious, that the borrower is a validly formed partnership or corporation with the authority to enter into the transaction, that the parties executing the loan documents have the authority to bind the borrower, and that the loan is valid and enforceable in accordance with its terms (which is frequently not true, so the attorney must point out those areas in which the documents are not enforceable or make broad generalizations as to the enforceability of the loan documents).

Documents Relating to Leases.   The rent roll is the blueprint for the items which will be required with regard to all existing tenants. The rent roll, submitted during the underwriting process, should be updated immediately after the Commitment Letter is signed. From the rent roll, the loan closer should develop a subsidiary checklist of the names of all tenants, whether or not copies of their leases have been sent to the lender and approval obtained, and whether estoppel certificates, subordination and attornment agreements, and nondisturbance agreements (if any) have been obtained.

It is the responsibility of the borrower to provide the rent roll and all existing leases to the lender for review by the lender and its attorney. In the example, only the two most important leases are listed in the right column: the ground lease to the bank and the lease to the supermarket. Naturally, it would be necessary to obtain the lender's approval of all leases before the loan can close. If the lender does not like some of the provisions of existing leases, tenants have no obligation to amend their leases but will often do so if the tenant receives concessions in return. If the lender wants such changes, it should initiate the discussion with the borrower, which will result in a three-way negotiation.

It is necessary to obtain estoppel certificates from all tenants, because an estoppel certificate will show whether a tenant disagrees with any of the matters reflected in both the estoppel certificate and the lease, whether the tenant believes the borrower (landlord) has defaulted on any obligations to the tenant (e.g., failure to complete tenant improvements) and other problems. It is surprising how often estoppel certificates bring to light problems or side agreements not reflected in the lease itself. The lender's attorney provides the borrower with the form of estoppel certificate, but it is generally the responsibility of the borrower to tailor the estoppel certificate to facts specific to each lease and to distribute and obtain executed estoppel certificates from all tenants in a timely manner.

Most leases which predate the date of the loan are superior to the lender's lien; that is, if there is a default and the lender forecloses, the buyer at the foreclosure sale takes the property subject to such preexisting leases and has no right to terminate the leases in the absence of the tenants' default. The lender should be aware that in the absence of a subordination and attornment agreement, in some states even unrecorded leases may have higher priority than the lender's lien. To resolve this problem, lenders generally ask existing tenants (except, sometimes, anchor tenants) to sign a subordination and attornment agreement by which the tenant agrees that its lease is subordinate to the lender's lien. Many leases require the tenant to sign such agreements or attempt to impose subordination by virtue of the lease language itself.

When the tenant has no obligation to subordinate the lease to the lender's lien, the tenant usually can obtain a nondisturbance agreement from the lender in exchange for the subordination and attornment agreement. Whether combined with or separate from the subordination and attornment agreement, the nondisturbance agreement provides that, although the tenant agrees that the lender's lien is superior to the tenant's lease, in case of the borrower's default on the loan, the lender (or its successor in interest) will not disturb the tenant's use of the premises in accordance with its lease. When both a subordination and attornment agreement and a nondisturbance agreement are obtained, any practical difference from the original position in which the tenant's lease was superior to lender's lien is difficult to ascertain. Nevertheless, this ritual is regularly observed in loan transactions. Nondisturbance agreements are generally not referred to in the Commitment Letter but nevertheless may be required before loan closing.

As with estoppel certificates, the subordination and attornment agreements and nondisturbance agreements are generally on forms provided by the lender or drafted by lender's counsel, but they are distributed and collected by the borrower. They may or may not be recorded; the tenant, as well as the borrower and lender, has the right to have such agreements recorded. The process of obtaining completed estoppel certificates, subordination and attornment agreements, and nondisturbance agreements is often one of the stumbling blocks to closing the loan in a timely manner. The loan closer should regularly check with the borrower on this problem and report any delays to the lender.

The borrower should submit to the lender and lender's attorney the form lease to be used for future tenants, which has generally been drafted by borrower's counsel. The lender is in a position to demand changes in the form lease and often does so.

The rent roll should show that the requirements of the Commitment Letter for occupancy of the property (see example) are met; if not, the lender must waive or amend its requirement or the loan cannot close.

A reciprocal easement agreement, also known by such terms as a declaration of covenants, conditions, and restrictions (CC&Rs), is a document frequently found in shopping center transactions in which different portions of the shopping center are owned by different entities or are ground-leased to major tenants. Such an agreement governs responsibilities and costs for things such as insurance, taxes, repair, maintenance and capital improvements to the shared areas, and remedies available to the parties if one of the parties fails to fulfill such obligations or pay such costs. Such agreements also guarantee automobile and pedestrian ingress and egress over the portions of the shopping center owned or leased by the other parties. Reciprocal easement agreements are often highly negotiated between the parties, but the lender does not ordinarily become involved in negotiations. If the lender has serious objections to an existing reciprocal easement agreement, again, the issue will be one for a three-way negotiation. If the parties to such an agreement are a ground lessee and the property owner, the agreement may actually be incorporated into the ground lease rather be the subject of a separate agreement. If the parties are separate owners of different portions of the shopping center, the reciprocal easement agreement is almost always recorded.

Escrow Agreement.   When loans are made for projects which are not fully leased and which will require tenant improvements before premises are usable by new tenants, the lender commonly holds back certain amounts for the cost of such tenant improvements. Such an escrow agreement will be drafted by lender's counsel and negotiated between lender and borrower and their respective counsel.

Payment of Commitment Fee.   Commitment fees are often subject to negotiation prior to but rarely after the signing of the Commitment Letter. In the sample Commitment Letter, none of the commitment fee is refunded or applied against principal owed, which means that the borrower has paid the lender a loan fee (or points) equal to the amount of the commitment fee. Commitment fees are ordinarily paid upon the borrower's execution of the Commitment Letter and rarely become a problem if the loan closes without any problems. When loans do not close, battles frequently occur over the disposition of the commitment fee.

Costs. The borrower customarily pays all costs of processing the loan. Any costs not billed directly to the borrower are generally deducted from the borrower's loan proceeds and paid directly to the appraiser, surveyor or title insuror, etc. The closing statement prepared by the escrow holder or title company should specify the costs and must be approved by the borrower. It is rare for any of the costs to cause major controversy with one exception: attorney's fees incurred by the lender. If the lender is a large institutional investor using inside counsel (for whose services a fee is not generally charged), the amount of attorney's fees is not likely to bother the borrower. However, when the lender uses outside counsel and the negotiations have been lengthy, the borrower often objects to the amount of the attorney's fees. This problem can create last-minute snags in the closing, especially if the amount of fees is not known to the borrower until a day or two before the closing.

Borrower's Affidavit. A document normally required prior to the close is a statement by the borrower, under penalty of perjury, which addresses several items of concern to the lender, such as whether any condemnation proceedings have been commenced, whether any casualty has occurred which has damaged the property or improvements, and whether there has been any material change in the information previously supplied. In the example, it may be necessary to obtain an affidavit from each general partner, in addition to an affidavit from the partnership signed by the general partners. Sometimes the lender requests the opinion of counsel (an opinion letter from borrower's counsel, discussed above) to address the condemnation and casualty issues, in addition to including such items on the borrower's affidavit. The borrower's affidavit is always drafted by lender's counsel and reviewed by the borrower and borrower's counsel. Sometimes the subject of minor negotiations, this affidavit rarely raises a major stumbling block to the loan closing.

Other Unwritten Requirements. Nowhere does the Commitment Letter refer to an appraisal of the property. The lender has undoubtedly formed an opinion of the value of the property prior to making a commitment, usually based on an appraisal. However, the appraisal may have been an informal appraisal, and the lender may want an updated or formal appraisal prior to the closing of the loan. It is particularly important to have an updated appraisal if the original appraisal was made before construction was completed.

The loan closer must make sure that the transaction is properly reported to the Internal Revenue Service, as required by the Tax Reform

Act of 1986, because the loan closer may be subject to fines for failure to do so.

Although a guarantee is not required by the example used in this chapter, it is not unusual for lenders to require guarantees of the loan by principal shareholders of borrower corporations or parents of subsidiary borrowers. Many controversies arise in regard to such guarantees, including whether they are enforceable if the proceeds of the foreclosure sale are not sufficient to pay all the remaining debt. A loan closer should be aware of the importance of such guarantees, which are always drafted by lender's counsel and negotiated between attorneys for lender and borrower.

The form addressing prorations of costs is another unwritten requirement on which all parties must agree prior to closing the loan.

Whenever the party to the transaction is a corporation, the other party must contact the appropriate state official to make sure that the corporation is a validly formed corporation, in good standing, and authorized to do business in the state where the property is located. Verification is usually easy to do by letter or phone call to the appropriate state official. Failure to make this determination can cause problems if it is ever necessary to sue the entity which the lender thought was a validly formed corporation. Lenders often remember this task if the borrower is a corporation, but borrowers sometimes overlook checking on the corporate status of the lender.

Even if the corporation is validly formed and in good standing in the state where the property is located, the loan documents must be signed by someone with authority to bind the corporation. Such authority may be found in the bylaws of the corporation or in a resolution of the board of directors of the corporation authorizing certain officers to bind the corporation to certain kinds of documents; a copy of such bylaws or resolution must be obtained. In addition, it is necessary to ascertain that the individual who executes the documents on behalf of the corporation actually holds the office so empowered; a certificate of incumbency issued by the secretary of the corporation certifies that the particular individual holds the office and should be obtained for each individual executing any document on behalf of any corporation.

The Closing Itself

Although variations are common, there are two basic types of closings: an escrow closing and a New York style closing. New York style closings are not limited to New York State, but they are more common in eastern than western states.

Escrow Closing

In an escrow closing, the funds from the lender, the loan documents, and the title documents are given to a neutral third party, called an *escrow holder* or *escrow company*, with written escrow instructions from each of the parties to the transaction. Escrow instructions from the parties, usually written by their respective legal counsel, list the conditions to the close of the loan.

The loan closer must always read and understand all escrow instructions from all parties. Escrow instructions may be lengthy and detailed and may even change some of the basic terms of the loan agreement and/or purchase and sale agreement. In some cases, parties submit joint escrow instructions signed by all parties, in which case there is usually no danger of conflict. In other cases, escrow instructions from one of the parties may conflict with the instructions of another party. In either case, escrow instructions may raise new problems. The loan closer must draw the attention of the parties to the conflicts or problems and require resolution before the loan closing.

The parties will vary depending on the transaction. In many areas, the escrow company is the same as the title insuror. If the loan is being used to purchase the property, there will be a seller whose instructions will generally require funds to be paid to its existing lenders, with the surplus to be disbursed to seller. If the borrower already owns the property and is using all or part of the loan funds to pay off the construction loan, the borrower's instructions will usually require funds to be paid to the construction lender and the construction lender's lien to be released, with the surplus (if any) to be disbursed to the borrower. Borrower and lender will both have instructions with regard to the title insurance policy and exceptions to title.

The lender's escrow instructions will generally be more detailed than those of the borrower and will list all the loan documents which must be delivered and specify those which must be notarized and/or recorded with the appropriate public official. The list is usually accompanied by exhibits of the (unexecuted) loan documents with a written requirement that the executed loan documents be identical to the exhibits.

When negotiations on loan documents are resolved only shortly before the closing or at the closing meeting itself, revised documents will be produced which look similar to prior versions at first glance. Because the versions are easily confused, the documents should be carefully checked prior to the closing for conformance to the latest version on which the parties have agreed.

In an escrow closing, there is frequently but not always a closing meeting. The meeting will usually take place at the office of the escrow holder or the attorney for one of the parties on the day before documents are to be recorded and money wired. The escrow holder, title insuror (if separate from the escrow holder), borrower, lender, and seller (if any) will attend, along with their respective attorneys, and the construction lender (if any) or seller's lender may attend. All documents will be executed at this meeting. Because it is necessary to notarize signatures on all documents which need to be recorded, a notary will always be present.

In particular transactions, it is common for some of the documents to pass through the loan closer rather than through the escrow holder, but the documents which will always pass through the escrow holder are the note, deed of trust, title insurance policies for both borrower and lender, and the loan funds.

In a pure escrow closing, no closing meeting is held. Instead, the parties sign all documents ahead of time and submit them to the escrow holder, relying solely on their written escrow instructions to make sure the loan closes properly.

New York Closings

In a New York closing, there is always at least one closing meeting, usually two, and there is no third-party escrow holder. The first meeting is usually held a day or two before the documents are to be recorded and the money wired and is held at the office of the attorney for one of the parties. The parties are the same as those who would attend an escrow closing meeting. Before the closing, the title insuror will have issued a title commitment or preliminary title report, and, at the closing meeting, the title insuror will have title insurance policies available. At the first meeting in a New York closing, all documents are executed and, where necessary, notarized, and all documents to be recorded are exchanged. The documents are then taken by the title company to be recorded.

At the second meeting, usually held the same day as the documents are recorded, the title insuror will actually deliver the title insurance policies to the borrower and the lender. The borrower will deliver the note to the lender, and the lender will deliver to the borrower (and the construction lender or other previous lender) a Lender's Disbursement Statement which recites where the funds will be wired that day. The second meeting may be attended by only the attorneys and the title insuror, rather than by the parties themselves.

Transfer of Funds

In commercial loan transactions, funds are generally not conveyed by check but by wire transfer of the money from the lender directly into the bank accounts of the escrow holder or (in a New York closing) the various designated recipients. The loan closer should know the name and telephone number of the individual at the lender's bank who is in charge of wiring the funds. Otherwise, the parties may experience the frustration of being bounced around the bureaucracy of the bank when delays are intolerable and costly.

The timing of the transfer of funds is frequently a problem with commercial loans because the amounts are big enough that one day's interest is substantial. Thus it is not wise to plan to transfer funds on a Friday or the day before a bank holiday. Different time zones must be considered when the lender or lender's bank is in a different time zone from the other parties. Last-minute problems are frequently encountered which must be resolved before the loan can close, which will delay the disbursement of the funds. In these cases, the parties must agree on who bears the cost of the interest on the funds for the duration of the delay. This issue often causes painful negotiations.

Recording

The title company takes the documents to the office of the appropriate public official where they are logged in by time, date and number, or book and page number. In some jurisdictions, rather than returning the documents to the person submitting them at the time, the public official retains the documents and returns them only after the lapse of some days, weeks, or months. In these cases, the person submitting the documents must make a note of the time, date, and document number of all recorded documents and convey this information to the various parties. The loan closer should also have a reminder system to check receipt of the actual, recorded documents.

Other Final Considerations

Whether the closing is an escrow closing or a New York closing, there are always business decisions which must be made at the last minute. These decisions often include what conditions, if any, may be waived. For example, it may be discovered at the closing meeting that an estoppel certificate has not been obtained for a particular tenant; if the tenant rents 1500 square feet in a large shopping center, the lender may choose to waive the estoppel certificate for the particular tenant. Thus, business people who have the authority to bind the parties to business decisions must attend the closing meeting or, at a minimum, be accessible by telephone.

Documents need to be distributed to the parties. The loan closer makes sure all parties receive copies of all documents, with original signatures where necessary. Often the documents are compiled into indexed binders or files distributed to each party. These distributions are usually made at the closing meeting, except for recorded documents which are distributed after recordation. In escrow closings with no closing meeting, all executed documents are generally exchanged through the escrow holder. Agreements are usually signed in sufficient numbers for every party to have a fully executed original. In the case of the Note, Deed of Trust, and Assignments of Rents and Leases, usually only the lender receives a fully executed original; photocopies of the documents recorded but not yet returned should be included, and when the actual recorded documents are returned, the originals should go to the lender; photocopies showing the actual recording seal of the public official and date and time of recording should be sent to all other parties. Each party should retain its original documents in a valuable documents file or safety deposit box.

After recording, disbursement of funds, and distribution of the documents, the loan closer turns the file over to the loan-servicing department of the lender or mortgage banker. It is important to remind the loan-servicing department of matters, in addition to the loan payments, which must be checked on periodically such as receipt of annual operating and financial statements and notices for changes in variable interest rates.

26
Construction Loan Administration

Alfred Wilner, P.E.
President, Alfred Wilner, Inc., New York, New York

Introduction

Most construction loan professionals agree that the hard work begins after the loan closes. If construction lending is indeed part of the process of creating real estate value, such value does not actually exist until completion of the physical improvement. Given the constraints of time and the loan amount, completion of the project is sometimes quite elusive. Construction lending is considered by many to be the riskiest form of lending, posing substantial exposure for the lender. However, a well-organized and tightly administered construction loan department can be an important profit center for a lending institution, as well as a source for other business.

This chapter will discuss construction loan administration procedure commonly used in many lending institutions. The institution must decide on how its construction loan administration responsibilities will be handled. Put quite simply, will the loan origination officer who solicited the project and underwrote the loan be the same person who oversees the loan during the construction period? Who will monitor the periodic disbursement of funds? Two common solutions are offered here.

331

The "All-Purpose" Loan Officer

Although the exact title may vary from lender to lender, smaller institutions frequently assign a loan officer to a particular customer, geographic area, or type of loan. This person then becomes responsible for the entire loan process, from loan origination through closing and construction to the final takeout or ultimate disposition of the loan. The advantage of this approach is that the borrower deals with one person throughout the term of the loan. Because the loan officer is familiar with the borrower and any special conditions of the project, special needs can be better met. The borrower, in turn, never feels shunted from desk to desk or from department to department.

Loan Administration versus Loan Origination

There are, however, disadvantages to this system. Because the loan officer is closely involved with the borrower, difficult decisions may not be made objectively. The other disadvantage concerns skill levels: As loans become larger and projects become more complex, loan administration requires different skills than does loan origination, analysis, and underwriting. Lenders have recognized these problems. The all-purpose loan officer is therefore usually found only in smaller institutions offering more personalized services.

Most interim lending institutions divide their construction loan departments into two major groups. The loan origination group deals with new business and incoming loan products. Loan sources, which vary widely, may include existing bank customers and borrowers brought to the bank by brokers, attorneys, or other lenders. Through the lender's wide range of contacts in the business community, other sources of new business are constantly in touch with the construction loan officer. The origination department begins the application, evaluation, and approval process. Earlier chapters have dealt with the submission, loan negotiation, and closing process. Once these steps have been taken for a specific loan, the loan package is handed to the second major lending group—the loan servicing or loan administration department.

The goal of the loan administration department is to deliver a complete project with the loan ready for payoff. To achieve that goal, the department has the responsibility of monitoring the orderly distribution of funds to the borrower, in accordance with the terms of the loan commitment and good lending practice.

Getting Started

Upon notification that a loan has been approved, the loan administrator must get a series of documents. The majority of these items are readily available or have been required as part of the loan approval process. These documents include the following:

1. *Loan commitment.* The loan administrator should review the overall loan commitment for the project, to understand the scope of the loan, the background of the borrower, and any special provisions applying to this particular loan.

2. *Appraisals.* The process of understanding the loan should include a review of the appraisal for the job by the loan administrators. They will quickly understand the project, proposed lease rates, and comparable jobs.

3. *Plans and specifications.* The loan administrator should become familiar with the details of the proposed improvements. Even without detailed construction expertise, the loan officer must understand the nature of the project, including the type of construction, site features, location, and highway access.

4. *Plan review.* In becoming familiar with the project, the loan officer refers to a plan review prepared during the loan underwriting process. The review is frequently prepared by an outside engineering or architectural consultant retained by the lender. The report usually contains a summary of the physical features of the project, a review of the soils report and structural system, and an examination of the mechanical systems. The report confirms to the lender that the project is designed in accordance with good engineering and architectural practice. Portions of the report may also deal with the proposed costs of construction and examine estimates and contracts submitted by the borrower.

5. *Construction agreements.* The loan administrator generally requires that copies of the contract with the general contractor (if a general contractor is used) or contracts with major trades and suppliers be submitted for review. These contracts are frequently submitted to the engineering consultant for further review.

6. *Building permit.* The existence of a valid building permit covering the proposed improvement must be confirmed by the loan officer. In most municipal jurisdictions, the permit confirms that the project has been approved by the local zoning board and that the project, as designed, conforms to the local building code requirements.

7. *Loan budget—hard costs.* The loan administrator must have the

latest cost estimates prepared by the borrower. This estimate must have a line-by-line cost breakdown of all the elements of construction required for the job. An allowance for contingency costs is usually included as a separate line item in the cost estimate.

8. *Loan budget—soft costs.* The soft costs are nonconstruction costs, including the cost of land, interest reserve, legal fees, commissions, sales and promotional expenses, design fees, insurance, taxes, and other such items. A separate cost breakdown is prepared for these items.

9. *Progress schedules.* The loan commitment specifies the term of the loan and expiration date of the loan agreement. The loan administrator must review progress schedules prepared by the borrower and confirm that the project is scheduled to be completed prior to the loan expiration date. In conjunction with the progress schedule, the loan officer may also require that a proposed cash flow schedule be prepared. This cash flow schedule is a valuable forecasting tool that allows the lending institution to plan for its overall disbursing requirements for all projects underway.

10. *Insurance certificates.* The loan officer must assemble the insurance certificates, as specified in the loan commitment. Coverage may include comprehensive general liability, worker's compensation, builder's risk, and flood damage policies.

11. *As-built survey.* To confirm that a building has been correctly placed on the parcel, many lenders require that the borrower submit an "as-built foundation survey." This procedure guards against a costly but not unusual error in building layout or encroachment onto adjacent property or specially zoned areas.

12. *Certificate of occupancy.* Upon completion of the work, a Certificate of Occupancy (CO) is usually issued for the project by the local municipality. In certain jurisdictions, a separate CO is issued for each building or rental space in a complex project. These documents must be assembled by the loan officer as part of the loan closing process.

The Requisition Process

Monitoring the flow of funds to the borrower is the prime responsibility of the loan administration department. The entire success of the loan process can be judged by the accuracy and efficiency of the flow of funds to a project.

Hard-Cost Distribution

The loan commitment usually outlines the overall procedures for periodic distribution of hard-cost funds. Typically the borrower prepares a monthly requisition using a format such as the American Institute of Architects form 702 or 703. These are accompanied by backup data required by the lender. These data usually include supporting requisitions from contractors, delivery receipts, purchase orders, partial or complete lien waivers, cancelled checks, and such other data as the lender may request. Concurrent with the preparation of the requisition, the project is inspected by the lender's technical representative. This physical inspection may be performed by the lender's in-house personnel, by a consulting engineer, or by an architect retained by the lender.

Each line item of the requisition is examined by the inspector in relation to the work actually in place at the site. The inspector must answer a simple question for each such item: Are the funds requested by the borrower a fair representation of the work actually in place at the site? The question may be answered by a combination of percentage of completed work or by an examination of actual costs. The inspector then evaluates other significant factors of the construction project: Is the quality of materials and work consistent with the requirements of the plans and specifications? Is such compliance confirmed by documents such as concrete test reports, compaction reports, or other verifiable documentation? Is the project well organized and well supervised? Does the project have an adequate work force? Is the work proceeding in an orderly manner and on schedule? Conversely, are there any delays attributable to weather or shortages of labor or materials?

All these factors, as well as a description of the status of the major trades, are summarized in a written report and forwarded to the loan officer for review. A series of progress photos is usually taken each month by the inspector as part of the field observation.

Soft-Cost Distribution

In addition to the hard-cost requisition, the borrower prepares a soft-cost requisition, submitting it to the loan administrator. This soft-cost requisition will provide soft-cost funding for interest and other soft costs incurred. Similar backup for the soft costs is required prior to funding by the loan administrator. These soft costs include such items as land costs, interest, leasing commissions, legal fees, design fees, insurance, taxes, and other project-related costs not categorized as hard-cost items.

Requisition Approval

With the two requisitions and an inspection report from the inspecting engineer or architect in hand, the loan administrator is now in a position to conduct an overall evaluation of the project for the prior month. A judgment must be made as to whether the project is proceeding in a satisfactory manner based on the facts presented. Is the requisition approved for hard costs? Are there sufficient funds in the interest reserve and other soft-cost items to permit funding? These and other questions are reviewed each month, on each job, by a qualified loan officer. If the loan officer has received positive responses to all of the inquiries, then the last major step can be taken prior to actual funding.

The loan commitment invariably requires the borrower to conduct business in such a manner as to keep the property free of any liens. To confirm this fact, an examination of the title is conducted each month just prior to the funding date. This updated examination of the mortgage records is usually performed by a local title company in the municipality where the mortgage is filed. Good lending practice requires that, if a lien has been filed, no further funding can proceed. Technically, the loan is in default. The lien must either be removed or a suitable bond provided by the borrower.

"Bonding a lien" is a procedure whereby a surety bond is provided to the court having jurisdiction, to ensure the court that funds are available in the event the lienor is successful.

The actual funding may consist of a transfer of funds to the borrower's account, if the borrower has an account with the lender's bank. If the borrower banks elsewhere, funds are bank-wired to the borrower's account. Lenders frequently set up a procedure where they deduct the loan interest and, in effect, pay themselves the interest.

As the job progresses, this procedure is repeated each month until the project is completed. Upon completion, the lender seeks to be paid in accordance with the provisions of the loan documents. If there is a long-term takeout, evidence of satisfactory completion of the work usually must be submitted to the takeout lender. A separate inspection of the property by representatives of the long-term lender is usually made. Other materials, such as the certificate of occupancy and fire underwriter's certificate, are also provided to the takeout lender. Another closing is scheduled to allow the interim lender to be paid off.

Internal Controls

Because of the complexity of the interim loan process, good records and files must be maintained by the lender. Additionally, the accounts are subject to audit by various agencies. The lender also has a fiduciary responsibility in the event that there are loan participants and the lender is acting as lead lender.

Although filing procedures vary from organization to organization, certain basic concepts are important. The major groupings usually established are:

1. *Document file.* The document file contains all the agreements signed by the parties and include loan commitment, participation agreements (if any), buy-sell agreements, tripartite agreements, and any special documents executed by the major parties to the loan.

2. *Project file.* The project file contains the plans, specifications, surveys, and other documents listed earlier that relate directly to the proposed improvement. This file could also include soil reports, appraisals, special market studies, etc.

3. *Time file.* The time file is more properly labeled a reminder or tickler file. It flags for the loan officer such crucial dates as the original date of closing, expiration of takeout, dates of owner contribution, and other milestones during the life of the loan.

4. *Requisition file.* The requisition file is actually a series of files for each requisition made by the borrower as the loan progresses. For each disbursement of hard costs, a file is established that contains the borrower's loan request, engineer's inspection report, backup data, lien waivers, copies of cancelled checks, if required, title update, and other data. Similar information is maintained for all soft costs, including records of disbursements for land, interest, fees, taxes, and all backup for such items.

5. *Special conditions.* Records are maintained for other aspects of the disbursement process. For example, if payment for tenant finishes is required in an office building, a separate record of such disbursements is maintained. If the lender is to receive portions of closing funds for condominium sales, a separate file is maintained for such transactions. The loan administrator may be required to approve leases or contracts of sale as part of the disbursement process.

6. *Correspondence file.* A general correspondence file may be kept separately to hold a wide range of correspondence created during the course of the project. Many of the accounting tasks lend themselves to computer applications. Portions of the "files" may, in fact, be maintained on computer by a series of programs specially prepared for the loan administration department.

Other Considerations

Retainage

"Retainage," as defined in a recent text, is "a sum of money withheld from progress payments to the contractor in accordance with the terms of the owner-contractor agreement."[1] The purpose of retainage is to allow the developer or the lender recourse if there is any failure in the work or if additional work is required to fulfill the terms of the contract. Traditionally, the amount retained is 10 percent of the contract.

Problems arise because many contracts, particularly in the private sector, do not specify how the amount is to be withheld or when it is to be released. If 10 percent of payment is held back, contractors (who are often underfinanced in any case) are forced to work with only 90 percent of their funds; consequently, they need to know when the balance will be available.

Retainage may present particular difficulties for the subcontractor whose work is completed early in the building process but who must wait for final project approval before receiving the last 10 percent. For example, the excavator is a subcontractor who suffers most unfairly from retainage. To retain part of the excavator's fee is unnecessarily punitive because not only is this job finished early but also once the foundation work begins, the excavator's involvement in the project is completely over.

As a result of continuing protests and pressures from subcontractors (who claim they must raise their prices to compensate for retainage), owners, contractors, and lending institutions are being forced to pay more attention to the problems of retainage. Contracts now frequently specify that the retainage will be 10 percent up to a specified time and then, if the work is satisfactory, the retainage will be reduced to 5 percent until the project is complete. In many cases, subcontractors involved in the early stages of construction may have their retainage released soon after their work is completed.

The loan administration department should have a clearly stated policy concerning retainage of hard costs. This policy, or any modification thereof, should be included in the commitment or as the subject of separate correspondence.

Payment for Stored Materials

Borrowers often request payment for materials delivered to the site but not yet installed. However, many lending institutions will not fund ma-

[1]From Cyril Harris, ed., *Dictionary of Architecture and Construction*, McGraw-Hill, New York, 1975.

terials until they are actually installed in the job. Contractors, who may be required by suppliers to pay upon delivery to the site, may need additional financing to cover the period until payment—in some cases, as much as 60 to 90 days.

The problem increases during a period of escalating costs. Contractors wishing to save money by ordering materials early may be hesitant to do so or may find it impossible to do if they must wait too long for reimbursement. As a result, the material prices may rise in the time gap between estimating costs and actual purchase. Many subcontractors now have standard contract forms providing that prices for certain materials will be those in effect at the time of delivery so that the subcontractor is protected. This practice can cause loan overruns.

From the point of view of owners and lenders, there are, of course, real dangers in funding materials before they are incorporated into a project. Materials stored on site are commonly subject to theft, pilferage, and vandalism. There may be damage by the elements if the stored materials are not sufficiently protected. There have also been cases of unscrupulous borrowers who have moved materials from one site to another in order to be paid twice for the same shipment.

Some lenders will fund if materials are stored in a bonded warehouse and are evidenced by bona fide bills of sale. Without such documentation, the construction lender or owner risks the possibility that the goods may be subject to vendors' liens. Certain materials that are custom-made for a particular job, such as precast concrete, may be safely paid for by lenders on delivery. Specially fabricated items are often paid for in advance. Lenders generally will not pay for goods that cannot be readily identified (such as sand, brick, block, cement). Lenders also frown on funding for materials that are easily transportable and may be used interchangeably in many jobs.

To solve some of the lender's difficulties relating to payment for materials delivered but not yet installed, the lender's commitment should clearly state the lender's policy toward such payments:

- Will payment be made for certain materials if they are on the site, or is storage in a warehouse required?
- Will advance payments or deposits be made to manufacturers while materials are being fabricated and stored?
- What documentation is required if such payments are to be made?

Furthermore, subcontractors' terms should be consistent with the terms of the general contractor's agreement with the owner or lender regarding such payments. The loan administrator carefully monitors payments for stored materials and coordinates with the field reports from inspection personnel.

Change Orders, Extra Work Orders, and Amendments to Work

The nature of the construction process is such that every job experiences some changes during its course. Changes too often become a source of irritation between the borrower and lender, or between the general contractor and the owner, especially when substantial amounts of work are involved. A number of factors determine how much change will become necessary in a job:

1. *Adequacy of the plans.* Good plans—well-detailed, easy to follow, and prepared by a competent architect—require fewer changes. If plans are sketchy, misleading, or not sufficiently detailed, changes can usually be anticipated.

2. *Competency of the contractor.* The developer or owner should ask many questions before choosing a contractor. Has the contractor completed jobs of a similar scope and nature? Has the job been planned carefully, or does the contractor have the reputation of operating under crisis management? Is the base bid realistic, or does the contractor hope to make a profit on multiple change orders?

3. *Nature of the work.* Certain types of jobs where the work cannot be readily defined are more prone to change orders. An example is a renovation where existing conditions cannot be determined because they are concealed within the building shell.

4. *Owner's indecision.* Some owners have trouble expressing their wishes or have difficulty visualizing the finished building from plans. Consequently, as construction proceeds, there may be frequent changes.

5. *Tenant requirements.* Changing leasing conditions frequently lead to sealed changes. Special tenant requirements sometimes become known only after construction has started. These invariably lead to expense charges.

In any event, the loan administrator must be constantly aware of the status of the overall hard costs of a job. The lender must make provisions in the loan allocation for some amount of additional hard-cost expenditure. If such an arrangement is not possible, there must be a clear understanding that any change orders that increase the cost of the project will be funded by the borrower. The lender must also be aware of change orders that downgrade or cheapen the value of the improvement. Such changes are sometimes made by a borrower in an effort to pay for cost overruns in other items. Under certain conditions, changes or deletions that decrease the value of an improvement could jeopardize the position of an interim lender if it were a significant deterioration from the approved plans and specifications. This could create a situation in which a long-term lender would decline to fund the takeout commitment on the grounds that the improvement did not conform to plans and specifications. Constant periodic inspection by the lender's technical personnel, as well as by the loan administrator, can help minimize this type of risk.

27

Servicing the Loan

Donald L. Tripp
Vice President, Dorman & Wilson, Inc.
White Plains, New York

Understanding the Loan Documents

The primary function of the income property asset administrator is monitoring compliance with the terms of the loan documents. To perform this function properly, the administrator must fully understand the loan agreement and all related documents, including current leasing arrangements. Although standardized mortgage loan documents have been in use for many years for single-family mortgages, income property loan agreements are individually tailored to match the risks and rewards associated with the specific transaction.

Familiarity with the Asset (Collateral)

To obtain a working knowledge of the asset that serves as collateral for the loan, the administrator must consider the individual characteristics of each loan. The location, property type, and loan amount distinguish each transaction and determine the amount and degree of attention required from the administrator. A loan on an office building net-leased to a *Fortune* 500 company for a period equal to or greater than the loan term may not require as much attention as one on a speculative office building that is only partially leased.

Some critical areas of concern to the administrator of the speculative loan are the current leasing market, the types of leases currently being negotiated in the local area, and—of greater importance to the income stream—the market rent trend. Over a relatively short period, favorable or unfavorable market conditions will determine the project's degree of success. Monitoring the leasing in a multitenanted building will provide the asset administrator with information on the future income stream, thereby serving as an indicator of success or a warning of a decline in the value of the asset.

Establishing Borrower Relationships

As stated above, the asset administrator's primary task is to ensure that the borrower complies with the terms of the loan documents. Therefore, administrators should review the documents prior to the loan closing so that they understand the terms of the transaction as set forth in the commitment letter. Various documents such as leases, surveys, insurance policies, title reports, and certifications from tenants, architects, and tradespeople generally require review and approval before closing and, in the case of lease and insurance policy renewals, continual monitoring after closing. In addition, these latter items must meet investors' requirements prior to closing, since insufficient or deficient documentation accepted by lenders may be interpreted by many borrowers as a waiver or relaxation of written requirements.

As a means of highlighting misunderstandings or misinterpretation of the loan documents, the administrator should send a letter to the borrower as soon as practical after closing, confirming the transaction and reiterating the important commitment terms. The first part of the letter should cover the date of closing, the amount advanced, how the funds were delivered, e.g., by wire or checks, whether any funds were held in escrow (with a brief description of their purpose), and any amounts remaining to be funded in the future. The second part should summarize briefly the payment terms—the due date of payments and the payment amount (specifically identifying applicable components of principal, interest, ground rents, various escrows, etc.). It is also important to mention any provisions for assessing penalties for late payments. The letter should conclude by providing the names of persons in the loan administration department that borrowers can contact if they have questions on their loan.

Establishing a line of communication with the borrower is very important, as some transactions may require a "breaking-in" period, particularly with borrowers who are unfamiliar with the mortgage banking company. During the first several months after closing, the administrator should contact the borrower immediately if any item required under the documents is even one day late. This strategy will send a strong signal to the borrower that strict adherence to the loan terms will be required. A less than aggressive attitude on the part of the administrator may be interpreted as an informal waiver of those terms by many borrowers. Since a great deal of time and experience have gone into the writing of loan documents by the investor, it is the administrator's responsibility to the investor to enforce the compliance expected of the borrower.

Payments and Collections

Another of the administrator's important functions is the collection of mortgage payments, preferably on or before their due dates. The administrator must understand the basic cash flow structure of an income-producing property and the distinction between it and that of a residential loan. The funds required to make monthly payments on single-family residential loans come from the homeowners' income and average about 28 to 30 percent of their gross monthly income. If the borrowers' income is interrupted because of illness or temporary unemployment, they have a good chance of catching up in subsequent months.

In contrast, in most cases income property is highly leveraged. For leverage to be profitable, the rate of return on the investment must be higher than the cost of the money borrowed. The economic forces determining the cash flows for income properties differ markedly from the market forces that determine the cost and related financing for single-family homes. On average, over time, commercial rents are governed by costs associated with land, construction, maintenance, and financing. Added to this is a return on investment needed to attract equity. Therefore, careful analysis of these costs will result in a financial model that sets forth minimum rents required for success. If these rents are not attainable in the marketplace, the project will fail. Conversely, attainable rents will be an early indicator, although not an insurer, of a project's success.

Since rents generally are fixed over the life of a lease, the cash flow is fairly predictable over time. This scenario assumes that there will be no interruption in rental collections. In addition, it assumes that there will be no unanticipated expenses that will divert cash away from debt service payments. Accordingly, the options available to an income property borrower in times of tight cash flow may be limited. The most common causes of rental interruptions are unstable tenancies and bankruptcies. Once the loan has been underwritten with preexisting tenants, the property's success will be governed by the financial stability of those tenants. When the property is not fully leased prior to closing, the lender no doubt will require review and approval of new leases, not only for form, but to review the credit of the lessee.

Unfortunately, the relationship between the cash flow and the debt service payment, which typically consumes a greater portion of cash flow than the single-family model, presents a more difficult problem when an income property payment is missed. If the amount that should have been allocated for the debt service payment is spent elsewhere, there is little hope of recovering this payment in future months, because of the high leveraging. Any diversion of funds from those budgeted for a property's operation usually creates a problem. The most common type of diversion is deferring maintenance. Over time, this deferral results in poorly maintained property, affecting its marketability to tenants, and eventually a depressed cash flow.

Income property loans generally require some type of restructuring if payments are missed because of insufficient cash flow caused by vacancy factors, the most common cause of income property delinquency. The management of this problem is discussed in greater detail in the next chapter.

Real Property Taxes and Assessments

Real estate taxes and other miscellaneous assessments are superior to the lien of the mortgage; if they are not paid, the mortgage loan is placed in jeopardy. In many cases, the taxing authority has the right to sell its tax lien, which accrues interest and penalties beyond the payment due date. The purchaser of the tax lien then has the right to foreclose against the property. Even if the tax lien was not purchased by a third party, the taxing authority or municipality has the right of foreclosure. In either case, the foreclosure will negatively affect the lender's collateral, and the lender will have to decide whether to advance funds to remove the tax lien to maintain the mortgage lien in a secure position.

The preferred method for monitoring timely payment of real estate taxes is for the loan agreement to require the payments into an escrow account of the amounts estimated for real estate taxes. In general, the escrow is added to debt service payments and paid by the borrower simultaneously to the lender. The administrator is responsible for estimating the correct amount of future taxes and then for making the appropriate disbursements to the taxing authority in a timely manner from the funds accumulated in the escrow account. In the event that there will be no tax escrow account, the administrator must be certain that the taxes have been paid.

Although the loan documents contain the legal description of the mortgaged property, they do not always cite the tax description. The best reference for the tax description is the title insurance policy. In estimating the monthly escrows, the asset administrator should also refer to the property appraisal, which will indicate current taxes, as well as future estimates. Again, the title policy should be reviewed to ensure that the tax information in both the appraisal and title policy are in agreement. Any discrepancies should immediately be reconciled with the loan originator or appraiser.

Insuring Income Property

It is quite common for the lender to have a greater financial interest in the property than the borrower. Consequently, the lender's risk is greater, and an important safeguard is the maintenance of adequate insurance to protect the collateral. The insurance industry, similar to the real estate financing industry, is continually adapting its products to meet the requirements of the marketplace. Many types of coverage are available, but generally the mortgage lender is primarily concerned with the risk of loss to the collateral. There are many variations of this type of coverage, ranging from basic fire insurance to broad coverage against various hazards. In earthquake-prone areas, the broader type of coverage is advisable. Coverage is also available against flood and should be required if the property is located in a specially designated flood zone. This information is available from local municipalities and surveyors. Prior to the loan closing, the loan manager should, as part of the commitment review or loan closing documentation process, determine the types of insurance required consistent with the risks to which the property may be exposed.

In addition to property coverage, the lender frequently requires the borrower to maintain liability insurance. Although liability does not extend to the lender, it is good business practice to make sure the borrower has this insurance. A liability award against an uninsured property owner, while junior to the lien of the mortgage and therefore not jeopardizing the mortgage lien, could disrupt the borrower's financial stability, possibly leading to a loan default. Therefore, requiring liability insurance assures the lender that the property's operations will not be impaired by a personal injury award. Other types of coverage commonly required are as follows:

Rent insurance. This coverage reimburses the landlord for loss of rents if the property is damaged to the extent that the tenants are unable to occupy their space and as a result do not make rental payments. This coverage should ensure that the landlord will have sufficient cash flow to meet operating expenses, property taxes, and debt service payments over a period sufficient to allow the restoration of the premises.

Business interruption. This coverage is in lieu of rent insurance on owner-occupied properties. It provides a source of funds to pay operating expenses, taxes, and debt service if damage to a property causes the occupant to stop business operations, thus impairing its ability to carry the property.

Boiler and machinery. Since heating, ventilation, air conditioning, and other mechanical equipment are vital to many income properties, and further, since the cost of this equipment is substantial, lenders frequently require insurance to facilitate the immediate repair of any damage so as to maintain these services to tenants and avoid defaults of leases by the landlord. Another related form of coverage available insures machinery and electrical apparatus. This coverage is particularly appropriate for electrically heated buildings and air conditioning and ventilation equipment.

Earthquake insurance. In earthquake-prone areas, this coverage is advisable.

Insurance costs have been escalating substantially over the past few years, and the premium expense is significant. In general, premiums are paid up front at the time coverage begins, and policies are written for one-year terms. In many cases, lenders now require that monthly payments be made into an escrow account, similar to the tax escrow programs, to accumulate sufficient funds to renew insurance coverage when the current policies expire. In the event there is no insurance escrow, the administrator must nevertheless be certain that the payment is made.

Since an insurance policy is a contract between the insurer and the insured (the property owner), the mortgagee must receive notice if this contract is terminated. Accordingly, the standard mortgagee clause should be made a part of the policy. Under this arrangement, any payments made by the insurer to the insured as a result of a loss settlement will be made payable to the mortgagee. By having control of the loss settlement proceeds, the mortgagee has the flexibility to apply the funds to the restoration of the building or the reduction of the loan balance. In addition, the mortgagee clause requires notice to the mortgagee from the insured, prior to cancellation or termination of coverage other than at the scheduled expiration of the policy.

Inspections and Operating Statements

Nearly all mortgage loan agreements contain a provision allowing entry and inspection of the mortgaged premises by the lender. The loan manager should arrange to have all income properties inspected periodically to ensure that the asset is being properly maintained. Inspection frequency is generally annual or biannual, depending on loan amounts and/or specific investor requirements.

Property inspections are useful in spotting trends, both at the mortgaged premises and in surrounding neighborhoods. Evidence of neighborhood decline, such as excessive vacancies in formerly occupied buildings, abandoned properties or properties in disrepair, and littered streets should be noted and reported to the investor. In addition, the borrower should be informed of the inspection findings, and concern should be expressed as to the declining trends.

Although the borrower may have little or no control over the maintenance of neighboring properties, this certainly is not the case with the subject property. All items of deferred maintenance and poor housekeeping should be brought to the attention of the property owner. Small problems, when left unrepaired, develop into major problems.

One critical item that should be inspected closely is the roof to ensure that there is proper drainage, since water seepage into the interior of a building is likely to create major problems with interior and exterior walls and ceilings. The roof should be clean and free of debris and standing water. Standing water, called "ponding," is the result of improperly installed roof drains. Interior corridors, stairwells, and elevators should be clean and free of debris and equipment. Maintenance of the boiler and equipment rooms is particularly important, as undiscarded trash and improperly stored equipment are fire and safety hazards.

Finally, for commercial tenants, the lender should review the rent roll to determine whether there have been any changes in major tenants since the last inspection. Any discrepancies should be discussed with the property's manager and noted on the report. Frequent tenant turnover may indicate a developing problem.

Active versus Passive Servicing

During the life of a loan, it is not uncommon for a borrower to request a favor from the mortgagee. The request could be in the form of a partial release of a portion of the mortgaged premises, an easement to or in favor of an adjoining property, or a renegotiation of specific loan terms.

This generally is an ideal time for the administrator to review the original loan transaction in an effort to enhance the mortgagee's position. This review is a perfectly legitimate opportunity, since the mortgagor is also looking for a concession from the mortgagee. Some of the items that may be renegotiated with the mortgagor in an exchange from the mortgagee are an increased interest rate, shorter maturity, or a portion of any monetary gain to be obtained from a third party.

In summary, active loan and asset administration is essential, not only to protect the investment but also to take advantage of opportunities to enhance the lender's position.

28

Handling Distress Real Estate

Daniel S. Berman, Esq.

Partner, Fink, Weinberger, Fredman, Berman & Lowell, New York and White Plains, New York

General Information

When confronted with problem real estate loans, the best solution is to have none. Unfortunately, in a time of inner city income property market glut, this is no longer possible. Even institutions with very healthy property loan portfolios are affected by distress real estate. As the disease of distress spreads rapidly, it is difficult to visualize a healthy office building, shopping center, or apartment house which remains unaffected by a neighboring problem property. Distress real estate means lowered rents, undesirable tenants, and overall reduced market values.

Organizing for Problem Loans

Most lenders wish the problem would go away by itself; many are not sufficiently organized to cope with it. Problem property loans need specialized treatment and full-time attention. The first thing to do about problem loans is to assign experienced and trained personnel to them.

When the problem arises, the file on the loan is often sent back to the original underwriter, on the theory that he or she knows the property best. But the property may be in trouble because of faulty underwriting—the last person who can admit that mistake is the original underwriter. The loan workout person should add a new face to the package. If nothing else, the new person is able to start fresh, to admit that the loan may have been ill-conceived in the first place, and to reject any implied personal commitment to the owner or the developer that derives from past relationships. A problem loan needs a long, hard, fresh look to answer the question: "Why is it a problem, and what are we going to do about it?"

Adequate Staffing Indispensable

The problem loan officers should report to an experienced workout executive and should have access to legal counsel familiar with real estate problems. Since problem real estate loans involve both business and legal decisions, the loan workout officer needs to be able to tap both kinds of knowledge.

Construction Loans—Spotting Problems in the Field

The sooner a problem loan is recognized, the easier it is to cut losses and turn the property around, whether the loan is a construction or permanent loan. An early-warning system is especially important in an incomplete construction loan. If the developer or contractor is "stealing from the job," the sooner the problem is discovered, the less money will be wasted. If honest cost overruns are involved and are detected early in the construction loan, the wise decision might be to abandon the job entirely. Abandoning a 20-percent-advanced construction loan may be cheaper than completing the job in a soft rental market.

Symptoms of cost overruns, overdrawn jobs, dissatisfied tradespeople, poor work, and a failure to monitor the project become apparent long before the project becomes hopeless. In troubled times, lenders should constantly review construction progress in the field, compare loan balances with the projected cost to complete, and make certain that sufficient reserves are available to build the job with the balance of the loan. If the job cannot be kept in balance, cut losses or reconsider the investment before more funds are drawn down. In some cases, architectural inspectors will be able to help, and their job should be newly defined to spot current troubles. In other cases, perusal of the owner's books and records before further disbursement of funds, as well as accounting assistance to review the borrower's financial statements, may prove useful.

Getting Financial Information

Find out what is the developer's current total overall cash flow by securing a list of all the other jobs in which the developer is involved and checking with other lenders, commercial banking sources, and accountants to see if the developer is in trouble anywhere else.

If either the developer or the job is in trouble, the next question is: "What is the size and cause of the trouble, and what are the possible solutions?" This question may seem too general, but there are no rules for distress property loans. The only rule is to get as much current information as possible. With this information at hand, the best solution will become apparent.

Find the Real Cause of the Trouble

The question of why the job is in trouble must be answered before any solution can be found. If the job is in trouble because the developer does not know how to control costs or timing schedules, controls can be built in to get the job back on the track. If the trouble is inattention or understaffing, the solution is obvious. If the trouble is stealing, the answer becomes apparent. But you must be in the field to spot this. You cannot determine the trouble from a file in your office. The sooner someone goes out to the job and walks into the job shack and visits with local suppliers and commercial banking sources, the faster you will be able to decide what to do. Visit the job.

Sometimes just asking questions on the job site is an eye opener. Before that, it may be desirable to request an audit of the developer's books. That simple request can uncover the fact that the developer has no books, no controls, and has no idea of where the job is going and how it will finish.

Marketplace Changes

Often the problem is not the developer but the marketplace. Have market conditions changed since the original underwriting? When the lender has the legal right to halt advances on a condominium construction loan, it may be essential to do so in an overbuilt area with a huge glut of unsold units.

The local representative should alert the lender to problem market areas as well as problem developers. Up-to-date information on changing conditions is indispensable. In some cases, there is time to change the marketing concept when the job is 75 percent complete. Condominiums could be converted into rental apartments, or full-floor office space into subdivided units; jobs may be slowed down to await better timing, or they may be boarded up rather than being fully equipped or outfitted.

Once marketing problems are spotted, up-to-date comparables should be sought, current rental and sales prices compiled, and the entire underwriting concept rethought. The lender will then be in a position to decide whether to complete, who is to complete, and what will happen when the job is completed. One may decide to take a loss and determine what the loss will be, or one may decide to hold the property through rent-up to try for third-party financing. The lender may want to sell the property subject to liberal financing that it supplies, thus deferring realization of loss to a later period. Check with the accounting department to discover how financing will be treated on the firm's books and for regulatory purposes.

Permanent Loans—Spotting Problems in the Field

The best way to spot permanent-loan problems in advance also involves going out into the field to visit the property. What is the condition of the property? Does it appear to be run down? Is the property fully rented, or is it partly vacant? Are the tenants satisfied? Would they renew their leases today, and at what rentals? Poor maintenance and vacancies are an indication of trouble to come. Real estate taxes should be current. Get income and expense statements for the property and see if they are up to date; analyze these statements to see whether the cash flow cushion is sufficient to keep the property solvent, or whether the property is about to slip into trouble.

Someone from the home office should inspect the property and assemble the information required. No request for deferral of loan interest or amortization should be considered without two or three years of the latest income and expense figures, together with a projection of the forthcoming year. Submissions should also include an up-to-date leasing and renting schedule and facts on competing properties. Are the current rentals shown on the property at market too low or too high when compared to the competition?

Financial Trend of the Property

What are the trends as reflected in the financial reports on the project? Reevaluate the project based on current numbers on next year's projections before making any decision about deferring interest or amortization. Do not waive interest or amortization until the entire problem is thought through, because deferral may get the debtor into deeper and deeper trouble. If the equity is already gone as a result of present conditions, visualize how the debtor is going to work out of trouble and rebuild equity. Any deferral is only carte blanche to allow the property to slip further into trouble.

If a deferral of interest or amortization is decided upon, be clear as to its objective. What should the owner be doing during the breathing period? How will the owner's performance be measured?

Get a Written Understanding

A written understanding should accompany deferral of interest or amortization, and it should result in some sort of mortgage modification. Perhaps assure that during the deferral period all rents are collected by lender staff and all disbursements are made through the lender's agent, rather than entrusting the funds to the hands of a desperate borrower who may collect rents, pay nothing to the lender and nothing toward real estate taxes or suppliers, and give the property back to the lender in arrears. If there are junior lienholders, make sure that they too defer collections during troubled periods. But check the legal ramifications of these controls; the lender's lawyer will want to make sure they do not jeopardize its rights as a secured creditor.

The usual workout agreements provide for interest or principal deferrals for short or long periods; for interest rate reductions; for smaller amortization payments and a longer maturity; or, on some occasions, for additional funding to be supplied by the lender for specific purposes.

If the lender agrees to defer interest and amortization, lengthen the mortgage term, or add money of its own, it should get something back—perhaps collecting the rents or making the disbursements. Perhaps there should be monthly payments of real estate taxes; monthly or quarterly financial reporting; or, in some cases, personal guarantees on the new loan or new real estate as security. Before giving something, review the entire file to make sure something is given in exchange.

Protecting the Permanent Loan
Takeout

The construction lender wants to protect the commitment for a permanent loan or takeout. The takeout may be the best way for the construction lender to salvage its funds, even if there is a small loss of principal.

The commitment letter should be carefully read to see if it can be fulfilled. If extensions of time are required, the construction lender should not leave this important job to the developer but should have its own team see to it. The strength of the permanent lender should also be considered, as well as the permanent lender's capacity to deliver the permanent loan.

Construction Loan Problems

The construction lender has some problems that a permanent lender does not. The construction lender must lock everything up to prevent on-site fixtures and equipment from being stolen. It must take control as soon as possible, making sure that on-site materials do not get "reclaimed" by unhappy subcontractors and that the neighbors do not help themselves to the refrigerators, washing machines, and other readily portable building supplies. It must take precautions to prevent damage due to inclement weather.

At the same time, someone should be putting together a cost-to-complete analysis. The lender must make sure that the building permits are current and that they are transferred or transferable. The existing subcontracts should be reviewed, together with a cost-to-complete analysis. Punch lists should be prepared for all completed work. If there has been unauthorized substitution or downgrading of materials, find out who was responsible and what can be done about it.

Checking Subcontracts and Cost to Complete

Check the existing subcontracts and the credit standing of subcontractors. If problems exist, do not be afraid to consider alternative contractors and subcontractors. However, in many cases options will be limited. Face the realities of subcontractors' strength in the union hall and their knowledge of what must still be done and where the connections can be found. Still, alternatives must be considered, at least for trading purposes.

The cost to complete should be reviewed in a practical and realistic manner. Can unstarted buildings and the total number of units be reduced? Can amenities be cut? Should the project be upgraded to improve market value? A new cash flow budget should be prepared on a trade-by-trade basis and on a month-by-month basis. A detailed plan and budget should be laid out, and the job should be continued on a piecemeal basis until someone is sure what the total cost is going to be, and whether the additional funding is going to make the project more successful.

Bargaining with Trade Creditors

If the workout plan involves getting trade creditors to take less than 100 cents on the dollar, the lender needs to know two things:

1. Who is going to take the public relations burden of being the "bad guy"? It is best to have the original developer do this, but the negotiating job should not be left to the developer alone, who may have an ax to grind. The lender's local attorney or field representative should also be present to protect its interests.
2. How should future payments to this distress job be controlled? Disbursement through another corporation belonging to the lenders, through a title company, through the old developer, or through the new contractor? Make sure that inspection procedures are changed so that the mistakes are not repeated. Finally, check how these controls will affect the lender's secured position.

Some Interim Remedies— Without Foreclosing

Foreclosure is the standard that all interim procedures are measured against, and the cost and time needed to obtain good title must be considered. Accepting a deed in lieu of foreclosure should be considered because of speed. But if a deed is accepted, what will be given up for it? A deed in lieu of foreclosure does not cut off mechanics' liens and possible third-party creditors. If they must be wiped out, one must go back to the longer, more expensive foreclosure proceedings. Also, the borrower is released from any guarantees or liabilities in exchange for the deed. Are these guarantees and liabilities worth anything?

One needs to consider the effect of having a new developer step in to finish the job and the effect of extending the time of performance on the liabilities of third parties. In other words, by making a new deal with the developer, the contractor, or the subcontractors, are the lender's rights against the bonding company, the title insurer, or third-party guarantors wiped out?

Getting Up-to-the-Minute Facts

In making these decisions, facts must be faced. Even clear title may not yield what is needed. A fully insured, bonded job may not mean finishing in time to meet the takeout commitment. And what can be done may not save as much of the principal of the original loan as possible.

In planning what to do next, the construction lender should consider the additional funding that may be available from third parties. The lender is not the only one with a checkbook. Limited partners may be prepared to add fresh money to avoid the tax impact of a foreclosure. (More about this later.)

Contributions can come from bonding companies, title companies, and general contractors. Also, trade creditors may subordinate their mechanics' liens, make cash contributions themselves, or reduce their contract price to salvage their junior positions.

Prospective tenants or contract buyers are sometimes sources of funds. A tenant who needs to open a store at a particular time may help bail out the project. A warehouse tenant or prospective owner of an industrial plant that needs the facility by a particular date may also be willing to put some more money into the project.

Junior lenders, construction loan participants, and permanent lenders may all invest funds to rescue a distressed property. Other potential contributors may be the inspecting and supervising architects or the developer's commercial banker who prefer to see the project successful rather than face liability, lawsuits, and bankruptcy risks.

Importance of Timing

What comes first, of course, is meeting the completion date set by the permanent commitment. Other key dates are the completion dates called for by leases to major tenants, by contracts to sell the property, by building and sewer permit expirations, and by market timing. Completing a condominium project in time to hit the sales or rental season may be important, and so may weather conditions.

Before planning to make further advances, make sure those new advances are protected as first liens. Also, before making additional advances, check the lender's rights against the bonding company and other sureties and guarantors. Review any defenses these third parties may have and, if further advances are required, make sure the lender's rights are protected.

Get Rights to Assign

Once the lender takes on a construction job, the next question to consider is whether construction contracts, the building and sewer permits, the permanent loan, and the contracts to sell condominium units are assignable.

Reexamine the file with a jaundiced eye, and make sure the completed structure will comply with building codes, zoning requirements, title insurance, survey restrictions, and condominium registration requirements. Be sure the property has the required access roads and utilities. A view of a project when in trouble may often reveal sloppy paperwork on the initial closing. Before advancing further funds, make sure that the building will be able to get certificates of occupancy, title insurance, etc.

Consider Alternative Plans

With all the facts on the table, the lender should consider its options. How will it control the project during the workout period? If it finds the developer or contractor honest but incompetent, it may let them remain in possession but will exercise more careful payment control. If the lender does not wish to exercise payment control directly, it may bring in another general contractor to watch the job and act as the controlling joint venturer with the defaulted borrower.

If the developer is in trouble but not yet insolvent, a request for additional equity is reasonable. Or the lender can go to court to ask for appointment of a receiver and start foreclosure. Consider both the cost of the receivership and the kind of receiver which is likely. Will the receiver be a political hack who will dissipate the proceeds of the job, or someone who will try to earn the fee? Consider selling the mortgage to a third party at a discount and letting the third party do the workout. Perhaps the lender may have to commit to supply permanent financing when the job is finished, but that may be cheaper than finishing the job on its own. Perhaps the title company or the bonding company will take over the job and complete it.

Using Nominees

If taking title, consider having a nominee hold title rather than putting one's institution on the line. This may avoid the local tax problem of "doing business" in the area during the workout period. Perhaps additional funds can come from the permanent lender, who might advance them in exchange for a higher interest charge, or for some kind of sale-leaseback guarantee. Perhaps additional funds can be raised by selling the tax loss position to a new syndicate.

Mortgagee in Possession

If the lender is to be a mortgagee in possession or will take a deed from the developer or foreclose, consider:

1. What is the impact of a takeover on the lender's balance sheet, loss reserves, and future earnings? Will this mean having to amortize the lender's own property? What rights of redemption does the present owner have? Would one rather have title and foreclosure or try to collect from the developer on the note or guarantee? Can one do both? What effect will the bankruptcy laws have on obtaining title?

2. If the lender is a real estate investment trust, a thrift, life insurance company, or other regulated entity, is its charter broad enough to permit active management of the project? What will the federal income tax impact be if it engages in active property management? Are there any other regulatory problems? An inventory of unsold condominium units raises questions of complying with local condo registration laws and possibly questions of interstate sales of securities. These are particularly sticky questions that should be studied in advance. At the very least, the inventory of unsold condo units should be held in a separate subsidiary—not by the parent.

Perfect solutions may not be obtainable. One may have to weigh the need to meet timing deadlines, the desire to cut off the rights of inferior lienholders, the availability of a deed in lieu of foreclosure, and the impact of whatever solution is chosen on proposed deficiency judgments, rights against guarantors, bonding companies, and title insurers.

The new general contractor or job supervisor must have the responsibility of completing the project. That will include the responsibility of getting a certificate of occupancy, of forwarding to the lender detailed reports showing where funds are going, and the responsibility of getting "clean" mechanics' lien waivers.

Be prepared to pay a good price for this. A cost-plus contract with substantial fees for the new contractor/developers will have to be developed. Although it is expensive, remember the greater expense required for 24-hour-a-day guards on the project to prevent mysterious disappearances, to protect the builders' risk and casualty insurance, and to make sure everything is accounted for.

If new documents are prepared and if you have junior loan participants, make sure that all of them give written approval for the proposed course of action.

Tax Aspects of Distress Real Estate

There are three reasons why one must understand the tax aspects of distress properties:

1. Much of the distress real estate now on the market is held in limited partnerships. Most of these entities were organized in limited partnership form to take advantage of tax write-offs. Even those parcels of real estate that were planned to be held as economic transactions and not as tax shelters find tax write-offs valuable. So the fact that the property is now losing money is not necessarily a detriment. The limited partner investors may be a source of additional funds which can be put into the deal as long as write-offs continue. Understanding their position will help raise outside money for the project.

2. Even if there were no limited partners in the project initially, depreciation write-offs may still be worth money to investors. A group of new investors packaged with an enterprising management team can add the new funds and skills needed to turn the project around.

3. If there are already limited partner investors in the project, a mortgage foreclosure is a tax disaster to them. Cognizance of the ramifications of this disaster can give the lender bargaining leverage in negotiating with the existing limited partners.

Every limited partnership that has held real estate for a period of time will have some tax benefits out of depreciation and some tax consequences on foreclosure. Therefore, the limited partner investors are forced to answer the following questions:

1. What will it cost me in new dollars to prevent the foreclosure by giving some money to the lender?

2. How does the cost of preventing foreclosure compare with the money I will have to give to the tax collector if the property is foreclosed?

3. What other benefits, including tax shelter savings and future appreciation, do I get out of the property if I prevent foreclosure?

One can be sure that the investors make these computations themselves. The lender may use these computations so that it can thereby evaluate its bargaining strength when it sits down with the investors. At the very least, if owners can pay less to avoid foreclosure than to pay the tax collector, one should be able to convince them to come up with some new funds.

One of the largest problems in dealing with limited partner investors is locating them. When the job gets into trouble, the general partner or developer no longer has any interest in it, having diverted all the funds possible and perhaps even having gone broke because of mismanagement, greed, or overextension. The fact that the property is about to be foreclosed rolls off the back of the general partner who cannot lose anything more and is no longer interested in making money from the project.

The general partner often has difficulty with limited partner investors. They are already dissatisfied, since the general partner has fulfilled neither his or her promises nor their dreams. Once a project gets into trouble, the relationship between the general partner and the limited partner investors is strained. It is not likely that the general partner will convince limited partners to invest more with the mortgage lender soon to protect themselves against a large income tax.

It is up to the lender itself (or its local counsel) to locate the limited partners (through the recorded limited partnership certificate), to see that they are represented by their own lawyer, and to negotiate with them as well as the general partner. One must recognize that the interests of the limited partners differ from those of the general partners. Limited partners can be a source of new funds, local know-how, and management.

Effect of the Bankruptcy Laws on Mortgage Lenders

The bankruptcy and reorganization laws are complex and are constantly changing. Congress derives the right to pass bankruptcy laws from the Constitution, and the first federal bankruptcy statute is dated before 1800. However, mortgage lenders were rarely affected by the bankruptcy laws until the 1960s. The pattern of the last 25 years, with the large number of real estate syndications, many limited partners, and the coming of the public real estate investment trusts, has given the bankruptcy courts a new interest in the field.

Recent reorganizations illustrate the increasing interest of the bankruptcy courts in protecting the rights of equity investors. The courts try to balance the rights of secured mortgage lenders with their efforts to salvage something for the general creditors and the small equity investor.

What to Do about Bias Against Secured Lenders

Currently, many lenders feel that bankruptcy courts favor the small creditor and equity investor. Institutional lenders are made to feel like Scrooge foreclosing a mortgage at Christmas.

It is the job of the mortgage lender's local bankruptcy attorney to convince the bankruptcy court that the owner or developer, and not the lender, is the real villain. The court must be shown by skilled trial counsel that the lender represents hundreds of small depositors and/or policyholders, whereas the developer fits any one or all of the following categories: a young opportunist who has not invested his or her own equity in the project, mismanaged the project, pocketed all the funds, failed to supervise properly, took kickbacks from subcontractors, and went broke on another job. Also, the villain misled poor tradespeople into working on the job and never told them it was in trouble. Such a person, the attorney claims, should not be protected by the bankruptcy courts, because such protection would only encourage questionable operators to perpetrate similar frauds.

Further, the developer-borrower has no equity in the project. The job cannot be finished unless the lender forbears or adds additional funds of its own, and the lender cannot do so, lender's counsel argues, while the villainous developer controls and continues to milk the project. Finally, it is argued, it is unconstitutional to deprive the lender of a secured lien, and, in most cases, the bankruptcy court has no right to interfere with that lien, although it can delay foreclosure and make sure the lien does not exceed fair market value.

What the Court Can Do to Secured Lenders

The bankruptcy court can hurt the secured lender by delaying foreclosure (through the use of a "stay") while the bankruptcy court takes a look around to see if some equity can be salvaged for the general creditors and the limited partners. Unfortunately, while the bankruptcy court is "supervising" the property, the property may slide downhill through lack of management and direction. But, if the court can be convinced that, ultimately, there will be little or nothing for general creditors and equity investors, it can permit the lender to get on with its foreclosure and sell the property.

In all likelihood, the bankruptcy court can delay foreclosure during some period to explore reorganization (and that period may be long), but, ultimately, the mortgage lender should get its payments again or will be permitted foreclosure and possession of the real estate unless there is a "cram down"—about which more will be said.

So the ideal approach to bankruptcy and reorganization proceedings is to demonstrate, as early as possible, that there is no equity for the owners and that a continued delay will harm everyone. In general, one should come up with some kind of plan which yields something to the general creditors and possibly the equity investors in return for a faster sale. Lender counsel must be committed in advance to pursue the lender's rights through the courts and must be prepared to fight rather than to delay.

Counsel must insist that the rents be used to maintain the lender's property, that the real estate taxes be paid, and, hopefully, that the lender gets paid interest while the court ponders what to do. Furthermore, the lender requires good interim property management. Therefore, counsel and local workout officers must not actively influence the bankruptcy proceedings.

How the Bankruptcy and Reorganization Laws Affect Mortgages

Chapters 1 through 7 of the Bankruptcy Act relate to straight bankruptcy and liquidations. They seek sale and liquidation of the bankrupt property and the distribution of the proceeds to the creditors. In straight bankruptcy, the secured creditors get paid first, and the general creditors get paid second. In most cases, straight bankruptcy (including the sale and liquidation of the property) is not what the borrower wants at all; the borrower wants delay.

Here we will deal mainly with the reorganization sections in which the debtor seeks rehabilitation to salvage something for the equity investors and general creditors. The main reorganization chapters under the old law were X, XI, and XII, but those chapters have been merged into a single reorganization section called Chapter 11.

Look at the bankruptcy laws through the eyes of the secured mortgage lender, and bear in mind the following:

1. The holder of a real property mortgage, if it is a valid lien, is unaffected by the filing of a bankruptcy petition. But the bankrupt can try to get the liens set aside (as a preference, a failure to comply with local recording and docketing laws, a failure of consideration, etc.).

2. Theoretically, the reorganization and bankruptcy courts cannot destroy the preferred position of a lienholder, but, in bankruptcy, the secured lender's mortgage may be limited to the current value of the property held as security. Put another way, a $5 million lien on a property that is now worth only $3 million is going to be limited to $3 million by the bankruptcy court. The rights to the other $2 million are considered by the court those of a general creditor rather than a secured one.

The procedural rights (the rights of foreclosure) of a mortgage holder may be limited, controlled, or otherwise modified or altered by the bankruptcy court. Since the court has a right to postpone foreclosure while the property is managed by the debtor in possession or by a court-appointed trustee, the property's value may be undermined. So the court's power to stay foreclosure and sale can seriously affect the rights of the mortgage holder. It is important to note, however, that the court must operate within the law and that there are appellate procedures and constitutional guarantees to secured mortgage holders who find themselves threatened with indefinite delay.

Control by the Bankruptcy Court

Once the bankruptcy court takes over, it has exclusive jurisdiction to determine the validity, amount, and priority of liens upon the property. The court has the exclusive jurisdiction to authorize the sale of the property free and clear of the liens, with the lien to attach to the proceeds of the sale, up to the amount of the lien, if the court decides that there is some equity in the property above the mortgage.

The bankruptcy court can require previously appointed state court receivers and trustees to turn the property over to the custody of the bankruptcy court, provided the state court receiver or trustee took possession within four months prior to the bankruptcy. But the bankruptcy court cannot generally interfere with a trustee or receiver who has been appointed more than four months prior to the filing of the petition. The bankruptcy court does have jurisdiction to stay and prevent foreclosure proceedings and receiverships begun within four months of the filing of the bankruptcy petition.

One of the first things the bankruptcy court looks into is whether the alleged secured lien is actually "perfected." Often, the first efforts of the court are to find a technical ground for setting aside the mortgage. If the court is successful in setting aside the mortgage, the lender had better hope it has sufficient title insurance or that its closing lawyer has adequate malpractice insurance, because it is in deep trouble. If the lender's secured lien is set aside for technical reasons, i.e., noncompliance with the recording statutes, notwithstanding demonstration of valid consideration therefore, the lender may nonetheless be deemed an unsecured creditor. And unsecured creditors do not always fare well in bankruptcy proceedings.

Chapters 7 and 11 and the
Secured Lender

Chapter 7 is a liquidation section: The property will be sold either at auction or on a negotiated basis and the proceeds distributed to the unsecured creditors, subject, of course, to its mortgage lien. Ordinarily, liquidation offers little threat to the secured real estate lender who holds a mortgage. The real problems in bankruptcy involve Chapter 11 proceedings, where debtors claim that if they had some time they could reorganize the real estate, pay the unsecured creditors all or a major portion of their claims, recover mortgage payments, and protect the equity holders. The typical Chapter 11 debtor always starts out in filing a bankruptcy or reorganization petition by making that claim.

The two major problems facing the secured creditor in a reorganization proceeding under Chapter 11 are:

1. The stay
2. The cram down

The *stay* is a court order "staying" the secured creditor from foreclosing on the real estate. It is automatic and takes effect the moment the reorganization petition is filed by the debtor. The theory behind the stay is simple: What good will it do to reorganize the entity, if the property which is the entity's major asset is in the hands of the secured lender rather than the general creditors and the equity owners? Therefore, the courts protect the unsecured creditors and equity holders by keeping the property in the hands of the debtor, or an especially appointed trustee, under the protection of the bankruptcy court, until the court determines what is best for all the parties and whether the property can be rehabilitated.

The secured creditor is probably advised to ask at the outset that the stay be lifted so as to keep pressure on the debtor. But early efforts to lift the stay are not likely to succeed. The courts' experience, especially in recent inflationary times, has been that if the debtor is given enough time through "stay" of foreclosure, things get worked out and everyone profits.

Therefore, instead of attempting to lift the stay by arguing that the foreclosure should proceed and that reorganization is unlikely to be successful, the secured mortgage holder will attempt to get some conditions imposed by the court if it is to continue the stay. At the very minimum, the mortgage lender will ask that the trustee or debtor make regular payments on real estate taxes, keep the buildings in repair, keep the interest current (although the principal may stay in arrears), etc.

Therefore, the mortgage lender's attorney should make one or both of the following motions:

1. To lift the stay and complete the foreclosure, selling the property to the highest bidder
2. To get adequate protection against waste while the debtor retains possession of the real estate—this may be one of the conditions which the court will impose on the debtor, if the automatic stay is to be continued

The other weapon used to obtain concessions from the secured lender is the *cram down*. The debtor's reorganization plan usually covers two groups of creditors: the unsecured creditors (everyday supplies necessary to on-site operations) and the secured creditors (mortgage and lien holders). This chapter will ignore the treatment of the unsecured creditors and deal only with the holders of mortgages who are considered secured creditors.

Most real estate debtors cannot make the full mortgage payments under the original mortgages or they would not be in reorganization proceedings. Therefore, if the mere passage of time does not help them rent up vacancies, increase income, or decrease expenses, the only way for the debtor to reorganize is to force some kind of a mortgage modification.

The debtor usually starts out trying to negotiate with the lender. Would it take a lower interest rate? How about stretching out the payments so that each principal payment amortizing the mortgage is less? Can we leave a balloon until the end? Would the lender reduce the total amount of the mortgage from, say, $3 million to $2 million or $2.5 million? These are the kind of negotiations the debtor attempts to work out with a secured lender. If successful, the negotiations obviate the need to deal further with the bankruptcy courts.

However, both sides—the secured lender and the debtor—must understand that the cram down hangs over those negotiations. For a reorganization plan to be successful, the various groups of creditors—secured and unsecured—must each consent to the plan (or at least a majority of each class must consent to the plan). Otherwise, if they vote against the plan, the court must find a way to compensate them. As far as the secured creditors are concerned, there will be only one mortgage holder at each level (senior and junior mortgage holders). Therefore, for the plan to be adopted without court intervention, the secured mortgage holder will have to consent to the plan, which is the reason for the negotiations discussed above.

However, what if all the unsecured creditors and all the junior creditors vote for the plan, and the first mortgage holder refuses to alter the terms of the mortgage and to consent to the plan? One possibility is to reinstate the payment schedule called for under the original mortgage. If this were to take place, the debtor would have to make up any payments in arrears and the mortgage would be reinstated and be "unimpaired." Thus whether or not the mortgage holder consented to the reorganization plan it would be imposed, since, in truth, the debtor's status was unimpaired. The debtor's arrears would have been remitted and the mortgage reinstated. Except for a period of delay by the bankruptcy court, the mortgage holder would be unimpaired, and the property could be reorganized.

However, what if it is not possible to make up all those arrearages, or what if making up the arrearages is only a temporary solution, and the borrower knows that it may go into default again within several months unless the mortgage is modified? In that case, the debtor's plan should provide for modification of the mortgage. The mortgage holder, of course, would argue that the plan was confiscatory, unconstitutional, and in breach of its secured mortgage.

The Bankruptcy Code has a procedure for the court to impose a modification of secured lenders' position over and above the lenders' objections. That procedure is called the *cram down*. It is covered by Section 1129(b) of the Bankruptcy Code. Under the cram down, the mortgage may be modified by the court, under certain conditions, even if the secured creditor objects.

Section 1129(b)(2)(A) states that the court may "cram" a plan down the secured creditor's throat, if the plan is:

a. fair and equitable to the secured mortgage lender; or if it
b. provides that the mortgage lender shall retain its lien in its present form; or if it
c. gives the secured mortgage lender a new schedule of payments which have a present value equal to the value of its secured claim.

There are a lot of "ifs" in the above language. For example, what is the value of the secured claim? All the secured lender is entitled to receive under Section 1129 of the Bankruptcy Code is the fair market value of the property at the date of the filing of the bankruptcy petition. Note that this number may be entirely different from the amount of the mortgage. As discussed earlier, one may have made a $5 million loan some years ago, yet at the time of the filing of the petition, the property may only be worth $3 million. What happens to the other $2 million? The lender will get a $3 million secured claim—which is equal to the fair market value of the property on the date of the reorganization petition—and will have a $2 million unsecured claim, which falls into a pool with the claims of the other general creditors.

If the lender fails to get cash equal to the value of its secured claim, it may get a deferred payment schedule. But the deferred payment schedule must yield a present value equal to the value of the secured claim. What interest rate shall be used in discounting the payment schedule? The court will decide the current fair interest rate. Thus a number of controversial subjects involve valuation by the court and the use of such words as *fair* and *equitable*. It is the court's ability to determine a fair and equitable interest rate and a fair and equitable value of the property that gives it leverage over both the debtor and the secured lender in forcing compromise. In short, the court may cram down its valuation on recalcitrant debtors and creditors alike.

To avoid the expense and uncertainty of a valuation trial, both debtors and creditors often come to an understanding as to how the mortgage can be recast. If the secured lender is certain of prevailing in a cram down and assured of obtaining an interest rate and valuation close to the terms of its existing mortgage, it will resist overtures on the part of the borrower to make extensive changes, and it will not compromise. If the lender feels vulnerable, it will compromise rather than face a trial which may result in a cram down. These decisions require the advice of an experienced bankruptcy counsel.

One last point: If the value of the property securing the loan at the date the plan was filed is less than the face value of the mortgage, the lender will become an unsecured creditor for a portion of its claim. This will give the lender two bites of the apple, and it may have an opportunity to participate as a general creditor in the pool of funds available for general creditors, as well as in the secured lenders' pool. The lender will have a vote there as well.

Figure 28.1 is a workout officer's checklist; it identifies the legal, financial, and managerial issues discussed in this chapter which the lender–mortgage banker should thoroughly address when handling distress real estate.

Figure 28.1. Checklist for workout officers.

I. Legal and Practical Problems of Income Property Loans in Trouble
Preparing for distress loan management:
Staffing up for adequate supervision
Updating the budget to "today's realities"
Personal inspection of the site and marketplace
Problem property or problem people?
Control:
Who has it?
Is it transferable?
Respective rights and obligations of owner, developer, permanent lender, mechanics and other lienholders, fee owner, long-term and space tenants, unsecured creditors, receivers, bankruptcy trustees, limited and general partners, brokers, and managers.

(Continued)

Figure 28.1. Checklist for workout officers. (*Continued*)

II. Legal Problems: Construction and Development Loans
Is there default?
Rights, duties, and liabilities of a mortgagee in possession
Acceleration provisions
Self-help
Protecting the job—guards, subcontract rights, books and records
Appoint a receiver?
Lease and rent assignments
Protecting the buy-and-sell agreement
Protecting rights against a bonding company, personal guarantors
of completion, and payment
Particular problems on leasehold mortgages
Protecting credit leases
Deed in lieu of foreclosure
Other nonjudicial remedies
Protecting disbursement procedures
Obtaining lien waivers

III. Cost to Complete
Timing and urgency (weather)
Cost to complete—how firm? Who guarantees cost and quality?
Hidden liabilities in existing partnership or other title-holding
entity?
Creditors' rights, torts, tax, and securities law problems,
assignability of leases, mortgages, and subcontracts
Status of title, income tax status, permits, and ecological problems
Cost of guard service

IV. Interim Losses and Sources of Funds
Budget to completion, including rent-up, sales costs, promotion,
and interim operating cash deficits
Source of funds: new investors, tax shelter buyers, old limited partners, developer, general contractor, subcontractors, bonding company, title company, insurers, borrowers, and commercial bankers
Effect of transfer or timing on liability to fund any of the above commitments (can they walk?)
Are existing leases an asset or a liability?

V. What Have You Got after Completion?
Rethinking feasibility in present circumstances
Completion from existing and from other distress deals
Current rental trends and projections
Income tax projections and tax risks during and after rent-up
Computation of recapture risk
Interim and permanent financing rates, terms, and timing
Compare return on investment and risk-reward ratios with other
real estate offerings and other types of investment

(*Continued*)

Figure 28.1. Checklist for workout officers *(Continued)*

VI. Permanent Loan Problems
   Early warning signs
   Current financial statements
   Inspection and tax search
   Lease modification
   Rent-impairing activities
   Tenancy or neighborhood changes
   Defer interest or amortization
   Forebearance?
   Documentation
   Quid pro quo
   Nonjudicial remedies

VII. Bankruptcy and Reorganization Laws
   Consulting specialized counsel
   Real estate versus bankruptcy counsel
   Role of house counsel
   Powers of bankruptcy courts
   Restraining orders
   Preferences
   Turnover proceedings
   Relief from stay
   Representation on creditors' committees
   Voidable preferences
   Liens
   Venue
   Fraudulent conveyances
   Rights of secured creditors
   Cram down
   Estimating bankruptcy costs and legal fees

VII. Legal Problems of Workouts
   Foreclosure or not foreclosure?
   "Good" versus "bad" creditor jurisdictions
   Nonjudicial remedies
   Receivership
   Mortgagee in possession
   Defenses and delay
   Counterclaims
   Lien priority of advancing additional funds
   Mechanics' lien waivers
   Rights to continue guarantee, bonding, and other contractural
       obligations
   Anticipating bankruptcy and preference problems
   Collecting rents
   Extending leases and buy and sell provisions

(Continued)

Figure 28.1. Checklist for workout officers. (*Continued*)

IX. Legal Problems of Partnership Entities

Default provisions
Rights and duties of general versus limited partners
Tax aspects of modifying, liquidating, foreclosing, and entity
  modification
Resolving conflicts among partnership and contracting groups at
  various levels
Protecting first-user and construction loss status
Securities laws problems

X. Legal Risks of New Investment Group

check: real estate, lien, trust, tax, securities, bankruptcy, debtor and
  creditor, corporate, partnership, usury laws.
Is long-term tenant really a tenant whose lease can be cancelled, or
  a mortgagor with an equity of redemption to which bankruptcy
  trustee may have rights?
Responsibility to third parties or tax authorities for antecedent debts,
  torts or acts
Legal and practical obligations to creditors, tenants, contractors, employees, managers, developers, unions, receivers, assignees or rents,
  trustees in bankruptcy, junior mortgagees, and other lienholders
Effects on new investor group of new general partner, new limited partner, and partnership entity
Cash flow and tax priorities and obligations of new versus old group
Effect of bankruptcy laws on general partner, partnership entity, mul-
  tiproperty partnership, and permanent and construction lenders

29

The Secondary Market in Income Property Mortgages

Eric Stevenson, Esq.

Senior Staff Vice President, Mortgage Bankers Association of America, Washington, D.C.

An income property mortgage is usually held by the investor until the term of the mortgage ends, and the investor—the one that holds the mortgage as an investment—is usually the same institution that lent the money to the borrower. This is much less the custom in the single-family mortgage market, where the customary practice is for a mortgage banker, bank, or savings and loan association to lend money to the borrower based on the security of a mortgage, and then, usually within a few months, to sell the mortgage to the Federal National Mortgage Association (FNMA) or the Federal Home Loan Mortgage Corporation (FHLMC) or to pool the home mortgage with others for the issuance of government-backed securities (GNMAs) based on the mortgage pool of government-insured or -guaranteed mortgages.

The majority of single-family mortgages are traded on the secondary market for several reasons, whereas income property mortgages are seldom traded. The amount of any one single-family mortgage is small compared to the amount in a pool of single-family mortgages. If a home mortgage goes into default, it can easily be replaced. Single-family mortgages are generally a standard product. Moreover, in the single-family mortgage market, mortgages sold on the secondary market are often insured by the Federal Housing Administration or guaranteed by the Veterans Administration, or part of the risk is insured by one of the private mortgage insurance companies, all of which have established strict underwriting criteria for single-family mortgages. There are large and active secondary mortgage markets that have been created by FNMA, FHLMC, the securities firms, and others.

In the income property market, however, the default of any one mortgage represents a substantial loss to the investor, and the loans are dissimilar: One shopping center cannot be substituted for another. Furthermore, there is no large and active secondary market for commercial mortgages. However, there are exceptions, and one is the secondary market in insured mortgages.

The Secondary Market in Insured Mortgages

In the income property mortgage market, only a small portion of the mortgages are insured or guaranteed. There is a federal insurance program for apartment projects (described in Chapter 17) and for certain hospitals. The Government National Mortgage Association (GNMA) guarantees the timely payment of principal and interest on apartment project mortgages which are insured by the Federal Housing Administration. Consequently, GNMA securities collateralized by insured apartment mortgages can be sold on the secondary market.

Several other federal programs insure or guarantee income property mortgage loans. The Small Business Administration guarantees loans, which are often mortgages, made by state or local development companies, and those loans can be sold on the secondary market. The Department of Housing and Urban Development has a guarantee program for certain income-producing mortgages issued in connection with urban development, and securities have been sold which are backed by those guaranteed mortgages. The Farmers Home Administration and the Economic Development Administration in the departments of Agriculture and Commerce, respectively, have had guarantee programs for commercial mortgages, but these programs are inactive in the mid-1980s.

Other types of mortgages on income-producing property have been bought and sold in the secondary market because they have the backing of credit-rated financial institutions. One type of mortgage financing is an industrial revenue bond, usually issued by a municipality and sold to investors. The payments to the investors are supported by the revenues from the real estate project, not by any guarantee from the municipality. To ensure that the investors receive their money, the industrial revenue bond is often backed by a letter of credit from a bank or by a guarantee from a surety company. Industrial revenue bonds for specified purposes have been entitled to tax-exempt interest rates, and therefore the borrowers have been able to afford the costs of credit enhancement, namely the letter of credit or surety bond. Taxable bonds, secured by real estate and backed by a surety company, have occasionally been used to finance real estate.

Another type of mortgage which can be sold on the secondary market is the mortgage on a building which is leased by a credit-rated financial institution or major company. For example, a bank wishes to raise funds, so it sells to an issuer of securities the office building in which its corporate headquarters is located. The sale is subject to the bank's long-term lease of the space in the building. The rental amount from the bank is sufficient to cover the payments at current yields to the group of investors who buy securities collateralized by the building and the lease payments. If the bank has a credit rating, then the securities should have the same credit rating.

Federally insured buildings, industrial revenue bonds, and sale-leasebacks to credit-rated companies are a relatively small portion of the commercial real estate market. The remainder of this chapter discusses the secondary market in conventionally financed mortgages through whole loan sales, participation sales, and the use of securities.

Whole Loans

A small portion of income property mortgages originated each year are sold by the original lenders to other investors. No one knows the size of this secondary market: There is no central facilitating agency to handle such sales; the contact for the sale may have come through a mortgage banker, a securities firm, or other intermediary, but often it comes about because representatives of the seller and the buyer are acquainted with each other.

An income property loan may be sold shortly after it is closed by the original lender, or it may be held in the lender's mortgage portfolio for a time and then sold. If the yield on the mortgage is higher than the yields expected on similar mortgages at the time of sale, the buyer will pay a premium. However, if the yield on the mortgage is lower than existing yields expected, the buyer buys at a discount. For tax purposes, the seller takes the gain or loss on the sale of the mortgage at the time of sale.

In the secondary market for whole loans, the buyer is usually given a complete loan package, covering not only information obtained when the original loan was made but also the information on the performance of the rental property since the mortgage was closed. This information would include a list of leases and tenants, profit and loss statements, maps, repair and utility information, the mortgage commitment, and the loan documents. The buyer will review all the information and then will make a site inspection.

Usually a whole loan is sold without recourse. In other words, the seller gives no assurance to the buyer that the mortgagor will continue to pay the mortgage payments. Sometimes, however, the seller will agree to buy the loan back if, within a limited period of time (often three months), the loan goes into default or the information provided to the buyer is incorrect in any material respect.

The mortgage will be transferred on the land records from the name of the seller to the name of the buyer. The buyer will henceforth arrange for the servicing of the mortgages, although, for some sales, the seller retains the servicing.

Participations

A single mortgage loan may be divided into interests, and each of the interests may be sold. Similarly, a mortgage holder can pool together a group of mortgages and then issue and sell undivided interests in the pool of mortgages. The interest that is sold is called a *participation* or a *participation interest*. The financial institution which originally made the loan and is now selling participations is sometimes called the *lead lender*. Those who buy the participations are called the *participants*.

When participations are sold in a mortgage or pool of mortgages, the mortgage documents are not altered. The lead lender remains the lender of record, and the borrower or borrowers make the mortgage payments to that lender. The lead lender either services the mortgages itself or has its correspondent mortgage bankers do so. If the servicing is done by agents of the lead lender, the lender nevertheless takes responsibility for servicing. The loan documents are recorded in the lead lender's name and usually remain in the possession of that lender.

The participants each receive a participation certificate, and a participation agreement covers the legal relationship between the seller and the buyer of the participation certificate. This agreement often provides that a third party, or custodian, will collect the funds received from the mortgage or mortgages and then distribute those funds to the participants in accordance with their respective shares.

Some agreements provide that the seller (lead lender), in case of default, will cover the monthly payments to the participants for a limited period. Other agreements put the risk of default entirely on the holders of the participations.

The participation agreement also covers what happens when major decisions have to be made about a mortgage in which participations have been sold. Sometimes the lead lender can decide to foreclose; sometimes the decision can be made only upon a vote of the participants, usually voting in proportion to the interests they own. Sometimes the lead lender can agree to take a deed to the property in lieu of foreclosure or can agree to change the terms of the loan, but in some situations such decisions must be agreed to by the participants. The lead lender, if it fails to service the mortgage or mortgages property, can usually be removed by vote of the participants.

A participation certificate can be bought or sold on the secondary market as long as the custodian (if there is one) or the seller (if the seller is handling the responsibilities of the custodian) is notified. The disbursements are then made to the new owner of the participation certificate.

The participant has to worry about two risks: the safety of the loan itself and the continued financial stability of the lead lender servicing the loan. For these reasons, the participants should not only verify all the information on the mortgage itself but also ascertain that the lead lender will remain in business and is financially strong. There is always the danger that mortgage payments could be made to a lead lender who goes out of business, or has its assets attached, before it distributed those payments to the custodian or directly to the participants.

A participation, like a whole loan sale, is always used to sell interests and is not a form of borrowing collateralized by mortgages. Participations are placed privately, by the seller itself, by a mortgage broker, or by an investment banking firm. A participation is not usually registered with the Securities and Exchange Commission (SEC), provided that it is sold primarily to financial institutions and companies that would be regularly engaged in financing real estate.

A participation is usually sold to a limited number of investors. If offered for sale to "the public" or to a large number of individuals (the federal law on this subject is complex on this point), the participation becomes a public sale, and an offering prospectus or memorandum must be prepared and submitted to the SEC.

One difficulty in selling participations is convincing the buyer of the safety of the loan. If the buyer has to reunderwrite the loan and inspect the property as though the participation were a new loan offering, the buyer will want a yield on the mortgage equivalent to a new loan.

One way to provide the buyer with a lower-risk loan is to have the seller take the initial losses from default and foreclosure. Suppose, for example, a lead lender (seller) sells $10 million worth of participations on a single property and agrees to cover all losses up to 10 percent of the outstanding principal at the time of loss. Suppose thereafter that the principal amount has been reduced to $9 million, and then the property goes into default and foreclosure. When the property is sold, assume that the participants have a $1 million loss before reimbursement. The seller, however, has agreed to cover losses up to 10 percent of the $9 million outstanding, or $900,000. This amount is paid to the participants, and they have lost only $100,000.

An alternative to an agreement that the seller will take a percentage of the loss is to have the seller retain a second lien on the property. The first lien is sold to a buyer. If there is a loss, the second lienholder (mortgagee) takes the loss before the first lienholder suffers any loss.

Arrangements providing for a junior and a senior position (in event of loss, the loss is applied to the junior interest before the senior interest is tapped) are unusual. Most participations are sold as whole loans are sold.

Securities

A security, as used in the mortgage business, is a certificate that is collateralized by mortgages. It can be a bond which pays interest only at regularly scheduled periods until the entire principal of the mortgage is paid at the end of the term. It can be a security, as is common in the single-family mortgage field, that passes through to the security holder all payments, whether principal or interest, as they are received, modified by a monthly basis.

When there is an issue of securities, an offering memorandum is prepared which sets forth the details on the security offering, including the risks that there may be in the offering. The securities may be placed privately or sold publicly.

The advantage of using securities is that the market for securities includes many buyers who would not buy mortgages. These buyers are willing to take yields below that which they would require if they were buying whole mortgage loans, provided that the mortgage security is considerably safer than the usual income property mortgage.

In addition to expanding the market, another advantage of securities is that the seller can take advantage of the yield curve. If 3-year Treasury bonds are selling, for example, for 6⅞ percent, 5-year Treasuries are selling for 7⅛ percent, and 10-year Treasury bonds are selling for 7¾ percent, then mortgage yields for 3-year and 10-year terms will probably change in somewhat the same way, the higher yields for the longer terms.

If an owner has a mortgage which has been made at the interest rate for 10 years, then it may make money if it can sell the 10-year mortgage in different classes, paying a lower rate to those who purchase for a shorter term. Breaking the loan into classes, moreover, permits the seller to provide call protection for some of or all the securities. Thus even if the mortgage is prepaid, the buyer of the security based on the mortgage will receive interest and principal according to the schedule set forth in the security offering.

Dividing the income stream from a pool of mortgages into classes, or *tranches,* is a way of achieving a blended interest rate. It can be done with participations, but it is more commonly done with securities which are widely sold. In the single-family mortgage market, the method is used for collateralized mortgage obligations. In income property, the technique is used for fixed-payment bonds and pass-through securities, and it will be used with real estate mortgage investment conduits (REMICs), explained below.

For example, a subsidiary of Connecticut Mutual Life Insurance Company issued bonds backed by mortgages for the European market in August 1985. The 5-year bonds were offered at 10⅛ percent, the 10-year bonds were offered at 11 percent, and zero coupon bonds due in 15 years were offered to yield slightly more than 11 percent. The zero coupon bonds in this offering were sold at $18.80 for each $100 that will be paid on maturity.

The Tax Reform Act of 1986 created REMICs, which from 1987 to 1992 will be used with alternative methods for issuing mortgage-backed securities. In 1992, REMICs will become the only method for issuing these securities.

A financial institution or mortgage banker will pool mortgages and sell them to the REMIC. An individual income property mortgage may also be sold to a REMIC. In either event, the REMIC will be the issuer of securities based on the mortgage or mortgages. The REMIC will not be taxed as a corporation but instead will be merely a conduit designed to receive the payments of principal and interest on the mortgages and pass those payments to the shareholders of the REMIC. The REMIC may take such action as is necessary to protect the value of the mortgages it holds, including foreclosure actions, but its purpose is limited to the management of its real estate mortgage portfolio. The REMIC may establish several classes of securities holders, as described above, and may direct that principal payments for one class of mortgages be paid before the principal payments on the second class of mortgages are paid.

Senior-subordinated debt structures will be used with REMICs. For example, an issuer may divide a pool of mortgages into two classes of securities. The security with a first lien on the properties may be backed by a letter of credit and be sold at a lower interest rate, whereas the second class of securities, offering a higher interest rate, is supported by a second lien on the properties and will be retained by the issuer or sold to those interested in higher yields despite the greater risk.

Pools of Commercial Mortgages

Income property mortgages are not usually pooled as the basis for the issuance of securities because the buyers of the securities must be assured that the mortgages will not go into default. Securities buyers do not want to investigate the leasing structure of a shopping center, determine whether the center is in a good location, or assess whether the owner of the shopping center has enough management skill. The buyers of securities want to be assured that, even if the shopping center goes into default, they will continue to get their payments.

Consequently, the securities that have been issued to the public and based on existing commercial mortgages held in an investor's portfolio primarily have been those which are backed by life insurance companies with strong financial capability. One guarantee involves a life insurance company that issues a bond or a pass-through security and promises the buyer of the security that if any mortgage goes into default, the issuer will continue making the payments on the mortgage for up to two years. If the mortgage is foreclosed during that time, or if the borrower gives the life insurance company the deed to the property in lieu of foreclosure, the life insurance company will buy the mortgage back at its outstanding principal value. Consequently, the buyer of the security does not take the risk of default and foreclosure. It does take some risk of prepayment of mortgages, although most of the mortgages have lock-in periods.

As of March 1987, fewer than a dozen issues by life insurance companies of fixed payment bonds or of pass-through securities were secured by commercial mortgages. Nevertheless, the average issue was well over $100 million each, and The Prudential Insurance Company of America was responsible for a single sale on the European market of $1.3 billion. All these issues had been offered between November 1984 and October 1986. In the latter half of 1987, several financial institutions sold commercial mortgage pools.

Originations

The secondary market for securities based on portfolios of commercial mortgages is growing slowly, but there is a faster-growing effort to finance specific properties with securities. Senior subordinated debt structures are being used. An example where apartment buildings were financed originally with securities is an issue that was placed privately in the late summer of 1986 by First Boston Corporation, the investment banking firm, on behalf of Oxford Development, a large apartment builder, and CIGNA Investments, Inc., a subsidiary of CIGNA, a large financial holding company. For this issue, 11 limited partnerships, each owning a recently built apartment building, obtained mortgages on those apartments from Connecticut General Life Insurance Company, a subsidiary of CIGNA. The apartments were all built by Oxford, and the general partner of each of the partnerships was a subsidiary of Oxford.

The loan-to-value ratio of each of the mortgages was about 80 percent. Connecticut General then retained 25 percent of each mortgage as a second mortgage. CIGNA Investments pooled the remaining 75 percent amount of each mortgage and issued securities collateralized by 11 first mortgages. The securitized mortgages equaled about 66 percent loan-to-value of the apartments as a whole. If there were a loss on one of the apartment buildings, the loss would first be taken by the second mortgagee, Connecticut General, up to its 25 percent interest. In addition to this safety factor, the issuer, CIGNA Investments, obtained a bank letter of credit which is designed to cover any shortfall of the mortgage payments for a limited period of time. As a result of this letter of credit and the safety provided by the second mortgage arrangement, Standard & Poor's Corporation, a rating agency, gave the $79 million issue a Double A-minus rating. With the rating from Standard & Poor's, the securities could be sold on a comparable basis to corporate bonds of the same term with the same rating.

Credit Ratings for Mortgages

Standard & Poor's, Moody's Investment Services, and Duff & Phelps Inc., all rate bonds and other corporate obligations and are now beginning to rate certain commercial mortgages. One test that they apply is a worst-case scenario. They look at the cash flow generated by property or group of properties and determine whether it would be sufficient to cover debt service if, in a troubled real estate market, rents went down and vacancies increased. They determine the likelihood of a worst case based in part on the historical record of real estate in that particular city.

Despite the relatively limited experience with ratings, investment bankers believe that an increasing number of securities will be backed by commercial mortgages and sold on the secondary market. It should become possible for a financially strong issuer to assemble mortgages from several owners, or to draw those mortgages from its own portfolio, and then issue securities backed by a letter of credit or supported by the issuer using second mortgages.

Securities are particularly important for large transactions and for transactions in which one owner is pooling mortgages on a number of properties that it owns. For example, securities have been offered on hotel casinos in Las Vegas, Reno, and Atlantic City, on Rockefeller Center in New York, on the construction of two major office buildings in Atlanta and Pittsburgh, and on several groups of hotels or motels owned by one owner. In an acquisition situation—the purchase of a chain of department stores—the buyer cross-collateralized the mortgages on each of the stores in the chain, which means that if the mortgage on one of the stores goes into default, the income from the other stores can be used to make up the shortfall. Securities were issued on the pool of department store mortgages to raise money for the purchase of the chain.

The major investment banking firms have developed staffs to handle what is expected to be a strong growth in securities for income property mortgages. The most active player in the field of securitization, however, is the Federal Home Loan Mortgage Corporation which, in a two-year period (1985 to 1986), has issued almost $2 billion of securities backed by multifamily mortgages. FHLMC buys mortgages on existing apartment buildings according to precise specifications: 15-year term, 30-year amortization, no prepayment allowed for at least 54 months. Other standard underwriting requirements and standardized documents are used. During this same two-year period, FHLMC has purchased over $3 billion of these multifamily mortgages.

FHLMC issues its securities as participation certificates in a public sale. It has also sold participation certificates to the European market. It guarantees the securities so that they are rated with FHMLC's rating, a Triple A rating from Standard & Poor's and Moody's. Thus, for taking the risk of default of mortgages, FHLMC purchases mortgages that pay at a current market rate for 15-year mortgages and sells securities on which it has to pay interest rates comparable to other Triple A corporate bonds.

Summary

Well-established financial institutions may well decide to follow FHMLC's lead and pool mortgages for the purpose of issuing securities.

Nevertheless, those institutions will probably attempt to arrange a form of financing, perhaps through a REMIC, that will permit the pool of mortgages to be rated on its own merits and not on the basis of the credit or the issuer. Most financial institutions are not willing to take on their financial statements the very substantial amount of debt that would be represented by a guarantee of commercial mortgages, even though that debt would be offset by the assets from the sale of securities.

The recent development of commercial mortgage-backed securities offers a way of opening up the mortgage market to those who buy securities but are unfamiliar with income property mortgages. Whether financial institutions without credit ratings of A or better will be able to participate in the market depends in part on the extent to which forms of credit enhancement become available. If letters of credit of surety bonds support the mortgages in a pool, the credit rating of the pool will be based on the financial institution issuing the letter of credit or the insurance company backing the surety bond, not on the mortgages themselves.

PART 7

The Changing Income Property Market

30

Changes in the Income Property Market and Their Effect on Mortgage Banking

Ronald F. Poe, CMB

President, Chief Executive Officer, Dorman & Wilson, Inc., White Plains, New York

The residential lending process experienced sweeping changes, as well as explosive and dynamic growth, during the latter part of the 1970s and through the first half of the 1980s. Leading the growth was the explosion in mortgage-backed securities. In a period of 10 years, the mortgage-backed securities market grew from the embryo stage to more than $750 billion, making this market second only to direct U.S. Treasury obligations in terms of outstanding public debt. This ability to access the public capital markets, known generally as securitization, changed the shape, in a very positive manner, of the entire residential mortgage market. During this period, however, four other general trends also shaped the residential lending market. They can serve as a guide to future trends that will equally substantially affect commercial lending. These trends in residential lending were specialization, increased competition, the need for sophistication and quality control-oriented underwriting, and, finally, a need for problem loan management and disposition.

In terms of specialization, the residential market is divided into three areas: origination, marketing, and servicing. In terms of competition, the residential market saw large numbers of nontraditional companies such as corporate industrial giants enter into the field of residential mortgage banking. Further, traditional mortgage banking firms, at least on the origination side, saw large numbers of very small, almost boutique-type origination firms, spring up at an ever-growing rate. The Federal National Mortgage Association (FNMA) and the Federal Home Loan Mortgage Corporation (FHLMC)—the major underwriting quality control forces in the residential lending business—continually increased their call for quality underwriting, and that call has filtered down to all residential firms. Finally, to protect the integrity of the U.S. single-family residential mortgage, mortgage firms in the first half of the 1980s were required to internally restructure so as to manage delinquent loans and foreclosures, and ultimately dispose of foreclosed single-family real estate, far more effectively than they had ever done.

As we enter the latter half of the 1980s, it is interesting to note that the same trends and major forces which reshaped the residential market are moving to restructure the commercial income property real estate financing market as it relates to the origination, marketing, and servicing of commercial loans. This chapter will deal with five major forces affecting commercial real estate, discuss how they are analogous to the factors which have affected residential lending, and show how these factors will ultimately shape the future of the commercial real estate market. In addition, it will discuss strategies whereby those involved in the commercial real estate financing market can best adjust their operations to more effectively serve their borrower clients, investors, and shareholders. The five major forces are:

- Securitization
- Specialization
- Competition
- Quality underwriting
- Problem loan management and disposition

Securitization

As mentioned earlier, securitization dramatically changed the face and scope of residential lending. However, for a combination of reasons, securitization has not played a major part in commercial lending—of approximately $2 trillion in outstanding residential debt, approximately $750 billion, or 37.5 percent, has been securitized. Of an estimated $600 billion in outstanding income property debt, only $40 billion has been securitized. Various forces have worked to slow the growth of commercial securitization, not the least of which has been the lack of standard underwriting criteria and standard loan documentation. Adequate, and in some instances, surplus availability of income property funds from insurance companies, thrifts, and pension funds have not made access to the public capital markets a high priority, and, consequently, slow progress has been made in resolving the standard underwriting and documentation questions. Nonetheless, powerful forces have been building to push toward more rapid securitization. The major suppliers of commercial real estate finance, insurance company funds through general or separate accounts, have grown increasingly short in terms of maturities. The standard 20- to 25-year loan common in the 1960s and 1970s has shrunk to a maturity in the 10- to 12-year range. Commercial borrower disenchantment with these shorter maturities has led to a demand for public capital market access which, by its very nature, and following the performance of the residential securities market, will make available funds at longer maturities. In addition, commercial borrowers are well aware of the rate economies achieved by public capital market access. This availability of large pools of public capital funds, coupled with the possibility of credit ratings, provide hopes of such substantial interest savings for commercial borrowers that a demand swell is rapidly pushing toward a major commercial securitization market.

Traditionally, commercial mortgage loan portfolios were extremely static and, by their very nature, highly illiquid. On reflection, one finds it difficult to conceive of an institutional investment less liquid than the standard long-term fixed-rate commercial mortgage loan. As tax laws change and the overall investment climate becomes increasingly more volatile, the ability to quickly and efficiently restructure institutional portfolios becomes critical. Obviously, this ability to restructure rapidly is highly contingent on liquidity. Again, as institutions realize the need to add liquidity to their real estate investment portfolios, in turn they will reach out more and more for the securitization process and the development of an efficient secondary market for income property loans.

Legislation passed in 1986 as part of the Tax Reform Act created real estate mortgage investment conduits (REMICs), eliminating many of the tax impediments previously restricting commercial securitization but, more importantly, enabling the issuer to subordinate one class of mortgage securities to another. This subordination has enabled commercial mortgage securities to receive, far more easily than through the traditional process, credit ratings, making them acceptable in the public capital markets.

On another front, the traditional credit agencies have continued to make progress in determining the appropriate processes for rating commercial mortgage obligations. The lack of standardized underwriting and documentation previously alluded to has been a major impediment to this rating process, but the subordination made possible under the terms of REMICs has clearly alleviated the problem.

The traditional originator of commercial mortgage loan debt, functioning in a climate of ever-increasing securitization, will need not only to understand the process but also to restructure its organization to attempt to function within this securitized market. An education process and the commitment of capital dollars and resources not formerly utilized in the commercial lending origination and closing process will be required.

The residential mortgage loan originator or mortgage banker has well understood the need for substantial amounts of capital to fund, on a short-term basis, pools of loans being accumulated for ultimate securitization and public sales. However, almost all commercial real estate lending, at least on the origination side, has been done on a best-efforts, private placement basis. In this scenario, the ultimate portfolio lender normally funds the investment on the date of closing with its funds. As it is a private placement transaction, the originator has acted only as a broker or intermediary and has provided no funding whatsoever because, without a secondary market for commercial lending, only substantial portfolio lenders who can hold investments for long periods could possibly take the risks inherent in funding even for short periods. As a securitized secondary market develops for commercial real estate debt, originators will be required to follow the established residential process, namely obtain warehouse lines of credit, close loans with their own funds, and then ultimately sell in the capital markets after taking appropriate hedging positions. Commercial mortgage originators must develop sufficient net worth to generate the lines of credit to fund their commercial operations and, further, must understand the protective hedging steps necessary to ensure against interest rate risks during the warehouse period. Mortgage originators unable to obtain the credit lines and to develop the necessary interest rate risk strategies will find themselves at a serious disadvantage in the marketplace.

Another requirement for capital resources results from the need for the originator–securities issuer to keep the loan current to maintain a steady stream of income for the ultimate bond holder. This is a unique, if not heretofore unknown, concept within the commercial lending area. To make commercial mortgage securities competitive with residential securities, the income stream guarantee must be ensured. Consequently, commercial mortgage issuers will need to ensure that they have the availability of sufficient cash reserves for their delinquent principal and interest payments until properties are foreclosed and loans satisfied. Following the precedent of the residential mortgage market, the most profound change of the decade of the 1980s will be the securitization and development of the secondary mortgage market for commercial properties.

Specialization

On the residential side, increasingly the business of mortgage banking is divided and/or specialized along functional lines: origination, servicing, and marketing. Specialization has also taken place on the commercial income property side, but not in terms of function; this specialization has occurred in the areas of product and geography.

First consider product specialization. The major area of product specialization has been in debt and equity financing arrangements. Income property mortgage bankers and/or originators traditionally originated exclusively debt financing. From the late 1970s on, life insurance companies—the major income property lenders—became major fund managers for pension funds, either through general account investment accounts or through the mechanism of real-estate-oriented separate accounts. Some exclusively equity-oriented pension funds desired to become direct real estate equity owners.

During the first half of the 1980s, few income property originators directed their operations to fulfill the gradual but growing investment appetite of pension fiduciaries for real estate equities. Gradually the origination operation began to split into either debt or equity operations, with a few companies performing well in both areas. The problem was further exacerbated by the fact that, in the early part of the 1980s, the advantages of pre-reform tax laws worked to impede pension fiduciaries in their quest for real estate equities. In many cases, due to a combination of the inexperience of their origination system, as well as an inability to compete with the values offered by tax-oriented syndication, pension fiduciaries were unable to fulfill many of their equity acquisition goals.

Tax reform eliminated most competitive disadvantages of the tax-exempt pension fund for real estate purchases. It is reasonable to assume tax-exempt fiduciaries will play an increasingly active, if not dominant, role in real estate equity acquisitions. This appetite will further force traditional mortgage originators to develop equity skills and to heighten the focus on the areas of specialization which have occurred between debt and equity originators. In many cases, this will be a difficult endeavor. By their very nature, mortgage financings proceed more smoothly and securely than do equity transactions. Equity transactions have incredibly higher incidences of lack of completion. The very nature of the real estate equity transaction makes it highly volatile, and potential buyers or sellers often change their minds, positions, or offers—it seems to the intermediary—on almost a moment's notice. This volatility is rare in the debt transaction. These psychological and internal difficulties will need to be overcome by investors if mortgage bankers are to successfully provide the full range of origination services their investors require to compete in contemporary financial markets.

The second area of specialization is transaction size and geography. Gradually, the nationwide origination market has adjusted itself so that originators are normally divided into those arranging small- to mid-size loans, that is, $5 million and under, and those normally arranging loans in excess of this amount. Small local and regional mortgage bankers and originators have traditionally handled the under-$5-million market with a small number of large mortgage banking firms, along with a number of nationwide mortgage brokers controlling the over-$5-million market. As underwriting sophistication and quality control became increasingly more important in the income property process, it is reasonable to assume that this product division or specialization will continue.

Note that with the exception of a few nationwide mortgage brokers, the market for income property originations, both debt and equity, is extremely locally or regionally oriented. Knowledge and insight of local markets has traditionally been one of the investor's primary tools for ensuring quality underwriting and a secure investment. Time and again, nationwide origination systems have been unable to produce the quality product required by the institutional investment community. As real estate markets continue to change and fragment into even more submarkets within traditional markets, this emphasis on local or regional geographic specialization will continue, and nationwide origination systems will prove the exception rather than the rule.

Competition

The third major trend affecting income property lending is competition. Again, to use an analogy with residential lending, competition over and above that which can be expected has affected both income property and residential financing. On the residential side, the trend clearly has been for nontraditional lending sources to enter the business. These nontraditional sources include industrial giants, along with a number of computerized loan origination firms and real estate networks not previously associated with real estate finance. Conversely, on the commercial side, competition has come not from nontraditional or outside sources but rather from sources which had previously been either users or providers of funds. Looking ahead, the three major areas of additional competition to be confronted by income property mortgage banking companies are:

- Institutional investors
- Investment bankers
- Developers' financing subsidiaries

Institutional Investors

A number of catalysts have caused institutional investors to enter into mortgage banking and origination activities. One major factor for the investor is to ensure both quality control and product control, as investment products change in an unpredictable economy and a volatile market. As investment appetites changed away from traditional fixed-rate lending and into joint ventures, direct equity investments, and a wide variety of other investments needed to balance institutional cash flows, some institutional investors were disappointed with the ability of their independently operated origination systems to produce the required investment mix. This disappointment was coupled with disappointment on the servicing side in that many servicing agents were unable to cope with the sophistication needed to service an increasing array of complex real estate investments.

In addition, institutional investors, in many cases, created real estate investment structures outside the institutional corporate structure to provide incentive-based compensation for institutional employees.

One-stop shopping, or the desire for synergism, again caused many institutional investors to attempt to provide a full service package to their investment clients and, in an effort to be as profitable as possible, to attempt to provide services to clients which generated fees in addition to standard forms of investment compensation.

Investment Bankers

The investment banking community, the next area of competition, grows daily. Investment bankers had been responsible for most, if not all, of the major innovations that have taken place in the public capital markets regarding mortgage securities. Gradually, mortgage securities has become an increasingly large proportion of the investment banking business. Realizing that only a small amount of the commercial real estate financing business proportionately was handled by investment bankers and that this was a growing and lucrative market, investment bankers turned more and more to the direct business of mortgage banking. This was a natural progression.

Real estate, moreover, had become a principal financial asset for many corporations. Corporate clients often turned to their investment bankers for the financial restructuring of their real estate assets. In addition, the trend to securitization, discussed previously, caused the investment banking community to enter the area of real estate financing in a major fashion.

Innovations to date brought by the investment banking community to real estate finance have been securitization, the development of a fledgling secondary market, construction financing funded through commercial paper, and interest rate protection through various hedging and swapping techniques. As the involvement of the investment banking community in real estate finance continues to grow, traditional mortgage bankers must become familiar with financing techniques attuned to public capital markets and be aware of opportunities for profit and greater borrower service which may become available throughout investment banking and mortgage banking partnerships.

Developers' Financing Subsidiaries

The third area of competition to face mortgage bankers has been the phenomenon of the creation of in-house financing divisions by the development community. The purpose in creating these divisions has been threefold. The first is obviously cost. Major developers have concluded, rightly or wrongly, that effective cost savings can be brought about by directly arranging their own financing. Secondly, with financing operations in place, many developers have attempted to market financing placement services for a fee, thereby creating within the developer's organization not only a service center for internal financing, but also a profit center for the generation of fees throughout the financing of other developers. The trend toward securitization, coupled with the innovation and expansion of REMICs, will, in all likelihood, cause developer involvement in financing to continue to grow.

Thirdly, developers create their own financing capability because they perceive a need for responsiveness and confidentiality. As some mortgage originators move into other areas related to real estate such as development, leasing, and sales brokerage, certain developers have perceived their traditional financing sources as competition. Others have felt, from time to time, that their financing requests were not necessarily met with the responsiveness they had anticipated. Consequently, costs notwithstanding, occasionally developers have felt the attainment of confidentiality and responsiveness has compensated for the cost of their in-house financing operations.

All these new competitive forces notwithstanding, the mortgage originator–banker who is attuned and knowledgeable within the market and is oriented to both borrower and investor service, should be able to meet the various threats brought to real estate finance by the various new competitors. By representing a broad spectrum of investors and being locally based, the traditional mortgage banker is continually in the market ready to serve both his investor and borrower clients. This continued market presence assures the mortgage banker's investor clients of an opportunity to finance the majority of investment-grade deals within the market. In turn, it also assures the mortgage banker's borrower clients that the mortgage banker is completely aware of all the competitive aspects of the market and will make available the best possible financing vehicles to the borrower clients.

Quality Underwriting

The trauma of the massive overbuilding, especially the office glut of the 1984 to 1986 period, will profoundly affect how most commercial investments are underwritten. Looking to history, the period of 1974 to 1975 is instructive as to commercial investors' reaction to adverse market conditions. At this time, most income property lenders found that a major problem was a concentration on neighborhood rather than regional underwriting. Corrections were made in terms of underwriting processes so that entire regions and the forces affecting their economic success or lack thereof would be taken into consideration. As we look at the trauma of the mid-1980s and the losses which investors will experience, clearly underwriting will need to expand to transcend regional considerations and look toward national trends. Energy, agriculture, and the decline of heavy industry have all contributed to the overbuilding glut. These three areas of the economy, as well as other areas prone to cyclicality, such as the high-tech industry and the investment banking community, could also, from time to time, falter and affect real estate absorption and values.

For better or for worse, over the past 15 years, income tax policy has been used as a method of economic stimulation and control. This has changed tax policy from a reasonably stable economic influence to a volatile one. A review of the first half of the 1980s indicates that much real estate appreciation, or lack thereof, may have been directly attributable to changes in tax policy on an almost constant basis.

The 1986 Tax Reform changes which highlight the economic and cash flow benefits of real estate, and deny many tax-shelter benefits, will need to be factored more heavily into the underwriting processes. Future underwriting must consider nationwide trends and very carefully track absorption patterns and trends. The overemphasis given to inflationary effects in the underwriting process will need to be modified, and real estate will need to be seen in terms of its national context.

Disinflation, as well as the economic dislocations in energy, agriculture, and industry, have caused residential delinquencies and foreclosures on a nationwide basis to reach record highs in 1986. If any good came from this situation, it was the pool of residential delinquent and foreclosed properties large enough to draw statistical information and indications as to specific causes of default. This ability to specifically identify individual areas of concern has enabled residential lenders to adjust underwriting practices and guidelines on a rifle rather than a shotgun basis and make individual changes which treat large problem areas. The office building and hotel delinquency and foreclosure situation brought by the 1984 to 1986 glut will enable income property lenders and underwriters to benefit from the same statistical pool as did their residential counterparts. This will necessarily lead to underwriting guideline changes for the future to preclude repeats of the 1984–1986 situation.

All income property underwriters must stay carefully attuned to the underwriting changes taking place and to ensure that those changes are factored as rapidly as possible into current underwriting practices.

Problem Loan Management and Disposition

For the 10 years ending in 1985, commercial real estate was, in general, the beneficiary of substantial income tax advantages and an inflationary economy. Consequently, during this period real estate values escalated dramatically, and commercial real estate gained the reputation of being the surest hedge against inflation. Skills required to monitor, correct, and ultimately dispose of real estate problems were rarely used in this period in that "inflation corrected most of real estate's mistakes."

A combination of overbuilding, driven by both unrealistic absorption expectations and tax incentives, as well as severe economic problems in certain sectors of the economy caused the commercial real estate sector to quickly turn into a problem area as the second half of the decade of the 1980s began.

More than ever, those involved in commercial real estate, to protect the integrity of both the commercial mortgage and commercial real estate equity investment, will need to completely revise and enhance their skills in regard to early problem detection systems, delinquency management, and ultimate foreclosure and disposition management.

Early Problem-Detection Systems

All too often, lenders have found, as have nonmanaging equity investors in commercial real estate, that problems frequently spring up and become serious, literally on a short-term basis, because either servicing agents or property managers have not carefully monitored the investments under their control and have not been prepared to deal with problems prior to the crisis stage. As commercial mortgage servicers revamp their operations to be more attuned to signs of problems, regular property inspections, detailed operating statement analyses, and an aggressive and sophisticated review of properties, seen in light of their comparables in given real estate markets, will need to be done on a far more frequent basis. Servicing data systems will need to be expanded to take into consideration these additional analyses. Rather than waiting for the first delinquency or default to occur, those involved in the servicing of commercial real estate investments will have to aggressively and innovatively pursue vacancy problems within the markets, to anticipate the problems which can be reasonably expected to flow from overbuilt markets with exceptionally high vacancy rates. It will be necessary to develop close, working, and hopefully trust-oriented relationships between mortgage bankers and their borrower clients so that a team concept can be invoked early in the problem scenario to preclude default and bring to bear all the real estate skills of the parties on the specific problem.

Delinquency and Problem Loan Management

All too often, the system of loan administration, at both the originator-servicer and investor levels, defers action on the problem loan until legal involvement, loan acceleration, and foreclosure are the only courses of action. In general, if the problem is related to the general economy, the servicer and investor must work together with the developer-owner in resolving the problem. However, if even the slightest inkling of mis-management is involved, swift and decisive steps need to be taken as soon as possible to remove the borrower from the property.

The complications and burdens of taking over management of a property all too often play into an unscrupulous borrower's hands, and that borrower is often allowed to continue to manage the property. The astute mortgage banker will, early in the process, develop a management plan of action which can be quickly implemented when the legal steps are taken to remove the poorly performing borrower.

Few mortgage bankers have the capability of truly being hands-on property managers for the properties securing each and every loan type and size within their portfolios. Nonetheless, modern portfolio management demands that the mortgage banker be able to formulate a strategic problem-solving plan and contract with an outside management team which can implement the plan. Without aggressive problem property management, investors will clearly question the need for the outside local servicer. Survival literally demands that, as the investment climate becomes more competitive, this type of aggressive problem-loan management be the standard rather than the exception.

Foreclosure and Disposition Management

Again, to use the residential sector as an indicator of the future, one needs only to look at the tremendous strides which have been made over the past few years as residential mortgage bankers and servicers have worked efficiently to protect the integrity of the residential mortgage. The entire disposition and foreclosure process has been continually reviewed and revised with the aim of making it less time-consuming and more efficient.

To reduce commercial losses, the same steps must be taken on the income property side. Progressive income property mortgage bankers, working in conjunction with their attorneys and investors, need to review, well in advance of it happening, all of the impediments to foreclosure and disposition. Aggressive plans must be instituted as early as possible so that long periods do not elapse between the initial default and ultimate sale.

All too often, equity in a property is completely eroded by the carrying costs accrued during long and acrimonious periods of foreclosure. Finally, the same vigor in pursuing more favorable mortgagee creditor bankruptcy rules, which are being pursued on the residential side, is needed on the commercial side. Bankruptcy, or the threat thereof, has played as great a role in eroding commercial real estate equity as has any adverse economic consequence.

Conclusion

The income property mortgage market has undergone both dramatic growth and volatile change for a sustained period. Nonetheless, with some notable exceptions caused by economic problems, it has proved to be a major nationwide economic stimulant and the basis for favorable investment cash flows for many of the nation's largest institutional investors. By adapting to the changing forces of securitization, specialization, competition, quality underwriting, and problem loan management and disposition, the modern commercial mortgage banker will insure his or her continuing place in the ever-growing, ever-changing world of commercial real estate finance.

Appendix

Glossary of Income Property Terms

Cassie Kupstas

Librarian, Mortgage Bankers Association of America, Washington, D.C.

A number following a glossary entry indicates that the definition came from one of the sources listed below. If a number does not follow an entry, it is an original definition.

1. The Institute of Financial Education, *Income Property Lending,* Chicago, 1983.
2. James A. Douglas and Jean R. Goldman, *The Arnold Encyclopedia of Real Estate 1985 Yearbook,* Warren, Gorham & Lamont, Boston, 1985.

When a definition for an entry contains a TERM in all capital letters, that term is also an entry in the glossary.

A&D LOAN: See ACQUISITION AND DEVELOPMENT LOAN.

ABSTRACT OF TITLE: A written history of the title transaction of conditions bearing on the title to a designated parcel of land. It covers the period from the original source of title to the present and summarizes all subsequent instruments of public record by setting forth their material parts.

ACCELERATION CLAUSE: A common provision of a mortgage or note providing the holder with the right to demand that the entire outstanding balance be immediately due and payable in the event of default. Without this clause, the mortgagee may have to file separate foreclosure suits as each installment of the mortgage debt falls due and is in default.

ACCEPTANCE LETTER: A letter that is signed by a construction loan borrower that says all work is complete and of acceptable quality.

ACQUISITION AND DEVELOPMENT LOAN (A&D LOAN): A loan for the purchase and preparation of raw land for subdivision use. Usually a construction loan or sale is the source of repayment.

ACQUISITION LOAN: See LAND ACQUISITION LOAN.

ADJUSTABLE MORTGAGE: A mortgage or deed of trust that allows the lender to periodically adjust the interest rate in accordance with a specified index and as agreed to at the inception of the loan. Also referred to as ADJUSTABLE-RATE MORTGAGES (ARMs) and VARIABLE-RATE MORTGAGES (VRMs).

ADJUSTABLE-RATE MORTGAGE (ARM): See ADJUSTABLE MORTGAGE.

ADVANCE: In real estate, a partial disbursement of funds under a note. Most often used in connection with construction lending.

ADVANCE COMMITMENT (CONDITIONAL): A written promise to make an investment at some time in the future if specified conditions are met.

ALIENATION CLAUSE: A special type of acceleration clause that demands payment of the entire loan balance upon sale or other transfer of the title; also known as a *due-on-sale clause*.

AMENITY: An aspect of a property that enhances its value. Off-street reserved parking within a condominium community; the nearness of good public transportation, tennis courts, or a swimming pool are examples.

AMERICAN LAND TITLE ASSOCIATION (ALTA): A national association of title insurance companies, abstractors, and attorneys specializing in real property law. The association speaks for the title insurance and abstracting industry and establishes standard procedures and title policy forms.

AMORTIZATION: Loan payment by equal periodic payments calculated to retire the principal at the end of a fixed period and to pay accrued interest on the outstanding balance.

ANCHOR TENANT: A prime tenant in a shopping mall or center such as an established department store; other smaller tenants are referred to as SATELLITE TENANTS.

ANNUITY CAPITALIZATION: A method for determining value by capitalizing the annual net income that presumably remains constant.

APARTMENT: A complete and separate living unit in a building containing other units, usually at least four.

APARTMENT HOTEL: A multiunit residence which usually includes apartments and hotel rooms and usually provides some hotel services, such as cleaning and linen services, to the tenants.

APPRAISAL: A report made by a qualified person setting forth an opinion or estimates of value. The term also refers to the process by which the estimate is obtained. Synonymous with VALUATION.

APPRAISED VALUE: An opinion of value reached by an appraiser based upon knowledge, experience, and a study of pertinent data.

APPRAISER: One qualified by education, training, and experience to estimate the value of real and personal property. The estimate is based on a process in which the appraiser judges the facts discovered in an investigation of the property.

APPRECIATION: An increase in value, the opposite of DEPRECIATION.

ASSEMBLAGE: The process of acquiring adjacent parcels of land to combine into a single site for development.

ASSESSMENT: The value placed on property for the purpose of taxation. May also refer to a levy against property for a special purpose, such as a sewer assessment.

ASSIGNMENT: The transfer of a right or contract from one person to another.

ASSIGNMENT OF LEASE: A requirement as a condition of making a loan that the lender has control of leases, with covenants requiring the lender's consent on any modifications or changes in the lease; also, to assure mortgage payments, rental payments sometimes are made directly to the mortgagee.

ASSIGNMENT OF MORTGAGE: A document that evidences a transfer of ownership of a mortgage from one party to another.

ASSIGNMENT OF RENTS: An agreement between the property owner and mortgagee that transfers to the mortgagee the right to collect rents from tenants in the event of default by the owner.

ASSUMPTION OF MORTGAGE: Assumption by a purchaser of the primary liability for payment of an existing mortgage or deed of trust. The seller remains secondarily liable unless specifically released by the lender.

ATTACHMENT: The act of taking property into the custody of the law to provide security for payment of a judgment in an impending suit.

BALLOON MORTGAGE: A mortgage with periodic installments of principal and interest that do not fully amortize the loan. The balance of the mortgage is due in a lump sum at a specified date in the future, usually at the end of the term.

BALLOON PAYMENT: The unpaid principal amount of a mortgage or other long-term loan due on a specified date in the future. Usually the amount that must be paid in a lump sum at the end of the term.

BAND OF INVESTMENT: An approach to developing a CAPITALIZATION RATE by creating a weighted average rate reflecting the percentage of value represented by each debt and ownership position.

BANKRUPT: A person, firm, or corporation who, through a court proceeding, is relieved from the payment of all debts after the surrender of all assets to a court-appointed trustee, for the protection of creditors. Bankruptcy may be declared under one of several chapters of the federal bankruptcy code: Chapter 7 covers liquidation of the debtor's assets; Chapter 11 covers reorganization of bankrupt businesses; Chapter 12 covers certain farm bankruptcies; or Chapter 13 covers workouts of debts by individuals.

BASE RENT: The minimum fixed guaranteed rent in a commercial property lease.

BASIC RENT: The rent charged in a subsidized housing project and computed on the basis of a maximum subsidy.

BASIS POINT: 1/100th of 1 percent. Used to describe the amount of change in YIELD in many debt instruments, including mortgages.

BASKET PROVISION: A provision contained in the regulatory acts governing the investments of insurance companies, savings and loan associations, and mutual savings banks. It allows for a certain small percentage of total assets to be placed in investments not otherwise permitted by the regulatory acts.

BELLY-UP: Term used to describe a failed real estate project.

BELOW-MARKET INTEREST RATE (BMIR): Applies to certain mortgage insurance programs where the interest rate on the mortgage is below that charged for conventional financing in the area in order to assist low- and moderate-income families to rent or purchase dwelling units.

BLANKET: Refers to the coverage of more than one piece of property under one instrument, such as blanket insurance policy, BLANKET MORTGAGE, blanket assignment, or blanket survey.

BLANKET MORTGAGE: A lien on more than one parcel or unit of land, frequently incurred by subdividers or developers who have purchased a single tract of land for the purpose of dividing it into smaller parcels for sale or development. Also called *blanket trust deed*.

BLIND POOL: A securities offering of interests in property that has yet to be acquired.

BOND: An interest-bearing certificate of debt with a maturity date; an obligation of government or a business corporation. A real estate bond is a written obligation usually secured by a mortgage or a trust deed.

BOWTIE LOAN: A variable-rate loan instrument that derives its name from the fact that it attempts to smooth the impact of rate increases and decreases on borrowers by deferring a portion of high interest rates until maturity. Usually, all interest above a certain rate is deferred to maturity of the loan.

BREAKDOWN METHOD: A way of figuring DEPRECIATION by separating elements into physical, functional, and economic types, and classifying each as curable or incurable.

BREAKEVEN POINT: In residential or commercial property, the figure at which occupancy income is equal to all required expenses and debt service.

BRIDGE FINANCING: A loan spanning the gap between the termination of one loan (generally short-term) and the start of another (generally permanent long-term) loan.

BROKER: An individual employed on a fee or commission basis as agent to bring parties together and assist in negotiating contracts between them.

BUILDER'S AND SPONSOR'S PROFIT AND RISK ALLOWANCE (BSPRA): A credit against the required equity contribution in HUD/FHA insurance programs granted the developer for its services in sponsoring and building the project.

BUILDER-SELLER SPONSOR: Sponsor of a project specifically organized to build or rehabilitate and sell, immediately upon completion, a project to a private nonprofit organization at the certified cost of the project. The nonprofit sponsor buys a total package.

BUILDER'S RISK INSURANCE: Fire and extended coverage insurance for a building under construction. Coverage increases automatically as the building progresses and terminates at completion.

BUILDING CODE: Regulations that control design, construction, and materials used in construction. Building codes are based on safety and health standards.

BUILDING EFFICIENCY: A percentage ratio of net rentable area to gross building area.

BUILDING OWNERS AND MANAGERS ASSOCIATION INTERNATIONAL: The trade association of owners and managers of income properties, who benefit from exchange of information and management techniques.

BUILDING PERMIT: Written permission by a local government for the construction of a new building or for making improvements.

BULLET LOAN: Financing for leased-up properties often used to repay the construction loan; typically an interest-only loan for 2 to 10 years that cannot be prepaid.

BUY-SELL AGREEMENT: An agreement entered into by an interim and a permanent lender for the sale and assignment of the mortgage to the permanent lender when a building has been completed. Often the mortgagor is a party to this agreement on the theory that the mortgagor should have contractual right to insist that the permanent lender buy the mortgage.

CALL PROVISION: In a mortgage or deed of trust, the mortgagee's or beneficiary's ability to speed up payments of the obligation under certain conditions. In bonds, the issuer's right to redeem the bond before maturity.

CAP (INTEREST RATE): The maximum allowable interest rate increase for VARIABLE-RATE MORTGAGES.

CAPITAL ASSET: An asset of a permanent or fixed nature or employed in carrying on a business or trade.

CAPITAL EXPENDITURES: The cost of an improvement made to extend the useful life of a property or to add to its value.

CAPITAL GAIN or LOSS: The gain or loss incurred from the sale or disposition of a capital asset.

CAPITAL IMPROVEMENT: Any structure or component erected as a permanent improvement to real property that adds to its value and useful life.

CAPITALIZATION: The process of converting into present value a series of anticipated future installments of net income by discounting them into a present worth using a specific desired rate of earnings.

CAPITALIZATION RATE: Rate of return on net operating income considered acceptable for an investor and used to determine capitalized value—this rate should provide a return on, as well as a return of, capital.

CAPITALIZED VALUE: Estimated market value computed by dividing annual net income by capitalization rate. Capitalized value is thus appraised value that would yield a given annual net income at an assumed rate of return.

CARRYING CHARGES: The charges or costs incurred for holding property when it is idle, nonproductive, or in an interim use.

CASH FLOW (AFTER TAXES): The cash throwoff less income taxes paid or plus any personal (property owner's) or special income tax benefits.

CASH FLOW (BEFORE TAXES): Money left from a project's gross income after all expenses—operating and debt service—have been deducted.

CASH-ON-CASH RETURN: The rate of return on an investment measured by the cash returned to the investor based on the investor's cash investment without regard to income tax savings or the use of borrowed funds.

CERTIFICATE OF COMPLETION: A document issued by an architect or engineer stating that a construction project is completed in accordance with the terms, conditions, approved plans, and specifications.

CERTIFICATE OF OCCUPANCY: Written authorization given by a local municipality that allows a newly completed or substantially completed structure to be inhabited.

CHANGE ORDER: A change in the original plan of construction by a building owner or the general contractor.

CLOSING: The conclusion of a transaction. In real estate, closing includes the delivery of a deed, financial adjustments, the signing of notes, and the disbursement of funds necessary to the sale or loan transaction.

COINSURANCE: A sharing of insurance risk between insurer and insured depending on the relation of the amount of the policy and a specified percentage of the actual value of the property insured at the time of loss. In federal multifamily housing programs, it refers to a sharing of the risk of mortgage default between a mortgage firm and the federal government.

COMMINGLED FUNDS: Funds kept together in a single account but separately owned and/or accounted for. They are often set up to attract pension fund dollars and can either be open end (investors can take funds away at any time) or closed end (investors are committed once they invest).

COMMITMENT: An agreement, often in writing, between a lender and a borrower to loan money at a future date subject to compliance with stated conditions.

COMMITMENT FEE: Any fee paid by a potential borrower to a potential lender for the lender's promise to lend money at a specified date in the future. The lender may or may not expect to fund the commitment.

COMMON AREA: Land or improvements on land that are designated for common use and enjoyment by all occupants, tenants, or owners.

COMMUNITY SHOPPING CENTER: A shopping center with a gross leasable area of 100,000 to 300,000 square feet, and classified between the smaller neighborhood center and the larger regional center.

COMPARABLES: Comparable properties used for comparative purposes in the appraisal process: facilities of reasonably the same size and location with similar amenities. Also, properties that have been recently sold and have characteristics similar to property under consideration, thereby indicating the approximate fair market value of the subject property.

COMPLETION BOND: A bond furnished by a contractor to guarantee completion of construction.

CONDOMINIUM: A form of ownership of real property. The purchaser receives title to a particular unit and a proportionate interest in certain common areas. A condominium generally defines each unit as a separately owned space to the interior surfaces of the perimeter walls, floors, and ceilings. Title to the common areas is in terms of percentages and refers to the entire project less the separately owned units.

CONDOMINIUM DECLARATIONS: The basic condominium document that must be registered by the originating property owner prior to the conveyance of the first unit sold. The declaration thoroughly describes the entire condominium entity, including each unit and all common areas, and specifies essential elements of ownership that permanently govern its operation. Also known as a MASTER DEED.

CONSTANT: The percentage of the original loan paid in equal annual payments that provides principal reduction and interest payments over the life of the loan. For example, a $1 million loan with a 10.8 percent constant requires a $108,000 annual payment.

CONSTRUCTION LOAN: A short-term interim loan for financing the cost of construction. The lender advances funds to the builder at periodic intervals as the work progresses.

CONSTRUCTION LOAN AGREEMENT: A written agreement between a lender and a builder and/or borrower in which the specific terms and conditions of a construction loan, including the schedule of payments, are spelled out.

CONSTRUCTION LOAN DRAW: The partial disbursement of the construction loan, based on the schedule of payments in the loan agreement. Also called TAKEDOWN.

CONTINGENT INTEREST: A lender's equity-sharing provision normally appended to a loan at a fixed interest rate and calling for a percentage of annual gross or net project income exceeding an agreed base amount. Contingent interest is paid to the lender in addition to fixed interest.

CONTRACT OF SALE: A contract between a purchaser and a seller of real property to convey a title after certain conditions have been met and payments have been made.

CONTRACT RENT: Actual rent as called for in a rental or lease agreement.

CONVENTIONAL FINANCING: In real estate, mortgage financing which is not insured or guaranteed by a government agency.

CONVERTIBLE MORTGAGE: A mortgage in which the funds provided by the lender in the form of a loan convert into equity ownership after a predetermined period of time.

CONVEYANCE: The document, such as deed, lease, or mortgage, used to effect a transfer.

COOPERATIVE: A form of multiple ownership of real estate in which a corporation or business trust entity holds title to a property and grants the occupancy rights to particular apartments or units to shareholders by means of proprietary leases or similar arrangements. Also referred to as a co-op.

CORRESPONDENT: An abbreviation of "mortgage loan correspondent." A mortgage banker who services mortgage loans as an agent for the owner of the mortgage or investor. Also applies to the mortgage banker in the role of originator of mortgage loans for an investor.

COST APPROACH TO VALUE: A means of valuation in which the value of a property is determined by computing the replacement value of improvements, depreciation, and the value of the land.

COST CERTIFICATION: Itemization of all construction and other building and material costs for verification. Generally required in HUD/FHA multifamily insurance programs.

COST OVERRUN: The amount of money required or expended over and above such budgeted costs as labor, interest, materials, and land.

COUPON RATE: The annual interest rate on debt instrument. More generally, the annual interest rate on any indebtedness. In mortgage banking, the term is used to describe the contract interest rate on the face of the note or bond.

COVENANT: A legally enforceable promise or restriction in a mortgage. For example, the borrower may covenant to keep the property in good repair and adequately insured against fire and other casualties. The breach of a covenant in a mortgage usually creates a default as defined by the mortgage and can be the basis for foreclosure.

CREDIT REPORT: A report to a prospective lender on the credit standing of a prospective borrower, used to help determine creditworthiness.

CRITICAL-PATH METHOD: A construction method which calls for diagramming the interconnected individual tasks that are a part of the construction project.

DEBT-EQUITY RATIO: A ratio between the amount of capital borrowed and the amount of capital invested out-of-pocket or obtained through the sale of common stock; also known as the LEVERAGE RATIO.

DEBT SERVICE: A borrower's periodic payment comprising repayment of PRINCIPAL plus payment of interest on the unpaid balance.

DEBT SERVICE COVERAGE: The ratio of annual net income to annual principal and interest payments.[1]

DEED OF TRUST: In some states, the document used in place of a mortgage. A type of security instrument conveying title in trust to a third party covering a particular piece of property. It is used to secure the payment of a note. A conveyance of the title land to a trustee as collateral security for the payment of a debt with the condition that the trustee shall reconvey the title upon the payment of the debt, and with power of the trustee to sell the land and pay the debt in the event of a default on the part of the debtor.

DEFAULT: A breach or nonperformance of the terms of a note or the COVENANTS of a mortgage.

DEFAULT RATIO: The occupancy level at which the effective gross income from an income-producing property is insufficient to pay operating expenses and debt service, thus creating the risk of default; calculated[2] by dividing effective gross income into operating expenses plus debt service.

DEPRECIATION: A sum representing presumed loss in the value of a building or other real estate improvement, resulting from age, physical wear, and economic or functional obsolescence and deducted annually from net income. The opposite of APPRECIATION.

DEVELOPER: A person or entity who prepares raw land for building sites, and usually builds on the sites. The term also covers someone who rehabilitates existing buildings.

DEVELOPMENT LOAN: A short-term loan, advanced before a construction loan, used by developers to acquire land and install basic utilities such as roads, sewers, and water supply systems.

DEVELOPMENT PROCESS: The process through which development projects are conceived, initiated, analyzed, financed, designed, built, and managed.

DISBURSEMENTS: The payment of monies on a previously agreed to basis. Used to describe construction loan draws.

DRAW: Periodic advancing of funds according to a schedule of payments in a construction loan agreement; also called advance, disbursement, payout, progress payment, or TAKEDOWN.

EASEMENT: A right to the limited use or enjoyment of land held by another. An easement is an interest in land—to enable sewer or other utilities lines to be laid, or to allow for access to a property.

ECONOMIC LIFE: The estimated period during which a property can be utilized profitably.

ECONOMIC RENT: The rent that a property would bring if offered in the open market, the fair rental value. Not necessarily the CONTRACT RENT.

EFFECTIVE GROSS INCOME (PROPERTY): Stabilized income that a property is expected to generate after a vacancy and bad debt allowance.

ELLWOOD TECHNIQUE: An advanced method of developing a CAPITALIZATION RATE based on the proportion of investment represented by debt and by equity.[2]

ENCROACHMENT: The intrusion of any improvement partly or completely on property belonging to another.

ENCUMBRANCE: Anything that affects or limits the fee simple title to property, such as mortgages, leases, easements, or restrictions.

END LOAN: The final mortgage loan to the ultimate purchaser of a property, as opposed to a construction loan or other form of interim financing.

EQUITY: Net ownership; the difference between fair market value and current indebtedness, usually referred to as the owner's interest.

EQUITY OF REDEMPTION: The common law right to redeem property following an owner's default by paying the unpaid debt plus interest and costs prior to the foreclosure sale. In some states, the mortgagor has a statutory right to redeem property after a foreclosure sale.

EQUITY PARTICIPATION: The right of a lender to a share in the gross profits, net profits, or net proceeds in the event of sale or refinance of a property on which the lender has made a loan; also known as an *equity kicker*.

ERISA: Employee Retirement Income Security Act, adopted in 1974, affects many aspects of pension and profit-sharing plans, and regulates the investments such plans can make and the conduct of their fiduciaries.

ESCALATOR CLAUSE: A clause providing for the upward adjustment of rent payments to cover specified contingencies, such as the provision in a lease to provide for increases in property tax and operating expenses.

ESCROW: A situation in which a third party, acting as the agent for the buyer and the seller, carries out instructions of both and assumes the responsibilities of handling all the paperwork and disbursement of funds.

ESCROW AGENT: The person or organization having a fiduciary responsibility to both the buyer and seller (or lender and borrower) to see that the terms of the purchase or sale (or loan) are carried out. Synonyms are *escrow company* and *escrow depository*.

EXCEPTION: In legal descriptions, that portion of land to be deleted or excluded. The term is often used in a different sense to mean an objection to title or encumbrance on title.

FAIR MARKET VALUE: The price at which property is transferred between a willing buyer and a willing seller, each of whom has a reasonable knowledge of all pertinent facts and neither being under any compulsion to buy or sell.

FAST-TRACK CONSTRUCTION: The starting of construction before all the design drawings are complete.

FEASIBILITY STUDY: A detailed investigation and analysis conducted to determine the financial, economic, technical, or other advisability of a proposed project.

FIDUCIARY: One who acts in a capacity of trust and confidence for another.

FINANCING PACKAGE: The total of all financial interest in a project. It may include mortgages, partnerships, joint venture capital interest, stock ownership, or any financial arrangement.

FIXED DISBURSEMENT SCHEDULE: In construction financing, a system where the lender and borrower agree to a schedule of set payments, as opposed to VOUCHER SYSTEM.

FIXTURE ALLOWANCE: A cash allowance made by the lessor to the lessee to offset the cost of installing fixtures at a retail location.

FLAT RENTAL: Rental payments under a lease that are fixed and unchanged throughout the term of the lease.

FLOATING RATE OF INTEREST: An interest rate that instead of being a fixed percentage is stated as an amount above or below another rate, usually the prime rate, so that as the prime rate moves up or down, the interest rate moves with it.

FLOOR LOAN: The portion of a mortgage loan that the lender agrees to advance without regard to the fulfillment of project leasing requirements. For example, the floor loan, equal to perhaps 80 percent of the full amount, may be funded upon completion of construction without occupancy requirements, but substantial occupancy of the building may be required for funding the full amount of the loan.

FLOOR-TO-CEILING LOAN: A loan in which there are two separate fundings, one funding at acceptable completion of construction and a second funding upon compliance with occupancy or cash flow requirements as set forth in the loan.

FORECLOSURE: A legal procedure in which property mortgaged as security for a loan is sold to pay the defaulting borrower's debt.

FREE AND CLEAR RETURN: The YIELD from real estate expressed as a percentage of the total investment (debt plus equity) with no consideration given to debt service. Properties thus can be compared without distortions created by different financing costs.

FRONT-END or FRONT MONEY: Funds required to start a project and generally advanced by the developer or equity owner as capital contribution to the project. Also referred to as SEED MONEY.

FUNDING THE GAP: Financing obtained to fill the difference between the cost of construction and the amount of the FLOOR LOAN.

GAP FINANCING: An interim loan given to finance the difference between the FLOOR LOAN and the maximum permanent loan as committed.

GENERAL CONTRACTOR: A party that performs or supervises the construction or development of a property pursuant to the terms of a primary contract with the owner. The general contractor may use its own employees for this work and/or the services of other contractors (subcontractors).

GENERAL PARTNER: The coowner of a venture who is liable for all debts and other obligations of the venture as well as for the management and operation of the PARTNERSHIP. The general partner can have control of the business and can take actions that are binding on the other partners.

GRADUATED LEASE: A lease providing for a variable rental rate sometimes set forth in the lease, sometimes determined by a reappraisal using a predetermined formula. Also known as a *graded lease*.

GROSS AREA: The total floor area of a building, except that of unenclosed areas, measured from the outside of the exterior walls.

GROSS INCOME: Total income before any expenses are deducted.

GROSS LEASE: A lease where the lessor is responsible for all costs of maintaining the property. It is the opposite of a net lease, where the tenant pays these costs.

GROSS LEASABLE AREA (GLA): The total floor area designated for tenant occupancy and on which tenants pay rent. Usually used in describing property used for retail sale establishments.

GROSS RENT MULTIPLIER: A figure used to compare rental properties. It gives the relationship between the gross rental income and sales price. Also referred to as *gross income multiplier*.

GROUND LEASE or RENT: A lease of land alone, as distinguished from a lease of land with improvements on it, usually on a long-term basis.

GROUND RENT: The earnings of improved property allocated to the ground itself after allowance is made for earnings of the improvement. Also, payment for the use of land in accordance with the terms of a GROUND LEASE.

GUARANTY: A promise by one party to pay a debt or perform an obligation contracted by another in the event that the original obligor fails to pay or perform as contracted.

HARD COST: Land acquisition and construction costs.

HARD DOLLARS: Cash money given in exchange for an equity position in a transaction for real property.

HIGHEST AND BEST USE: The available present use or series of future uses that will produce the highest present property value and develop a site to its full economic potential.

HISTORICAL COST: Actual cost of a project when it was first constructed.

HOSKOLD FACTOR: A factor used to value an annuity and based on reinvesting capital recapture at a safe rate of interest. Named after H. E. Hoskold.

INCOME AND EXPENSE STATEMENT: The actual or estimated schedule of income and expense items reflecting net gain or loss during a specified period.

INCOME APPROACH TO VALUE: The appraisal technique used to estimate real property value by capitalizing net income.

INCOME/EXPENSE RATIO: The ratio between the gross income from a property and its operating expenses, computed by dividing operating expenses into gross income.

INCOME PROPERTY: Real estate developed or improved to produce income.

INCOME PROPERTY LOAN: A loan secured by income-producing property.

INDUSTRIAL PARK: A controlled development designed for specific types of businesses. These developments provide required appurtenances including public utilities, streets, railroad sidings, auto parking, and water and sewage facilities.

INDUSTRIAL REVENUE BOND: A form of financing whereby a municipality or development corporation issues bonds to finance revenue-producing projects. Project revenues are used to pay the debt service on the bonds.

INITIAL CLOSING: The date upon which the construction lender funds the CONSTRUCTION LOAN.

INSTITUTIONAL LENDER: A financial institution that invests its own funds or funds it is managing in real estate. Mutual savings banks, life insurance companies, commercial banks, pension and trust funds, and savings and loan associations are examples.

INTEREST RATE SWAP: A transaction in which two parties trade individual financing advantages to produce more favorable borrowing terms for each party. Usually one party will wish a fixed interest rate and the other a variable interest rate.

INTERIM FINANCING: Financing during the time from project commencement to closing of a permanent loan, usually in the form of a construction loan and/or development loan.

INTERNAL RATE OF RETURN: A method of determining investment yield over time assuming a set of income, expense, and property value conditions; combines the present worth of the right to receive future income streams with the present worth of the right to receive a particular profit when the property is sold.

INVOLUNTARY LIEN: A lien imposed against property without consent of an owner. Examples include property taxes, special assessments, federal income tax liens, judgment liens, mechanics liens, and materials liens.

JOINT AND SEVERAL NOTE: A note signed by two or more people, each of whom is liable for the full amount of the debt.

JOINT-STOCK COMPANY: A form of business ownership permitted in some states, which is a general partnership with some of the features of a corporation.

JOINT TENANCY: Joint ownership by two or more persons giving each tenant equal interest and equal rights in the property, including the right of survivorship.

JOINT VENTURE: An association between two or more parties to own and/or develop real estate. It may take a variety of legal forms including partnership, tenancy in common, or a corporation. It is formed for a specific purpose and duration.

JUNIOR MORTGAGE: A mortgage that is subordinated to the claims of a prior lien or mortgage.

KICKER: A term describing any benefit to a lender above ordinary fixed-interest payments. It may be an equity position in a property or a percentage participation in the income stream.

LABOR AND MATERIAL RELEASE: The written evidence from a contractor (or supplier of material) surrendering the right of lien to enforce collection of debt against property.

LAND ACQUISITION LOAN: A loan made for the purpose of purchasing land only, not improvements to or on land. Also referred to as just an ACQUISITION LOAN.

LAND BANK: Land purchased and held for future development.

LAND PURCHASE-LEASEBACK: A transaction whereby an entity purchases land, leases it back to the developer, and extends a LEASEHOLD MORTGAGE loan secured by the improvements on that land.

LAND SALE-LEASEBACK: Term used to describe a sale of land and simultaneous LEASEBACK of the land to the seller.

LEASE: A written document containing the conditions under which the possession and use of real and/or personal property are given by the owner to another for a stated period and for a stated consideration.

LEASEBACK: See SALE-LEASEBACK.

LEASEHOLD: An estate or interest in an estate in real property held by virtue of a lease.

LEASEHOLD MORTGAGE: A loan to a LESSEE secured by a LEASEHOLD interest in a property.

LEASE-PURCHASE: A method of acquiring ownership of real estate through gradual payments under which a lease is substituted for a mortgage obligation. Also referred to as a lease with option to purchase.

LEGAL DESCRIPTION: A property description recognized by law, that is sufficient to locate and identify the property without oral testimony.

LEGAL LISTS: Investments that life insurance companies, mutual savings banks, or other regulated investors may make under a state charter or court order.

LENDER PARTICIPATION: A financing arrangement in which the mortgage lender receives a portion of the cash flow, the gross revenue, or shares ownership of a real estate venture as a part of the loan. Also referred to as a KICKER.

LESSEE (TENANT): One holding rights of possession and use of property under the terms of a lease.

LESSOR (LANDLORD): One who leases property to a LESSEE.

LETTER OF CREDIT: A letter authorizing a person or company to draw on a bank or stating that the bank will honor their credit up to the stated amount.

LEVERAGE: The use of borrowed money to increase one's return on cash investment. For leverage to be profitable, the rate of return on the investment must be higher than the cost of the money borrowed (interest plus amortization).

LEVERAGE RATIO: See DEBT/EQUITY RATIO.

LIEN: A legal hold or claim of one person on the property of another as security for a debt or charge. The right given by law to satisfy debt.

LIEN WAIVER: A waiver of MECHANIC'S LIEN rights; a document signed by a supplier and subcontractors stating that the firm has been compensated for its work, thereby giving up its right to file a claim against the property.

LIMITED PARTNERSHIP: A partnership that consists of one or more general partners who are fully liable and one or more limited partners who are liable only for the amount of their investment.

LIQUIDITY: Cash position based on assets that can readily be converted to cash.

LIS PENDENS: A notice recorded in the official records of a county to indicate that there is a pending suit affecting the lands within that jurisdiction.

LOAN COVERAGE: The ratio of net income before depreciation divided by debt service.

LOAN SUBMISSION: A package of pertinent papers and documents regarding specific property or properties. It is delivered to a prospective lender for review and consideration for the purpose of making a mortgage loan.

LOAN-TO-VALUE RATIO: The relationship of a mortgage to the appraised value of a security. This ratio is expressed to a potential purchaser of property in terms of the percentage a lending institution is willing to finance.

LOAN WORKOUT: See WORKOUT AGREEMENT.

LOCK-IN PERIOD: That portion of the term of a mortgage loan during which the loan cannot be prepaid.

LONG-TERM FINANCING: A mortgage or deed of trust different from a CONSTRUCTION LOAN or INTERIM LOAN in that it has a term of 10 years or more.

LOT: A measured parcel of land having fixed boundaries as shown on the recorded plat.

MAI (MEMBER OF THE APPRAISAL INSTITUTE): The highest professional designation awarded by the American Institute of Real Estate Appraisers.

MAJOR TENANTS: A term used in shopping center, office building, and commercial property dealings to describe nationally recognized LESSEES with high credit standing, the amount of space they occupy, and the percentage of the development's gross rent they pay.

MARKETABLE TITLE: A title that may not be completely clear but has only minor objections that a well-informed and prudent buyer of real estate would accept.

MARKET APPROACH TO VALUE: In appraising, the market value estimate is predicated upon actual prices paid in market transactions. It is a process of correlation and analysis of similar recently sold properties.

MARKET RENT: The price a tenant pays a landlord for the use and occupancy of real property based upon current prices for comparable property.

MARKET STUDY: A projection of future demand for a specific type of project, usually with a recommendation for volume of space to be sold or rented and sale or rental price.

MARKET VALUE: The highest price that a buyer, willing but not compelled to buy, would pay, and the lowest a seller, willing but not compelled to sell, would accept.

MASTER DEED: The basic CONDOMINIUM document that must be registered by the originating property owner prior to the conveyance of the first unit sold. Also referred to as the CONDOMINIUM DECLARATION, the master deed thoroughly describes the entire condominium entity, including each unit and all common areas, and specifies essential elements of ownership that permanently govern its operation.

MATERIAL BOND: Insurance to the beneficiary (contractor) that the person posting the bond (supplier) will provide the materials necessary for the completion of contracted work.

MATURITY: The date on which an agreement expires; termination of the period a note or obligation has to run.

MBS: See MORTGAGE-BACKED SECURITIES.

MECHANIC'S LIEN: A claim created by law for the purpose of securing priority of payment for work performed and material furnished by a mechanic or other person for the construction or repair of a building; such claim attaches to the land as well as buildings and improvements erected thereon.

MERCHANTABLE TITLE: A title that a court of equity considers so clear that it will force acceptance of it by a purchaser. Also referred to as a MARKETABLE TITLE.

METES AND BOUNDS: A description in a deed of the land location in which the boundaries are defined by directions and distances.

MINIPERM: An income property mortgage, usually made in conjunction with a construction loan and usually three to five years in duration.

MORTGAGE: A formal document executed by an owner of property, pledging that property as security for payment of a debt or performance of some other obligation; the security instrument.

MORTGAGE-BACKED BOND: A bond or debt instrument which is backed by a pool of mortgages and for which the cash flow of the mortgages serves as the source of repayment.

MORTGAGE-BACKED SECURITIES: Bond-type investment securities representing an undivided interest in a pool of mortgages or trust deeds. Income from the underlying mortgages is used to pay off the securities.

MORTGAGE BANKER: A firm or individual who originates loans for sale to other investors. The mortgage banker generally continues to service the loans.

MORTGAGE BROKER: A firm or individual who brings the borrower and lender together, receiving a commission if a sale results. A mortgage broker does not retain servicing.

MORTGAGE COMMITMENT: A legal contract between a borrower and a lender to advance a mortgage loan when the borrower meets certain conditions, e.g., completing the project, acceptance by the lender's agent.

MORTGAGE CONSTANT: See CONSTANT.

MORTGAGE DISCOUNT: The difference between the principal amount of a mortgage and the amount it actually sells for. The percentage difference is in terms of POINTS.

MORTGAGEE: The lender in a mortgage transaction.

MORTGAGE OUT: To borrow the entire cost of a real estate project.

MORTGAGE PORTFOLIO: The aggregate of mortgage loans held by an investor, or serviced by a mortgage banker.

MORTGAGE REVENUE BOND: Bonds issued by public entity payable from revenues derived from repayments of interest on mortgage loans that were financed from the proceeds of the bonds.

MORTGAGE WINDFALL: Mortgage financing proceeds in excess of the cost of completing a project.

MORTGAGOR: The borrower or owner in a mortgage transaction who pledges property as a security for a debt.

MULTIFAMILY: A residential building consisting of more than four dwelling units.

MULTIFAMILY MORTGAGE: A residential mortgage on a dwelling that is designed to house more than four families, such as a high-rise apartment complex.

MUTUAL SAVINGS BANK: A state-chartered financial institution that invests mainly in mortgages.

NEGATIVE AMORTIZATION: A loan payment schedule in which the outstanding principal balance goes up, rather than down, because the payments do not cover the full amount of interest due. The unpaid interest is added to the principal.

NEGATIVE CASH FLOW: A situation in which expenditures required to maintain an investment exceed income received on the property.

NEGATIVE COVERAGE: A condition that occurs when a property is financed by a loan with a debt service that exceeds its earnings.

NEIGHBORHOOD SHOPPING CENTER: A group of retail businesses, providing a limited variety of convenience services for a limited area and having common parking and ownership or management. This is the smallest type of shopping center, usually ranging in size from 25,000 to 100,000 square feet.

NET INCOME: The difference between effective gross income and expenses, including taxes and insurance. The term is qualified as net income before depreciation and debt.

NET LEASE: A lease calling for the lessee to pay all fixed and variable expenses associated with the property. Also known as a pure net lease, as opposed to a GROSS LEASE. *Net Net* or *Net Net Net* are sometimes (unwisely) used to emphasize that the tenant will pay all costs in the mistaken belief that a net lease leaves some of the costs with the landlord.

NET OPERATING INCOME (NOI): The remainder left after total operating expenses (exclusive of interest payments) of a project are deducted from the GROSS EFFECTIVE INCOME.

NET PRESENT VALUE ANALYSIS: A method by which the present value of future returns is compared with present market value of the investment.

NET RATE: The rate of interest remitted to an investor after the servicing fee has been deducted from gross rate.

NET RENTABLE AREA: The actual square footage of a building that can be rented. Halls, lobbies, stairways, elevator shafts, maintenance areas, and other common areas may or may not be included depending on the custom of the locality.

NET RETURN: The remainder after total operational expenses and interest payments are deducted from GROSS INCOME.

NET SPENDABLE: The amount of cash that remains from the GROSS INCOME after deducting operating expenses, principal and interest payments, and income taxes. Synonymous with CASH FLOW.

NET WORTH: The value of all assets, including cash, less total liabilities; often used as an underwriting guideline to indicate creditworthiness and financial strength.

NET YIELD: That part of gross yield that remains after the deductions of all costs, such as servicing, and any reserves for losses.

NOI: See NET OPERATING INCOME.

NONDISTURBANCE AGREEMENT: An agreement that permits a tenant under a lease to remain in possession despite any FORECLOSURE.

NOTICE OF COMMENCEMENT: A document used in some states and recorded after a construction loan mortgage has been recorded. All MECHANICS' LIENS relate back to the date of recording of the notice, thereby enabling the mortgage to remain a first lien, not subordinated to any labor, supplier, or other claim for nonpayment of bills.

NOTICE OF COMPLETION: Notice recorded after completion of construction. MECHANICS' LIENS must be filed within a specific period thereafter.

NOVATION: The substitution of a new contract or obligation between the same parties or different parties. The substitution, by mutual agreement, of one debtor for another or one creditor for another, whereby the existing debt is extinguished.

NUT: In income property, it refers to the carrying charge on a property; i.e., the monthly *nut* for an investment piece of real estate.

OCCUPANCY RATE: The percentage of space or units that are leased or occupied.

OFFERING SHEET: A 1-page loan summary that points out its important features. The summary assists the investor in evaluating the mortgage loan being submitted by a mortgage originator.

OFFSITE IMPROVEMENTS: Improvements outside the boundaries of a property, such as sidewalks, streets, curbs, and gutters, that enhance its value.

ON-SITE IMPROVEMENTS: Any construction of buildings or other improvements within the boundaries of a property that increases its value.

OPEN-END COMMITMENT: A commitment to make a CONSTRUCTION LOAN where there is not a permanent mortgage TAKEOUT.

OPERATING EXPENSES: Generally regarded as all expenses of a property with the exception of real estate taxes, depreciation, interest, and amortization.

OPERATING RATIO: The percentage relationship between OPERATING EXPENSES and EFFECTIVE GROSS INCOME.

OPPORTUNITY COST: The rate of return available on the best alternative investment; the highest return that will not be earned if funds are invested in a particular project.

OPTION: A contract agreement granting a right to purchase, sell, or otherwise contract for the use of a property at a stated price during a stated period of time.

PACKAGE LOAN: INTERIM and TAKEOUT LOAN made by the same investor, as in construction lending.

PARKING INDEX: A standard ratio used to indicate the relationship between the number of parking spaces and the GROSS LEASABLE AREA or the number of leasable units.

PARTICIPATION LOAN: (1) A mortgage made by one lender, known as the lead lender, in which one or more other lenders, known as participants, own a part interest. (2) A mortgage originated by two or more lenders.

PARTICIPATION POOL: A loan or pool of loans in which two or more investors own a partial interest.

PARTNERSHIP: An association of persons joined by contract to combine their property, labor, skills, or any of or all these and to provide for sharing of profits and losses in a proportionate manner. The profits and losses are passed through to the partners, who report them on their individual income tax returns. The partnership itself pays no taxes.

PASSIVE INVESTOR: An investor who has no active role in operation or construction; participates only to earn a return on and of her or his investment.

PASS-THROUGH SECURITY: A form of a MORTGAGE-BACKED BOND for which the monthly collections on the mortgage pool are "passed through" to the investor.

PENSION FUND: An institution that holds assets invested in long-term mortgages, real estate, and high-grade stocks and bonds having acceptable yields and security. The purpose of a pension fund is to accumulate funds to hold and invest in such a manner that it will provide retirement income to individuals on an agreed upon plan.

PERCENTAGE LEASE: A LEASE in which the rental on a property is determined as a percentage of gross receipts from the business. Although a straight percentage lease is occasionally encountered, most percentage leases contain a provision for a minimum rent amount.

PERFORMANCE BOND: A bond to guarantee performance of certain specified acts, such as the completion of construction of a property or OFFSITE IMPROVEMENTS.

PERMANENT FINANCING: A mortgage loan, usually covering development costs, interim loans, construction loans, financing expenses, marketing, administrative, legal, and other costs. This loan differs from the construction loan in that the financing goes into place after the project is constructed and open for occupancy. It is a long-term obligation, generally for a period of 10 years or more.

PHYSICAL APPROACH TO VALUE: An appraisal method whereby property value is derived by estimating the replacement cost of improvements, less estimated depreciation, plus estimated land value by use of market data. Synonymous with the COST APPROACH.

PITI: Principal, interest, taxes, and insurance.

PLANNED UNIT DEVELOPMENT (PUD): (1) A comprehensive development plan for a large land area. It usually includes residences, roads, schools, recreational facilities, commercial, office, and industrial areas. (2) A subdivision having lots or areas owned in common and reserved for the use of some of or all the owners of the separately owned lots.

PLANS AND SPECIFICATIONS: Architectural and engineering drawings and specifications for construction of a building or project. They include a description of materials to be used and the manner in which they are to be applied.

PLAT: A map representing a piece of land subdivided into lots with streets, boundaries, easements, and dimensions shown thereon.

POINT: An amount equal to 1 percent of the principal amount of an investment or note. Loan discount points are a one-time charge assessed at closing by the lender to increase the yield on the mortgage loan to a competitive position with other types of investments.

PREPAYMENT: The payment of all, or a portion of, the mortgage debt before it is due.

PRESENT VALUE: Today's worth of monies to be received in future.

PRICE: When referring to the buying and selling of bonds and mortgages, price represents the percentage relationship between the amount paid for an instrument and the face value of that instrument. If sold for par, the price is 100; a premium price would be 105, for example, and a discount would be 95 percent of the face value.

PRIME LEASE: The lease from an owner of property to a tenant who subleases the property to others.

PRIME RATE: The interest rate that banks charge to their most preferred customers. It tends to be the yardstick for general trends in interest rates.

PRIME TENANT: A tenant, or related group of tenants, that is the largest single occupant of a building. Such occupancy is generally for 25 percent or more of the aggregate square footage.

PRINCIPAL: The amount of debt, exclusive of accrued interest, remaining on a loan. Before any principal has been repaid, the total loaned amount is the principal.

PRO FORMA STATEMENT: A financial or accounting statement projecting income and performance of real estate within a period based upon estimates and assumptions.

PROGRESS PAYMENT: A method for disbursing construction loan funds in which the contractor delivers to the lender for payment all bills and lien waivers covering work completed through a certain stage; also called *stage plan.*

PROJECT COST: Total cost of the project including professional compensation, land costs, furnishings and equipment, financing, and other charges, as well as the construction costs.

PRO RATA: To allocate proportionate shares of income (such as rents) or of an obligation (such as taxes and insurance premiums), paid or due, between seller and buyer at closing.

PUNCH LIST: A list of discrepancies in building plans or other construction flaws written by original architects during their final inspection of the structure.

PURCHASE-MONEY MORTGAGE: A mortgage given to the seller as all or part of the purchase consideration in exchange for property, most commonly used in land purchases, with prior rights over any subsequent lien, unless made subject to subordination.

REAL ESTATE: See REAL PROPERTY.

REAL ESTATE INVESTMENT TRUST (REIT): An investment vehicle established for the benefit of a group of real estate investors and managed by one or more trustees who hold title to the assets for the trust and control its acquisitions and investments. A major REIT advantage is that no federal income tax is paid by the trust if certain qualifications are met. The REIT is designed to provide an opportunity for large-scale public participation in real estate investment.

REAL ESTATE MORTGAGE INVESTMENT CONDUIT (REMIC): An entity which may hold mortgages and pass through the interest and principal payments to various classes of shareholders in differing proportions. A REMIC is not taxed separately but serves as a conduit.

REAL-ESTATE-OWNED (REO): A term frequently used by lending institutions to describe ownership of real property acquired as a result of foreclosure or by receipt of a deed in lieu of foreclosure.

REAL ESTATE SYNDICATE: A group of investors who pool funds for investment in real property.

REAL PROPERTY: Land and appurtenances, including anything of a permanent nature such as structures, trees, minerals, and the interest benefits and inherent rights thereof. Also called REAL ESTATE.

RECAPTURE: That amount of taxable gain from the sale or disposition which, though otherwise qualified for favorable capital gains rates, is taxed at ordinary income rates to recoup the tax benefits of certain ordinary income depreciation deductions taken prior to the sale or disposition.

RECAPTURE RATE: The rate at which an equity investment will be recouped over the life of the investment; the return of investment capital.

RECONCILIATION: In appraisals, the process of merging the indications of value derived by using the three approaches into a single, final estimate of value.

RECORDING: The noting in the registrar's office of the details of a properly executed legal document, such as deed, mortgage, a satisfaction of mortgage, or an extension of mortgage thereby making it a part of the public record.

REGIONAL SHOPPING CENTER: A shopping center with a GROSS LEASABLE AREA of 300,000 to 1,000,000 square feet and having two, three, or more full-line major department stores as ANCHOR TENANTS.

REHABILITATION: The restoration to good use, through repair of structure or improvements of a declining property or neighborhood; to arrest and reverse deteriorating influences.

REIT: See REAL ESTATE INVESTMENT TRUST.

RENTAL ATTAINMENT PROVISION: A mortgage commitment requiring a minimum occupancy level in a project before the full amount of the mortgage is advanced.

RENTAL CONCESSION: A landlord's agreement to forgo part of the advertised rent in an effort to attract tenants.

RENTAL HOLDBACK STANDBY LOAN: A provision in a TAKEOUT COMMITMENT that requires that only a portion of the permanent financing be funded on completion of construction, with the balance held back until specified occupancy levels or cash flow figures are met.

RENT ROLL: A list of tenants in a property listing terms of lease, area leased, and amount of rent being paid.

RENT-UP PERIOD: The time after construction that a rental property requires to achieve project stabilized income and occupancy levels.

REO: See REAL-ESTATE-OWNED.

REPLACEMENT COST: The cost to replace a structure with one of equivalent value and function, but not necessarily identical in design or materials.

REPRODUCTION COST: The money required to reproduce a building using the same or equivalent materials, design, and construction methods, less an allowance for depreciation; an element of the cost-approach method of appraisal.

RETURN OF INVESTMENT: The rate at which the investor recaptures the original capital invested in a project. It is calculated as equity over cash flow.

RETURN ON EQUITY: The ratio of cash flow on an investment (minus debt service and operating costs) to the amount invested (exclusive of financing).

RETURN ON INVESTMENT (ROI): The project's yield, or the amount earned over and above the original capital investment. It is calculated as cash flow over equity.[1]

REVERSE LEVERAGE: A situation that arises when financing is too costly. It results when total yield on cash investment is less than the financing constant on borrowed funds. Refer to NEGATIVE CASH FLOW.

ROI: See RETURN ON INVESTMENT.

SALE-BUYBACK: A financing arrangement in which the developer sells a property to an investor and then buys it back on a long-term sales contract; sometimes called an *installment-sale contract.*

SALE-LEASEBACK: A technique in which a seller sells property to a buyer for a consideration and the buyer simultaneously leases the property back to the seller, usually on a long-term basis.

SANDWICH LEASE: A lease in which the "sandwich party" is a LESSEE, paying rent on a leasehold interest to one party, and also is a LESSOR, collecting rents from another party or parties. Usually the owner of the sandwich lease is neither the fee owner nor the user of the property.

SATELLITE TENANT: A tenant in a retail area, such as a shopping center, that depends on the ability of the larger ANCHOR TENANTS to attract customers to the area.

SECONDARY MORTGAGE MARKET: A system whereby lenders and investors buy existing mortgages or MORTGAGE-BACKED SECURITIES and in doing so provide greater availability of funds for additional mortgage lending by banks, mortgage bankers, and savings and loan associations.

SEED MONEY: Funds required to start a development project and generally advanced by the developer or equity owner as a capital contribution to the project; also referred to as FRONT-END MONEY or FRONT MONEY.

SENSITIVITY ANALYSIS: A method of valuation of the rate of return on an investment with changes in a single factor.

SERVICING: The collection of payments and management of operational procedures related to a mortgage.

SERVICING AGREEMENT: A written agreement between an investor and mortgage servicer stipulating the rights and obligations of each party.

SINKING FUND: A fund that, with interest, will serve as payment for future replacements required for an income property.

SITE DEVELOPMENT: All improvements made to a site before the actual constructing of the building, such as utility installation.

SITE VALUE: The value of a piece of land without any improvements, as if it were vacant.

SOFT COSTS: Architectural, engineering, and legal fees as distinguished from land and construction costs.

SPECULATIVE CONSTRUCTION: Construction of a building without prior rental, lease, or sale agreements.

STABILIZED OPERATING STATEMENT: Detailed projection of all income and disbursements over a selected period of years and averaged for a single year.

STANDARD METROPOLITAN STATISTICAL AREA (SMSA): A term used by the U.S. Census Bureau describing a central city area and its surrounding suburbs and other small jurisdictions.

STANDBY COMMITMENT: A commitment to purchase a loan or loans with specified terms, both parties understanding that delivery is not likely unless circumstances warrant. The commitment is issued for a fee with willingness to fund in the event that a permanent loan is not obtained. Such commitments are typically used to enable the borrower to obtain construction financing at a lower cost on the assumption that permanent financing of the project will be available on more favorable terms when the improvements are completed and the project is generating income.

STANDBY FEE: A nonrefundable fee paid by a borrower to a lender for a STANDBY COMMITMENT.

STEP-UP LEASE: A lease in which the rent is fixed for the initial term and increases at specified intervals by predetermined amounts or by amounts based on periodic appraisals. Also referred to as a GRADUATED LEASE.

STRAIGHT-LINE DEPRECIATION: A method of depreciation where an equal amount of depreciation is taken annually over the economic life of a property.

STRAW MAN: A party who buys property on behalf of another in order to hide the identity of the real buyer; a nominee; a front.

SUBCHAPTER S: Provisions of the Internal Revenue Code under which certain qualifying small business corporations may elect to eliminate income tax at the corporate level, with the corporation's income taxed directly to the shareholders.

SUBCONTRACTOR: The person or company under contract to perform work for a developer or general contractor.

SUBDIVISION: Improved or unimproved land divided into a number of parcels for the purpose of sale, lease, or financing.

SUBLEASE: A lease executed by a LESSEE to a third person for a term no longer than the remaining portion of the original lease.

SUBORDINATED GROUND LEASE: A lease in which the ground lessor rights are junior to the rights of the holder of the first mortgage.

SUBORDINATION: The act of a party acknowledging, by written recorded instrument, that a debt is inferior to the interest of another in the same property. Subordination may apply not only to mortgages, but to leases, real estate rights, and any other types of debt instruments.

SURVEY: A measurement of land, prepared by a registered land surveyor, showing the location of the land with reference to known points, its dimensions, and the location and dimensions of any improvements.

SYNDICATION: The sale of equity interest (shares) in real estate projects to investors other than the original developers.

TAKEDOWN: The advance of money by a lender to a borrower under a loan agreement, loan commitment, or line of credit.

TAKEOUT COMMITMENT: A commitment by a lender to provide a long-term mortgage upon satisfactory completion of construction.

TAKEOUT LOAN: A first mortgage loan that is committed and expected to be made upon completion of a specified real estate project.

TANGIBLE ASSETS: Physical assets such as electrical fixtures as opposed to intangible assets such as a keen business sense.

TENANCY: A holding of real estate under any kind of right of title. Used alone, tenancy implies a hold under a lease.

TENANT CONTRIBUTIONS: All costs that are a PRO RATA responsibility of the tenant over and above the contract rent specified in the lease, such as common area maintenance.

TENANT MIX: An arrangement made up of tenants who offer different products or services that, when placed together, complement each other in their ability to attract customers.

TERM MORTGAGE: A mortgage in which, for a specified period of time, only interest is paid, after which the principal is due.

TITLE INSURANCE POLICY: A contract by which the insurer, usually a title insurance company, agrees to pay the insured a specific amount for any loss caused by defects of title to real estate, wherein the insured has an interest as purchaser, mortgagee, or otherwise.

TITLE SEARCH: An examination of public records, laws, and court decisions to disclose the past and current facts regarding ownership of real estate.

TRACK RECORD: The previous operating results of the sponsor (or developer) of a real estate program.

TRACT: An area of land.

TRACT LOAN: A loan to a developer secured by land being subdivided.

TRADE FIXTURES: Articles of personal property attached to real property but necessary to the conducting of trade and thus subject to removal by the owner.

TRIPARTITE AGREEMENT: An agreement between borrower, construction lender, and permanent lender to ensure delivery of a loan.

TURNKEY PROJECT: A builder-contractor-developer contracts to construct and deliver a completed facility that includes all items necessary for occupancy.

UNDERWRITING: The analysis of risk and the matching of it to an appropriate rate and term.

UNIFORM COMMERCIAL CODE (UCC): A commercial comprehensive law regulating commercial transactions. It has been adopted, with modification, by most states.

UNIMPROVED LAND: Raw land.

UNIT-IN-PLACE COST METHOD: A way to project construction costs by estimating the cost of each part or component installed, or in place, such as the foundation, roof, and so on. Also referred to as SEGREGATED COST METHOD.

VACANCY and RENT LOSS: Vacancy refers to any type of rental property or unit thereof that is unrented. In the estimate of gross income of a property, an allowance or discount for vacancy is usually made. Rent loss can result, for example, from periods of remodeling or rehabilitation of a project, low occupancy rates, rent loss because of the tenant's inability to pay.

VACANCY FACTOR: A percentage rate expressing the loss from gross rental income due to vacancy and collection losses.

VACANCY RATE: Ratio between the number of vacant units and total number of units in a multitenant building or development.

VALUATION: See APPRAISAL.

VARIABLE-RATE MORTGAGE (VRM): See ADJUSTABLE MORTGAGE LOAN.

VARIANCE: An approved special charge in construction codes, zoning requirements, or other property use restriction.

VOUCHER SYSTEM: In construction lending, a system of giving subcontractors a voucher in lieu of cash that they may redeem with the construction lender. The
opposite of a FIXED DISBURSEMENT SCHEDULE.

WAIVER OF LIEN: The written evidence from a contractor (or supplier of material) surrendering the right of lien to enforce collection of debt against property.

WAREHOUSING: The borrowing of funds by a mortgage banker on a short-term basis using permanent mortgage loans as collateral. This form of interim financing is used until the mortgages are sold to a permanent investor.

WHOLE LOAN: In the secondary mortgage market, the purchase or sale of an entire loan, as opposed to the purchase or sale of a participation or share in a loan.

WORKING CAPITAL: Liquid assets available for the conduct of daily business.

WORKING CAPITAL RATIO: Ratio of current assets to current liabilities. It is one of the most commonly used ratios to indicate a company's financial position.

WRAPAROUND MORTGAGE: A refinancing technique involving the creation of a subordinate mortgage that includes the balance due on the existing mortgage(s) plus the amount of a new secondary or junior lien.

YIELD: In real estate, the effective annual amount of income being accrued on an investment, expressed as a percentage of the price originally paid.

YIELD TO MATURITY: A percentage returned each year to the lender on actual funds borrowed, considering that the loan will be paid in full at the end of MATURITY.

ZERO-COUPON BONDS: A comparatively recent form of investment on which interest is accumulated and paid in full only on the maturity date. These bonds are usually suitable only for tax-exempt holders.

ZONING: The act of city or county authorities specifying the type of use to which property may be put in specific areas.

Index

Housing and Urban Development (HUD), U.S. Department of (*Cont.*):
  as investor: in continuing-care facilities, 229
    in nursing homes, 223

Implicit reinvestment, 137
Improvements analysis, 282
Income for shopping centers, 166
Income approach to real estate appraisal, 83–88
Income-expense statement, 105–118
Income-producing properties, 46
  insuring, 347–349
  underwriting computations for, 119–125
Income property asset administrator, 343
Income property market:
  competition as force in, 392–395
  impact of a default in, 374
  problem loan management and disposition as force, 396–398
  quality underwriting as force in, 395–396
  securitization as force in, 388–391
  specialization as force in, 391–392
Income statement, 50–51
  form of, 105–106
  model of, 116, 118
Income stream, 105
Income tax:
  credits in, 141, 145–146
  deductions in, 141
  for distress real property, 360–362
  of a partnership, 42–43
  of a regular corporation, 38–39
  of a subchapter S corporation, 39–40
Incomplete construction as risk in construction lending, 234–237
Incurable defaults, 97–98
Individual ownership:
  joint ownership, 36–37
  sole proprietorship, 35–36
Industrial leases:
  built-to-suit lease, 211
  leased ground, 211
  sale-leaseback, 211
  straight lease, 211
Industrial parks, 208
Industrial properties:
  building design and construction, 209
  building management, 210

Industrial properties (*Cont.*):
  categories of, 209
  checklist for, 207, 212–213
  leases in, 210–211
  location of, 208
  and past history of builder-developer, 209–210
  redevelopment of, 211
  tenant creditworthiness and responsibilities, 211
  types of, 207
  types of leases, 210–211
  zoning and development controls for, 5, 208–209
Industrial revenue bond, 374–375
Industrial tenants, market area for, 68
Institute of Real Estate Management Expense Reports, 115
Institutional investors, 393
Insurance for income property, 347–349
Insurance bills and policies, 298–299, 304, 315–316
Insurance certificates, 334
Insurance companies:
  as investor, 23–24
    in construction, 248, 249
    in continuing-care facilities, 229
    in hotels, 198
    in multifamily programs, 178
  liabilities of, 17
  as participating debt lenders, 263–264
Insured mortgages in the secondary market, 374–375
Interdisciplinary sessions, 74
Interest income, 113
Interim financial statements, 56
Interim joint venture, 266
Interim-term mortgages, interest rates for, 26
Intermediate-care facilities, 216
Internal rate of return (IRR), 127, 133–138
  computer programming for, 14, 138
  portfolio (reinvestment), 135–136
  real estate equity investment, 134
  reinvestment, 136–137
  single-investment (explicit reinvestment), 136
  single-investment (no reinvestment), 134–135
Interviews with prospective borrower's suppliers, 62

Loan closing:
  checklist for, 21
  and disbursement of funds, 329
  escrow closing, 326–327
  New York closings, 327–328
  recording of documents, 328–329
  transfer of funds, 328
Loan commitment, 333
  acceptance of, 20
  as binding document, 21
  contents of, 19–20
Loan documents:
  ALTA title policy, 303, 320–321
  articles of incorporation, bylaws,
    shareholder list, 300, 317
  assignment of leases, 297–298, 308–309,
    315–316
  assignment of rents, 297–298, 308–309,
    315–316
  borrower's affidavit, 310, 325
  building permits, 301, 318–319
  certificate of limited partnership, 295,
    311
  certificates of occupancy, 302, 319
  commitment fee, 308—309, 324
  declaration of covenants, conditions,
    and restrictions (CC&Rs), 323
  deed of trust or mortgage, 296,
    313–314
  documents relating to leases, 322–324
  due on sale or encumbrance, 299–300
  environmental engineers' report, 301,
    318–319
  escrow agreement, 307–308, 324
  estoppel certificate, 307, 321, 322
  evidence of utilities, 302
  financial statements, 304–305, 320–321
  financing statement, 296–297, 314–315
  form lease, 307
  ground lease to bank, 306
  income property construction loan,
    243–246
  insurance bills and policies, 298–299,
    304, 316–317
  landscaping plans, 300–3,10 317–318
  leases, 307, 322
  legal description of real property, 296,
    314
  management agreement, 300, 317–318
  nondisturbance agreements, 321, 323
  note, 295, 312–313
  operating statement, 304–305, 321

Loan documents (*Cont.*):
  opinion letter from borrower's counsel,
    305, 321—322
  partnership agreement, 295, 311—312
  plans and specifications, 300–301, 318,
    333
  preliminary title report, 303, 320–321
  property survey, 319
  rent roll, 307, 321, 323
  security agreement, 296–297, 314–315
  soils report, 300–301, 317
  subordination and attornment agree-
    ment, 307, 321, 323
  survey, 302–303
  tax bills, 298–299, 316
  title endorsements, 304
  understanding, 343
Loan evaluation technique and structur-
    ing of loan, 31–32
Loan offering:
  assessment of lender viewing, 12–13
  contents of, 12
  preparation of package, 12
Loan officer, "all-purpose," 332
Loan origination versus loan administra-
    tion, 332
Loan security of nursing homes, 221–221
Loan servicing, 9
  active versus passive, 350
  areas covered by agreement, 22
  documents in, 343
  establishing borrower relationships,
    344–345
  familiarity with the asset, 343–344
  inspections and operating statements,
    349–350
  insuring income property, 347–349
  payments and collections, 345–346
  real property taxes and assessments,
    346–347
Loan structuring, 31–32
Loan submission:
  inclusions with, 13
  lender's preferences for, 18
  preparation of, 11–14
Loan-to-value ratio, 31
Local credit agencies as lender, 26
Location:
  of continuing-care facilities, 226
  importance of, 19
  of industrial buildings, 208
  market area in, 66–68

About the Sponsor

The Mortgage Bankers Association of America (MBA) is the
only nationwide organization devoted exclusively to the field
of mortgage and real estate finance, both residential and
commercial. Founded in 1914, MBA today represents over
2500 member firms and financial institutions. Although
mortgage companies comprise the largest single group of
members, MBA has as members commercial banks, savings
and loan associations, mutual savings banks, life insurance
companies, and other financial service businesses related to
real estate finance.

The editor-in-chief, Eric Stevenson, is Senior Staff Vice
President of the MBA and in charge of its Income Property
Department. Wallace B. Katz, editor, is President of Wallace
B. Katz Associates, Washington, D.C. The Mortgage Bankers
Association of America is located at 1125 15th Street, NW,
Washington, D.C. 20005.